# Ted Sennett

# Comedy On Tape

## A Guide to Over 800 Movies that Made America Laugh

BILLBOARD BOOKS
An imprint of Watson-Guptill Publications/New York

For my grandchildren, Katie and Benjamin.
May their lives be filled with laughter.

First published 1999 by Billboard Books,
An imprint of Watson-Guptill Publications,
A division of BPI Communications, Inc.,
1515 Broadway, New York, NY 10036

**Library of Congress Cataloging-in-Publication Data**
Sennett, Ted.
        Comedy on tape / Ted Sennett.
            p.    cm.
        Includes index.
        ISBN 0-8230-8310-1
        1. Comedy films Catalogs.  2. Video recordings
    Catalogs.
        I.  Title.
PN1995.9.C55S396    1999
016.79143'617-dc21                    99-21110
                                CIP

Manufactured in the United States of America

First printing, 1999

1 2 3 4 5 6 7 8 9 / 07 06 05 04 03 02 01 00 99

Senior Editor: Bob Nirkind
Edited by: Amy Handy
Book and cover design: Jay Anning
Cover illustration: Dean MacAdam
Production Manager: Hector Campbell

# Comedy On Tape

# CONTENTS

Introduction  7

# The Comedy Icons and Lesser Clowns

The Marx Brothers  10

W. C. Fields  18

Mae West  22

Laurel and Hardy  25

Bob Hope  28

Jerry Lewis  34

Danny Kaye  38

Red Skelton  40

Abbott and Costello  42

Jim Carrey  46

# Great Comedy Filmmakers

Woody Allen  50

Mel Brooks  59

Frank Capra  64

Charlie Chaplin  68

Preston Sturges  70

Billy Wilder  75

# Comedy Genres

Love in Bloom:
Romantic Comedies  82

Wedded Bliss:
Marital Comedies  124

Home and Hearth:
Family Comedies  142

Slings and Arrows:
Satirical Comedies  170

Across the Footlights:
Comedies from the Stage  194

Flights of Fancy:
Comedy Fantasies  213

Dress Right:
Military Comedies  228

Cut to the Chase:
Comedy and Crime  235

Hats in the Ring:
Political Comedies  248

Nose-Thumbing:
Rude and Raucous Farces  253

One of a Kind:
Unclassifiable Comedies  273

Index of Titles  284

# Introduction

The sound of laughter. Whether it comes from a baby discovering his first rat-
tle or her own toes, or from a theater audience reacting to a pratfall or a witty
line of dialogue, laughter sustains us, renews us, and keeps us blissfully aware
of the absurdities all around us. In what Preston Sturges called "the cockeyed
caravan" of life, is there any sound more human? Lions, mice, and ducks may
chuckle now and again, but contrary to Walt Disney, they do not laugh.

Since the very first flickering images on a screen, laughter has been a mainstay of the movies. From an indomitable Little Tramp making his way through
a hostile world to a trio of crackpot brothers turning sacred cows into ham-
burger, from the acerbic wit of Billy Wilder to the iconoclastic lunacy of Mel
Brooks, comedy movies have allowed us to keep the darker side of life at bay
(at least for a few hours) with a steady barrage of quips, sight gags, witticisms,
and wisecracks. As we begin a new century, filmmakers may be more inclined
to shock us rather than tickle us into laughter, but their goal remains the same
as when it all began decades ago, to show us as we are: foolish, vain, romantic, outrageous, and very, very human. To light up the world with comedy.

This book is a guide to comedy films from the first years of sound to the
present. (The genius of such silent comedy filmmakers as Buster Keaton and
Harold Lloyd is, of course, undisputed, but space limitations prohibit their
inclusion.) The movies covered range from romantic comedies that comment on the never-ending war (and yes, the occasional truce) between men
and women to satirical comedies that puncture our follies and pretensions,
from films that celebrate family ties to raucous farces suggesting that we are
becoming a nation of horny teenagers. Here, too, are tributes to such emi-
nent comedy filmmakers as Frank Capra and Woody Allen. Coming from
different eras, these two have little in common except the feeling that the
world could suddenly become a threatening place for their beleaguered
heroes. (Longfellow Deeds, meet Alvy Singer.)

Inevitably, the content of comedy films changes from decade to decade,
from era to era, and as we enter a new century, it is abundantly clear that
much of movie comedy has taken on an approach that goes far beyond mere
brashness or impudence (the Marxes skewering warmongers). Filmmakers
such as the Farrelly Brothers are not only pushing the proverbial envelope,
they are tearing it to shreds. Their movie *There's Something About Mary*

startles in its graphic detail, in its glee in showing the ugliest and most degraded forms of human behavior, up front and close.

This movie's cruelty is not new to films. Bing Crosby could put Bob Hope in mortal danger without batting an eyelash. What *is* new is the way it celebrates its cruelty, asking us to feel liberated in an aren't-we-wicked way by laughing at excruciating bodily pain, mental retardation, and physical infirmity, among other none-too-hilarious subjects. The movie's huge success suggests that the Comedy of Cruelty and Violence is in full swing. Add to this the Comedy of Stupidity, celebrated in such movies as *Dumb and Dumber* and *Billy Madison,* and we have good reason to feel glum about the present state of movie comedy.

Still, comedy continues blithely on its way, as lovers meet, part, and then reunite, married couples bicker and reconcile, and families continue to behave in shameless and irrational ways. As long as people are people, and as long as the golden comedies of past years are available for us to watch, the sound of laughter will be heard in the land.

TED SENNETT

## KEY TO SYMBOLS

For each entry, the title of the film is followed by a block of information:

- Name of the producing or releasing company
- Year of release
- The letter "c" (indicating that the film was made in color). If not so noted, the film was made in black and white.
- Running time of the film
- Name of the director
- Name of the screenplay author(s), indicated with "SP"
- Principal cast members

### STAR RATINGS

| | |
|---|---|
| ★★★★ | Excellent |
| ★★★☆ | Very Good |
| ★★★ | Good |
| ★★☆ | Average |
| ★★ | Fair |
| ★☆ | Poor |
| ★ | The Worst |

The
Comedy Icons
and
Lesser Clowns

# The Marx Brothers

In America's Depression years, a time of breadlines and despair, three (originally four) brothers came along to poke fun at government, education, and art, while indulging in more than a little misanthropy (Groucho), chicanery (Chico), and lechery (Harpo). Their irreverent humor kept audiences laughing in a bad time. And even today, couldn't we use that fake mustache and loping gait, that honking horn, and that impossible Italian accent?

## Animal Crackers

★★★ Paramount, 1930, 98 min. Dir: Victor Heerman. SP: Morrie Ryskind, b/o musical play by George S. Kaufman, Morrie Ryskind. Cast: Groucho Marx, Chico Marx, Harpo Marx, Zeppo Marx, Margaret Dumont, Lillian Roth, Louis Sorin, Hal Thompson, Margaret Irving, Robert Greig.

The Marxes' second feature film, *Animal Crackers* sets the brothers loose at a Long Island estate and records the resulting pandemonium. Filmed at Paramount's Astoria Studio, the movie is virtually a literal transcription of their stage success. Groucho plays the not exactly reputable African explorer Captain Jeffrey Spaulding, who makes his entrance into the home of society matron Mrs. Rittenhouse (Dumont) borne on a litter by African natives. His monologue, one of Groucho's best-remembered pieces, takes off on flights of fancy. ("One morning I shot an elephant in my pajamas. How he got in my pajamas I don't know.") The plot involves a stolen painting, but who cares? From there on it's virtually nonstop chaos as Groucho insults Dumont, Chico mangles the English language, and Harpo honks his horn in pursuit of girls. *Animal Crackers* is antique and stagebound, but it's fun for all loyal Marxians.

## At the Circus

★★☆ MGM, 1939, 87 min. Dir: Edward Buzzell. SP: Irving Brecher. Cast: Groucho Marx, Chico Marx, Harpo Marx, Margaret Dumont, Florence Rice, Kenny Baker, Eve Arden, Nat Pendleton, Fritz Feld.

Yet another step down for the Marx Brothers. The brothers look tired, and the gags are not as fresh as they should be. Still, there are hilarious moments. This time Groucho is shady lawyer J. Cheever Loophole, summoned by Antonio Pirelli (Chico) to help keep the circus of his friend Jeff Wilson (Baker) out of the villain's clutches. Punchy (Harpo, and he is) arrives on the scene, led by a seal on a leash. Margaret Dumont is Jeff's wealthy aunt. Best bits: Groucho tangles with Eve Arden as Peerless Pauline, the human fly. Groucho's funniest insult to Dumont: "Those June nights on the Riviera. . . . We were young, gay, reckless. That night I drank champagne from your slipper. Two quarts. It would have been more, but you were wearing inner soles."

## The Big Store

★★☆ MGM, 1941, 80 min. Dir: Charles Riesner. SP: Sid Kuller, Hal Fimberg, Ray Golden, b/o story by Nat Perrin. Cast: Groucho Marx, Chico Marx, Harpo Marx, Margaret Dumont, Tony Martin, Virginia Grey, Douglass Dumbrille, Virginia O'Brien, William Tannen, Henry Armetta, Marion Martin.

The Marx Brothers at low ebb. Groucho is mangy master detective Wolf J. Flywheel and Chico and Harpo are his cronies as they tear about a department store. At least Margaret Dumont is on hand as the dowager who hires Groucho to protect her nephew (Martin), who owns the store, from the villainous machinations of the store's manager (Dumbrille). His goal: to kill Martin and marry Dumont. The jokes are often lame but as usual there are marvelous

Chico and Harpo Marx play at fisticuffs in *Animal Crackers* (1930), with Groucho Marx as referee. At the right, Margaret Dumont watches in dismay.

moments, mostly provided by Harpo. The movie was billed as the Marxes' farewell, but they came back twice more, sadly to no avail. Their best movie years were behind them.

## The Cocoanuts

★★★ Paramount, 1929, 96 min. Dirs: Joseph Santley, Robert Florey. SP: Morrie Ryskind, b/o musical comedy by George S. Kaufman. Cast: Groucho Marx, Chico Marx, Harpo Marx, Zeppo Marx, Margaret Dumont, Kay Francis, Mary Eaton, Oscar Shaw, Basil Ruysdael.

The Marxes' first movie, adapted from their Broadway success and filmed at a studio in Astoria, Queens. It's primitive and tacky, to be sure, but the movie set their characters in place for years to come: Groucho as the quipping, leering conman; Chico as the larcenous, piano-playing satyr; Harpo as the harp-playing genial idiot; and Zeppo (at least for the first five films) as the straight man. Forget the dumb plot and wait for the barrage of puns, wisecracks, and non sequiturs, plus songs by Irving Berlin. Highlights include the famous Groucho-Chico "viaduct—why a duck?" routine and Groucho's first movie courtship of Margaret Dumont. ("Your eyes! Your eyes! They shine like the pants of a blue-serge suit!")

## A Day at the Races

★★★☆ MGM, 1937, 111 min. Dir: Sam Wood. SP: Robert Pirosh, George Seaton, George Oppenheimer, b/o story by Robert Pirosh, George Seaton. Cast: Groucho Marx, Chico Marx, Harpo Marx, Allan Jones, Maureen O'Sullivan, Margaret Dumont, Douglass Dumbrille, Sig Rumann, Leonard Ceeley, Esther Muir.

The lunatic brothers close to their very peak, and that's high in the echelon of film comedy. This time, if you can believe it, they set their sights on both a sanitarium and a racetrack. Groucho is Dr. Hackenbush, the newly appointed sanitarium head (he's really a veterinarian), Chico is a racetrack tout, and Harpo is a jockey. Their job is keeping Maureen O'Sullivan's sanitarium out of the clutches of dastardly Douglass Dumbrille, while also dealing with High Hat, the horse owned by O'Sullivan's fiance, Allan Jones. But who cares about the plot? Comic highlights include the Marxes' examination of the indispensable Margaret Dumont, Chico's attempt to sell a library of racing tip books to a gullible Groucho, and the climactic Big Race.

## Duck Soup

★★★★ Paramount, 1933, 70 min. Dir: Leo McCarey. SP: Bert Kalmar, Harry Ruby. Cast: Groucho Marx, Chico Marx, Harpo Marx, Zeppo Marx, Margaret Dumont, Louis Calhern, Raquel Torres, Leonid Kinskey, Verna Hillie.

Generally regarded as the best of the Marxes' movies, and with good reason: it's a virtually

The Marx Brothers carry on with a bewildered Esther Muir in *A Day at the Races* (1937).

# Here's Groucho!

Here is a quiz for Marxists—fans of the Marx Brothers, that is. Can you name the movie in which Groucho fired off each of the following quips?

1. "We're fighting for this woman's honor, which is more than *she* ever did."

2. "One morning I shot an elephant in my pajamas. How he got into my pajamas I don't know."

3. To Margaret Dumont: "Marry me, and I'll never look at another horse!"

4. To a drunkard: "Didn't we meet at Monte Carlo the night you blew your brains out?"

5. To a waiter: "Have you got any milk-fed chicken? Well, squeeze the milk out of one and bring me a glass."

6. Beautiful woman: "I'm Beatrice Reiner. I stop at the hotel." Groucho: "I'm Ronald Kornblow. I stop at nothing."

7. To the student body: "As I look over your eager faces, I can readily understand why this college is flat on its back."

8. Woman: "You're awfully shy for a lawyer." Groucho: "You bet I'm shy. I'm a shyster lawyer."

9. Margaret Dumont: "This is a gala day for you." Groucho: "That's plenty. I don't think I could handle more than a gal a day."

10. To Margaret Dumont: "Martha, dear, there are many bonds that will hold us together through eternity." Dumont: "Really, Wolf? What are they?" Groucho: "Your government bonds, your saving bonds, your Liberty bonds."

**Answers**

1. *Duck Soup*
2. *Animal Crackers*
3. *A Day at the Races*
4. *Go West*
5. *A Night at the Opera*
6. *A Night in Casablanca*
7. *Horse Feathers*
8. *Monkey Business*
9. *Duck Soup*
10. *The Big Store*

nonstop barrage of outrageously funny quips, sight gags, and situations, all aimed at skewering the stupidity of war, diplomacy, and jingoism. Groucho is the new leader of Freedonia, Zeppo is his secretary, and Harpo and Chico are eager but inept spies—but they're not sure for which side. The glorious Margaret Dumont is on hand to take Groucho's insults with her usual dignified hauteur. Fans remember the exquisitely timed mirror sequence, which ends with no fewer than three Grouchos in nightshirts, or the demented war sequence at the movie's end. Yes, we know—you either love them or you don't. We happen to relish every drop of *Duck Soup.*

## Go West

★★☆ MGM, 1940, 81 min. Dir: Edward Buzzell. SP: Irving Brecher. Cast: Groucho Marx, Chico Marx, Harpo Marx, John Carroll, Diana Lewis, Walter Woolf King, Robert Barrat, June MacCloy, George Lessey.

Minor Marx, and another step on their way to decline. Groucho plays a shady lawyer named S. Quentin Quale, who arrives in a dusty Western town and is immediately fleeced by two ragtag characters instantly recognizable as Chico and Groucho. There's a plot of sorts—something about a deed to a mine—but the only interest lies in the gags and the slapstick. Groucho manages to fire off a few choice insults (he asks a drunken cowboy, "Didn't we meet at Monte Carlo the night you blew your brains out?") and Harpo has one hilarious showdown with the villain in a saloon. The best sequence is a climactic train chase modeled after the classic chase in Buster Keaton's *The General.* (Keaton, in fact, acted as advisor to the movie.)

## Horse Feathers

★★★☆ Paramount, 1932, 68 min. Dir: Norman Z. McLeod. SP: Bert Kalmar, Harry Ruby, S. J. Perelman, Will B. Johnstone. Cast: Groucho Marx, Chico Marx, Harpo Marx, Zeppo Marx, Thelma Todd, David Landau, Florine McKinney, Nat Pendleton, James Pierce, Reginald Barlow, Robert Greig.

Can higher education survive the Marx Brothers? Only by the skin of its teeth, as this hilarious comedy demonstrates. There's more satirical humor than usual in this madcap collegiate romp, with Groucho as Prof. Quincy Adams Wagstaff, the newly appointed head of Huxley College, Chico and Harpo as overage students, and Zeppo as Groucho's son. Watch happily as the boys take over a classroom session on biology, or spout non sequiturs in the "password" scene at a speakeasy; or wreck a climactic football game. In all, the brothers spoof the pomposity and long-windedness often associated with higher education and come up with a winner.

## Love Happy

★★☆ United Artists, 1949, 91 min. Dir: David Miller. SP: Frank Tashlin, Mac Benoff, b/o story by Harpo Marx. Cast: Groucho Marx, Chico Marx, Harpo Marx, Ilona Massey, Vera-Ellen, Marion Hutton, Raymond Burr, Bruce Gordon, Melville Cooper, Leon Belasco, Paul Valentine, Eric Blore, Marilyn Monroe.

The bottom of the barrel for the Marx Brothers and their last film together. The movie's only virtue (and for Marx fans, it's a blessing) is Harpo, who is given the lion's share of the footage and has several funny turns. In one, he is victimized in comic fashion by a series of tortures inflicted by a scheming Ilona Massey, and in the movie's climax, he scampers on a rooftop amid advertising billboards. Groucho plays private eye Sam Grunion in a nonsensical plot about some diamonds, but he's used mostly as a wraparound narrator for the story. He also has a scene in which he ogles the young Marilyn Monroe.

## Monkey Business

★★★☆ Paramount, 1931, 77 min. Dir: Norman Z. McLeod. SP: S. J. Perelman, Will B. Johnstone; additional material by Arthur Sheekman. Cast: Groucho Marx, Chico Marx, Harpo Marx, Zeppo Marx, Thelma Todd, Douglass Dumbrille, Rockcliffe Fellowes, Tom Kennedy, Ruth Hall, Harry Woods, Ben Taggart.

Even loyal Marx fans sometimes have trouble remembering which movie is which. This funny opus takes place mostly aboard an ocean liner, where the brothers are stowaways. It was their third movie, and the first made at Paramount Studios in Hollywood. The boys scramble about the ship, imitating Maurice Chevalier, tangling with bootleggers, and disconcerting everyone else with their madcap antics. Groucho's foil is blonde Thelma Todd, the wife of one of the bootleggers, with whom he shares a hilarious stateroom scene. "I know you're a woman who's gotten nothing but dirty breaks," Groucho tells her. "We can clean and tighten those brakes, but you'll have to stay in the garage overnight."

## A Night at the Opera

★★★★ MGM, 1935, 92 min. Dir: Sam Wood, SP: George S. Kaufman, Morrie Ryskind; additional material by Al Boasberg, b/o story by James Kevin McGuinness. Cast: Groucho Marx, Chico Marx, Harpo Marx, Allan Jones, Kitty Carlisle, Margaret Dumont, Walter Woolf King, Sig Rumann. Rampant hilarity from the Marxes, and certainly one of the funniest of all their movies. This time the boys are out to demolish the world of opera with their antics, and they succeed beyond measure. Groucho is Otis P. Driftwood, shady manager to opera matron Mrs. Claypool (Dumont). He enlists the dubious help of Fiorello (Chico) and Tomasso (Harpo) to keep Mrs. Claypool's money from straying elsewhere. There's also a subplot involving tenor Allan Jones and his inamorata, Kitty Carlisle. Everyone, of course, recalls the classic stateroom scene, a slapstick model for all time, but the movie is studded with madcap moments. Save some laughter for the hilarious climax in which the brothers wreck a performance of *Il Trovatore.*

## A Night in Casablanca

★★☆ United Artists, 1946, 85 min. Dir: Archie Mayo. SP: Joseph Fields, Roland Kibbee; additional material by Frank Tashlin. Cast: Groucho Marx, Chico Marx, Harpo Marx, Sig Rumann, Lisette Verea, Lois Collier, Charles Drake, Dan Seymour.

The team's next-to-last film, and a far distance from their glory days at Paramount and MGM. Still, they manage to win some laughs, mostly due to Harpo. He looks considerably older, but he's still in top form, dueling while munching an apple, performing a charade to warn Groucho about impending danger, and—best of all—leaning casually against a building. A cop chastises him, "Say, what do you think you're doing, holding up the building?" Harpo moves away, and of course the building collapses. The rest of the material is substandard, with the Marxes tangling with spies in Casablanca. Groucho gets off a few good quips as the manager of a seedy hotel, but the old manic energy is missing. And where is Margaret Dumont?

## Room Service

★★☆ RKO, 1938, 78 min. Dir: William A. Seiter. SP: Morrie Ryskind, b/o play by John Murray, Allen Boretz. Cast: Groucho Marx, Chico Marx, Harpo Marx, Lucille Ball, Ann Miller, Frank Albertson, Donald MacBride, Philip Loeb, Charles Halton.

The first Marx Brothers film to draw on material not written expressly for them—and it shows. Drawing on the hit Broadway comedy, *Room Service* has a shortage of laughs, and the virtually single set of a hotel room is much too confining. Groucho is a shoestring theatrical producer trying to keep his troupe of actors from being thrown out of a hotel until he can scrounge up money for his show. Harpo and Chico are his cohorts and the usual manic troublemakers. Despite the presence of such reliable actors as Lucille Ball and Ann Miller, there is a dispirited air about the proceedings. Harpo gets the best scene: ferociously hungry, he downs an entire salad in almost the flicker of an eye, pausing only to catch a handful of salt tossed by Chico.

The famous stateroom scene from *A Night at the Opera* (1935). The brothers refined the scene in vaudeville before filming it at MGM.

# W. C. Fields

He was lazy, larcenous-minded, alcoholic, and hostile toward children, women, dogs, automobiles, and clean living. He was also one of the funniest, most audacious figures who ever strolled onto a movie screen: an irreverent comedian who, to this day, provokes either annoyance or adoration. His movies, most of them ramshackle, are still tributes to his peculiar art.

## The Bank Dick

★★★★ Universal, 1940, 74 min. Dir: Edward Cline. SP: Mahatma Kane Jeeves (W. C. Fields). Cast: W. C. Fields, Cora Witherspoon, Una Merkel, Evelyn Del Rio, Grady Sutton, Jesse Ralph, Franklin Pangborn, Shemp Howard, Richard Purcell, Russell Hicks.

One of W. C. Fields's funniest films: a crazy-quilt with copious laughs for his legion of fans. (Nonfans need not apply.) He plays Egbert Sousé, the Number One customer of the Black Pussy Cat Café in the town of Lompoc. Purely by accident, Sousé foils not one but two bank robberies and is named the bank detective. His main job is to keep bank auditor J. Pinkerton Snoopington (Pangborn) from examining the bank's books. (Egbert just happens to have "borrowed" bank money to pay for some bonds.) Fields was not a believer in family values, and here he is saddled with the family from hell, each one determined to insult or humiliate him at every chance. Not to worry—fortune finally smiles on Egbert Sousé. Fields wrote the screenplay under a pseudonym.

## It's a Gift

★★★★ Universal, 1934, 73 min. Dir: Norman Z. McLeod. SP: Jack Cunningham, b/o story by Charles Bogle (W. C. Fields), J. P. McEvoy. Cast: W. C. Fields, Jean Rouverol, Julian Madison, Kathleen Howard, Tommy Bupp, Tammany Young, Baby LeRoy, Charles Sellon.

One of W. C. Fields's funniest movies, *It's a Gift* has the master comedian as Harold Bissonette, a small-town grocer who is the regular target for everyone, including his wife and his customers. When he buys an orange ranch in California, it turns out to be something of a goldmine. That's the plot, but Fields surrounds it with some of his hilarious set pieces, notably one in which he keeps trying to fall asleep on his porch and is constantly interrupted. (Mention the name "Karl La Fong" to a Fields fan, and you'll earn a laugh.) There's also Fields's running battle with little Baby LeRoy.

## Man on the Flying Trapeze

★★★☆ Universal, 1935, 65 min. Dir: Clyde Bruckman. SP: Ray Harris, Sam Hardy, Jack Cunningham, Bobby Vernon, b/o story by Charles Bogle (W. C. Fields). Cast: W. C. Fields, Mary Brian, Kathleen Howard, Grady Sutton, Vera Lewis, Lucien Littlefield, Oscar Apfel, Walter Brennan.

Poor office worker Ambrose Wolfinger (Fields), saddled with a battle-ax wife (Howard), a mean mother-in-law (Lewis), and a shiftless brother-in-law (Sutton), all of whom despise or abuse him. Only his daughter (Brian) loves him. He can't seem to get a break—when he is given one day off from his job to attend a wrestling match, he gets into deep trouble. The movie's highlight is an extended sequence—actually a beautifully orchestrated piece of slapstick mayhem—involving one of Fields's favorite props, the automobile. Best quip: Ambrose lies that he needs the day off to attend his mother-in-law's funeral. His sympathetic boss remarks, "It must be hard to lose a mother-in-law." "Yes, it is," Ambrose replies. "Almost impossible." A field day for Fields fans.

# My Little Chickadee

★★★ Universal, 1940, 83 min. Dir: Edward Cline. SP: Mae West, W. C. Fields. Cast: W. C. Fields, Mae West, Joseph Calleia, Dick Foran, Margaret Hamilton, Donald Meek, Ruth Donnelly.

The story makes little sense. The production is strictly bargain-basement. Some of the quips fall flat. Does all this matter? No. Fans of Mae West and W. C. Fields will find enough pleasure in this one and only teaming of the iconic comedians. Fields plays Cuthbert J. Twillie, a confidence man with a penchant for cards, liquor, and voluptuous women like West. West is Flower Belle, who is thrown out of town for bad behavior. The two meet on a train, and when she spots the hard cash in his carpetbag, she cons him into a marriage strictly of convenience. The stars wrote the screenplay, and each gets a chance to shine: Fields at a card game or bar, West as a sashaying saloon singer or, in one hilarious scene, as an unlikely schoolmarm. It's ramshackle but fun.

Myrtle Sousé (Una Merkel) has words with her shifty father, Egbert (W. C. Fields), in *The Bank Dick* (1940).

Con man Cuthbert J. Twillie (W. C. Fields) shines up to Flower Belle Lee
(Mae West) in *My Little Chickadee* (1940).

## Never Give a Sucker an Even Break

★★★☆ Universal, 1941, 71 min. Dir: Edward Cline. SP:
John T. Neville and Prescott Chaplin, b/o story by Otis
Criblecoblis (W. C. Fields). Cast: W. C. Fields, Gloria Jean,
Leon Errol, Margaret Dumont, Susan Miller, Franklin
Pangborn, Jody Gilbert, Mona Barrie.

The master comedian's last starring movie is an
often hilarious and sometimes incomprehensi-

Gloria Jean as Fields's singing niece and the inimitable rubber-legged comedian, Leon Errol. Favorite Fields quip: falling off a high cliff, he remarks philosophically, "It's the last foot that's dangerous."

## Six of a Kind

★★★ Paramount, 1934, 62 min. Dir: Leo McCarey. SP: Walter DeLeon, Harry Ruskin. Cast: W. C. Fields, George Burns, Gracie Allen, Mary Boland, Charles Ruggles, Alison Skipworth.

Not a Fields starring vehicle but vintage nonsense that can still offer a good deal of fun. Flora and J. Pinkham Whinney (Boland and Ruggles) decide to drive to California on a second honeymoon, and they advertise for a second couple to share expenses. The couple turns out to be Burns and Allen, plus their huge Great Dane. When bank clerk Whinney is suspected of embezzlement (unwittingly, he is carrying $50,000 in bank money), Sheriff "Honest" John Hoxley (Fields) goes after him. At one point, "Honest" John declares that everything pleasant "is either illegal, immoral, or fattening."

## You Can't Cheat an Honest Man

★★★☆ Universal, 1939, 76 min. Dir: George Marshall. SP: George Marion, Jr., Richard Mack, and Everett Freeman, b/o story by Charles Bogle (W. C. Fields). Cast: W. C. Fields, Edgar Bergen, Constance Moore, Mary Forbes, Thurston Hall, Eddie "Rochester" Anderson, John Arledge, Edward Brophy.

W. C. Fields's first comedy for Universal finds him playing one Larson E. (read "Larceny") Whipsnade, owner of a circus that features two ordinary men as "the world's shortest giant and tallest midget." Of course Whipsnade is always short of cash or in trouble with the law. He also has a running war of words with ventriloquist Edgar Bergen's impudent dummy, Charlie McCarthy. The movie's best scene is a society party at which Whipsnade turns up—in a chariot—as an unwanted guest. The movie is credited to George Marshall, but Edward Cline actually directed most of Fields's scenes.

ble mess. The story makes no sense whatever—Fields, it seems, is trying to sell his script to producer Franklin Pangborn and then enacts his story about landing in a mountain retreat owned by the imperious Mrs. Hemoglobin (Dumont). Somehow it all ends with a car chase that is a model of its kind. Other participants include

# Mae West

Undulating hips, insinuating voice, unabashed sexuality—what other movie icon could claim these characteristics other than Mae West? In thirties movies that made no claim to art, West scandalized her critics and delighted her audiences with her naughty innuendoes and her frank enjoyment of men. Censorship finally tamed her, but her movies remain a testament to a true original.

## Belle of the Nineties

★★★ Paramount, 1934, 73 min. Dir: Leo McCarey. SP: Mae West, b/o her story. Cast: Mae West, Roger Pryor, John Mack Brown, John Miljan, Katherine DeMille, Libby Taylor, James Donlan, Duke Ellington and His Orchestra.

Who is "the most talked-about woman in America?" Why, Ruby Carter (West), of course, the buxom blonde music hall entertainer and courtesan who turns men into her slaves. Arriving in New Orleans, Ruby is asked if she is in town "for good." "I expect to be here," she replies, "but not for good." Audiences of the day knew exactly what she meant. Here, Mae West is in top form as she mixes it up with lovers and villains in a melodramatic plot. Her opening music hall number, in which she appears in a variety of fantastic guises, is spectacular. "Some of the wildest men make the best pets," she insists. The lady should know.

## Every Day's a Holiday

★★☆ Paramount, 1938, 80 min. Dir: A. Edward Sutherland. SP: Mae West. Cast: Mae West, Edmund Lowe, Lloyd Nolan, Charles Butterworth, Charles Winninger, Walter Catlett, Chester Conklin, Louis Armstrong.

Mae returns to the Gay Nineties in this middling vehicle. She's Peaches O'Day, a con artist with a long police record at New York's City Hall. When she sells the Brooklyn Bridge to an immigrant, police chief McCarey (Lowe) has her exiled to Boston. She returns disguised as Mademoiselle Fifi, the toast of Gay Paree. The plot not only thickens but also curdles as Peaches-Fifi becomes involved with ousting Tammany boss "Honest" John Quade (Nolan). Mae keeps on pitching but this time many of her quips fall flat. At least Louis Armstrong turns up to end the movie on an exuberant note.

## Goin' to Town

★★★ Paramount, 1935, 74 min. Dir: Alexander Hall. SP: Mae West, b/o story by Marion Morgan, George B. Dowell. Cast: Mae West, Paul Cavanagh, Gilbert Emery, Marjorie Gateson, Tito Coral, Ivan Lebedeff, Fred Kohler, Sr., Monroe Owsley, Luis Alberni.

A fairly snappy Mae West vehicle, with Mae as Cleo Borden, a dance hall dame who uses her charms to rise from the saloons of the old West to the mansions of Southampton and Buenos Aires. Inheriting a fortune from her late boyfriend, Cleo has wealth, power, and a posh ranch house—but no man. She sets her sights on a surveyor named Carrington (Cavanagh), who, as usual with Mae's male targets, resists her and then finally surrenders. But not before other complications involving a playboy millionaire (Owsley). Movie highlight: Mae sings an aria from *Samson and Delilah*, defined by the lady as an opera about "a lady barber who made good."

## Go West, Young Man

★★★ Paramount, 1936, 82 min. Dir: Henry Hathaway. SP: Mae West, b/o play by Lawrence Riley. Cast: Mae West, Randolph Scott, Warren William, Alice Brady, Elizabeth Patterson, Lyle Talbot, Isabel Jewell, Margaret Perry, Etienne Girardot, Xavier Cugat and His Orchestra.

Mae in a modern mode. Forgoing the usual period gowns and bric-a-brac, she plays Mavis

Arden, "the talk of the talkies," who finds herself stranded in a small country town. Obliged to stay in a local boarding house, she meets all sorts of odd rural types, plus one likely male conquest named Bud Norton (Scott). Her goal, of course, is seduction, and West's scenes with Scott are the funniest in the film. Bud is repairing her Rolls Royce: "Sorry I don't carry spare parts." Mavis looks him over: "I didn't expect you to." There's more plot, but it's not really important. It's Mae West all the way, strutting and gyrating for her legion of fans.

## I'm No Angel

★★★☆ Paramount, 1933, 87 min. Dir: Wesley Ruggles. SP: Mae West; adaptation by Harlan Thompson. Cast: Mae West, Cary Grant, Edward Arnold, Ralf Harolde, Russell Hopton, Gertrude Michael, Kent Taylor, Gregory Ratoff, Gertrude Howard.

Three cheers for Tira, lion-tamer extraordinary and queen of the carnival, otherwise known as the inimitable Mae West. Determined to better her status in life, Tira bumps and grinds her way to a smitten socialite (Taylor), then takes up with his equally smitten cousin (Grant).

Dressed to the nines (or maybe tens), Mae West addresses the jury at the trial in which she is suing Cary Grant for breach of promise in *I'm No Angel* (1933).

When Grant leaves her, she sues him for breach of promise, and the trial is the movie's highlight. Wearing a floor-length black gown, a fur wrap, and a feathered hat, she flirts with the judge and confounds the witnesses brought to sully her reputation. After her inevitable victory, she tells her adoring audience, "It's not the men in your life that counts, it's the life in your men." Nobody is surprised when Grant returns to her. *I'm No Angel* is the essence of Mae West, and probably her best film.

## Klondike Annie

★★★ Paramount, 1936, 80 min. Dir: Raoul Walsh. SP: Mae West, b/o play by Mae West; story by Marion Morgan, George B. Dowell. Cast: Mae West, Victor McLaglen, Phillip Reed, Helen Jerome Eddy, Harold Huber, Soo Yong, Lucille Webster Gleason.

One of Mae West's better—but also lesser-known—movies. Mae is Rose Carlton, the white queen of San Francisco's Chinatown, who kills her lord and master, a sinister Chinaman named Chan Lo (Huber). Fleeing aboard a freighter bound for Alaska, she attracts the amorous attention of the ship's captain, Bull Brackett (McLaglen). The movie takes a surprising turn when Rose, to avoid being arrested, takes over the identity of a dead missionary named Annie. Her West-style zeal not only brings in hordes of repentant sinners but also wins her the love of a dashing Mountie named Jack Forrest (Reed). Soon both Jack and Bull are vying for her affection. Highlight: Mae sings "An Occidental Woman in an Oriental Mood for Love."

## She Done Him Wrong

★★★☆ Paramount, 1933, 66 min. Dir: Lowell Sherman. SP: Harvey Thew, John Bright, b/o play by Mae West. Cast: Mae West, Cary Grant, Gilbert Roland, Noah Beery, Rafaela Ottiano, Rochelle Hudson, David Landau.

Say hello to Lady Lou, Queen of the Bowery, and, by her own admission, "one of the finest women who ever walked the streets." Of course it's the one and only Mae West, all aglitter in her diamond-spangled gown, in the film version of her biggest Broadway hit, *Diamond Lil.* (Only the name changed.) The voluptuous lady is entangled in a corny melodramatic plot, but she's also involved with many admirers, mainly a Salvation Army officer (Grant) who may not be what he seems. ("Why don't you come up sometime 'n' see me?" she asks him, famously.) The Westian quips turn up on a regular basis: "It was a toss up whether I go in for diamonds or sing in the choir. The choir lost." She also brays a few songs, notably "I Wonder Where My Easy Rider's Gone."

# Laurel and Hardy

British-born Stan Laurel and Georgian Oliver Hardy were going their separate ways in vaudeville and silent films when they teamed up in 1926 to become Laurel and Hardy, the incomparable duo whose hilarious, exquisitely timed antics kept audiences laughing for many years. Laurel's sweet, blank innocence and Hardy's pomposity and gentility in the face of endless disasters are the hallmarks of their comic genius.

## Babes in Toyland

★★★ MGM, 1934, 73 min. (originally 79 min.). Dir: Charles Rogers, Gus Meins. SP: Nick Grinde, Frank Butler. Cast: Stan Laurel, Oliver Hardy, Charlotte Henry, Felix Knight, Henry Brandon, Johnny Downs, Jean Darling, Marie Wilson, Florence Roberts, William Burress.

Yes, it's a musical, and a rather elaborate one at that, but Laurel and Hardy have prominent roles, and they are funny as Stannie Dum and Ollie Dee. Adapted from the Victor Herbert operetta, the movie has them helping to keep the mortgaged home of Mother Peep (Roberts) out of the clutches of evil Silas Barnaby (Brandon). More plot than usual for a Laurel and Hardy film, plus some songs, but the boys hold their own, winning laughs with their genial bungling. Reissued as *March of the Wooden Soldiers.* Remade in 1961.

## Bonnie Scotland

★★★ MGM, 1935, 80 min. Dir: James W. Horne. SP: Frank Butler, Jeff Moffitt. Cast: Stan Laurel, Oliver Hardy, June Lang, William Janney, David Torrence, Anne Grey, Vernon Steele, James Finlayson.

Stan and Ollie inadvertently join a Scottish military regiment stationed in India. Inevitably, they wreak havoc wherever they go, continually inviting the displeasure of their sergeant (Finlayson). By the movie's end, however, they are heroes who thwart a native uprising. As usual, the best moments are the simplest: Stan and Ollie singing and dancing to "One Hundred Pipers"; Stan driving Ollie into a fury with one of his tricks.

## The Flying Deuces

★★★ RKO, 1939, 69 min. Dir: A. Edward Sutherland. SP: Ralph Spence, Alfred Schiller, Charles Rogers, Harry Langdon. Cast: Stan Laurel, Oliver Hardy, Jean Parker, Reginald Gardner, James Finlayson, Charles Middleton.

Good Laurel and Hardy vehicle, with the comedians joining the French Foreign Legion to assuage Hardy's broken heart over losing Jean Parker. (Laurel goes along to keep him company.) When they try to desert, they are caught and sentenced to be hung at sunrise. (Laurel hopes the morning will be cloudy.) The nonsense concludes with a wild plane ride. Best scene: the boys sing and dance to "Shine on, Harvest Moon."

## Our Relations

★★★ MGM, 1936, 74 min. Dir: Harry Lachman. SP: Richard Connell, Felix Adler, b/o story by William Wymark Jacobs. Cast: Stan Laurel, Oliver Hardy, Sidney Toler, Alan Hale, Daphne Pollard, Betty Healy, Iris Adrian, James Finlayson.

Twice as much fun with Stan and Ollie discovering that they have twin brothers, British sailors named Alf and Bertie. When the four converge on the same beer garden, there's the expected identity mixup involving the waiter (Hale), the chief engineer (Finlayson) of their boat, and their respective wives (Pollard and Healy). The pleasure, as usual, comes with the inventiveness of the gags and the matchless interplay of the comedians.

## Saps at Sea

★★★ United Artists, 1940, 57 min. Dir: Gordon Douglas. SP: Charles Rogers, Felix Adler, Gil Pratt, Harry Langdon. Cast: Stan Laurel, Oliver Hardy, James Finlayson, Ben Turpin, Richard Cramer.

When Ollie has a nervous breakdown working in a horn factory, he tries to relax with Stan on a small boat. Trouble ensues when an escaped convict (Cramer) comes on board and takes over. Highlight: the boys are forced to eat a fake dinner they prepared for the convict—string for spaghetti, soap for cheese, sponge for meat balls, and so forth. One of the writers was comedian Harry Langdon.

## Sons of the Desert

★★★☆ MGM, 1933, 69 min. Dir: William A. Seiter. SP: Byron Morgan, b/o story by Frank Craven. Cast: Stan Laurel, Oliver Hardy, Charlie Chase, Mae Busch, Dorothy Christy, Lucien Littlefield.

Generally regarded as the best of Laurel and Hardy's feature films, *Sons of the Desert* has a simple premise: in order to attend the convention of the fraternal order of Sons of the Desert, Stan and Ollie concoct a series of lies that spiral comically out of control. At the convention they are plagued by a repulsively hearty lodge member (Chase), and at home they must elude their battle-ax wives (Busch and Christy) by hiding on the roof of Ollie's house. Stan gets some of the funniest routines: he consumes a wax apple with gusto and suddenly begins to use multisyllabic words in the manner of an idiot savant. Through all of this, Ollie maintains that priceless look of exasperation.

## Swiss Miss

★★☆ MGM, 1938, 72 min. Dir: John G. Blystone. SP: James Parrott, Felix Adler, Charlie Melson, b/o story by Jean Negulesco, Charles Rogers. Cast: Stan Laurel, Oliver Hardy, Walter Woolf King, Della Lind, Adia Kuznetzoff, Eric Blore.

Okay Laurel and Hardy comedy with music. Stan and Ollie, selling mousetraps in the Swiss Alps, find themselves without funds. They have assorted comic mishaps as they become involved with a famous composer (King) and his inamorata (Lind). Highlights include Stan and a St. Bernard; the boys trying to drag a piano across a swinging rope bridge; and Ollie's attempt to serenade his sweetheart, with Stan accompanying him on the tuba.

## Way Out West

★★★☆ MGM, 1937, 65 min. Dir: James W. Horne. SP: Charles Rogers, Felix Adler, James Parrott, b/o story by Jack Jevne, Charles Rogers. Cast: Stan Laurel, Oliver Hardy, James Finlayson, Sharon Lynn, Rosina Lawrence, Stanley Fields.

How many laughs can you crowd into a mere sixty-five minutes? Watch this feature film and you'll find the answer: many. In this trim little caper, the boys venture out West to deliver the deed to a gold mine to a demure young girl (Lawrence), only to be opposed by a larcenous saloon owner (Finlayson) and his wife (Lynn). Most of the movie consists of the team's beautifully timed routines, especially their attempt to reach the second floor of a house (where a crucial safe can be found) by way of a rope and a mule. Watch Laurel try to consume his hat (as the payoff on a boast), and you'll see this inspired comedian at his peak. The duo also delivers one marvelous song-and-dance routine.

Oliver Hardy and Stan Laurel play unseaworthy sailors in *Saps at Sea* (1940).

# Bob Hope

America's most durable comedian (although he was born in London), Bob Hope enjoyed an amazingly long career: on stage in musical comedy, on screen in scores of movies, on television as star of his own show, as frequent master of ceremonies at annual Oscar events, and as the nation's ambassador to its armed forces in war and peace. His brash, quipping style was unique (why try to match it?—nobody could do it better), and to several generations, he has become a legend. Following are only some of his comedy films.

## Casanova's Big Night

★★★ Paramount, 1954, c, 86 min. Dir: Norman Z. McLeod. SP: Hal Kanter, Edmund Hartmann, b/o story by Aubrey Wisberg. Cast: Bob Hope, Joan Fontaine, Basil Rathbone, Audrey Dalton, Raymond Burr, Vincent Price, Robert Hutton, Lon Chaney, Jr.

Lively comedy, set in eighteenth-century Italy, with Hope as Pippo, a tailor's apprentice who is obliged to impersonate the fabled lover and swordsman Casanova. When the true Casanova (Price) runs out on his debtors, Pippo is selected by them to test the virtue of the fair Elena (Dalton), who is marrying the Duke of Genoa (Hutton). Their reward will be the money Casanova owes them. Soon Pippo becomes involved in court intrigue, with his life in jeopardy at every moment. Never mind the plot—the movie has lavish costumes, a game cast, and quipping Hope in good form.

## The Cat and the Canary

★★★ Paramount, 1939, 74 min. Dir: Elliott Nugent. SP: Walter DeLeon, Lynn Starling, b/o play by John Willard. Cast: Bob Hope, Paulette Goddard, John Beal, Douglass Montgomery, Gale Sondergaard, Nydia Westman, George Zucco, Elizabeth Patterson.

Bob Hope cemented his stardom with this remake of the old haunted-house thriller. He fashioned the story's combination of laughs and thrills to his own persona of the fast-quipping but basically cowardly go-getter and came up with a winner. He joins heiress Paulette Goddard at a creepy mansion where skulldug-gery is afoot and soon they are being terrified by all sorts of mysterious occurrences: dimming lights, sliding door panels, shrieks in the night, and the like. Hope manages his usual share of wisecracks, but sensibly, the movie plays for suspense as well as comedy. First filmed in 1927 and remade in 1978.

## Caught in the Draft

★★★ Paramount, 1941, 82 min. Director: David Butler. SP: Harry Tugend, b/o his story. Cast: Bob Hope, Dorothy Lamour, Eddie Bracken, Lynne Overman, Clarence Kolb, Paul Hurst, Phyllis Ruth, Ferike Boros.

Standard-issue Bob Hope service comedy, very typical of its day, with some laughs. He plays a movie star who finds himself in the army, despite his strenuous efforts to avoid the draft. From then on, there's nothing but trouble. His sergeant ignores the "Do Not Disturb" sign on his tent. He almost expires of fright when he must fly with airborne troops. And for reasons too silly to explain, he spends one evening rushing about in his underwear. Does he eventually become a hero? Of course, and he also wins the heart of Dorothy Lamour. Although still early in his movie career, Hope carries off this nonsense with aplomb.

## Critic's Choice

★★☆ Warners, 1963, c, 100 min. Dir: Don Weis. SP: Jack Sher, b/o play by Ira Levin. Cast: Bob Hope, Lucille Ball, Marilyn Maxwell, Rip Torn, Jessie Royce Landis, Jim Backus, Marie Windsor.

A loose adaptation of the Broadway comedy, tailored to suit the talents of Bob Hope and Lucille Ball. Hope is a caustic drama critic whose wife (Ball) writes her first play. When he must agonize over whether to review it, he falls to pieces, giving himself over to liquor, psychoanalysis, and the waiting arms of his ex-wife (Maxwell). Meanwhile, his disgruntled wife is inexplicably attracted to a mumbling Method director (Torn). Only mildly amusing, despite the stars' best efforts.

## The Facts of Life

★★★ H-L-P Productions, 1960, 103 min. Dir: Melvin Frank. SP: Norman Panama, Melvin Frank. Cast: Bob Hope, Lucille Ball, Ruth Hussey, Don DeFore, Louis Nye, Philip Ober, Marianne Stewart, Peter Leeds.

Something of a departure for Hope (and Lucille Ball as well): a reasonably adult and very amusing marital comedy without the usual quota of quips. Hope and Ball play married folk who are *not* married to each other. Larry Gilbert (Hope) and Kitty Weaver (Ball) are neighbors who accidentally find themselves in Acapulco without their mates and proceed to fall in love. Their desperate efforts to keep their affair a secret—at a country-club dance and a "no-tell" motel—are frequently funny, as is their ill-fated attempt at their own "honeymoon." Ruth Hussey and Don DeFore are on hand as the couple's other halves.

## Fancy Pants

★★★ Paramount, 1950, c, 92 min. Dir: George Marshall. SP: Edmund Hartmann, Robert O'Brien, b/o story by Harry Leon Wilson. Cast: Bob Hope, Lucille Ball, Bruce Cabot, Jack Kirkwood, Lea Penman, Eric Blore, John Alexander, Hugh French.

A loose—very loose—adaptation of *Ruggles of Red Gap, Fancy Pants* transforms the gently humorous tale of an English butler in the Wild West into a vehicle for Bob Hope. This time the hero is not a reserved "gentleman's gentleman" but an American actor posing as one, and brought to the American West by the nouveau riche Floud family. Clumsy and cow-

ardly (the usual Hope persona), Humphrey—as he calls himself—is mistaken for an earl by the townsfolk. He also makes a mortal enemy of a nasty varmint (Cabot) who is courting the Floud daughter (Ball). Ball is hampered by having to play a disagreeable character, and her interaction with Hope is nowhere as successful as it had been in *Sorrowful Jones*.

## The Ghost Breakers

★★★ Paramount, 1940, 85 min. Dir: George Marshall. SP: Walter De Leon, b/o play by Paul Dickey, Charles W. Goddard. Cast: Bob Hope, Paulette Goddard, Richard Carlson, Paul Lukas, Willie Best, Anthony Quinn, Pedro de Cordoba.

The success of *The Cat and the Canary* (1939) encouraged Paramount to produce another mix of mystery and farce starring Bob Hope and Paulette Goddard. This time they chose an old play that had been filmed before, in 1922. Goddard plays an heiress who inherits a spooky Cuban mansion and brings along a nervous Hope (not intentionally—he gets locked in her trunk). Sure enough, the two are assailed or threatened on all sides by sinister types looking for the buried treasure in the mansion. All that really matters is the barrage of gags fired by Hope to mask his terror. As Hope's quaking valet, Willie Best wins some laughs, although many of the jokes at his expense might make viewers wince in today's climate. Remade in 1953 as *Scared Stiff*.

## The Lemon Drop Kid

★★★ Paramount, 1951, 91 min. Dir: Sidney Lanfield. SP: Edmund Hartmann, Robert O'Brien, b/o story by Damon Runyon. Cast: Bob Hope, Marilyn Maxwell, Lloyd Nolan, Jane Darwell, Andrea King, Fred Clark, J. C. Flippen.

Another amiable excursion by Bob Hope into Damon Runyon territory. He's the Lemon Drop Kid—he dotes on the confection—a racetrack tipster who finds himself in deep debt when he touts a gangster's moll onto a losing horse. Ordered to come up with ten thousand dollars or suffer the dire consequences, the Kid sets up a phony charity for Nellie Thursday (Darwell), one of those old Broadway residents Runyon loved to write about. Naturally, it all goes wrong, and the Kid is soon dashing about frantically in a Santa Claus suit or impersonating a genteel old lady. *The Lemon Drop Kid* is not Runyon, but it's breezy fun. Previously filmed in 1934.

## Monsieur Beaucaire

★★★ Paramount, 1946, 93 min. Dir: George Marshall. SP: Melvin Frank and Norman Panama, b/o novel by Booth Tarkington. Cast: Bob Hope, Joan Caulfield, Patric Knowles, Marjorie Reynolds, Cecil Kellaway, Joseph Schildkraut, Constance Collier, Reginald Owen.

A jaunty Bob Hope comedy, with scant relation to the Booth Tarkington book, but fun nonetheless. Hope plays a seventeenth-century French barber in the court of Louis XV (Owen), who is whisked off to Spain to impersonate a nobleman designated to marry a princess. His goal, of which he is blithely unaware, is to avert a full-scale war between the two countries. His true love is a chambermaid named Mimi (Caulfield). As always, the story is merely a peg on which to hang Hope's quips in the face of danger, few of which have anything to do with France, Spain, or the seventeenth century. Best scene: Hope's reception by the king of Spain. Most expected gag: a reference to Bing Crosby.

## My Favorite Blonde

★★★ Paramount, 1942, 78 min. Dir: Sidney Lanfield. SP: Don Hartman, Frank Butler, b/o story by Norman Panama, Melvin Frank. Cast: Bob Hope, Madeleine Carroll, Gale Sondergaard, George Zucco, Victor Varconi.

Silly but breezy wartime Bob Hope vehicle has the comedian as a vaudevillian who gets mixed up with British agent Madeleine Carroll. She is is trying to keep secret information out of the hands of enemy agents, and Hope is the patsy she enlists to help her elude the villains. Inevitably, they are also pursued by the police, who think Hope is a murderer. The comedian keeps the jokes flying in his familiar brash style, and while some of them were stale even in 1942, his ebullient style and

assured timing carry him through as usual.

## My Favorite Brunette

★★☆ Paramount, 1947, 87 min. Dir: Elliott Nugent. SP: Edmund Beloin, Jack Rose. Cast: Bob Hope, Dorothy Lamour, Peter Lorre, Lon Chaney, Jr., John Hoyt, Charles Dingle, Reginald Denny.

Bob Hope plays a photographer who turns detective in this sprightly but standard comedy.

By helping a lady in distress (Lamour) who holds a valuable map, our self-inflated hero finds himself (among other places) in a mysterious country home, a sanatorium for wealthy clients, and a Washington hotel. By now a master at keeping up the pace with machine-gun gags even when the plot turns preposterous, Hope tangles with such assorted villains as Peter Lorre and Lon Chaney, Jr.

Bob Hope and Dorothy Lamour in *My Favorite Brunette* (1947). Dorothy Lamour was, indeed, Hope's favorite brunette, appearing with him in all of the popular "Road" movies.

## My Favorite Spy

★★★ Paramount, 1951, 93 min. Dir: Norman Z. McLeod. SP: Edmund Hartmann, Jack Sher, additional dialogue by Hal Kanter, b/o story and adaptation by Edmund Beloin, Lou Breslow. Cast: Bob Hope, Hedy Lamarr, Francis L. Sullivan, Arnold Moss, Tonio Selwart, Stephen Chase, John Archer, Morris Ankrum, Marc Lawrence, Iris Adrian.

Once again Bob Hope tangles with spies in this fast-moving entry. He plays Peanuts White, a burlesque comedian who is sent to Tangier to double as a notorious international spy named Eric Augustine. In Tangier, nervously armed with a battery of quips, Peanuts searches for an important strip of microfilm while sinister types circle around him. He also encounters the beauteous Lily (Lamarr), who switches sides and joins with Peanuts in eluding the villains. There's a funny Mack Sennett–type chase, and Hope even gets to sing.

## The Paleface

★★★ Paramount, 1948, c, 91 min. Dir: Norman Z. McLeod. SP: Edmund Hartmann, Frank Tashlin. Cast: Bob Hope, Jane Russell, Robert Armstrong, Iris Adrian, Robert Watson, Jack Searle.

Bob Hope's movie persona over the years was that of an inept, cowardly man who fancied himself a womanizer. Not exactly lovable characteristics, but Hope covered his inadequacies with a barrage of jokes for every occasion and a devil-may-care attitude that audiences enjoyed. *The Paleface* was one of Hope's most popular forties movies—a lively Western spoof with Hope as a novice dentist named Painless Peter Potter. He meets Calamity Jane (Russell), who is on a government mission to find a group of nasty renegades. She marries him purely as a cover, and you can guess the rest. Oscar-winning song: "Buttons and Bows." Sequel: *Son of Paleface* (1952). Remade as *The Shakiest Gun in the West* (1968), with Don Knotts.

## The Princess and the Pirate

★★★ Goldwyn, 1944, c, 94 min. Dir: David Butler. SP: Don Hartman, Mel Shavelson, Everett Freeman; adapted by Allen Boretz, Curtis Kenyon. Cast: Bob Hope, Virginia Mayo, Walter Brennan, Walter Slezak, Victor McLaglen, Marc Lawrence, Hugo Haas.

One of Bob Hope's better features of the forties, lively and brightly Technicolored. Hope plays Sylvester the Great, an entertainer in the days of the Spanish Main who, along with a princess (Mayo), is captured by buccaneers. They escape to a port where pirates gather to divide their loot and after some wild adventures, they prevail. Naturally, historical accuracy is tossed aside as Hope delivers one contemporary wisecrack after another. (Seeing the governor's opulent palace, he exclaims, "Some drive-in!") Victor McLaglen and Walter Slezak are the chief villains, and Walter Brennan plays a dimwitted pirate appropriately named Featherhead.

## Road to Singapore

★★★ Paramount, 1940, 84 min. Dir: Victor Schertzinger. SP: Don Hartman, Frank Butler, b/o story by Harry Hervey. Cast: Bob Hope, Bing Crosby, Dorothy Lamour, Charles Coburn, Anthony Quinn, Jerry Colonna, Judith Barrett.

Paramount Studios had a brainstorm that turned into a goldmine: why not team two of their biggest stars in a knockabout comedy with music? Laid-back, mellow-voiced Bing Crosby and quipping comedian Bob Hope would play pals who find themselves in trouble in Singapore as they both pursue sultry Dorothy Lamour. The result was a smash hit, and the first of a popular series of "Road" movies. Never mind that some of the gags were lame, or that Crosby seemed to go out of his way to humiliate or betray his "pal." Audiences loved the jokes, the slapstick, and the songs and wanted more of the same. *Road to Singapore* was followed by travels to Zanzibar (1941), Morocco

(1942), Utopia (1945, actually Alaska), Rio (1947), Bali (1952), and Hong Kong (1962).

## Son of Paleface

★★★ Paramount, 1952, c., 95 min. Dir: Frank Tashlin. SP: Frank Tashlin, Robert L. Welch, Joseph Quillan. Cast: Bob Hope, Jane Russell, Roy Rogers, Bill Williams, Lloyd Corrigan, Paul E. Burns, Douglass Dumbrille, Harry Von Zell, Iron Eyes Cody.

A followup to Bob Hope's hit 1948 comedy *The Paleface,* this farce had the rapid pace and the gag-laden style of the best "Road" films. Bob Hope is Junior, the Harvard-educated son of that old Indian fighter Painless Potter, who comes back to Sawbuck Pass to claim the fortune he thinks his father stashed away for him. Russell, his *Paleface* costar, returns as a saloon singer who is really a lady bandit called "The Torch." Roy Rogers, appropriately named Roy Rogers, is a federal agent. Ignore the plot and wait for the Hopeful wisecracks and situations. This was the first film directed by comedy writer Tashlin, who proved to be an expert at this sort of slapstick nonsense.

## Sorrowful Jones

★★★ Paramount, 1949, 88 min. Dir: Sidney Lanfield. SP: Melville Shavelson, Edmund Hartmann, Jack Rose, b/o story by Damon Runyon. Cast: Bob Hope, Lucille Ball, William Demarest, Bruce Cabot, Mary Jane Saunders, Thomas Gomez, Tom Pedi.

Another—and fairly tangy—version of Damon Runyon's tale "Little Miss Marker," *Sorrowful Jones* lacks some of the raffish charm of the 1934 movie with Shirley Temple, but it will do as a Bob Hope vehicle. Hope plays the title role, a down-on-his-luck gambler who becomes the accidental guardian of a little girl (Saunders). He tangles with gangsters and detectives, all the while becoming reluctantly fond of his tiny charge. Sorrowful also finds the time to court a nightclub singer played by Lucille Ball. A few of the cast members, notably William Demarest, catch some of the Runyon pungency, but mostly the movie is intended as a gag-fest for its star. Remade again in 1980 as *Little Miss Marker.*

## They Got Me Covered

★★☆ Goldwyn-RKO, 1943, 95 min. Dir: David Butler. SP: Harry Kurnitz, b/o story by Leonard Q. Ross, Leonard Spigelgass. Cast: Bob Hope, Dorothy Lamour, Lenore Aubert, Otto Preminger, Edward Ciannelli, Marion Martin, Donald Meek, Phyllis Ruth.

Bob Hope at medium level in a wartime farce. This time he's a newspaper reporter who is fired for neglecting to report Germany's invasion of Russia. In Washington, he stumbles on a hot story involving Nazi saboteurs and their plot to blow up the city. With the help of his dubious girlfriend (Lamour), he sprints about the nation's capital, getting deeper into trouble and finally tangling with the spies. Once again the gags ("even my shoelaces are unstrung") are meant to disguise the fact that he's a bungler, a coward, and a liar, but likable for all that. The laughs come intermittently.

# Jerry Lewis

Whether working solo or as half of the phenomenally popular team of Martin and Lewis, Jerry Lewis built a successful career on playing innocent misfits whose mental age never seemed to have caught up to their chronological years. With the right roles, he revealed a gift for slapstick and mimicry, but, right or wrong, he enjoyed the loyalty and affection of his many fans.

## Artists and Models

★★★ Paramount, 1955, c, 109 min. Dir: Frank Tashlin. SP: Frank Tashlin, Hal Kanter, Herbert Baker; adapted by Don McGuire from play by Michael Davidson, Norman Lessing. Cast: Jerry Lewis, Dean Martin, Shirley MacLaine, Dorothy Malone, Eddie Mayehoff, Eva Gabor, Anita Ekberg.

More elaborate than most Martin-Lewis outings, *Artists and Models* also offers a few funny sequences for Lewis fans. He's a comic-book addict whose nightmares are turned into plots for artist Martin, who is writing gruesome comic books. Shirley MacLaine (in her second movie) and Dorothy Malone are aboard for romance and/or decoration. The funniest scene has Lewis grappling with several masseuses in a tangle of arms and legs. He also wins laughs as a guest on a television talk show.

## At War with the Army

★★☆ Paramount, 1950, 93 min. Dir: Hal Walker. SP: Fred F. Finklehoffe, b/o play by James B. Allardice. Cast: Jerry Lewis, Dean Martin, Polly Bergen, Mike Kellin, Jimmy Dundee, Jean Ruth, Dick Stabile, Tommy Farrell.

This first starring feature for Dean Martin and Jerry Lewis offers the setup that they would repeat in most of their movies: Martin as the laid-back womanizer and crooner who harasses his bungling, childlike friend Lewis. Lewis is an inept army recruit who must cope with everything from KP duty to a soda machine gone berserk. He even gets to sing a tune called "The Navy Gets the Gravy but the Army Gets the Beans." The team's enormous popularity continued into other branches of the service and beyond for a number of years.

## The Bellboy

★★☆ Paramount, 1960, 72 min. Dir and SP: Jerry Lewis. Cast: Jerry Lewis, Alex Gerry, Bob Clayton, Sonny Sands.

Jerry Lewis made his debut as a director and also wrote and produced this middling farce. There's no plot, only a series of slapstick episodes with Lewis as a hapless bellhop at Miami's luxurious Fontainebleau Hotel. He copes with a quartet of ringing telephones, removes the rear-end motor from a foreign car instead of the luggage, and uses camera trickery to blot out some scantily clad girls from a room. Little dialogue, much slapstick.

## Cinderfella

★★☆ Paramount, 1960, c, 88 min. Dir and SP: Frank Tashlin. Cast: Jerry Lewis, Anna Maria Alberghetti, Ed Wynn, Judith Anderson, Henry Silva, Robert Hutton, Count Basie.

The Cinderella story, revamped for Jerry Lewis, with Ed Wynn as the Fairy Godfather and

Jerry Lewis and Dean Martin scored in their first starring feature, *At War with the Army* (1950). They remained popular until they parted company in 1956.

Judith Anderson as the Wicked Stepmother. This time there are two wicked stepbrothers, Maximilian and Rupert (Silva, Hutton). The production is elaborate and there are a few musical sequences, but the antics are conventional slapstick, with Lewis spreading havoc, on himself and everyone else, as the clumsy simpleton Cinderfella.

## The Delicate Delinquent

★ Paramount, 1957, 100 min. Dir and SP: Don McGuire. Cast: Jerry Lewis, Martha Hyer, Darren McGavin, Horace McMahon, Milton Frome.

Jerry Lewis's first movie after splitting with Dean Martin leaves everything to be desired. A woefully unfunny, uneasy mixture of comedy and sentiment, it has Lewis playing a hapless janitor who is everybody's favorite victim, a nerd who is considered the neighborhood jinx. Cop McGavin mistakes him for a delinquent (why?) and sets about trying to reform him, with the expected results. It's hard to decide which scene is the most abysmal: Lewis performing a solo of "By Myself" (paging Fred Astaire), or his suddenly introspective, self-analytical monologue to McGavin, which is totally against the character he has played. Most of Lewis's later solo efforts would be better than this.

## The Disorderly Orderly

★★ Paramount, 1964, c, 90 min. Dir and SP: Frank Tashlin. Cast: Jerry Lewis, Glenda Farrell, Susan Oliver, Everett Sloane, Karen Sharpe, Kathleen Freeman, Del Moore, Alice Pearce, Jack E. Leonard.

More slapstick hijinx from a solo Jerry Lewis. He plays Jerome Littlefield, a "disorderly"—read clumsy and inept—orderly at a mental hospital, and after a while, you begin to wonder who should be wearing the straitjacket. The movie is largely a series of slapstick incidents involving Jerome: he tries to fix a television set (naturally real "snow" pours out of the set), tries to bandage a patient, nearly destroys another patient in traction, creates havoc with spilled pills, and so on. One sequence draws laughs: Jerome reacting with sympathy pains to Alice Pearce's description of her ailments. At times Lewis's character becomes disconcertingly serious. In all, another movie only diehard fans will enjoy.

## The Family Jewels

★★☆ Paramount, 1965, c, 100 min. Dir: Jerry Lewis. SP: Jerry Lewis, Bill Richmond. Cast: Jerry Lewis, Donna Butterworth, Sebastian Cabot, Jay Adler, Neil Hamilton.

How much Jerry Lewis are you prepared to tolerate? The Family Jewels will allow you to answer that question, since he plays no less than seven roles. Little Donna Butterworth, nine years old and the heir to a fortune, is asked to choose the uncle who will be her guardian. Lewis plays all the uncles, including a gung-ho airline pilot, a ghoulish photographer, and a cross-eyed gangster, and whether you laugh depends entirely on your feelings about the comedian.

## Hollywood or Bust

★★ Paramount, 1956, c, 95 min. Dir: Frank Tashlin. SP: Erna Lazarus. Cast: Jerry Lewis, Dean Martin, Pat Crowley, Anita Ekberg, Maxie Rosenbloom. Jack McElroy.

Martin and Lewis's last film as a team is mostly feeble, with few laughs scattered through the familiar territory. Gambler Martin and starstruck Lewis set off for Hollywood, accompanied by a Great Dane named Mr. Bascomb, and most of the movie concerns their adventures on the highway. They have the usual troubles with their automobile, Lewis gets to confront a dangerous bull, and Martin sings a few tunes. Anita Ekberg plays herself, the girl of Lewis's dreams.

## Jumping Jacks

★★☆ Paramount, 1952, 96 min. Dir: Norman Taurog. SP: Richard Lees, Fred Rinaldo, Herbert Baker, b/o story by Brian Marlow. Cast: Jerry Lewis, Dean Martin, Robert Strauss, Mona Freeman, Don DeFore, Dick Erdman, Marcy McGuire.

More of the same hi-jinx from Dean Martin and Jerry Lewis. This time Lewis is forced to impersonate a paratrooper at the urging of his pal and partner, Martin, who is already in the service. Soon enough he is at the mercy of the proverbial tough sergeant (Strauss) and also required to pack a parachute, leap out of a plane, and participate in maneuvers, all to much bellowing and screaming in terror. Of course he comes through unscathed and a virtual hero. Standard fare, with laughs only for fans who find the comedian's antics amusing. Martin gets to sing a few tunes and romance Mona Freeman.

## The Nutty Professor

★★ Paramount, 1963, c, 107 min. Dir: Jerry Lewis. SP: Jerry Lewis, Bill Richmond. Cast: Jerry Lewis, Stella Stevens, Del Moore, Kathleen Freeman, Henry Gibson.

Many Jerry Lewis fans regard *The Nutty Professor* as one of his best films, and your own reaction will depend entirely on whether you are among his legion of admirers. A kind of Jekyll-and-Hyde farce, the movie has Lewis as Julian Kelp, an inept, gargoyle-like professor who wreaks havoc wherever he goes. Experimenting with a secret formula, he turns himself into Buddy Love, an obnoxious singer who may have been modeled on Lewis's former partner, Dean Martin. Eventually, the two personalities begin to interact, causing confusion. The main problem is that neither Julian Kelp nor Buddy Love is a funny or sympathetic human being. It's also spooky instead of amusing when Love starts speaking in Kelp's voice. If you're an avid Lewis fan, ignore the above. Remade in 1996 with Eddie Murphy.

## You're Never Too Young

★★☆ Paramount, 1955, c, 102 min. Dir: Norman Taurog. SP: Sidney Sheldon, b/o story by Fannie Kilbourne. Cast: Jerry Lewis, Dean Martin, Diana Lynn, Nina Foch, Raymond Burr, Mitzi McCall, Veda Ann Borg.

In Billy Wilder's *The Major and the Minor* (1942), as a young woman who disguises herself as a gawky twelve-year-old, Ginger Rogers was not always believable, but she was starkly realistic in comparison with Jerry Lewis's performance in this remake. Fleeing from gangster Burr, he impersonates an antic preteenager at a fashionable boarding school for girls. Slapstick galore, with Dean Martin as a teacher and Diana Lynn, who appeared in *The Major and the Minor,* as his romantic interest.

# Danny Kaye

After years of entertaining at Catskill resorts and in Broadway musicals, Danny Kaye signed a contract with Samuel Goldwyn and became a comedy star: a red-headed clown with an antic disposition and a gift for delivering clever patter songs. His best work came later when he restrained his manic style to play more credible characters.

## The Court Jester

★★★☆ Paramount, 1956, c, 101 min. Dir and SP: Norman Panama, Melvin Frank. Cast: Danny Kaye, Glynis Johns, Basil Rathbone, Angela Lansbury, Cecil Parker, Mildred Natwick, Robert Middleton, John Carradine.

One of Danny Kaye's most successful movies, a lavish, entertaining comedy with Kaye at his most appealing. He plays Hawkins, the lowliest member of a band of renegades led by the Black Fox in medieval England. Their goal is to remove nasty King Roderick (Parker) from the throne. To penetrate the castle, Hawkins impersonates the court jester, leading to all sorts of complications. Kaye gets to display his gift for rapid-fire comedy, especially the well-remembered routine in which he must remember which drink is poisoned ("The pellet with the poison is in the vessel with the pestle. The chalice from the palace has the brew that is true.") He also performs a few excellent songs, including "Life Could Not Better Be" and "The Maladjusted Jester."

## The Inspector General

★★★ Warners, 1949, c, 102 min. Dir: Henry Koster. SP: Philip Rapp, Harry Kurnitz, b/o play by Nikolai Gogol. Cast: Danny Kaye, Walter Slezak, Elsa Lanchester, Barbara Bates, Gene Lockhart, Alan Hale, Walter Catlett.

A funny vehicle for Danny Kaye, who plays Georgi, the assistant to abusive taskmaster Yakov (Slezak), whose medicine show roams the Eastern European countryside. Forced out on his own, Georgi is mistaken for the Inspector General by the corrupt Mayor (Lockhart) and council of a town. Georgi is lionized until comic complications take over. Kaye gets to do his manic routines, consuming a huge dinner in rapid motion (very Chaplinesque), or frantically trying to conceal all the officials who have come to bribe him in parts of his room. Kaye also drops all pretense of a characterization to perform a few good songs.

## The Kid from Brooklyn

★★ Goldwyn, 1946, c, 114 min. Dir: Norman Z. McLeod. SP: Grover Jones, Frank Butler, Richard Connell, b/o play by Lynn Root, Harry Clork; adapted by Don Hartman, Melville Shavelson. Cast: Danny Kaye, Virginia Mayo, Vera-Ellen, Walter Abel, Steve Cochran, Eve Arden, Lionel Stander, Fay Bainter, Clarence Kolb.

Danny Kaye's third film, and a remake of Harold Lloyd's *The Milky Way.* Kaye plays a timid milkman who accidentally knocks out boxing champion Steve Cochran and becomes a headlined hero. His life is turned upside down when a scheming boxing manager (Abel) uses him as the fall guy for fixed fights. Success goes to his head, but he finally returns to his senses and the dairy business. Virginia Mayo is the girl he loves, and Vera-Ellen plays his sister. As a comic actor Kaye can be irritating, but his genuine talent shines through when he performs "Pavlova." *The Kid from Brooklyn* is strictly for Kaye fans with lots of tolerance.

## The Secret Life of Walter Mitty

★★ Goldwyn, 1947, c, 110 min. Dir: Norman Z. McLeod. SP: Ken Englund, Everett Freeman, b/o story by James Thurber. Cast: Danny Kaye, Virginia Mayo, Boris Karloff, Fay Bainter, Ann Rutherford, Florence Bates, Gordon Oliver, Thurston Hall.

It must have seemed a good idea at the time to adapt James Thurber's famous story about a day-dreaming Milquetoast into a vehicle for Samuel Goldwyn's star comedian. Unfortunately, despite Kaye's strenuous efforts and elaborate Technicolor trappings, the result is dreary. Here, Walter Mitty is a timid soul browbeaten by his monster mother (Bainter), his harebrained fiancée (Rutherford), and his boss (Hall). Spinning off from Thurber, the movie has him involved in a dangerous real-life adventure with beautiful Virginia Mayo. Mitty's dramatized daydreams are only faintly amusing, and the only reasons to watch are Kaye's musical numbers, especially his funny "Anatole of Paris."

## Up in Arms

★★★ Goldwyn, 1944, c, 106 min. Dir: Elliott Nugent. SP: Don Hartman, Allen Boretz, Robert Pirosh, b/o play by Owen Davis. Cast: Danny Kaye, Dana Andrews, Dinah Shore, Constance Dowling, Louis Calhern, George Mathews.

Up in Arms is a musical, complete with songs by Dinah Shore, decorative appearances by the Goldwyn Girls, and one ghastly musical dream sequence. But it's also the comedy that introduced Danny Kaye to feature films. As such, it displayed Kaye's gift for rendering clever patter songs. Unfortunately, the movie also saddled him with the role of a jittery hypochondriac who is drafted reluctantly into the army, and he is forced to behave like a bumbling—and charmless—idiot. (This was the third version of Owen Davis's play The Nervous Wreck.) The only palatable moments with Kaye come when he performs several musical routines, the best being his trademarked "Melody in 4-F." Dinah Shore's velvety voice provides a few soothing interludes.

## Wonder Man

★★★ Goldwyn, 1945, c, 98 min. Bruce Humberstone. SP: Don Hartman, Melville Shavelson, Philip Rapp; adapted by Jack Jevne, Eddie Moran from story by Arthur Sheekman. Cast: Danny Kaye, Virginia Mayo, Vera-Ellen, S. Z. Sakall, Donald Woods, Allen Jenkins, Ed Brophy, Steve Cochran, Otto Kruger.

Danny Kaye's second film, made after his success in Up in Arms. Here he played a dual role: a nightclub entertainer who is murdered by the mob and the entertainer's bookworm brother, who takes over his slain sibling's body. Spurred on by the frolicsome ghost of his dead brother, the bookworm gets the chance to register comic fear, confusion, and even some romantic feeling towards Virginia Mayo. As always, the movie's best portions are Kaye's specialty numbers, particularly a hectic "Orchi Tchornya" as performed by a Russian baritone with a sneezing fit. Vera-Ellen is the lithe dancer who was the girlfriend of the dead brother.

# Red Skelton

Billed as "America's Clown," Red Skelton parlayed his rubbery features and his gift for pantomime into a long career in films and on television. He could, at times, wax overly sentimental or he would trade too often on the good will of his audience, but he proved to be an able performer in comedy and musical films.

## The Fuller Brush Man

★★☆ Columbia, 1948, 93 min. Dir: S. Sylvan Simon. SP: Frank Tashlin, Devery Freeman, b/o story by Roy Huggins. Cast: Red Skelton, Janet Blair, Don McGuire, Hillary Brooke, Adele Jergens, Trudy Marshall, Ross Ford.

Standard Skelton slapstick, with occasional hearty laughs, as Red plays a meek street cleaner who becomes a brush salesman to please his girl (Blair). The job involves him in a murder, which has him scrambling about to escape the killers. At one point, he draws on his trademarked imitation of "Junior, the mean widdle kid," and at another, he tangles amusingly with housewife Adele Jergens.

## The Show-Off

★★☆ MGM, 1947, 83 min. Dir: Harry Beaumont. SP: George Wells, b/o play by George Kelly. Cast: Red Skelton, Marilyn Maxwell, Marjorie Main, Virginia O'Brien, Eddie "Rochester" Anderson, George Cleveland, Jacqueline Wells, Leon Ames, Marshall Thompson.

A third version of George Kelly's durable play, filmed before in 1926 with Ford Sterling and in 1934 with Spencer Tracy. This time around Red Skelton plays Audrey Piper, a loudmouth railroad clerk who marries Amy Fisher (Maxwell) and nearly ruins the Fisher family of Philadelphia with his bluster and free advice. Naturally, by the film's end, Audrey proves himself to be the family's savior. Skelton plays with more restraint than usual, and he has the benefit of an amiable supporting cast.

## A Southern Yankee

★★★ MGM, 1948, 90 min. Dir: Edward Sedgwick. SP: Devery Freeman, Frank Tashlin, b/o story by Devery Freeman. Cast: Red Skelton, Arlene Dahl, George Coulouris, Lloyd Gough, John Ireland, Charles Dingle, Joyce Compton.

One of Red Skelton's best comedies, *A Southern Yankee* stars the comedian as Aubrey, a bumbling bellhop during the Civil War who dreams of joining the Union Secret Service. Eventually he finds himself in the thick of the battle, where he impersonates a Confederate spy known as the Gray Spider. Although the plot was merely a peg on which to hang Skelton's comedy routines, many of the movie's gags were well handled, probably because Buster Keaton served as advisor. The funniest moment by far, echoing Keaton's *The General,* comes when Aubrey is trapped between enemy lines and wears halves of two jackets, blue and gray, which he displays to the cheers of both armies.

## Whistling in the Dark

★★★ MGM, 1941, 77 min. Dir: S. Sylvan Simon. SP: Robert MacGunigle, Harry Clork, Albert Mannheimer, b/o play by Laurence Gross, Edward Childs Carpenter. Cast: Red Skelton, Ann Rutherford, Conrad Veidt, Virginia Grey, Rags Ragland, Henry O'Neill, Eve Arden.

After featured roles, Red Skelton was given a starring role in this comedy-mystery—a remake of a 1932 film. Here he plays a radio criminologist known as the Fox, who is kidnapped by a gang of phony clairvoyants in order to have him construct the plan for a perfect murder. It is no surprise that the movie mixes gags and chills in the manner of Bob Hope's hits *The Cat and the Canary* and *The Ghost Breakers.* Still, Skelton proved himself to be an able slapstick comedian. Two sequels followed, *Whistling in Dixie* (1942) and *Whistling in Brooklyn* (1943).

## The Yellow Cab Man

★★☆ MGM, 1950, 85 min. Dir: Jack Donohue. SP: Devery Freeman, Albert Beich. Cast: Red Skelton, Gloria De Haven, Walter Slezak, Edward Arnold, James Gleason, J. C. Flippen, Paul Harvey.

Red Skelton had a popular hit with *The Fuller Brush Man* in 1948. So why not assign him another occupation and send him off again into the slapstick mills? Here he is a Yellow Cab man with something else on his mind beside passengers—as Augustus "Red" Pirdy, he has invented a type of unbreakable glass, and now dastardly villains are out to wrest the formula from him. There are wild chases and one amusing session on a psychiatrist's couch before the happy ending.

Red Skelton has Arlene Dahl on his arm in *A Southern Yankee* (1948). This was probably Skelton's best comedy, with gags devised by the great Buster Keaton.

# Abbott and Costello

Bud Abbott and Lou Costello enjoyed huge popularity in the forties as a movie comedy team, beginning with their first starring vehicle, *Buck Privates.* Rotund Costello's timid, childlike demeanor made him a natural victim for dour Abbott's bullying and schemes, which usually ended with Costello in trouble. Their box-office draw waned in the fifties.

## Abbott and Costello Meet Frankenstein

★★☆ Universal, 1948, 83 min. Dir: Charles T. Barton. SP: John Grant, Robert Lees, Frederic I. Rinaldo. Cast: Bud Abbott, Lou Costello, Lon Chaney, Jr., Bela Lugosi, Lenore Aubert, Jane Randolph, Glenn Strange, Frank Ferguson.

A notch or two better than most of the Abbott and Costello comedies, but hardly the classic horror-comedy it is rated by some critics. The team plays baggage handlers named Chick (Abbott) and Wilbur (Costello), who find themselves involved with Universal's favorite monsters, the Wolf Man (Chaney, a.k.a. Larry Talbot), Dracula (Lugosi), and the Frankenstein Monster (Strange). The principal joke, as expected, is Wilbur's fright as each monster materializes before his eyes only. The creatures are all played perfectly straight, which is a refreshing change, and Chaney is actually sympathetic as the reluctant Wolf Man.

Lou Costello is hypnotized by Count Dracula (Bela Lugosi), who turned up in the horror comedy *Abbott and Costello Meet Frankenstein* (1948).

The comedy team of Bud Abbott and Lou Costello flourished in the forties, then declined in the fifties.

## Abbott and Costello Meet the Invisible Man

★★★ Universal, 1951, 82 min. Dir: Charles Lamont. SP: Robert Lees, Frederic I. Rinaldo, John Grant, b/o story by Hugh Wedlock, Jr., Howard Snyder. Cast: Bud Abbott, Lou Costello, Nancy Guild, Arthur Franz, Sheldon Leonard, Adele Jergens, William Frawley.

Some clever special effects highlight this slightly superior entry from the comedians. They play a pair of detectives with an invisible client—a boxer who must prove that he did not murder his manager. The best scene has Costello in the ring with a middleweight contender while his unseen client actually throws the punches. Naturally the client leaves the ring, with Costello obliged to fight for real. Some genuine laughs here.

## Buck Privates

★★★ Universal, 1941, 84 min. Dir: Arthur Lubin. SP: Arthur T. Horman. Cast: Bud Abbott, Lou Costello, Andrews Sisters, Lee Bowman, Alan Curtis, Jane Frazee, Nat Pendleton, Samuel S. Hinds.

The first starring movie for the hugely popular comedy team of Bud Abbott and Lou Costello is little more than a string of their vaudeville routines, but audiences loved them, especially Costello in his usual role of the childlike, constantly put-upon clown. Here they join the army by mistake, and Lou is the natural target of the standard service comedy jokes. Abbott is the straight man, fast-talking and a little acerbic. Comedy historians will welcome their famous "Who's on first?" baseball routine, and nostalgia fans will enjoy the Andrews Sisters and their rendition of "Apple Blossom Time." Surprisingly, *Buck Privates* was one of the year's big hits.

## Buck Privates Come Home

★★★ Universal, 1947, 77 min. Dir: Charles Barton. SP: John Grant, Frederic I. Rinaldo, Robert Lees, b/o story by Richard Macaulay, Bradford Ropes. Cast: Bud Abbott, Lou Costello, Tom Brown, Joan Fulton, Nat Pendleton, Beverly Simmons, Don Beddoe.

Abbott and Costello add some sentiment to their usual slapstick mix in this sequel to their 1941 hit, *Buck Privates*. They play the same bumbling characters who now scheme to win legal custody of a little French orphan (Simmons), whom they smuggle into the country aboard a troopship. Slapstick is not neglected: the climax finds Costello behind the wheel of a racing car he drives wildly through congested city streets.

## Hold That Ghost

★★★ Universal, 1941, 86 min. Dir: Arthur Lubin. SP: Robert Lees, Frederic I. Rinaldo, John Grant, b/o story by Robert Lees, Frederic I. Rinaldo. Cast: Bud Abbott, Lou Costello, Joan Davis, Mischa Auer, Richard Carlson, Evelyn Ankers, Marc Lawrence, Shemp Howard.

A notch or two better than the standard Abbott and Costello caper, as the boys inherit a haunted house vacated by a murdered gangster. All the usual "haunted house" gimmicks are on hand: secret passageways, sliding panels, clutching hands, and so on, and Costello registers fright, of course, at every turn, but some of the gags are funny. Good support from Joan Davis as a professional radio screamer.

## In the Navy

★★☆ Universal, 1941, 85 min. Dir: Arthur Lubin. SP: Arthur T. Horman, John Grant, b/o story by Arthur T. Horman. Cast: Bud Abbott, Lou Costello, Dick Powell, Andrews Sisters, Dick Foran, Claire Dodd.

Abbott and Costello in the navy, where Costello has hallucinations and nearly wrecks the entire fleet. In the meantime, we have the chubby Costello grappling unsuccessfully with a navy hammock, falling victim to Abbott's shell game, and directing maneuvers in an outsize admiral's suit. Songs are provided by Dick Powell and the Andrews Sisters.

## Keep 'Em Flying

★★☆ Universal, 1941, 86 min. Dir: Arthur Lubin. SP: True Boardman, Nat Perrin, John Grant, b/o story by Edmund R. Hartman. Cast: Bud Abbott, Lou Costello, Martha Raye, Carol Bruce, Dick Foran, William Gargan.

The boys at large in the air force, having already demolished the army and navy. Once again the setting is merely a cue for their slapstick antics: Costello on a runaway air-torpedo; both men trapped in a wildly careening airplane; Costello registering terror at a carnival spook house, and so forth. There's also a plot of sorts, but don't pay attention. Martha Raye provides some raucous fun playing twins.

## The Time of Their Lives

★★★ 1946, 82 min. Dir: Charles Barton. SP: Val Burton, Walter DeLeon, Bradford Ropes. Cast: Bud Abbott, Lou Costello, Marjorie Reynolds, Binnie Barnes, John Shelton, Gale Sondergaard, Jess Barker, Donald McBride.

A nice switch for the team, with Lou Costello as the ghost of one Horatio Prim, a tinker who was falsely branded a traitor during the Revolutionary War. Now, along with another maligned ghost (Reynolds), Horatio gets even by playing havoc with some people (including Abbott) spending the night in a restored colonial mansion. Highlight: Horatio drives a seemingly driverless police car around the grounds.

## Who Done It?

★★☆ Universal, 1942, 75 min. Dir: Erle C. Kenton. SP: Stanley Roberts, Edmund Joseph, John Grant, b/o story by Stanley Roberts. Cast: Bud Abbott, Lou Costello, Patric Knowles, William Gargan, Louise Allbritton, Mary Wickes, Thomas Gomez, William Bendix.

When the president of a network is murdered, two aspiring radio writers (Bud and Lou) pretend to be detectives. As usual, Lou Costello gets the lion's share of the laughs, tussling with a drinking fountain, teetering on a high window ledge, or listening to a transcribed murder. Nice supporting cast, especially the indispensable Mary Wickes as a sardonic secretary.

# Comedy Series to Remember

From the 1930s to the 1950s, movie audiences at the local bijous certainly received their money's worth. You could see a double feature: an "A" movie with stars and a "B" movie with no stars, usually a low-budget "programmer" that lasted about an hour. Chances are that the program would include a newsreel, previews of coming attractions, and an animated cartoon. Often the second feature would be another entry in a popular series of movies churned out by the smaller studios every year. These compact little films made no claim to art—they were no more than "fillers" but they were fun. And frequently, they were comedies.

## Blondie

Pert, sensible Blondie first stepped off the pages of Chic Young's popular comic strip and onto movie screens in 1938 and immediately won the audience's heart. Columbia, known as the "Poverty Row" of studios, had found a winning formula in the domestic adventures of the Bumstead family: Blondie (Penny Singleton, originally known as Dorothy McNulty); her hapless husband, Dagwood (Arthur Lake); and their children, Baby Dumpling (later Alexander, played by Larry Simms) and Cookie (born in 1942 and played by Marjorie Kent). Dagwood was usually the center of the comedy, forever inept, flabbergasted, and in trouble. Nor can we forget the Bumstead dog, Daisy, whose human reactions to all situations were always good for a laugh. (Those expressive ears!) The series ran from 1938 to 1950, chalking up an astonishing twenty-eight entries. Future stars Rita Hayworth and Glenn Ford, among other familiar faces, turn up in the films.

## Ma and Pa Kettle

In 1947, Universal released *The Egg and I,* adapted from Betty MacDonald's best-selling book about her misadventures as a farm wife. The stars were Claudette Colbert and Fred MacMurray, but audiences responded enthusiastically to two rustic characters named Ma and Pa Kettle. Played by Marjorie Main and Percy Kilbride, the Kettles and their huge brood of children engaged in slapstick antics that tickled viewers. Universal quickly spotted the dollar signs and began a series of nine Kettle movies that began in 1949 with *Ma and Pa Kettle* and ended in 1957 with *The Kettles on Old MacDonald's Farm.* (Kilbride left the series in 1955.) The number of Kettle kids ranged from twelve to fifteen, depending on the movie. The Kettles were corny, to be sure, and their gags were timeworn, but movie audiences liked them.

## Francis the Talking Mule

Mr. Ed, the talking horse, was not the first animal to win audience favor with his impudent wisecracks. There was Francis, the talking mule, who brought in huge sums for Universal Studios from 1950 to 1956. Created in a novel by David Stern and voiced by character actor Chill Wills, blunt-speaking Francis could be counted on to get bumbling, none-too-bright Donald O'Connor into trouble in six movies, with Mickey Rooney replacing O'Connor in the seventh and last. Critics, of course, dismissed the series as silly, but true to form, Francis just kept on talking. Arthur Lubin, who directed the first six movies, went on to create a TV series centering on . . . yes, who else? Mr. Ed.

# Jim Carrey

Until recently the nation's foremost contortionist comedian, Jim Carrey proved, in *The Truman Show,* that he could play a believable human being, rather than a collection of tics, grimaces, and bizarre rearrangements of body parts. It remains to be seen whether he can move his promising career to a more durable, more credible level of comedy.

## Ace Ventura, Pet Detective

★★ Warners/Morgan Creek, 1994, c, 87 min. Dir: Tom Shadyac. SP: Jack Bernstein, Tom Shadyac, Jim Carrey. Cast: Jim Carrey, Sean Young, Courtney Cox, Tone Loc, Dan Marino, Noble Willingham.

Jim Carrey's breakthrough movie role, after a few seasons on television's *In Living Color,* has him playing Ace Ventura, a manic detective whose specialty is finding and retrieving lost pets. Here he's hired to find a dolphin named Snowflake, the mascot of the Miami Dolphins football team. When team quarterback Dan Marino is also missing, the plot (such as it is) thickens. Carrey can barely get through a line without twitching, grimacing, or twisting his features into grotesque shapes, and in no time at all, his routine becomes exhausting and/or irritating, but seldom funny. Even Jerry Lewis permitted himself a minute of repose. Young children may laugh, but everyone else should beware. Sean Young has an embarrassing role as a police officer with a secret.

## Ace Ventura: When Nature Calls

★ Warners, 1995, c, 91 min. Dir and SP: Steve Oedekerk. Cast: Jim Carrey, Ian McNeice, Simon Callow, Maynard Eziashi, Bob Gunton.

If you should see this awful movie, you may not forget the sight of Ace Ventura regurgitating to feed a starving bird, or spitting so profusely that he covers himself and two other characters with mucus. You may want to forget, but you won't. This sequel to *Ace Ventura, Pet Detective* begins with a spoof of *Cliffhanger* (he tries and fails to save a raccoon),

then sends the depressed Ace to a Tibetan monastery. He comes out of retirement to find the sacred bat that is the symbol of an African tribe. The jokes are crude and seldom funny, and Carrey is in his usual ultra-manic state.

## The Cable Guy

★ Columbia, 1996, c, 94 min. Dir: Ben Stiller. SP: Lou Holtz, Jr. Cast: Jim Carrey, Matthew Broderick, Leslie Mann, George Segal, Diane Baker, Jack Black, Eric Roberts, Janeane Garofalo, Andy Dick.

A dark, disturbing, and painfully unfunny comedy, and a serious mistake for Jim Carrey. He plays a weird cable TV installer who forces his friendship on customer Matthew Broderick, who has just moved out of his girlfriend's apartment. Step by step, Carrey turns Broderick's life into a waking nightmare, causing him to lose his job and alienate his family, while steering him toward a nervous breakdown. Apparently, the Cable Guy's life was shaped by television, and the movie may have been intended as a warning about the ultimate destructive effect of watching television incessantly, but it plays more like a horror film about a sociopathic stalker than a cautionary tale or a satire.

Jim Carrey as *Ace Ventura, Pet Detective* (1994). The manic detective proved to be the breakout role for this rubber-faced comedian.

## Dumb & Dumber

★ New Line, 1994, c, 110 min. Dir: Peter Farrelly. SP: Peter Farrelly, Bennett Yellin, Bobby Farrelly. Cast: Jim Carrey, Jeff Daniels, Lauren Holly, Karen Duffy, Victoria Rowell, Mike Starr, Charles Rocket, Teri Garr.

An early entry from the brothers Farrelly, before they pushed the gross-humor envelope further with *There's Something about Mary*. Here, Jim Carrey and Jeff Daniels play Lloyd and Harry, two brain-dead idiots who travel cross country to return a briefcase to a girl (Holly) whom Lloyd fancies, not knowing that the briefcase contains ransom money. Never mind the stupid plot; the movie is merely an exercise in the Comedy of Cruelty and Pain: Lloyd gives a headless bird to a blind boy; Harry's tongue becomes frozen on a ski lift; Lloyd puts a strong laxative into Harry's drink, and so on. Witless from first to last, and a good actor like Jeff Daniels should find a career counselor.

## Liar Liar

★★☆ Warners, 1997, c, 87 min. Dir: Tom Shadyac. SP: Paul Guay, Stephen Mazur. Cast: Jim Carrey, Maura Tierney, Justin Cooper, Cary Elwes, Jennifer Tilly, Anne Haney.

Fletcher Reede (Carrey), a divorced hotshot lawyer who can cheerfully lie his way through any court case, is suddenly in deep trouble. When his neglected young son (Cooper) wishes that his father would tell the truth for one whole day, the wish comes true, and Fletcher, to his dismay and agony, finds himself unable to lie to anyone. Of course it all ends with smiles, reconciliations, and a confirmation of family values. This time Carrey has a more coherent screenplay to work with, but he still finds time to do his usual twitching contortionist's routines. The screenplay includes one of those stupid sequences in which the hero, in his honesty mode, insults all the top members of his law firm, and they react by laughing uproariously. Oh, sure.

## The Mask

★★☆ New Line, 1994, c, 101 min. Dir: Charles Russell. SP: Mike Webb. Cast: Jim Carrey, Cameron Diaz, Peter Riegert, Peter Greene, Amy Yasbeck, Richard Jeni, Orestes Matacena, Nancy Fish, Ben Stein.

Timid bank clerk Stanley Ipkiss (Carrey) finds himself in possession of a magical mask which, when worn, turns him into a superhero capable of assuming any shape in the blink of an eye. Soon he's being chased by the police while tangling with a vicious mobster and nightclub owner (Greene) and his hoodlums. He's also fallen for Greene's singer girlfriend (Diaz, in her film debut). The plot is handled clumsily, but then there are the amazing special effects. Stanley's manic behavior as the Mask is animated in the style of Tex Avery, whose cartoons in the forties and fifties were unique for their combination of violence and free-wheeling slapstick.

## The Truman Show

★★★★ Paramount, 1998, c, 104 min. Dir: Peter Weir. SP: Andrew Niccol. Cast: Jim Carrey, Ed Harris, Laura Linney, Noah Emmerich, Natascha McElhone, Holland Taylor, Brian Delate, Paul Giamatti, Adam Tomei, Harry Shearer.

Meet Truman Burbank (Carrey), and why not? Everyone else has. For thirty years, an unsuspecting Truman has been the center of a television show chronicling his every move from the day of his birth. Truman lives in the tidy, pleasant town of Seahaven where everything—and everyone (wife, children, neighbors)—is perfect. Then he begins to suspect that something is wrong, and his world begins to collapse all around him. The people's obsession with the media, their absorbing interest in lives other than their own, and their readiness to accept anything they see or hear—these are the central ideas in Peter Weir's fascinating, ingeniously wrought film. Jim Carrey gives his first genuine performance as a man who finds himself trapped inside a totally controlling lie that is an idealized nightmare.

# Great
# Comedy
# Filmmakers

# Woody Allen

First an original stand-up comedian-writer, then an extremely funny stage and screen actor-writer, Woody Allen has evolved into one of our foremost creators of comedy films. Although many viewers claim to prefer the quipping, satirical early Allen of *Bananas* and *Sleeper,* there has always been a dark element in his work, evident in *Manhattan* and even *Annie Hall.* In such films as *Husbands and Wives* and *Crimes and Misdemeanors,* he combines bracing wit with somber reflections on life and love.

## Alice

★★★☆ Orion, 1990, c, 106 min. Dir and SP: Woody Allen. Cast: Mia Farrow, William Hurt, Joe Mantegna, Cybill Shepherd, Alec Baldwin, Blythe Danner, Gwen Verdon, Bernadette Peters, Judy Davis, Julie Kavner, Keye Luke.

As the nineties dawned, many movies took it on themselves to chastise audiences for their greed and selfishness in the eighties. Woody Allen's *Alice* drew on this theme but added Allen's sharp wit mixed with sadness about missed chances. Mia Farrow plays Alice, a woman who should be content with her lot, yet somehow drifts into a guilt-ridden affair with a divorced musician (Mantegna). She also takes the concoctions of a mysterious Oriental herbalist (Luke), which render her invisible. Now she is able to eavesdrop on other people's lives and even recall a past lover (Baldwin), with whom she flies over the nighttime city in a memorable sequence. In the end she comes to terms with all her past and present relationships. Funniest scene: the Christmas party.

## Annie Hall

★★★★ United Artists, 1977, c, 94 min. Dir: Woody Allen. SP: Woody Allen, Marshall Brickman. Cast: Woody Allen, Diane Keaton, Tony Roberts, Paul Simon, Shelley Duvall, Carol Kane, Colleen Dewhurst, Christopher Walken, Janet Margolin.

A triumph from Woody Allen, and one of his most popular and praised films. It won four Oscars, including Best Picture, Best Actress (Keaton), Best Direction, and Best Original Screenplay. The movie was Allen's first fully rounded view of the bright, angst-ridden New Yorkers who would populate many of his later efforts. Allen plays Alvy Singer, an intensely neurotic comedian who reflects on his life, including his childhood, his ex-wives and girl-friends, and especially his romance with Annie Hall (Keaton). Allen veers from fantasy to reality as he moves into Alvy's cluttered mind, in which fears and obsessions are transformed into comedy of a high order. Keaton achieved stardom (and, for a time, influenced fashion) as the dithering, lovable Annie.

## Bananas

★★★☆ United Artists, 1971, c, 82 min. Dir: Woody Allen. SP: Woody Allen, Mickey Rose. Cast: Woody Allen, Louise Lasser, Carlos Montalban, Natividad Abascal, Jacobo Morales, Miguel Suarez, Howard Cossell.

Early Woody Allen and very funny despite its loose construction and occasionally misfired gags. Allen is Fielding Mellish, a product tester who somehow becomes involved with the revolution in the tiny South American country of San Marcos. Through circumstances, he becomes the leader of the rebels, and when the current regime is overthrown, he becomes the country's president. Many uproarious moments: guerrilla Mellish ordering one thousand grilled cheese sandwiches and seven hundred cups of coffee at a lunch counter; soldiers torturing a man by forcing him to listen to the score of *Naughty Marietta;* Mellish arriving for dinner at

the dictator's home, carrying the requisite box of cookies, and so on. Great fun for Allen fans.

## Broadway Danny Rose

★★★ Orion, 1984, c, 86 min. Dir and SP: Woody Allen. Cast: Woody Allen, Mia Farrow, Nick Apollo Forte, Sandy Baron, Corbett Monica, Morty Gunty, Will Jordan, Milton Berle, Edwin Bordo.

An amusing Woody Allen entry, with Allen as a theatrical agent who represents such small-time performers as a stammering ventriloquist and a blind xylophonist. Suddenly he finds himself in big trouble revolving around his married Italian singer client (Forte) and the singer's birdbrained girl-on-the-side (Farrow). When Danny is mistaken for Farrow's boyfriend by a murder-mind-

Woody Allen is world-class neurotic Alvy Singer and Diane Keaton is Annie, the quirky, enchanting girl he loves, in the Oscar-winning *Annie Hall* (1977).

ed family of gangsters, he and the girl must flee for their lives. Allen is in his usual overwrought-loser mode, but Farrow is a hilarious revelation as a brassy blonde. Forte, an actual lounge singer, contributes some laughs with his rendition of his "specialty," a song called "Agita."

## Bullets over Broadway

★★★☆ Miramax, 1994, c, 99 min. Dir: Woody Allen. SP: Woody Allen, Douglas McGrath. Cast: John Cusack, Dianne Wiest, Chazz Palminteri, Jennifer Tilly, Joe Viterelli, Jack Warden, Tracey Ullman, Mary-Louise Parker, Jim Broadbent, Rob Reiner, Harvey Fierstein.

"I'm still a star! I never played frumps or virgins!" cries Helen Sinclair (Wiest) in this delightful bauble from Woody Allen. Wiest's performance as the self-dramatizing stage actress won her a Supporting Oscar. The year is 1929, and she's the leading lady in a "serious" new play by young David Shayne (Cusack), who has had more integrity than success. When David is forced to hire the dumb girlfriend (Tilly) of a top mobster (Viterelli), he learns more about playwriting from the mobster's henchman (Palminteri) than he bargained for. The movie is funny, even without the Allenesque quips, and sometimes it's even insightful about the theater and creativity. Still, you're likely to remember Wiest's Helen Sinclair exclaiming, "Don't speak!" to her amorous playwright.

## Celebrity

★★★ Miramax, 1998, 112 min. Dir and SP: Woody Allen. Cast: Kenneth Branagh, Judy Davis, Melanie Griffith, Winona Ryder, Joe Mantegna, Charlize Theron, Famke Janssen, Leonardo DiCaprio.

British actor Kenneth Branagh gives an accurate but disconcerting imitation of Woody Allen in this sometimes funny, sometimes strained, but always savage comedy on the desperate pursuit of fame. Branagh plays Lee Simon, a failed novelist and writer of celebrity profiles, who is recently separated from his neurotic wife, Robin (Davis). Clutching his screenplay, this fawning loser tries frantically to make contact with the famous people he encounters, most of whom seem to be self-serving, destructive, sexually voracious monsters. These are played by an impressive group of actors, all of whom are apparently anxious to accept any role in an Allen movie. Sometimes Allen wickedly captures the pretensions of these celebrities; other times the movie just seems sour and cluttered.

## Deconstructing Harry

★★☆ Fine Line, 1987, c, 90 min. Dir and SP: Woody Allen. Cast: Woody Allen, Kirstie Alley, Richard Benjamin, Eric Bogosian, Billy Crystal, Judy Davis, Hazelle Goodman, Mariel Hemingway, Amy Irving, Julie Kavner, Julia Louis-Dreyfus, Demi Moore, Elisabeth Shue, Stanley Tucci, Robin Williams.

Bluntly speaking, writer Harry Block (Allen) is a mess, and his writer's block is the least of his problems. He is despised by all the women in his life, including his ex-wives and his sister. Sexually obsessed, he finds comfort only with prostitutes. Even as he is about to be honored by his old alma mater, he views his life as a failure. Flashbacks and short comical tales from his writer's imagination dramatize his sorry state of mind, and sometimes fiction and reality intertwine. There are some fine Allenesque moments (his visit to a hell of his own making is a highlight), but the stellar cast is underused, and the movie is a bad-tempered and muddled affair, far from his best.

## Everyone Says I Love You

★★★★ Miramax, 1996, c, 101 min. Dir and SP: Woody Allen. Cast: Alan Alda, Woody Allen, Drew Barrymore, Goldie Hawn, Julia Roberts, Tim Roth, Lukas Haas, Gaby Hoffman, Natasha Lyonne, Edward Norton, Natalie Portman, David Ogden Stiers.

Yes, it's a musical, but filtered through the unique sensibility of Woody Allen, *Everyone Says I Love You* is an original musical like no other, and also a complete delight. Set mostly in upscale New York City (with dreamlike views of the city and—as a marvelous bonus—Venice and Paris), the movie centers on lawyer Alan Alda, his cause-

espousing wife Goldie Hawn, their children and stepchildren, and others who impinge on their lives. When the urge strikes, everyone sings (sometimes barely) or dances, with exhilarating results. Highlights include a jewelry store romp (to "My Baby Just Cares for Me"), a zany hospital number (to "Making Whoopee"), and a giddy Parisian dance, with everyone wearing Groucho masks. Allen and Hawn's dance along the Seine is pure movie magic.

## Everything You Always Wanted to Know About Sex (But Were Afraid to Ask)

★★★ United Artists, 1972, c, 87 min. Dir: Woody Allen. SP: Woody Allen, b/o book by Dr. David Reuben. Cast: Woody Allen, John Carradine, Lou Jacobi, Louise Lasser, Anthony Quayle, Tony Randall, Lynn Redgrave, Burt Reynolds, Gene Wilder, Tito Vandis.

Woody Allen's uneven collection of sketches, some ribaldly funny, some merely tasteless, all loosely suggested by Dr. David Reuben's bestselling book with the same title. The funniest by far is "What Happens During Ejaculation?" in which Allen depicts a gigantic control center during the key moments of intercourse, with Allen himself as a cowardly sperm. Other sketches include "What Is Sodomy?" in which Gene Wilder plays a doctor who falls passionately in love with a sheep; "Are Transvestites Homosexual?" which offers Lou Jacobi as a husband who likes to wear pretty feminine things, and "What's My Perversion?" involving a television panel show.

## The Front

★★☆ Columbia, 1976, c, 94 min. Dir: Martin Ritt. SP: Walter Bernstein. Cast: Woody Allen, Zero Mostel, Andrea Marcovicci, Herschel Bernardi, Michael Murphy, Remak Ramsay, Joshua Shelley, Lloyd Gough.

In 1952, during the period of Senator McCarthy's publicized "hunt" for Communists in government and the arts, a cashier named Howard Storm (Allen) becomes the "front" for a black-listed writer-friend (Murphy). Soon the success of his television scripts prompts him to front for other writers and he becomes a hidden celebrity. Complications ensue, leading to his appearance before a congressional committee. Allen neither wrote nor directed this serious comedy, and it shows. His character is not especially appealing, and the premise of the screenplay—that everyone who was blacklisted was honorable, and that all government investigators were fools or monsters—is shaky. The director and many cast members were also blacklisted in real life.

## Hannah and Her Sisters

★★★★ Orion, 1986, c, 106 min. Dir and SP: Woody Allen. Cast: Mia Farrow, Woody Allen, Michael Caine, Dianne Wiest, Barbara Hershey, Lloyd Nolan, Maureen O'Sullivan, Julie Kavner, Daniel Stern, Sam Waterston, Tony Roberts.

One of Woody Allen's finest films, funny and observant, as expected, but also infused with a becoming warmth and generosity. The movie centers on a family that has known both grief and happiness; at the center are three sisters: nurturing Hannah (Farrow); Lee (Hershey), a reformed alcoholic; and Holly (Wiest), distracted and unsure of herself. The people in their lives include Hannah's ex-husband (Allen), a world-class hypochondriac, and Hannah's current husband (Caine), who secretly adores Lee. The complex relationships between these people are exposed in ways that are both hilarious and poignant. Caine and Wiest both won supporting Oscars. In all, peak Allen.

## Husbands and Wives

★★★☆ TriStar, 1992, c, 107 min. Dir and SP: Woody Allen. Cast: Woody Allen, Mia Farrow, Judy Davis, Sydney Pollack, Juliette Lewis, Liam Neeson, Lysette Anthony, Blythe Danner, Benno C. Schmidt, Jr.

There are some laughs in this stinging comedy-drama, but mostly this vivisection of marriage and romance draws blood. It all begins when Jack (Pollack) and Sally (Davis) announce to their best friends, teacher Gabe (Allen) and his

wife, Judy (Farrow), that they are splitting up. Soon the seemingly perfect marriage of Gabe and Judy begins to unravel as well. Allen brings together a group of unhappy New Yorkers, and although they are sometimes sustained by their wit, they lack the warmth that would make audiences truly care. Also, it was difficult to separate the Gabe-Judy relationship in the movie from the Woody-and-Mia headlines of the day. Still, Allen's Oscar-nominated screenplay is brilliant and often perceptive. An Oscar nomination also went to Judy Davis.

## Love and Death

★★★☆ United Artists, 1975, c, 82 min. Dir and SP: Woody Allen. Cast: Woody Allen, Diane Keaton, Harold Gould, Alfred Lutter, Olga Georges-Picot, Zvee Scooler, C.A.R. Smith.

Woody Allen's *Love and Death* is not nearly as well known as many of his other films, but it's funny indeed, and many viewers remember lines and sequences with pleasure. Here, Allen not only spoofs classic Russian literature but also pays tribute to great foreign filmmakers from Eisenstein to Bergman. He plays Boris, a cowardly, bookish young Russian who survives the Napoleonic Wars, only to be executed for killing Napoleon. (Well, not really, but the charge remains.) From his prison cell, Boris tells about his experiences on the battlefield and his unrequited love for his cousin Sonia (Keaton), with whom he conspires to assassinate Napoleon. Allen enjoys satirizing the agonized soul-searchings and dense philosophical discussions in Russian literature.

## Manhattan

★★★★ United Artists, 1979, 96 min. Dir: Woody Allen. SP: Woody Allen, Marshall Brickman. Cast: Woody Allen, Diane Keaton, Michael Murphy, Mariel Hemingway, Meryl Streep, Anne Byrne.

Woody Allen's bittersweet, dark-hued comedy can be numbered among his best efforts. As rueful as it is funny, *Manhattan* looks at the lives of a group of neurotic New Yorkers headed by Allen

himself. He plays a comedy writer who is plagued by his ex-wife (Streep), at the same time that he is conducting a troubling affair with a seventeen-year-old girl (Hemingway). Things get even more complicated when a third woman (Keaton), the neurotic mistress of his married friend, enters the scene. There is no easy resolution to any relationship, and Allen ends up baffled and regretful. Stunningly photographed in black and white by Gordon Willis and richly scored with Gershwin music, *Manhattan* mixes laughter and melancholy, with memorable results.

In the shadow of the Queensboro Bridge, Mary Wilke (Diane Keaton) and Isaac Davis (Woody Allen) chat on a bench in *Manhattan* (1979).

## Manhattan Murder Mystery

★★★ TriStar, 1993, c, 108 min. SP: Woody Allen, Marshall Brickman. Cast: Woody Allen, Diane Keaton, Alan Alda, Anjelica Huston, Jerry Adler, Lynn Cohen, Ron Rifkin, Joy Behar, Marge Redmond, Aida Turturro.

Allen and Keaton are a Manhattan couple with a reasonably happy, slightly shaky marriage. When their next-door neighbor (Cohen) dies suddenly of a heart attack and the husband (Adler) shows little grief, Keaton gets the notion that the woman was murdered. To Allen's dismay, she begins her own investigation that puts them both in jeopardy. Alda and Huston play friends who help Keaton with her relentless snooping. A lightweight comedy-mystery in the *Thin Man* tradition, *Manhattan Murder Mystery* benefits from Allen's often funny quips. ("For crying out loud," he tells Keaton in exasperation, "save a little craziness for menopause.") The movie is enjoyable but forgettable.

## A Midsummer Night's Sex Comedy

★★★ United Artists, 1982, c, 88 min. Cast: Woody Allen, Mia Farrow, Mary Steenburgen, Tony Roberts, Jose Ferrer, Julie Hagerty.

A lightweight but charming bauble, clearly influenced by Ingmar Bergman's *Smiles of a Summer Night*. At the turn of the century, a group of people are brought together at the country home of Andrew Hobbs (Allen) and his wife, Adrian (Steenburgen), for a weekend of sexual intrigue. Partners change as assignations occur or go comically awry, and there are a few magical moments in the midsummer night. One guest dies while making love, but the weekend ends satisfactorily for everyone else. The film's best feature is Gordon Willis's exquisite cinematography.

## Mighty Aphrodite

★★★ Miramax, 1995, c, 95 min. Woody Allen. Cast: Woody Allen, Helena Bonham-Carter. Mira Sorvino, Michael Rapaport, Peter Weller, F. Murray Abraham, Olympia Dukakis, David Ogden Stiers, Jack Warden, Claire Bloom.

A slight but enjoyable Woody Allen comedy, with one offbeat gimmick that should have you howling with laughter. Allen is Lenny Weinrib, a sports writer who adopts a child with wife Amanda (Bonham-Carter). Years later, he searches for the child's natural mother, only to learn that she is a none-too-bright but likable prostitute (Sorvino in an Oscar-winning performance). He becomes involved in her life at the same time that his marriage is in trouble. The gimmick: Allen uses a Greek chorus—some members are well-known actors—that comments on the events in contemporary style ("Here comes the party-pooper") and breaks occasionally into song

and dance. At the movie's end, the chorus performs a nifty routine to "When You're Smiling" that will leave you smiling.

## New York Stories ("Oedipus Wrecks")

★★★ Touchstone, 1989, c, 123 min (entire film). Cast: Woody Allen, Mia Farrow, Julie Kavner, Mae Questel.

One segment of a three-part film, Woody Allen's "Oedipus Wrecks" returned him to the familiar character of the neurotic, victimized New Yorker. He plays Sheldon, a fifty-year-old lawyer burdened with the ultimate Jewish mother, a shrill, overbearing harridan (Questel). At a magic show, the magician inadvertently makes Momma disappear, to Sheldon's secret relief. He is mortified when she rematerializes in the sky, still continuing to berate him. When he turns to a medium (Kavner) for help, the outcome is unexpected. "Oedipus Wrecks" is pure Allen in its theme and execution, and funny indeed. The other segments of the movie are Martin Scorsese's "Life Lessons" and Francis Coppola's "Life Without Zoe," neither as good as Allen's entry.

## Play It Again, Sam

★★★ Paramount, 1972, c, 87 min. Dir: Herbert Ross. SP: Woody Allen, b/o his play. Cast: Woody Allen, Diane Keaton, Tony Roberts, Jerry Lacy, Susan Anspach, Jennifer Salt, Joy Bang, Viva.

Writer Allan Felix is the very essence of his creator's persona in the seventies: a terminally neurotic, movie-obsessed, pill-popping—but likable—loser. Repeatedly rejected by women, including his ex-wife (Anspach), he has taken to conjuring up the presence of Humphrey Bogart (Lacy), who dispenses advice about life and "dames." Ultimately, Allan begins a jittery affair with Linda (Keaton), the neglected wife of his best friend, Dick (Roberts). The affair ends with Allan and Linda reprising the famous airport scene between Rick and Ilsa at the end of *Casablanca*. Adapted by Allen from his Broadway play, the movie is steadily amusing but without the wild flights of fancy in his self-directed films of the period.

## The Purple Rose of Cairo

★★★ Orion, 1985, c, 82 min. Cast: Mia Farrow, Jeff Daniels, Danny Aiello, Dianne Wiest, Van Johnson, Zoe Caldwell, John Wood, Milo O'Shea, Edward Herrmann, Karen Akers.

Less astringent than most of Woody Allen's comedies in the early eighties, *The Purple Rose of Cairo* is a slender but affecting period piece. During the Depression, a young housewife and waitress named Cecilia (Farrow) has a wretched life with her boorish husband (Aiello). Her only escape is the movies, where she lives her fantasies. Then one night at her local Bijou, dashing screen hero Tom Baxter, played by movie idol Gil Shepard (Daniels), steps from the screen to proclaim his love for Cecilia. The resulting brouhaha brings the vain actor from Hollywood, and soon Cecilia, to her astonishment, is being courted by both the fictional Tom and the very real Gil. At the end, she is left only with her dreams, but in a cold, threatening world, that may be enough. Allen has always professed his love for movies and his belief in the needs they fulfill, and *The Purple Rose of Cairo* expresses his sentiments in bittersweet style.

## Radio Days

★★★☆ Orion, 1987, c, 85 min. Cast: Mia Farrow, Michael Tucker, Julie Kavner, Dianne Wiest, Seth Green, Josh Mostel, Wallace Shawn, Danny Aiello, Jeff Daniels, Diane Keaton, Tito Puente, Kitty Carlisle Hart, Kenneth Mars.

Woody Allen recalls the golden days of radio in the forties in one of his most pleasing movies. With affection and on-target accuracy, he focuses on several groups of people for whom radio is an essential part of their lives. Most often the movie returns to the members of one family, including mother (Kavner), father (Tucker), their young son (Green), and various relatives (Wiest, Mostel, and others) who dote on the popular radio personalities. Many of these personalities are depicted in their natural habitats of radio stations and nightclubs, unaware of their fleeting place in the sun. One is a squeaky-voiced hat-check girl (Farrow)

who rises to radio stardom at the start of World War II. Allen's screenplay won an Oscar nomination.

## Scenes from a Mall

★★ Touchstone, 1991, c, 87 min. Dir: Paul Mazursky. SP: Roger L. Simon, Paul Mazursky. Cast: Woody Allen, Bette Midler, Bill Irwin.

In his movies, Woody Allen has often suggested a man who covers his many wounds with a bracing wit. And at her best Bette Midler has played a brazen, proudly vulgar woman. Now take away Allen wit and extract Midler's brassiness, and what do you have? Paul Mazursky's *Scenes from a Mall.* He's a lawyer, and she's his psychiatrist wife, and they've been married for sixteen years. One afternoon at the mall, at Christmas time, he confesses to having an affair, just recently ended. They thrash about and fight furiously, until she confesses to cheating on him as well. Do they make up? Will you care? Probably not. Allen and Midler try to give the situation some bite and tang, but *Scenes from a Mall* is undernourished.

## Shadows and Fog

★☆ Orion, 1992, 86 min. Cast: Woody Allen, Kathy Bates, John Cusack, Mia Farrow, Jodie Foster, Fred Gwynne, Julie Kavner, Madonna, John Malkovich, Kenneth Mars, Kate Nelligan, Donald Pleasence, Lily Tomlin, Wallace Shawn, David Ogden Stiers.

A Woody Allen mistake—dull, murky, and unamusing. In an Eastern European village, a serial killer is loose, and a timid clerk—a self-styled "ink-stained wretch" named Kleinman (Allen) is not only suspected of being the killer but is also badgered, berated, and humiliated by everyone. On one dark night, he encounters various people, especially a sword-swallower (Farrow) from a traveling circus, who has fled from her clown-husband (Malkovich). Is Allen satirizing an art film, or is he engaging in a pointless parody of the Kafkaesque nightmare story? A large and stellar cast tries to make something of it all, without success.

## Sleeper

★★★★ United Artists, 1973, c, 88 min. SP: Woody Allen, Marshall Brickman. Cast: Woody Allen, Diane Keaton, John Beck, Mary Gregory, Don Keefer, John McLiam.

One of Woody Allen's funniest films of the seventies, a hilarious mixture of science fiction and satire. Allen's hapless hero is Miles Monroe who, in 1973, goes into the hospital for a minor operation and wakes up in the year 2173 after having been frozen when complications developed. He finds himself in a futuristic world where every turn brings another visual or verbal joke. He also becomes involved in a rebellion against the totalitarian government and falls for a light-headed girl named Luna (Keaton). Allen's barrage of one-liners will keep you laughing, and even many of the sets are splendid visual jokes. Among other things, you're likely to enjoy the outsize vegetables, the peculiar robots, and Allen's barb at the Miss America pageant.

## Stardust Memories

★★★ United Artists, 1980, 91 min. Cast: Woody Allen, Charlotte Rampling, Jessica Harper, Marie-Christine Barrault, Tony Roberts, Daniel Stern, Amy Wright.

Woody Allen's first film of the eighties was one of his most personal, most eccentric efforts. Allen plays Sandy Bates, a filmmaker not unlike himself who attends a festival of his films at a resort hotel at the New Jersey shore. A world-class neurotic, Sandy is assaulted on all sides by worshipful but often grotesque fans, pretentious movie freaks, and pompous academics who read deep meaning into his movies. As his past and present interact, he must also deal with tax problems, women problems, and troubles with his new movie. Allen's venomous view of his fans and admirers may put off some viewers, but he is equally hard on himself. Of course there are funny Allenesque lines but not enough to turn *Stardust Memories* into a popular hit.

## Take the Money and Run

★★★ United Artists, 1969, c, 85 min. SP: Woody Allen, Mickey Rose. Cast: Woody Allen, Janet Margolin, Marcel Hillaire, Jacquelyn Hyde, Lonny Chapman.

For all its lapses, Woody Allen's debut film as a director, writer, and star revealed an original new comic voice on the movie scene. Allen plays Virgil Starkwell, a thief of monumental ineptness whose attempts to rob banks end in disaster and prison. Basically a spoof of prison and gangster movies, the film is studded with funny Allenesque moments: in jail, he fashions a gun from soap but it melts in the rain; his road-gang punishment consists of one meal a day, "a bowl of steam"; when a prison guard snarls, "Any questions?" Virgil asks coyly, "Do you think a girl should pet on her first date?" Some scenes are awkwardly staged, but you may be laughing too hard to notice.

## Zelig

★★★☆ Orion-Warners, 1983, c & b/w, 79 min. Cast: Woody Allen, Mia Farrow, Garrett Brown, Stephanie Farrow, Will Holt, Sol Lomita, Mary Louise Wilson, Michael Jeter.

Just who is Leonard Zelig (Allen)? Zelig, it seems, is a rare phenomenon: a slight, bespectacled man who has so little personality of his own that he takes on the characteristics of whomever he's with—their appearance, their language, their entire being. For a while Zelig enjoys fame as the Chameleon Man—even a dance step, the Chameleon Hop, is named after him. Then he meets and falls in love with Dr. Eudora Fletcher (Farrow), who would like to "cure" him. Zelig's ultimate fate makes up the rest of this fascinating movie, which is filmed as a pseudo-documentary with "newsreels," interviews with real people, and the like. It's also a remarkable technical achievement as Allen moves Zelig in and out of actual historical events with great ingenuity.

# Mel Brooks

Starting in 1968 with *The Producers,* Mel Brooks brought his special brand of undisciplined and lunatic humor to the screen after years as a television comedy writer. Many of his movies in the seventies were uproarious spoofs of familiar genres, with jokes that were funny, tasteless, and funny *and* tasteless. In recent years, his broad satires have become a bit mechanical and old-hat but his lopsided view of the world and his ability to startle us into laughter remain intact.

## Blazing Saddles

★★★☆ Warners, 1974, c, 93 min. Dir: Mel Brooks. SP: Mel Brooks, Richard Pryor, Andrew Bergman, Norman Steinberg. Cast: Mel Brooks, Cleavon Little, Gene Wilder, Madeline Kahn, Harvey Korman, Slim Pickens, David Huddleston, Alex Karras, Burton Gilliam, Liam Dunn, John Hillerman.

One of Brooks's funniest movies, *Blazing Saddles* takes aim at the movie Western and manages to hit the target most of the time. The plot, if you care, concerns Bart (Little), a black drifter who is named sheriff of the town of Rock Ridge (the others met untimely deaths). He not only wipes out the corruption but also bests the state's dim-witted governor (Brooks) and scheming attorney general (Korman). Gene Wilder is the Waco Kid, Bart's once-famous gun-slinging ally, and Madeline Kahn is saloon singer Marlene Von Shtupp, an hilarious parody of Marlene Dietrich's "Frenchy" in *Destry Rides Again.* The verbal and sight gags come thick and fast, and if you miss one, just wait for another. Best performance in a small role: Liam Dunn as the town's practical-minded preacher.

## Dracula: Dead and Loving It

★★★ Warners, 1995, c, 90 min. Dir: Mel Brooks. SP: Rudy De Luca, Steve Haberman, Mel Brooks, b/o story by Rudy De Luca, Steve Haberman. Cast: Mel Brooks, Leslie Nielsen, Peter MacNichol, Steven Weber, Amy Yasbeck, Lysette Anthony, Harvey Korman.

Brooks takes on the Dracula story and comes up with another mix of outrageous gags, quips, and satirical bits, many of which will have you laughing in spite of your better judgment. The story details are the same as always: the undead Count Dracula (Nielsen) leaves his coffin in Transylvania to occupy a castle in England, where his vampire ways wreak havoc until he is destroyed. Brooks has some fun with the familiar grim settings and ghoulish activities, and you will have to find your own favorite portions. Personal candidates: slow-witted Dr. Seward (Korman) has tea with demented, insect-loving Renfield (MacNichol); Count Dracula meets Dr. Van Helsing (Brooks); Dracula casts no reflection at a lavish ball. Silly, to be sure, but relax and enjoy.

## High Anxiety

★★★ Fox, 1977, c, 94 min. Dir: Mel Brooks. SP: Mel Brooks, Ron Clark, Rudy De Luca, Barry Levinson. Cast: Mel Brooks, Madeline Kahn, Harvey Korman, Cloris Leachman, Dick Van Patten, Ron Carey, Howard Morris, Jack Riley, Charlie Callas.

Brooks's scattershot comic style sometimes hits the mark in this broad parody of such Alfred Hitchcock thrillers as *Psycho, The Birds,* and *Vertigo.* Other times it misses by a mile. Brooks stars as Richard Thorndyke, a psychiatrist with a fear of heights ("high anxiety") who takes over as head of the Institute for the Very, Very Nervous. He uncovers a hornet's nest of villainy headed by Dr. Harvey Korman and his grim head nurse, Cloris Leachman. Madeline Kahn is the girl whose father is a trapped patient. Funnier than the obvious Hitchcock spoofs are the scenes in which Brooks's skewered sense of humor prevails. Favorite scene: Brooks and Kahn try to elude the police and board an airplane by impersonating a quarreling old Jewish couple.

## History of the World—Part 1

★★ Fox, 1981, c, 92 min. Dir and SP: Mel Brooks. Cast: Mel Brooks, Gregory Hines, Dom DeLuise, Madeline Kahn, Harvey Korman, Bea Arthur, Sid Caesar, Cloris Leachman, Pamela Stephenson, Mary-Margaret Humes, Howard Morris.

Yet another helter-skelter, self-indulgent entry from Brooks, this one more ambitious than others as he roams across history from the Stone Age to the French Revolution. As usual, no gag is too stale, too vulgar, or too outrageous to be omitted, and some of them will have you laughing and cringing simultaneously. Highlights include Sid Caesar as an overbearing cave man, Brooks himself (he plays several roles) as Comicus, a "stand-up philosopher" in the Roman Empire, and an elaborate musical number during the Spanish Inquisition that must be seen to be believed. Brooks's version of the Last Supper will either offend you or have you howling with laughter. Worst section by far: the French Revolution.

## Life Stinks

★★☆ Fox, 1991, c, 95 min. Dir: Mel Brooks. SP: Mel Brooks, Rudy De Luca, Ron Clark, Steve Haberman. Cast: Mel Brooks, Lesley Ann Warren, Jeffrey Tambor, Stuart Pankin, Howard Morris, Rudy De Luca, Teddy Wilson, Michael Ensign.

A different direction for Mel Brooks, but not necessarily a successful one. Eschewing broad gags and vulgarity, Brooks aims for a touch of poignancy in his tale of Goddard Bolt (Brooks), a greedy, ruthless billionaire who wants to demolish a poor section of Los Angeles to build a commercial center named after himself. To gain complete control of the land, he makes a wager with rival Vance Crasswell (Tambor) that he can survive living on the streets for thirty days. Among others, he meets street-wise Molly (Warren), who helps him regain his humanity. Homelessness is not exactly a hilarious subject, and Brooks tries hard to win laughs that seldom arrive. Best scene: Bolt's dream dance with Molly.

## The Producers

★★★ Embassy, 1968, c, 88 min. Dir and SP: Mel Brooks. Cast: Zero Mostel, Gene Wilder, Kenneth Mars, Dick Shawn, Lee Meredith, Estelle Winwood, Renee Taylor, Christopher Hewett, Andreas Voustinas.

Brooks's first feature film sets the tone for many of the others ahead. Later he would take to spoofing familiar genres; here he sets up an outlandish situation and sprinkles it with nonstop gags. Broadway producer Max Bialystock (Mostel) finances his shows by romancing

In Mel Brooks's *The Producers* (1968), accountant Gene Wilder and producer Zero Mostel choose die-hard Nazi Kenneth Mars (center) to play Adolf Hitler in their production of *Springtime for Hitler.*

rich elderly women. He joins with his hysterical accountant Leo Bloom (Wilder) in a scheme to oversubscribe a sure flop, then skim off the surplus money after paying production costs. The scheme backfires when *Springtime for Hitler*, the dismal show he chooses, becomes a hit. Zero Mostel is too much for the screen to handle, but the movie generates laughs, especially with the *Springtime for Hitler* centerpiece that most people remember. Brooks's screenplay won an Oscar.

## Robin Hood: Men in Tights

★★☆ Fox, 1993, c, 102 min. Dir: Mel Brooks. SP: Mel Brooks, Evan Chandler, J. David Shapiro. Cast: Cary Elwes, Richard Lewis, Roger Rees, Amy Yasbeck, David Chappelle, Mark Blankfield, Tracey Ullman, Eric Allan Kramer, Mel Brooks, Dom DeLuise, Dick Van Patten.

Another hit-and-miss spoof from Mel Brooks, *Robin Hood: Men in Tights* takes on the Robin Hood legend and peppers it with the usual assortment of quips, gags, and non sequiturs. Brooks follows the familiar outlines of the

story: Robin of Loxley (Elwes) returns from imprisonment in Jerusalem to lead his Merrie Men against the tyranny of Prince John (Lewis) and the Sheriff of Rottingham (Rees). Rees is very funny as the ferocious but inept sheriff, and there are some laughs from Tracey Ullman as the witch Latrine and Dick Van Patten as the abbott (sure enough, someone shouts "Hey, Abbott!"). Mel Brooks himself makes an appearance as the unflappable Rabbi Tuckman, ready at all times to perform a circumcision ("at half off!" he exclaims).

## Silent Movie

★★★ Fox, 1976, c, 86 min. Dir: Mel Brooks. SP: Mel Brooks, Ron Clark, Rudy De Luca, Barry Levinson. Cast: Mel Brooks, Marty Feldman, Dom DeLuise, Sid Caesar, Bernadette Peters, Harold Gould, Ron Carey, Liam Dunn. Guest stars: Burt Reynolds, James Caan, Liza Minnelli, Paul Newman, Anne Bancroft, Marcel Marceau.

*Silent Movie* is exactly what the title says: an attempt to revive silent comedy, laced, of course, with Brooks's usual outrageous humor. The setting is Hollywood, and Brooks is Mel Funn, a director on the skids, who wants to make a silent movie. With sidekicks Feldman and DeLuise, he invades a studio where Sid Caesar is the "Current Studio Chief." Most of the movie has Brooks involved in slapstick chaos with guest stars Reynolds, Minnelli, Bancroft, et al. As usual, Brooks's scattershot humor sometimes hits the target, but more often it misses with gags that are hoary or just plain dumb.

## Spaceballs

★★★ MGM, 1987, c, 96 min. Dir: Mel Brooks. SP: Mel Brooks, Thomas Meehan, Ronny Graham. Cast: Mel Brooks, John Candy, Rick Moranis, Daphne Zuniga, Bill Pullman, George Wyner, Dick Van Patten, Michael Winslow, voice of Joan Rivers.

Another uneven parody from Mel Brooks, *Spaceballs* takes aim at the *Star Wars* trilogy (rather late in the day) and comes up with a fair number of laughs. It seems that in "a galaxy far away," the planet Spaceball, headed by President Skroob (Brooks) but dominated by sinister Dark Helmet (a hilarious Moranis), is bent on destroying the planet Druidia. The Spaceballs kidnap Druidia's Princess Vespa (Zuniga), prompting space jockey Lone Starr (Pullman) and his sidekick, half-dog, half-man Barf (Candy) to come to the rescue. Never mind the plot; the movie is really a stream of Brooksian sight gags, wisecracks, and anachronisms—some very funny. Brooks also plays Yogurt, "the everlasting know-it-all" whose specialty is merchandising *Spaceballs* products.

## The Twelve Chairs

★★★ UMC Pictures, 1970, c, 94 min. Dir and SP: Mel Brooks. Cast: Ron Moody, Frank Langella, Dom DeLuise, Mel Brooks. Bridget Brice, Robert Bernal.

One of Mel Brooks's early films, *The Twelve Chairs* is more compactly made than many of his later movies, when self-indulgence took over. Once the son of a nobleman, now reduced to working as a government clerk in 1927 Russia, Vorobyaninov (Moody) is told by his dying mother that the family jewels were hidden ten years earlier in one of a set of a dozen chairs, to escape the clutches of the Bolsheviks. Joined by Ostap Bender (Langella), a scheming beggar, Vorobyaninov goes on a desperate search for the one chair that holds the jewels. The search leads them to a theatrical company, a circus, and other locations. Mel Brooks himself contributes a funny cameo as the one-time valet to Vorobyaninov's father. Shot on location in Yugoslavia.

## Young Frankenstein

★★★☆ Fox, 1974, 105 min. Dir: Mel Brooks. SP: Gene Wilder, Mel Brooks, b/o characters created by Mary Shelley. Cast: Gene Wilder, Madeline Kahn, Peter Boyle, Marty Feldman, Teri Garr, Gene Hackman (unbilled), Kenneth Mars.

Probably Mel Brooks's funniest movie to date: a wild and often hilarious spoof of the horror film, especially the Frankenstein cycle. Brooks gets it right this time—he takes the visual style and familiar conventions of the genre, and then tilts them in the direction of parody. Co-author Gene Wilder stars as the grandson of the original mad baron, who returns to Transylvania to recreate the Monster. Surrounding Frankenstein are the old familiar faces: a leering humpbacked gargoyle (Feldman) who assists him in his experiments; a housekeeper (Leachman) so grim she makes horses whinny in fright; and an untouchable fiancée (Kahn) with a secret streak of nymphomania. The Monster himself (Boyle) turns out to have hidden talents as an entertainer and a lover. Great fun.

Gene Wilder is Dr. Frederick Frankenstein (pronounce that "Frahnkenshteen") and Teri Garr is his assistant, Inga, in Mel Brooks's *Young Frankenstein* (1974).

# Frank Capra

Although some revisionist writing has suggested otherwise, filmmaker Frank Capra has usually been viewed as the champion of America's common man, the fundamentally decent person who, beaten and nearly destroyed by the forces of evil, can finally restore order to his world. In particular, Capra's comedies of the thirties and forties, despite their anachronistic ring, continue to resonate with optimism, humor, and pride of country.

## Arsenic and Old Lace

★★★ Warners, 1944, 118 min. Dir: Frank Capra. SP: Philip G. Epstein, Julius J. Epstein, b/o play by Joseph Kesselring. Cast: Cary Grant, Raymond Massey, Priscilla Lane, Josephine Hull, Jean Adair, Jack Carson, Edward Everett Horton.

Untypical of director Frank Capra, but very typical of Warners' blunderbuss approach to comedy, *Arsenic and Old Lace* offered a broad adaptation of the hit Broadway comedy. A mixture of murder and mirth, the story centers on drama critic Cary Grant, who discovers that his two sweet old aunts (Hull and Adair in their Broadway roles) are cheerfully poisoning lonely old gentlemen who come looking for a room. Enter the ladies' homicidal brother (Massey) and soon the bodies are everywhere, to Grant's consternation. Usually the deftest of comedy actors, Grant is at a loss here, overplaying every scene. Still, there are some uproarious moments, mostly contributed by the great Josephine Hull, who waddles better than anyone. Filmed in 1941 but released in 1944.

## A Hole in the Head

★★☆ United Artists, 1959, c, 120 min. Dir: Frank Capra. SP: Arnold Schulman, b/o his plays. Cast: Frank Sinatra, Edward G. Robinson, Eleanor Parker, Eddie Hodges, Carolyn Jones, Thelma Ritter, Keenan Wynn, Joi Lansing.

Later and lesser Frank Capra, derived from a Broadway play and television play, both by Arnold Schulman. Frank Sinatra plays Tony, a Miami drifter and dreamer who runs a hotel and who is also the father of a doting eleven-year-old son (Hodges). Down to Miami comes Mario (Robinson), Tony's businessman brother, who considers him "a bum." He would like to turn Tony into a conformist and also take possession of his son. On the sidelines are Mario's sensible wife (Ritter), a hotel resident (Jones) with her eye on Tony, and a widow (Parker) set up as a possible match for Tony. Best feature: the Oscar-winning song "High Hopes."

## It Happened One Night

★★★★ Columbia, 1934, 105 min. Dir: Frank Capra. SP: Robert Riskin, b/o story by Samuel Hopkins Adams. Cast: Clark Gable, Claudette Colbert, Walter Connolly, Roscoe Karns, Alan Hale, Ward Bond, Jameson Thomas.

The peerless romantic comedy that started a trend in movies, downgraded the undershirt industry, and surprised everybody by winning five Oscars. Despite the Depression setting, the screenplay is still fresh and funny. Colbert is Ellie Andrews, a spoiled heiress who defies her father (Connolly) and jumps aboard a New York–bound bus to be with her money-minded fiancé (Thomas). On board is Peter Warne (Gable), a cocky reporter who knows a good story when he sees one. Together, they begin a cross-country trek that begins in hostility and ends in romance. The two stars are marvelous in roles they never wanted to play. The movie had many imitations, none as good, and Oscars went to Gable, Colbert, Capra, Riskin, and the film itself.

Runaway heiress Claudette Colbert dozes on the shoulder of reporter Clark Gable in Frank Capra's landmark comedy *It Happened One Night* (1934).

## Lady for a Day

★★★☆ Columbia, 1933, 96 min. Dir: Frank Capra. SP: Robert Riskin, b/o story by Damon Runyon. Cast: May Robson, Warren William, Glenda Farrell, Jean Parker, Walter Connolly, Ned Sparks, Nat Pendleton, Barry Norton.

Capra's Depression fable still retains much of its appeal. It was also his first major success. The story revolves around Apple Annie (Robson), a whisky-soaked old derelict who has a secret: she has a young daughter (Parker) who thinks her mother is a society dowager, and who is now coming to America with her wealthy fiancé (Norton) and his father, a Spanish nobleman (Connolly). Annie's friends rally around her and turn her into the very picture of a society "swell." Veteran actress Robson, then seventy years old, won an Oscar nomination for her touching performance, and nominations also went to the movie, Capra, and writer Riskin. Capra himself remade the movie as *Pocketful of Miracles* in 1961, with Bette Davis as Annie.

## Mr. Deeds Goes to Town

★★★☆ Columbia, 1936, 115 min. Dir: Frank Capra. SP: Robert Riskin, b/o story by Clarence Budington Kelland. Cast: Gary Cooper, Jean Arthur, George Bancroft, Lionel Stander, Douglass Dumbrille.

More than a little musty, Capra's *Mr. Deeds Goes to Town* still has enough diverting moments to make it worth a viewing. In one of his best roles, Gary Cooper plays a guileless young man from Mandrake Falls who inherits a fortune from his uncle. Assailed by a scheming lawyer (Dumbrille), greedy people, and a reporter (Arthur) out to make him a laughing-stock, bewildered Deeds tries to give his money to the desperate poor and is called insane. In the end, he not only triumphs but wins the reporter's love. His insanity hearing is the movie's best-remembered sequence. Cooper is engaging, and Arthur shows why she was one of the most delightful actresses of the thirties and forties.

## Mr. Smith Goes to Washington

★★★★ Columbia, 1939, 129 min. Dir: Frank Capra. SP: Sidney Buchman, b/o story by Lewis R. Foster. Cast: James Stewart, Jean Arthur, Claude Rains, Edward Arnold, Thomas Mitchell, Eugene Pallette, Guy Kibbee, Beulah Bondi, Harry Carey, H. B. Warner.

One of Capra's most popular films, *Mr. Smith Goes to Washington* may now seem like little more than a rousing flag-waver in our more cynical age, but its exuberant mix of comedy and drama still prevails. Jefferson Smith (Stewart) is the memorable hero—a gawky, earnest young man who becomes a U.S. senator and is nearly crushed by the political machine that exercises control with an iron fist. Jeff's journey from naïveté to righteous fervor (in his famous filibuster) involves many other characters, including his dubious then loving secretary (the marvelous Arthur), a cor-

rupt senator (Rains), and a bibulous reporter (Mitchell). Top-notch entertainment.

## You Can't Take It with You

★★★☆ Columbia, 1938, 127 min. Dir: Frank Capra. SP: Robert Riskin, b/o play by George S. Kaufman, Moss Hart. Cast: Jean Arthur, James Stewart, Lionel Barrymore, Edward Arnold, Ann Miller, Spring Byington, Mischa Auer,

Donald Meek, Samuel S. Hinds, Halliwell Hobbes, Eddie "Rochester" Anderson.

Meet the Sycamores, the wildly eccentric family of Kaufman and Hart's Pulitzer Prize–winning stage comedy. Under Frank Capra's sympathetic direction, they are still a funny bunch on the screen, but in his characteristic style, Capra adds some of his usual sentiment about the "little people" and it drains away some of the fun. Still, there's much to enjoy, with Jean Arthur as the only sensible Sycamore and James Stewart as the tycoon's son she loves. The romance comes to a temporary impasse when their two families meet in an uproarious sequence. The movie won the year's Best Picture Oscar, and Capra also received his third Academy Award.

A happy ending for all in Frank Capra's Oscar-winning comedy *You Can't Take It With You* (1938), with (left to right) Lionel Barrymore, James Stewart, Jean Arthur, and Edward Arnold.

# Charlie Chaplin

One of the screen's undisputed geniuses of the silent era, Charlie Chaplin was reluctant to use the new technology of sound, even years after *The Jazz Singer* and many other films made it the only game in town. His 1931 masterwork *City Lights* eschewed all talk. He finally made a number of sound films that, despite their lapses, contained the same spark of genius that illuminated his earlier work.

## The Great Dictator

★★★☆ United Artists, 1940, 128 min. Dir and SP: Charlie Chaplin. Cast: Charlie Chaplin, Paulette Goddard, Jack Oakie, Henry Daniell, Reginald Gardiner, Billy Gilbert, Maurice Moscovich.

Charlie Chaplin skewers the lunacy of totalitarianism, and if the results in *The Great Dictator* are uneven, the best of the movie compensates for the lapses. The comedian plays two roles: he is both a humble Jewish barber and his egomaniacal look-alike, Adenoid Hynkel, ruler of Tomania. Paulette Goddard is the sweet Jewish girl who is loved and befriended by the barber. Some of the movie is drowned in sticky sentiment, but there are some classic sequences: Hynkel dancing with a buoyant world globe and his barber chair competition with Benzino Napaloni (Oakie), dictator of Bacteria. The barber's final speech, in which he pleads for peace and universal love, has its defenders and detractors.

## Modern Times

★★★☆ United Artists, 1936, 85 min. Dir and SP: Charlie Chaplin. Cast: Charlie Chaplin, Paulette Goddard, Henry Bergman, Chester Conklin, Stanley Sandford, Hank Mann.

Chaplin's immortal "little fellow" comes smack up against the age of mechanization, with hilarious results. When he goes to work in a factory, everything goes wildly wrong: he is used as a guinea pig for an out-of-order feeding machine, finds himself trapped on a conveyor belt that causes tics, and is obliged to feed lunch to a fellow worker (Conklin) who is enmeshed in the cogs of a giant machine.

Chaplin also takes the time to befriend a homeless waif (Goddard). The master comedian uses sound techniques sparingly in this mostly silent comedy—near the movie's end he sings a nonsense version of the song "Titina" in his own voice. Funny—and frightening—sequence: blindfolded Charlie, careening on roller skates through a department store.

## Monsieur Verdoux

★★★ United Artists, 1947, 123 min. Dir and SP: Charlie Chaplin. Cast: Charlie Chaplin, Martha Raye, Isobel Elsom, Marilyn Nash, Mady Correll, Fritz Leiber.

Seven years after *The Great Dictator,* Chaplin directed this bitterly misanthropic variation on the Bluebeard story. He plays a dapper bank teller with a crippled wife and child, who, after losing his job, earns his living by courting and marrying wealthy women under a pseudonym and then murdering them. Eventually, he is apprehended and sentenced to death. He defends himself by asserting that his crime is no worse than the mass murders committed in the world every day by weapons of destruction. *Monsieur Verdoux* is very uneven and poorly cast in most of the roles apart from Chaplin, but there are pearly moments, contributed mostly by Martha Raye as one of Verdoux's wives, a vulgar virago he cannot seem to kill.

In Charlie Chaplin's *Modern Times* (1936), the Little Tramp (Chaplin, right) and his coworker (Chester Conklin) are dwarfed by a monster machine.

# Preston Sturges

His film output was comparatively slim, but Preston Sturges remains one of the screen's foremost satirists. A writer-director who poked outrageous fun at America's most cherished ideals and lofty pretensions, Sturges created his own world of charlatans, blowhards, and stammering victims and embodied them through his stock company of players. His mocking wit and jaundiced view of the human condition are evident in all of his movies.

## The Beautiful Blonde from Bashful Bend

★★☆ Fox, 1949, c, 77 min. Dir and SP: Preston Sturges. Cast: Betty Grable, Cesar Romero, Rudy Vallee, Olga San Juan, Porter Hall, Sterling Holloway, Hugh Herbert, Alan Bridge, El Brendel.

A generally flat-footed farce from Sturges's declining years. A songless Betty Grable stars as a straight-shooting frontier girl who is mistaken for a schoolmarm. There's a funny climactic sequence in which bullets take the place of custard pies, but the rest is heavy-handed. The only real pleasure is the presence of some of Sturges's favorite actors, including Rudy Vallee (in his by-now standard fussbudget phase), Porter Hall, Alan Bridge, and Sterling Holloway. The inimitable Hugh Herbert gets laughs as a nearsighted doctor.

## Christmas in July

★★★ Paramount, 1940, 67 min. Dir and SP: Preston Sturges. Cast: Dick Powell, Ellen Drew, Raymond Walburn, William Demarest, Ernest Truex, Franklin Pangborn.

Early, minor Preston Sturges, with a few glimpses of the master satirist he would later become. Young Jimmy MacDonald (Powell) is an office worker who is tricked into believing that he has won $25,000 in a contest to find a slogan for Maxford House Coffee. ("If you can't sleep at night, it isn't the coffee, it's the bunk.") Somehow he convinces the Maxford people that he is indeed the winner, and he launches a frenzied shopping spree with the check. Not surprisingly, the funniest portions come from the members of Sturges's upcoming stock company of players, especially Raymond Walburn as Maxford's blowhard director and Franklin Pangborn as an overwrought radio announcer.

## Easy Living

★★★☆ Paramount, 1937, 86 min. Dir: Mitchell Leisen. SP: Preston Sturges, b/o story by Vera Caspary. Cast: Jean Arthur, Ray Milland, Edward Arnold, Mary Nash, Franklin Pangborn, William Demarest, Luis Alberni.

Yes, Mitchell Leisen directed this romantic charmer (and deftly, too) but *Easy Living* is best remembered as a prime example of early scripting by Preston Sturges. The piquant Jean Arthur is the Depression Cinderella who has a sable coat dropped onto her head when an irate financier (Arnold) flings it out the window. (His wife bought it for a mere $58,000.) In no time at all the bewildered girl is mistaken as Arnold's mistress and finds herself sitting in the lap of luxury. She also finds love with a young man (Milland) who turns out to be Arnold's son. (He's pretending to be a working stiff.) The movie's most famous scene—an inspired piece of controlled slapstick—takes place in the Automat. See for yourself.

## The Great McGinty

★★★ Paramount, 1940, 81 min. Dir and SP: Preston Sturges. Cast: Brian Donlevy, Akim Tamiroff, Muriel Angelus, William Demarest, Allyn Joslyn, Louis Jean Heydt, Arthur Hoyt.

Sturges's first solo as writer and director, and an Oscar winner as Best Original Screenplay. He would do better work afterward, but this ingratiating movie contains all the ingredients that would become familiar: the bursts of slapstick, the slightly off-center dialogue, and especially his fondness for the world's blowhards, frauds, and nincompoops. Brian Donlevy plays a hobo who becomes mayor, then governor, all with the backing of the state's cheerfully corrupt boss (Tamiroff). He gets into trouble when he turns honest at the urging of his wife (Angelus). Sturges throws a few darts at political chicanery, but the movie is rather tame next to his later efforts.

## Hail the Conquering Hero

★★★★ Paramount, 1944, 101 min. Dir and SP: Preston Sturges. Cast: Eddie Bracken, William Demarest, Ella Raines, Raymond Walburn, Freddie Steele, Franklin Pangborn, Elizabeth Patterson, Jimmy Conlin, Al Bridge.

Sturges's best film as writer-director: a pungent comedy that skewers a number of America's sacred cows, including mother love and patriotism. It also aims its darts at hero worship and wartime hysteria—and all this at the height of America's involvement in World War II! Eddie Bracken plays Woodrow Lafayette Pershing Truesmith, a glum 4-F whose father was a famous marine hero. A group of sympathetic marines concoct a deception—they bring him to his hometown as a war hero. Woodrow protests but things get out of control and he becomes a candidate for mayor. Ironically, the town loves him even after he admits the lie. The cast includes members of Sturges's stock company, including the unfailing William Demarest as the most determined of the marines.

## The Lady Eve

★★★☆ Paramount, 1941, 96 min. Dir: Preston Sturges. SP: Preston Sturges, b/o story by Monckton Hoffe. Cast: Barbara Stanwyck, Henry Fonda, Charles Coburn, William Demarest, Eugene Pallette, Eric Blore, Melville Cooper, Janet Beecher, Martha O'Driscoll.

Preston Sturges's comedy has all the ingredients associated with this talented writer-director: offbeat characters, sly, sparkling dialogue, and a fondness for the world's eccentrics and crackpots. This one adds a note of romance. Aboard an ocean liner, Charles "Hoppsy" Pike (Fonda), a cotton-headed millionaire whose only interest is snakes, meets cardsharp Jean Harrington (Stanwyck). He falls in love, but when he learns the truth about her, he leaves her bitterly, claiming that he knew about her scheme all along. Hurt and angry, Eve decides to wreak revenge by impersonating a bewitching Englishwoman named Lady Eve Sidwich, then marrying him only for his money. The premise is farfetched but Sturges adds his own deliciously goofy touches.

## The Miracle of Morgan's Creek

★★★☆ Paramount, 1944, 99 min. Dir and SP: Preston Sturges. Cast: Betty Hutton, Eddie Bracken, William Demarest, Diana Lynn, Porter Hall, Almira Sessions, Jimmy Conlin, Alan Bridge.

Sturges's Bronx cheer to small-town wartime America, *The Miracle of Morgan's Creek* was his boldest film to date. At a time when the myth held that the nation's young women waited for their men to return from battle with visions of marriage and motherhood, this movie upset the apple cart. Small-town girl Trudy Kockenlocker (Hutton) gets pregnant one evening by a soldier she can't even identity. She needs a husband—quickly—and settles on Norval Jones (Bracken), a bumbling 4-F who adores her. Many frantic sequences later, everything is resolved. Some of the movie shows signs of strain, but on the whole, it's a funny, audacious miracle that could only come from Preston Sturges. And how did he get away with the closing title?

## The Palm Beach Story

★★★ Paramount, 1942, 90 min. Dir and SP: Preston Sturges. Cast: Claudette Colbert, Joel McCrea, Rudy Vallee,

Movie director John L. Sullivan (Joel McCrea) sets out to learn about "real life," accompanied by "the girl" (Veronica Lake), in Preston Sturges's *Sullivan's Travels* (1942).

Mary Astor, Sig Arno, Robert Dudley, Franklin Pangborn, William Demarest, Jack Norton, Robert Greig, Roscoe Ates. This Sturges comedy is highly regarded by some, but it's really only fitfully amusing, with some sly, original touches. Claudette Colbert leaves her architect-husband (McCrea)—her reasons are fuzzy—and settles in Palm Beach, where she is courted by a crackpot millionaire (Vallee). When McCrea shows up, she identifies him as her brother, and he is soon being pursued by Vallee's oversexed sister (Astor). Vallee and Astor are the movie's funniest characters—he's a stuffy fussbudget and she's a giddy sort with many ex-husbands. The movie's reputation rests largely on one sequence in which Colbert, on the train to Palm Beach, tangles with a boisterous group of hunters known as the Ale & Quail Club.

## The Sin of Harold Diddlebock

★★ RKO, 1947, 90 min. Dir and SP: Preston Sturges. Cast: Harold Lloyd, Frances Ramsden, Jimmy Conlin, Raymond Walburn, Edgar Kennedy, Rudy Vallee, Arline Judge, Lionel Stander, Franklin Pangborn, Margaret Hamilton.

A sorry attempt to bring silent-movie icon Harold Lloyd into the sound era, under the aegis of writer-director Sturges. Sturges's marvelous stock company is on hand, but the material is feeble. The movie begins well with the climactic sequence from Lloyd's silent *The Freshman*, then picks up twenty-three years later, with football hero Harold Diddlebock (Lloyd) now a meek bookkeeper. When he is fired, Harold gets wildly drunk on a single cocktail and ends up owning a circus! Harold's efforts to sell the circus to a nasty banker (Vallee) lead to various slapstick complications. Of course there's the requisite "thrill" scene, with Harold perched on a high ledge with a lion. The movie was reedited and rereleased in 1950 as *Mad Wednesday*. It still didn't work.

## Sullivan's Travels

★★★☆ Paramount, 1942, 91 min. Dir and SP: Preston Sturges. Cast: Joel McCrea, Veronica Lake, William

Demarest, Robert Warwick, Eric Blore, Robert Greig, Jimmy Conlin, Franklin Pangborn, Porter Hall.

One of Sturges's most unusual films, an odd but also brilliant mixture of slapstick comedy and grim drama. Joel McCrea stars as Sullivan, a movie director who, tired of making lightweight comedies, sets out to discover life as a tramp with only ten cents in his pocket. He finds more than he bargained for in a nightmarish experience that puts him in prison. His ultimate lesson: making people laugh with comedy films is just as essential as creating "deep-dish" dramas. *Sullivan's Travels* shifts too often between knockabout humor (one chase scene is a slapstick gem) and stark reality, but Sturges gives it all his own original imprint. Veronica Lake plays the nameless girl who accompanies Sullivan on his odyssey and comes to love him.

# Unfaithfully Yours

★★★☆ Fox, 1948, 105 min. Dir and SP: Preston Sturges. Cast: Rex Harrison, Linda Darnell, Rudy Vallee, Barbara Lawrence, Kurt Kreuger, Lionel Stander, Robert Greig, Edgar Kennedy.

One of Sturges's least-remembered but funniest movies—an often uproarious mixture of satire, slapstick, and fantasy. A famed symphony conductor (Harrison) comes to believe that his wife (Darnell) is cheating on him with his secretary (Kreuger). In a rage, he fantasizes about different ways of dealing with her infidelity, all while he is conducting his orchestra. The fantasies, which involve noble sacrifice, Russian roulette, and murder—are all played out in Harrison's mind. They are cleverly handled, but Sturges gets the biggest laughs with his secondary characters, especially Darnell's unpleasant brother-in-law (Vallee) and a music-loving detective (Kennedy). Remade in 1984, with Dudley Moore as the jealous conductor.

# Billy Wilder

One of the screen's finest, most original filmmakers, Billy Wilder delights in exposing the dark side of the American dream or skewering the nation's foibles and prejudices, usually (but by no means always) with laughter. Over a long and illustrious career, he has succeeded in creating a memorable gallery of grasping, greedy cheats, fools, and swindlers, not only in his comedies, but also in his dramas.

## The Apartment

★★★★ United Artists, 1960, 125 min. Dir: Billy Wilder. SP: Billy Wilder, I.A.L. Diamond. Cast: Jack Lemmon, Shirley MacLaine, Fred MacMurray, Ray Walston, Jack Kruschen, Edie Adams, David Lewis, Joan Shawlee.

There's a sour aftertaste to this Oscar-winning film, but admittedly it's offset by sharp dialogue, superb performances, and expert direc-

tion. A sardonic tale of the business world, *The Apartment* centers on C. C. ("Bud") Baxter (Lemmon), an ambitious office worker who, on the promise of getting ahead in the company, agrees to lend his apartment to colleagues for sexual assignations. Secretly, Bud is in love with Fran Kubelik (MacLaine), an elevator operator who turns out to be the discarded

Jack Lemmon is C. C. "Bud" Baxter and Shirley MacLaine is Fran, the girl he loves, in Billy Wilder's Oscar-winning film *The Apartment* (1960).

mistress of a married executive (MacMurray). Eventually, Bud regains his integrity and pride and also wins Fran's love. The scenes between Bud and Fran—a lonely man and a wounded girl—are touching, funny, and observant. The movie was turned into a 1968 Broadway musical called *Promises, Promises.*

## Avanti!

★★★ United Artists, 1972, 144 min. Dir: Billy Wilder. SP: Billy Wilder, I.A.L. Diamond, b/o play by Samuel Taylor. Cast: Jack Lemmon, Juliet Mills, Clive Revill, Edward Andrews, Gianfranco Barra, Franco Angrisano.

In this overlong, moderately amusing comedy, Jack Lemmon stars as a married business executive who comes to Italy to claim the body of his father, who has died in an accident. He learns that his father was killed along with his long-time mistress, and that the mistress's daughter (Mills) is also on the scene. Eventually the two re-create their parents' affair. After confronting a blizzard of bureaucratic red tape, they decide to bury their parents on an island they (the parents) had both loved. Lemmon and Mills are fine in their roles but the movie is stolen by Clive Revill as a suave hotel manager who is helpful with everything from blackmail to love affairs.

## Buddy Buddy

★★★ MGM/UA, 1981, c, 96 min. Dir: Billy Wilder. SP: Billy Wilder, I.A.L. Diamond, b/o play by Francis Veber. Cast: Jack Lemmon, Walter Matthau, Paula Prentiss, Klaus Kinski, Dana Elcar, Miles Chapin, Michael Ensign, Joan Shawlee.

Victor Clooney (Lemmon) is a mild-mannered CBS censor who has turned suicidal after learning that his wife (Prentiss) is cheating on him. Trabucco (Matthau) is a rumpled hit man assigned to assassinate a mob-squealer. When Victor and Trabucco rent adjoining hotel rooms, Billy Wilder's breezy comedy gets under way. In the tradition of hotel farces, *Buddy Buddy* also involves a stuffy desk clerk, a wisecracking bellboy, and a garrulous chambermaid. Matthau and Lemmon offer proof again (as if proof were needed) that they are— or at least were—one of the screen's most diverting comedy teams.

## A Foreign Affair

★★★☆ Paramount, 1948, 116 min. Dir: Billy Wilder. SP: Charles Brackett, Billy Wilder, Richard Breen. Cast: Jean Arthur, Marlene Dietrich, John Lund, Millard Mitchell, Peter Von Zerneck, Stanley Prager.

Call it either cynical or callous, but this Billy Wilder comedy somehow draws laughter out of a potentially depressing situation. Prim and proper Congresswoman Jean Arthur comes to bombed-out West Berlin with a delegation bent on investigating military morale. She encounters a captain (Lund) who has made the city his profitable domain, and whose sole concern is keeping Arthur away from his mistress (Dietrich), a nightclub singer who once consorted with Nazis. By the time Arthur learns the truth, she has fallen in love with Lund. Some critics found the movie distasteful, but the screenplay is pungent and witty in the Wilder style. Arthur has to cope with unflattering makeup and hairdo but Dietrich has a field day as the amoral mistress.

## The Fortune Cookie

★★★ United Artists, 1966, 125 min. Dir: Billy Wilder. SP: Billy Wilder, I.A.L. Diamond. Cast: Jack Lemmon, Walter Matthau, Ron Rich, Judi West, Cliff Osmond, Lurene Tuttle.

Say hello to "Whiplash" Willie Gingrich (Matthau), the proudly corrupt lawyer who is a shark among sharks. Willie gets the best case of his career when his brother-in-law Harry Hinkle (Lemmon), a TV cameraman, is injured by a football player during a game. Willie sees huge dollar signs, and so does Harry's greedy ex-wife (West). Soon everyone is involved: worried lawyers for the insurance company, doctors with opposite opinions, and the dismayed football player (Rich). As usual, Billy Wilder aims his barbed arrows at human behavior and draws some laughs, greatly abetted by Matthau's hilarious Oscar-winning (Best Supporting Actor) performance. Matthau and Lemmon became a movie team that has lasted for more than three decades.

## Kiss Me, Stupid
★ Paramount, 1964, 126 min. Dir: Billy Wilder. SP: Billy Wilder, I.A.L. Diamond. Cast: Dean Martin, Ray Walston, Kim Novak, Felicia Farr, Cliff Osmond, Barbara Pepper, Doro Merande, Henry Gibson, Mel Blanc.

A serious mistake from Billy Wilder, *Kiss Me, Stupid* was condemned as smut when it was first released. It's mild by today's standards, but it's also painfully unfunny, obnoxious, and indeed "stupid." Dean Martin plays Dino, a womanizing crooner who finds himself stranded in a town called Climax(!). When Dino needs a woman, local aspiring songwriter Orville Spooner (Walston), seeking Dino's favor, passes off a waitress called Polly the Pistol (Novak) as his wife. The ensuing confusion of identities is meant to be uproarious but it is merely offensive. Early in its excessive running time, the movie settles into a permanent leer from which it never recovers. One note of interest: Martin sings three unpublished songs by the Gershwins.

## Love in the Afternoon
★★★☆ Allied Artists, 1957, 130 min. Dir: Billy Wilder. SP: Billy Wilder, I.A.L. Diamond, b/o novel by Claude Anet. Cast: Audrey Hepburn, Gary Cooper, Maurice Chevalier, John McGiver.

Director Billy Wilder's homage to his mentor and idol Ernst Lubitsch, *Love in the Afternoon* is a lighter-than-air but witty souffle. In Paris, a wealthy American womanizer (a miscast Cooper) finds himself puzzled and intrigued by a lovely young music student (Hepburn) who comes to warn him about a jealous husband. Unknowingly, he hires Hepburn's detective father (Chevalier) to find out who she really is. Inevitably, his attempts at seduction give way to true romantic feeling. Many scenes emulate Lubitsch in their use of suggestion, most notably one in which the camera remains largely fixed on a closed door as Cooper attempts to seduce Hepburn with food, drink, and gypsy music. Other sly touches help distract the viewer from the age difference between the leads.

## The Major and the Minor
★★★ Paramount, 1941, 100 min. Dir: Billy Wilder. SP: Charles Brackett, Billy Wilder, b/o story by Fannie Kilbourne. Cast: Ginger Rogers, Ray Milland, Rita Johnson, Diana Lynn, Norma Varden, Lela Rogers.

Billy Wilder's first film as a director, *The Major and the Minor* is still amusing, although it moves into pre-*Lolita* territory. In her post-Astaire period, Ginger Rogers seemed to enjoy playing characters much younger than her true age, and here she impersonates a twelve-year-old. Without enough money to get home, she dresses up as a preteen to get half-fare. On the train, she finds herself involved with an army major (Milland), who thinks she really *is* twelve. The clueless major takes her to his military school, where he begins to have inexplicable feelings for this apparently prepubescent child. Rogers is not too convincing in pigtails, but she works hard to keep the comedy from sinking into tastelessness. Remade in 1955 as *You're Never Too Young*, with Jerry Lewis in the Rogers role.

## Midnight
★★★★ Paramount, 1939, 94 min. Dir: Mitchell Leisen. SP: Charles Brackett, Billy Wilder, b/o story by Edwin Justus Mayer, Franz Schulz. Cast: Claudette Colbert, Don Ameche, John Barrymore, Mary Astor, Francis Lederer, Rex O'Malley, Hedda Hopper, Elaine Barrie.

Pure sparkling champagne. The witty Brackett-Wilder screenplay centers on Claudette Colbert, at her stylish best, playing a penniless girl in Paris who is given a lavish apartment and an expensive wardrobe by an aristocrat (Barrymore)—but not for the usual reason. He wants Colbert to seduce the playboy (Lederer) with whom his wife (Astor) is having an affair. Also involved in Colbert's masquerade (she pretends to be a baroness) is a taxi driver (Ameche), who finds her fetching. Everyone converges on Barrymore's chateau, where there are further complications. It all ends in that familiar setting for thirties comedies: the courtroom. Barrymore steals the movie as the cuckolded aristocrat, bringing touches of irony and rue to the sly, often sardonic dialogue.

## One, Two, Three

★★★★ United Artists, 1961, 108 min. Dir: Billy Wilder. SP: Billy Wilder, I.A.L. Diamond. Cast: James Cagney, Horst Buchholz, Arlene Francis, Pamela Tiffin, Lilo Pulver, Howard St. John, Hans Lothar, Leon Askin, Red Buttons.

James Cagney's crackling machine-gun style was seldom shown to better advantage than in this fast-paced satirical comedy, his first in twenty years. He plays the high-powered head of Coca-Cola's operations in West Berlin, who is forced to deal with the dangers of life in a divided, occupied city. The problem: his boss's daughter (Tiffin) marries an East German Communist (Buchholz), which is trouble enough. Then the boss himself (St. John) shows up, and Cagney has to turn the young groom into an instant capitalist. He soon finds himself sprinting from one side of the wall to another. The Wilder-Diamond screenplay is frequently hilarious, and Cagney and the cast play it with dizzying speed.

James Cagney converses with Horst Buchholz, who is about to be transformed from Communist to capitalist in *One, Two, Three* (1961). Looking on at left and right are Hans Lothar and Pamela Tiffin.

## Sabrina

★★★☆ Paramount, 1954, 113 min. Dir: Billy Wilder. SP: Ernest Lehman, Billy Wilder, Samuel Taylor, b/o play by Samuel Taylor. Cast: Audrey Hepburn, William Holden, Humphrey Bogart, Martha Hyer, Walter Hampden, John Williams, Francis X. Bushman, Nancy Kulp.

Audrey Hepburn is the principal reason to see this charming romantic comedy. In her first movie after her success in *Roman Holiday*, she is enchanting as the chauffeur's daughter who pines for playboy Holden. Sent to Paris as a duckling, she returns as a swan, and when Holden now finds her fetching, his conservative older brother (Bogart) becomes alarmed at the possibility of an inconvenient alliance. He decides to court Sabrina himself, with not unexpected consequences. Both Bogart and Holden are years too old for their roles, but the writing and direction are handled artfully, and the movie has the sparkle of good if not vintage champagne. A 1995 remake was better cast in the male leads, but Julia Ormond, alas, was no match for Ms. Hepburn.

## The Seven Year Itch

★★☆ Fox, 1955, c, 105 min. Dir: Billy Wilder. SP: George Axelrod, b/o his play. Cast: Marilyn Monroe, Tom Ewell, Evelyn Keyes, Sonny Tufts, Victor Moore, Oscar Homolka, Doro Merande, Carolyn Jones.

George Axelrod's hit Broadway comedy was always an extremely slender conceit about a married New Yorker (Ewell) who, as a "summer bachelor," fantasizes his way through an innocent assignation with the light-headed, voluptuous girl upstairs. In the movie version, since the girl is played by Marilyn Monroe, guess who gets most of the footage. George Axelrod adapted his own play, and for some reason he coarsened and vulgarized the material, so it now seems like one long locker-room joke. Despite Ewell's best efforts in the role he created on stage, he cannot make his character seem anything more than a middle-aged simpleton with an overactive imagination.

Transformed from duckling to swan, Audrey Hepburn enchants Humphrey Bogart in Billy Wilder's *Sabrina* (1954).

## Some Like It Hot

★★★★ United Artists, 1959, 119 min. Dir: Billy Wilder. SP: Billy Wilder, I.A.L. Diamond, b/o story by Robert Thoeren, M. Logan. Cast: Tony Curtis, Jack Lemmon, Marilyn Monroe, Joe E. Brown, George Raft, Pat O'Brien, Nehemiah Persoff, Joan Shawlee.

Quickly, name the ten funniest comedy movies of the sound era. Chances are that one of your candidates would be this uproarious farce. You know the story: in twenties Chicago, two out-of-work musicians (Curtis and Lemmon) are forced to flee to Florida after witnessing gangland's St. Valentine's Day Massacre. They disguise themselves as members of an all-girl band whose singer is the voluptuous Monroe. Complications occur when the Chicago gangsters arrive on the scene. Here's a laugh-a-minute movie that never falters, with a screenplay that touches merrily on such noncomedic topics as transvestism, impotence, and gangland murder—plus a wondrously funny performance by Jack Lemmon as the manic "Josephine." The movie received five Oscar nominations but only Orry-Kelly's costumes won the statue.

## Stalag 17

★★★☆ Paramount, 1953, 120 min.. Dir: Billy Wilder. SP: Billy Wilder, Edwin Blum, b/o play by Donald Bevan, Edmund Trzcinski. Cast: William Holden. Don Taylor, Otto Preminger, Robert Strauss, Harvey Lembeck, Richard Erdman, Peter Graves, Neville Brand, Sig Ruman.

An absorbing comedy-drama, adapted from the hit 1951 Broadway play *Stalag 17* is set in a World War II German prison camp holding American airmen. Much of the movie is given over to the usual rowdy cavorting of the service comedy, but there is a serious plot: an abrasive airman named Sefton (Holden, in an Oscar-winning performance) is suspected of being an informer who is threatening plans to escape. The hostility toward him grows even as the danger increases. Director and coauthor Wilder improves on the play, keeping the comedy but strengthening the cynical main character and focusing more on the attitudes of men in confinement. The movie later inspired the television series *Hogan's Heroes*.

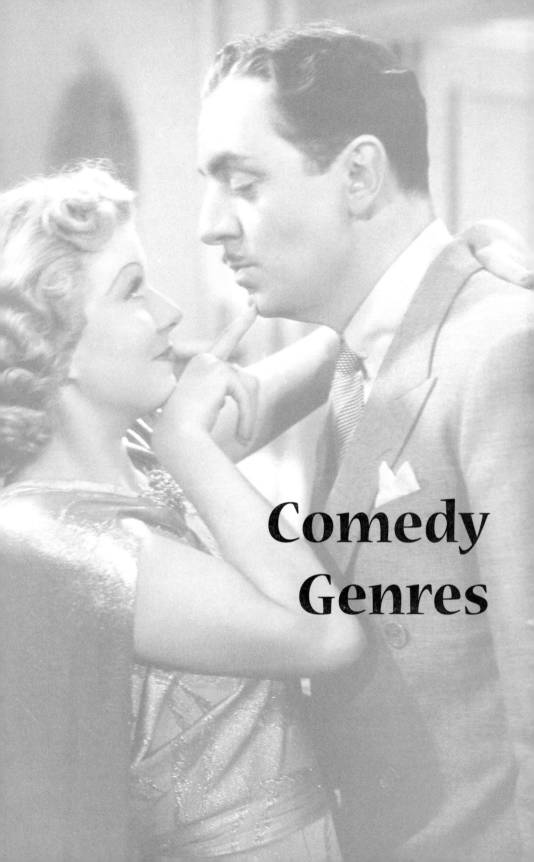

Comedy Genres

# Love in Bloom: Romantic Comedies

If, as they say, everyone loves a lover, then Hollywood and the moviegoing public have adored romantic stories since the first flickering images showed a couple exchanging a kiss. Of course, not all romantic stories have happy endings—Romeo and his Juliet spring to mind—but many have found abundant laughter in the rocky course of a love affair. The best romantic comedies combine wit, originality, and a perceptive view of tangled man-woman relationships, and you'll find many of them here.

## About Last Night...

★★☆ TriStar, 1986, c, 113 min. Dir: Edward Zwick. SP: Tim Kazurinsky, Denise DeClue, b/o play by David Mamet. Cast: Rob Lowe, Demi Moore, James Belushi, Elizabeth Perkins, George DiCenzo, Michael Alldredge, Robin Thomas.

A curious adaptation of David Mamet's one-act play *Sexual Perversity in Chicago, About Last Night . . .* both expands and dilutes the play's basic situation into a conventional romantic comedy about an on-again, off-again love affair between de-ethnicized Danny Martin and Debbie Sullivan (Lowe and Moore). The movie explores the singles scene in some detail but all the bite of the original rests in the performance of James Belushi as Danny's crude, self-assured pal Bernie Litko. The opening sequence, in which Bernie tells Danny about his night's wild sexual adventure, is the best in the movie.

## Addicted to Love

★ Miramax, 1997, c, 100 min. Dir: Griffin Dunne. SP: Robert Gordon. Cast: Meg Ryan, Matthew Broderick, Kelly Preston, Tcheky Karyo, Maureen Stapleton, Nesbitt Blaisdell, Remak Ramsay.

An eternal question in filmmaking: how could such competent actors as Meg Ryan and Matthew Broderick commit themselves to a project as witless and irritating as *Addicted to Love*? Broderick plays Sam, an astronomer who is suddenly jilted by his girlfriend Linda (Preston). Frantic, Sam tracks her to a New York apartment she is sharing with her new lover, Anton (Karyo), and sets up sophisticated surveillance equipment to watch them. Enter Maggie (Ryan), Anton's jilted—and seriously disturbed—girlfriend who is out for revenge. Sam and Maggie join forces in exacting revenge in painfully unfunny ways, until inevitably, the two fall in love with each other. Gruesome from first to last.

## All in a Night's Work

★★☆ Paramount, 1961, c, 94 min. Dir: Joseph Anthony. SP: Edmund Beloin, Maurice Richlin. Cast: Dean Martin, Shirley MacLaine, Charles Ruggles, Cliff Robertson, Norma Crane, Gale Gordon, Jerome Cowan, Jack Weston, Ian Wolfe, Mabel Albertson.

This lightweight farce would like to be wickedly suggestive in the sixties style, but it's all pretty tame. Shirley MacLaine plays an office worker who comes to Florida, only to find herself in a compromising situation. She is spotted fleeing from the hotel room of a publishing mogul, dressed only in a towel. (Actually, she was running in alarm from someone else.) The mogul is dead, and now his nephew (Martin), fearing the worst, must keep his name out of the scandal sheets. Martin wines, dines, and courts the lady, until (of course) he falls in love with her. Flimsy stuff, but good supporting players.

## All Night Long

★★★ Universal, 1981, c, 88 min. Dir: Jean-Claude Tramont. SP: W. D. Richter. Cast: Gene Hackman, Barbra Streisand, Dennis Quaid, Diane Ladd, Kevin Dobson, William Daniels.

A rather nice surprise: a romantic comedy with some original, offbeat touches and a charming, low-key performance by Gene Hackman. He plays the forlorn all-night manager of a super-market, saddled with a cheerless wife (Ladd) and a dumb son (Quaid). His life changes when he meets a neighbor's wife (Streisand), who has been carrying on with his son. Streisand is clearly miscast as the dissatisifed housewife (she took the role over from Lisa Eichhorn), but her budding romance with Hackman, who decides to do something about his dull existence, radiates unexpected warmth. Some oddball minor characters also help make a small but entertaining movie.

## Arthur

★★★ Orion, 1981, c, 97 min. Dir and SP: Steve Gordon. Cast: Dudley Moore, Liza Minnelli, John Gielgud, Geraldine Fitzgerald, Jill Eikenberry, Stephen Elliott, Barney Martin, Ted Ross.

Veteran actor John Gielgud is the true star of this popular comedy, giving an Oscar-winning

Perpetually tipsy millionaire Arthur Bach (Dudley Moore) embraces waitress Linda (Liza Minnelli), to the disapproval of his valet, Hobson (John Gielgud), in *Arthur* (1981).

performance (Best Supporting Actor) as the acerbic, protective valet to alcoholic playboy Dudley Moore. Moore is Arthur, and if you still think drunkards are funny, and if you can tolerate his endless cackling and prattling, you should enjoy the movie. Arthur has been instructed to shape up and to marry an available heiress (Eikenberry), but instead he falls for waitress Linda (Minnelli), and now he is in danger of being disinherited. There's a contrived climax in a wedding chapel, but until then, the movie ekes out a fair number of laughs. The theme song, "Best That You Can Do," won an Oscar. A sequel, *Arthur 2: On the Rocks* (1988) failed at the box office.

## As Good as It Gets

★★★ TriStar, 1997, c, 139 min. Dir: James L. Brooks. SP: Mark Andrus, James L. Brooks, b/o story by Mark Andrus. Cast: Jack Nicholson, Helen Hunt, Greg Kinnear, Cuba Gooding, Jr., Shirley Knight, Skeet Ulrich.

Meet Melvin Udall (Nicholson), although you may not want to. A prolific romance novelist with an obsessive-compulsive disorder, Melvin feels obliged to make an insulting, demeaning remark to everyone he meets, regardlesss of race, creed, or color. Will this latter-day Scrooge eventually become a veritable pussycat? Can you doubt it? Before the movie ends, he has been humanized by a small dog, a sensitive gay man (Kinnear), and mostly by a waitress (Hunt) with whom he falls in love. This enjoyable but overlong comedy-drama won Oscars for Nicholson and Hunt, but it is Hunt who stands out in a lovely performance. Wait for her big "money" scenes: when she tearfully confesses her hidden feelings to her mother (Knight), and when she tries awkwardly to thank Melvin for his help with her sick son. Oscar-nominated Kinnear is also fine.

## The Bachelor and the Bobby-Soxer

★★★ RKO, 1947, 95 min. Dir: Irving Reis. SP: Sidney Sheldon. Cast: Cary Grant, Myrna Loy, Shirley Temple, Rudy Vallee, Ray Collins, Harry Davenport.

How much suspension of disbelief are you willing to make? If you can believe that stern judge Myrna Loy has a teenage sister who resembles Shirley Temple, you may enjoy this frivolous comedy. Cary Grant plays a bachelor artist who is worshipped by bobby-soxer Temple. When Temple involves him in an innocently compromising situation, Judge Loy sentences him to "date" her sister, hoping this will cure her of her infatuation. Inevitably, Loy and Grant fall in love, to the dismay of Temple and of Loy's stuffy suitor, Rudy Vallee. Much of the humor comes from Grant's reluctant participation in high-school fun and games. As usual, he tolerates all the foolish shenanigans with charm and good humor, making the movie seem more amusing than it actually is.

## Bachelor Mother

★★★ RKO, 1939, 81 min. Dir: Garson Kanin. SP: Norman Krasna, b/o story by Felix Jackson. Cast: Ginger Rogers, David Niven, Charles Coburn, Frank Albertson, Ernest Truex, Ferike Boros, June Wilkins.

After leaving dance partner Fred Astaire, Ginger Rogers sought to establish herself as a nondancing comic actress. *Bachelor Mother* is one of her better efforts, an ingratiating comedy in which she gives an appealing performance. She plays a department store salesgirl who is mistaken for an unwed mother when she finds an abandoned baby. She becomes involved with the playboy son (Niven) of the store's owner, who, for a while, believes that she wants to abandon the baby. By the time everything is straightened out, the two are in love. The unfailing Charles Coburn is on hand as Niven's father, who insists on claiming the baby as his grandson. The movie was poorly remade in 1956 as the musical *Bundle of Joy,* with Debbie Reynolds and Eddie Fisher.

## Ball of Fire

★★★ Goldwyn-RKO, 1941, 111 min. Dir: Howard Hawks. SP: Charles Brackett, Billy Wilder, b/o story by Billy Wilder, Thomas Monroe. Cast: Barbara Stanwyck, Gary Cooper,

Dana Andrews Dan Duryea, Oscar Homolka, S. Z. Sakall, Henry Travers, Richard Haydn, Aubrey Mather, Allen Jenkins, Tully Marshall.

Fleeing from a subpoena that would incriminate her gangster boyfriend, burlesque dancer Sugarpuss O'Shea (Stanwyck) hides out in a house where seven staid old professors have been working on an encyclopedia. She is supposedly in residence to teach them about "slang," but when she meets an eighth professor (Cooper), she soon has other things on her mind. And so does the bewildered professor. Believe it or not, the screenplay was intended as a sly variation on *Snow White and the Seven Dwarfs,* and if Sugarpuss is not exactly Snow White, the character springs to life in Stanwyck's Oscar-nominated performance. By now Cooper was an expert at playing shy, befuddled men, and he is very funny trying to stave off Sugarpuss's advances. The movie sags at times, but it is far better than director Hawks's 1948 musical remake, *A Song Is Born.*

## The Beautician and the Beast

★★☆ Paramount, 1997, c, 103 min. Dir: Ken Kwapis. SP: Todd Graff. Cast: Fran Drescher, Timothy Dalton, Ian McNeice, Patrick Malahide, Lisa Jakub, Phyllis Newman.

Fran Drescher is, admittedly, an acquired taste, like kumquats or anchovies. The star of the long-running sitcom *The Nanny,* she is equipped with a nasal bray that makes Barbra Streisand sound like Queen Elizabeth. Here, in her starring debut, she plays Joy Miller, a beautician who, improbably, is invited to tutor the children of Boris Pochenko (Dalton), the dictator of a remote Eastern European country called Slovetzia. It is only a matter of time before Joy brings her personal-style democracy to Slovetzia and also wins the heart of Pochenko. You also know that at some point plain Joy will become "gaw-jus" Joy, dressed to the nines and looking regally beautiful. A reasonably amiable comedy that depends on your tolerance of its star.

## Beautiful Girls

★★★☆ Miramax, 1996, c, 107 min. Dir: Ted Demme. SP: Scott Rosenberg. Cast: Matt Dillon, Michael Rapaport, Martha Plimpton, Mira Sorvino, Lauren Holly, Timothy Hutton, Annabeth Gish, Natalie Portman, Uma Thurman, Pruitt Taylor Vince, Rosie O'Donnell, Noah Emmerich, Max Perlich.

An exceptionally strong cast brings some vitality to this comedy about high school friends reuniting in a small town after ten years. Not surprisingly, romance and sex are the main (possibly the only) forces guiding this group: Paul (Rapaport), who has a fixation on fashion models, has lost his longtime girlfriend (Plimpton) to another man. Tommy (Dillon) is in trouble—his girlfriend (Sorvino) knows he is seeing his old high school flame (Holly), now married. And Willy (Hutton) finds himself falling for a cheeky thirteen-year-old (Portman). Then along comes Andera (Thurman), beautiful and unattainable, and all bets are off. Rosie O'Donnell has a small but showy role as a neighborhood feminist with her own ideas about womanhood.

## Before Sunrise

★★★ Columbia, 1995, c, 101 min. Dir: Richard Linklater. SP: Richard Linklater, Kim Krizan. Cast: Ethan Hawke, Julie Delpy.

A slight, sweetly romantic story, told against the beautiful background of Vienna, *Before Sunrise* exudes a surprising amount of charm. Jesse (Hawke), a young American on his way back to the States after the end of a love affair, meets Celine (Delpy), a French student, on a train. Impulsively, he proposes that they spend the day together in Vienna, and she agrees. Nothing much happens—they move through the city and meet various people—but they are clearly falling in love. There is a great deal of talk—some of it amusing—and then they part, vowing to meet again. That's all, but the two actors are appealing, and the romantic spell they cast is palpable.

## Best Friends

★★ Warners, 1982, c, 116 min. Dir: Norman Jewison. SP: Barry Levinson, Valerie Curtin. Cast: Goldie Hawn, Burt Reynolds, Jessica Tandy, Barnard Hughes, Audra Lindley, Keenan Wynn, Ron Silver.

Paula (Hawn) and Richard (Reynolds) are a successful writing team. They are also in love, and when Richard proposes marriage, Paula accepts, reluctantly. Everything goes down hill from there. Her parents turn out to be terminally weird, and his parents are clearly impossible. Worse, not one of the characters is as amusing as the writers seem to believe they are. At a party in their honor, Paula overdoses on Valium and collapses in her food. Inevitably, they quarrel angrily, and Richard moves out. Their conclusion: "We got married and it ruined everything." Do they kiss and make up? Do you doubt it? None of the actors can be blamed, and the basic idea has possibilities, but the movie never takes off.

## Blind Date

★ TriStar, 1987, c, 93 min. Dir: Blake Edwards. SP: Dale Launer. Cast: Kim Basinger, Bruce Willis, John Larroquette, William Daniels, Phil Hartman, George Coe, Stephanie Faracy, Joyce Van Patten, Graham Stark.

At least until the utterly preposterous climax, there's a dark movie lurking around the edges of this wretched farce, but don't bother to look for it. Bruce Willis makes his starring debut as a nerdlike businessman who is warned that his blind date (Basinger) becomes wild when she has even one drink. Stupidly, he gives her champagne, and she causes chaos that has him losing his job and nearly his sanity. She also has a demented ex-beau (Larroquette) who is determined to kill Willis. There is much frantic activity, none of it even vaguely amusing, plus a wedding finale that must be seen to be disbelieved. A terrible movie in every possible way.

## Boomerang

★★ Paramount, 1992, c, 118 min. Dir: Reginald Hudlin. SP: Barry W. Blaustein, David Sheffield, b/o story by Eddie Murphy. Cast: Eddie Murphy, Robin Givens, Halle Berry, David Alan Grier, Martin Lawrence, Grace Jones, Eartha Kitt, Geoffrey Holder, Chris Rock, Tisha Campbell.

Marcus Graham (Murphy) is a dapper, hugely self-assured marketing executive with a string of women he treats with suave indifference. Along comes the ravishing Jacqueline (Givens), who turns out to be not only his new boss but a woman who is delighted to give Marcus the same stand-off treatment he gives to his many "conquests." After much back-and-forth banter and some sexual activity, Marcus comes to find true love and commitment with the demure Angela (Berry). Murphy's attempt at sophisticated romantic comedy is sabotaged by an exceptionally coarse screenplay without a trace of wit or style. Eartha Kitt, as a cosmetics queen, gives a preposterous imitation of Eartha Kitt.

## The Bride Came C.O.D.

★★☆ Warners, 1941, 92 min. Dir: William Keighley. SP: Julius J. Epstein, Philip G. Epstein, b/o story by Kenneth Earl, M. M. Musselman. Cast: Bette Davis, James Cagney, Stuart Erwin, Jack Carson, Eugene Pallette, Harry Davenport.

As a change of pace, Warners cast Bette Davis and James Cagney, two of their top dramatic stars, in a romantic comedy. The result, at best, was mediocre. By this time, the plot of the spoiled runaway heiress who falls for the man hired by her father to bring her home, hatched seven years earlier by *It Happened One Night,* was frayed to the breaking point, and neither Davis nor Cagney, although game, could carry off the necessary lighthearted style. (Davis is shrill, Cagney desperate.) Most of the dialogue echoes other films ("You glamor girls are a drug on the market!"), and few of the situations are more than mildly amusing. As a whole, the movie betrays the studio's heavy-handed approach to comedy.

## Bringing up Baby

★★★★ RKO, 1938, 102 min. Dir: Howard Hawks. SP: Dudley Nichols, Hagar Wilde, b/o story by Hagar Wilde. Cast: Cary Grant, Katharine Hepburn, May Robson, Charles Ruggles,

Barry Fitzgerald, Walter Catlett, Fritz Feld, Ward Bond.

One of the funniest screwball comedies of the thirties, *Bringing Up Baby* was not a hit when it was first released, but it showed Katharine Hepburn's capacity for farce after too many dreary dramas. She plays a light-headed rich girl who disrupts the life of absent-minded archaeologist Grant and wins him for her own in the end. Much of the comedy revolves about her pet leopard, Baby, and you won't want to miss the scene in which Hepburn and Grant roam the countryside looking for the missing Baby, while singing his favorite song, "I Can't Give You Anything But Love." There's also the couple's first meeting on a golf course, punctuated by one comic disaster after another. Diverting entertainment of the kind they can't seem to make any more.

In *Bringing up Baby* (1938), the antics of Cary Grant and Katharine Hepburn land them in jail, and constable Walter Catlett is inclined to throw away the key.

# Broadcast News

★★★☆ Fox, 1987, c, 131 min. Dir and SP: James L. Brooks. Cast: William Hurt, Holly Hunter, Albert Brooks, Robert Prosky, Lois Chiles, Joan Cusack, Peter Hackes, Jack Nicholson (unbilled).

The setting is a Washington, D.C., television station where sex and ratings are the two most prominent topics of interest. William Hurt is a handsome but superficial anchorman for the station; Holly Hunter is a take-charge producer with some hangups of her very own; Albert Brooks is an erudite but uncharismatic news writer. (The screenplay's best lines are his.) The station's battle for ratings occupies much of their time, but they never neglect personal relationships. The three actors are fine (they were all Oscar-nominated), but the funniest performance is given by Joan Cusack as a frenetic worker at the station. Jack Nicholson makes a brief, unbilled appearance as the station's star anchorman. The movie received four other Oscar nominations, including one as Best Picture.

# Bull Durham

★★★☆ Orion, 1988, c, 108 min. Dir and SP: Ron Shelton. Cast: Kevin Costner, Susan Sarandon, Tim Robbins, Trey Wilson, Robert Wuhl, Jenny Robertson, Max Patkin, William O'Leary, David Neidorf.

A rowdy, ribald romantic comedy, revolving about the twin games of sex and baseball. Kevin Costner gives one of his most assured performances as Crash Davis, a veteran player hired by the Carolina League's Durham Bulls, supposedly as a catcher, but actually to watch over Ebby "Nuke" LaLoosh (Robbins), a promising but undisciplined young pitcher. Susan Sarandon is Annie Savoy, a baseball devotee who chooses one player each year and then, in her own womanly way, teaches him to "mature." When she chooses Nuke, a fight ensues between Crash and Annie, but their heated opposition to each other eventually turns to love. Ron Shelton ably directs his own well-wrought screenplay, which captures the pungent flavor of minor-league baseball.

# Christmas in Connecticut

★★☆ Warners, 1945, 101 min. Dir: Peter Godfrey. SP: Lionel Houser, Adele Comandini, b/o story by Aileen Hamilton. Cast: Barbara Stanwyck, Dennis Morgan, Sydney Greenstreet, Reginald Gardiner, S. Z. Sakall, Robert Shayne, Una O'Connor, Frank Jenks, Joyce Compton.

This featherweight romantic comedy, typical of the period, stars Barbara Stanwyck as a magazine columnist whose expertise on home matters is pure sham. Forced by her boss (Greenstreet) to prepare a Christmas dinner for sailor and war hero Dennis Morgan at her nonexistent Connecticut farm, she scrambles about trying to acquire a home and family in a matter of hours. No surprise when she falls for the hero. She not only manages to produce a delicious Christmas dinner, courtesy of chef S. Z. Sakall, but also wins the sailor's heart. Remade for cable television in 1992. Why?

# Come September

★★★ Universal-International, 1961, c, 112 min. Dir: Robert Mulligan. SP: Stanley Shapiro, Maurice Richlin. Cast: Rock Hudson, Gina Lollobrigida, Walter Slezak, Sandra Dee, Bobby Darin, Brenda De Banzie, Rosanna Rory, Joel Grey, Ronald Howard.

A breezy comedy from the authors of *Pillow Talk, Come September* stars Rock Hudson as a wealthy American who comes to the Italian Riviera every September to spend time with his mistress (Lollobrigida). This time he arrives in July, only to find that the villa has been turned into a hotel by his major-domo (Slezak). The hotel is swarming with young, chaperoned girls on a tour, and when American college boys arrive to pitch a tent on the lawn, there are obvious comic complications. Some nice Italian scenery and a lighthearted air help to keep the movie afloat.

# Coming to America

★★☆ Paramount, 1988, c, 116 min. Dir: John Landis. SP: David Sheffield, Barry Blaustein. Cast: Eddie Murphy, Arsenio Hall, James Earl Jones, John Amos, Madge Sinclair,

Shari Headley, Eriq La Salle, Louie Anderson, Samuel L. Jackson, Cuba Gooding, Jr..

Eddie Murphy deprived of his street-smart sharpness and wit is virtually no Eddie Murphy at all. Proof positive: *Coming to America.* He plays Akeem, the wildly wealthy, sweet-natured prince of an African country who defies his father's choice of a bride by going to America to find his own woman. Accompanied by his one friend (Hall), he moves to the poorest section of Queens, New York, where he falls for beautiful Lisa (Headley). There are some amusing portions (Akeem interviewing New York candidates for his bride-to-be is funny), but on the whole the screenplay is clumsily written. Murphy's character is disconcertingly bland, but he also appears, disguised, in several cameo roles. A change of pace for the actor, but not a good one.

## Continental Divide

★★☆ Universal, 1981, c, 103 min. Dir: Michael Apted. SP: Lawrence Kasdan. Cast: John Belushi, Blair Brown, Allen Goorwitz, Carlin Glynn, Tony Ganios, Val Avery.

A few decades ago, this mild romantic comedy might have made a passable vehicle for Clark Gable and Loretta Young. Here it serves to give John Belushi a stab at playing a romantic leading man, and he does well enough. He plays Ernie Souchak, a hard-hitting Chicago investigative reporter who goes to Wyoming to interview a naturalist (Brown) who is trying to save the eagle. Predictably they clash, then fall in love, leaving them with a dilemma about the future. For much of the running time, it's just these two, and they make a pleasant pair.

## Crossing Delancey

★★★ Warners, 1988, c, 97 min. Dir: Joan Micklin Silver. SP: Susan Sandler, b/o her play. Cast: Amy Irving, Peter Riegert, Reizl Bozyk, Jeroen Krabbe, Sylvia Miles, Suzzy Roche, George Martin, Rosemary Harris, Amy Wright, David Hyde Pierce.

Isabelle, known as Izzy (Irving), enjoys her New York life. Intelligent and self-reliant, she works in a bookstore, getting to meet all sorts of literary types, especially an attentive, smooth-talking novelist (Krabbe). Her grandmother (Bozyk), however, thinks she needs a husband and, through a matchmaker (Miles, in a hilarious performance), arranges for Izzy to meet pickle-shop owner Sam (Riegert). Her feelings are ambivalent but ultimately her resistance melts as she comes to appreciate and even love him. A charming, endearing little comedy, leisurely paced but true to its characters.

## Desire

★★★ Paramount, 1936, 96 min. Dir: Frank Borzage. SP: Edwin Justus Mayer, Waldemar Young, Samuel Hoffenstein, b/o play by Hans Szekely, R. A. Stemmle. Cast: Marlene Dietrich, Gary Cooper, John Halliday, William Frawley, Ernest Cossart, Alan Mowbray, Zeffie Tilbury, Akim Tamiroff.

From its opening credits—a woman's gloved hand fondling a pearl necklace—*Desire* bears the stamp of its producer, Ernst Lubitsch. Although Frank Borzage directed, the Lubitsch "touch" is evident in the stylish decor, the sly uses of suggestion and indirection, and the air of sophistication. Swathed in Travis Benton gowns, Dietrich is alluring as a clever jewel thief who meets a vacationing engineer (Cooper). She's forced to plant a stolen necklace on him, but love blossoms, and she turns honest. The opening sequences, in which Dietrich steals the necklace with an elaborate ruse, are pricelessly funny, and if the rest of the film fails to match them, it is still frivolous fun.

## Desk Set

★★★ Fox, 1957, c, 103 min. Dir: Walter Lang. SP: Phoebe Ephron, Henry Ephron, b/o play by William Marchant. Cast: Katharine Hepburn, Spencer Tracy, Gig Young, Joan Blondell, Dina Merrill, Neva Patterson, Sue Randall.

Marking the eighth teaming of Katharine Hepburn and Spencer Tracy, *Desk Set* adds up to pleasant light entertainment. Hepburn plays the efficient head of the reference library for a television network; Tracy is the methods engineer who brings in a massive computer that threatens Hepburn's department. Of course they clash, and of course she ultimately demonstrates the superior worth of the human mind. Nor should anybody be surprised when the two fall in love. Adapted from a Broadway play, *Desk Set* is cheerful, inconsequential, and occasionally witty, and Hepburn and Tracy give their usual expert performances. Present, too, are such likable actors as the always welcome Joan Blondell as a member of Hepburn's staff and Gig Young as Hepburn's longtime suitor.

## Doc Hollywood

★★★ Warners, 1991, c, 104 min. Dir: Michael Caton-Jones. SP: Jeffrey Price, Peter S. Seaman, Daniel Pyne, b/o book by Dr. Neil B. Shulman. Cast: Michael J. Fox, Julie Warner, Barnard Hughes, Woody Harrelson, David Ogden Stiers, Bridget Fonda, George Hamilton.

On his way to a high-paying plastic surgeon job in California, new medical graduate Ben Stone (Fox) has a car accident in Grady, South Carolina ("Squash Capital of the South"), and is forced to stay a while. The Grady townspeople, needing medical help, conspire to persuade him to stay. He's reluctant until he meets lovely Julie Warner. There's not much else, but *Doc Hollywood* is disarmingly likable, thanks to Fox's easygoing style and a supporting cast of capable actors, including Barnard Hughes as the local doctor, David Ogden Stiers as the mayor, and Woody Harrelson as an insurance salesman who fancies himself as Fox's rival for Warner's affection. The movie also has some authentic-seeming small-town atmosphere: a parade, a carnival, and the like.

## The Doctor Takes a Wife

★★★ Columbia, 1940, 89 min. Dir: Alexander Hall. SP: George Seaton, Ken Englund, b/o story by Aleen Leslie. Cast: Loretta Young, Ray Milland, Reginald Gardiner, Gail Patrick, Edmund Gwenn.

A breezy romantic comedy, typical of the period. Young is a professional bachelor girl who writes a popular book called *Spinsters Aren't Spinach*. Milland is a surgeon who scoffs at independent-minded women. This is forties Hollywood, and naturally the two are forced to pretend that they are married. Sharing the same apartment, they exchange the sort of insults that can only lead to romance. Gail Patrick is the resident "other woman." There are funny moments, such as the new "bride" at a gathering of her "husband's" colleagues, where she tries to grapple with nonstop medical terminology.

## Every Girl Should Be Married

★★☆ RKO, 1948, 85 min. Dir: Don Hartman. SP: Don Hartman, Stephen Morehouse Avery, b/o story by Eleanor Harris. Cast: Cary Grant, Betsy Drake, Franchot Tone, Diana Lynn, Eddie Albert, Elisabeth Risdon, Alan Mowbray.

Betsy Drake made a charming if somewhat offbeat impression in her film debut in this light romantic comedy. She plays a disarmingly straightforward salesgirl who perseveres in her pursuit of a marriageable doctor (Grant). He is determined to remain a bachelor, but she tries every scheme possible, enlisting the aid of her best friend (Lynn) and a suave man-about-town (Tone) to land her prey. In real life, Ms. Drake also won her man, marrying Grant soon after the movie was released. They would appear together in one more film, *Room for One More,* in 1952.

## The Fabulous Baker Boys

★★★☆ Fox, 1989, c, 113 min. Dir and SP: Steve Kloves. Cast: Jeff Bridges, Michelle Pfeiffer, Beau Bridges, Elie Raab, Jennifer Tilly.

A nice surprise: a tangy, offbeat, and ruefully funny romantic comedy with some good jazz and top-notch performances by the leads. The brothers Bridges play Frank (Beau) and Jack (Jeff) Baker, two small-time nightclub pianists. Frank is the family man who is content with his lot; Jack is footloose and discontent. Along comes singer Susie Diamond (Pfeiffer), who joins their act and precipitates unsettling changes. Beau and Jeff Bridges are ideally cast, but it is Michelle Pfeiffer who will rivet your attention. As a woman who has probably seen too much, she captures Susie's mixture of toughness and vulnerability. She won a Best Actress nomination for her superb performance.

## For Love or Money

★★☆ Universal, 1993, c, 95 min. Dir: Barry Sonnenfeld. SP: Lawrence Konner, Mark Rosenthal. Cast: Michael J. Fox, Gabrielle Anwar, Anthony Higgins, Michael Tucker, Bob Balaban, Isaac Mizrahi, Udo Kier, Simon Jones, Dan Hedaya, Fyvush Finkel.

A slender romantic comedy set at a posh hotel, with Michael J. Fox as the young concierge who is adept at handling the needs of its guests—that is, until he falls in love with a millionaire's beautiful mistress. He also has the dream of building a hotel in Manhattan. Can he win the girl's heart and still get the millionaire's backing for his hotel? Will you care? Probably not, but Fox is a likable actor, and the movie is lightweight enjoyment. Fashion designer Isaac Mizrahi plays a fashion designer, and Fyvush Finkel is amusing as the world's oldest bellman. The movie perks up in a rowdy climax at the millionaire's summer house.

## Four Weddings and a Funeral

★★★☆ Polygram/Working Title, 1994, c, 117 min. Dir: Mike Newell. SP: Richard Curtis. Cast: Hugh Grant, Andie MacDowell, Kristin Scott Thomas, Simon Callow, Rowan Atkinson, James Fleet, John Hannah, Charlotte Coleman, David Bower, Corin Redgrave, Jeremy Kemp.

This blithe, richly amusing British comedy attracted a wide American audience. Hugh Grant, he of the nervous stammer and fluttering eyelids, plays a determined bachelor with a slew of past conquests. At several successive weddings, he meets a lovely American girl (MacDowell) with whom he is instantly smitten. However, they never get further than enjoyable one-night stands. Each wedding has its wry or comical aspects—and one is the girl's own wedding, but not to Grant. Ultimately,

love wins the day. Simon Callow nearly steals the film as an acerbically witty friend of the celebrants, and Rowan Atkinson is hilarious as a nervous priest officiating at his first wedding ceremony.

## French Kiss

★★ Fox, 1995, c, 111 min. Dir: Lawrence Kasdan. SP: Adam Brooks. Cast: Meg Ryan, Kevin Kline, Timothy Hutton, Francois Cluzet, Victor Garrivier, Susan Anbeh.

Some beautiful Paris scenery is not enough to compensate for the severe defects of this feeble romantic comedy. Meg Ryan plays a jilted girl (she was also jilted in *Addicted to Love*) who flies to Paris to win back her errant fiancé (Hutton). On the plane she meets an artful thief (Kline), who drops a stolen necklace into her purse. To retrieve the necklace, he pursues her around the City of Light, while she stalks her ex-boyfriend with his help. It's only a matter of time before the two realize that they care about each other. What a surprise! The two leads are able, although Ms. Ryan can overplay her quirkily adorable persona. Nice musical score.

## The Goodbye Girl

★★★☆ MGM-UA, 1977, c, 110 min. Dir: Herbert Ross. SP: Neil Simon. Cast: Richard Dreyfuss, Marsha Mason, Quinn Cummings, Paul Benedict, Barbara Rhoades.

Most versions of Neil Simon's Broadway plays, adapted by the writer himself, have turned out to be rather flat and juiceless. Simon wrote an original screenplay for this hugely entertaining romantic comedy and came up with a winner. Richard Dreyfuss gives a charismatic, Oscar-winning performance as a flamboyant actor who is obliged to share an apartment with Mason, a divorcée and ex-dancer with a young daughter (Cummings). There is no surprise when hostility gives way to love, but Simon fashions a warm, engaging screenplay that happily keeps his usual wisecracks to a minimum. As the perennial victim—the "goodbye girl"—who is usually deserted by her lovers, Mason

Richard Dreyfuss won an Academy Award for his engaging performance as a driven young actor opposite Marsha Mason in *The Goodbye Girl* (1977).

avoids being overwhelmed by her costar's theatrics. A stage musical adaptation, with Martin Short in the Dreyfuss role, failed to make the grade on Broadway in 1993.

## Green Card

★★★ Touchstone, 1991, c, 108 min. Dir and SP: Peter Weir. Cast: Gerard Depardieu, Andie MacDowell, Bebe Neuwirth, Gregg Edelman, Robert Prosky, Conrad McLaren, Jessie Keosian.

A standard but engaging romantic comedy, with French star Gerard Depardieu as a composer who needs a green card to stay in America and Andie MacDowell as a horticulturalist who needs a husband to rent a desirable Manhattan apartment. They meet, decide to marry for convenience only, and then have to pretend to be *really* married for the immigration authorities. Will they truly fall in love? No suspense here, but Depardieu, in his first major English-speaking role, grapples nobly with his dialogue and comes across as charming and MacDowell makes an attractive vis-à-vis. Funny business: Depardieu has his photograph taken in various costumes to show a happy "past."

## Hands Across the Table

★★★ Paramount, 1935, 80 min. Dir: Mitchell Leisen. SP: Norman Krasna, Vincent Lawrence, Herbert Fields, b/o story by Vina Delmar. Cast: Carole Lombard, Fred MacMurray, Ralph Bellamy, Astrid Allwyn, Marie Provost.

Of all the comic actresses who thrived in the thirties, Carole Lombard was perhaps the most memorable, with impeccable timing and a luminous quality that combined vulnerability and toughness. Here she played a manicurist, out to snare a rich husband, specifically wheelchair-bound aviator Ralph Bellamy, until she meets poverty-stricken ex-millionaire Fred MacMurray. The movie was produced by Ernst Lubitsch, whose famous "touch" is evident in more than one scene. Favorite sequence: MacMurray on the phone with his snobbish fiancée (Allwyn), while Lombard plays a dim-witted "long-distance" operator in the background.

## Harold and Maude

★★★ Paramount, 1971, c, 90 min. Dir: Hal Ashby. SP: Colin Higgins. Cast: Ruth Gordon, Bud Cort, Vivian Pickles, Cyril Cusack, Charles Tyner, Ellen Geer.

Yes, it's a comedy, even though it deals with such matters as suicide and death. And yes, it's a romance, even though Harold (Cort) is twenty and his inamorata, Maude (Gordon), is nearing eighty. Harold is a very strange young man who apparently relishes faking his suicide, again and again. Maude is feisty, exuberant, and fond of uttering hollow aphorisms about life. They meet at a funeral, fall in love, and carry out a number of pranks together. Eventually, their romance ends on a sadly ironic note. *Harold and Maude* is a cult film, best enjoyed by those who can appreciate its dark, offbeat humor. Ruth Gordon adds another eccentric old biddy to her latter-day list of one-note performances, and Bud Cort will have you either laughing or cringing.

## He Said, She Said

★★☆ Paramount, 1991, c, 115 min. Dirs: Ken Kwapis, Marisa Silver. SP: Brian Hohlfeld. Cast: Kevin Bacon, Elizabeth Perkins, Nathan Lane, Sharon Stone, Anthony LaPaglia, Charlayne Woodard, Phil Leeds, Rita Karin.

This attempt at old-fashioned romantic comedy fails largely because of a muddled screenplay. The movie traces the up-and-down relationship of Dan Hanson (Bacon) and Lorie Bryer (Perkins) over time. They begin as colleagues on a newspaper, writing rival columns, then move to television, where they score as anchors on the program "He Said/She Said." Together they run the gamut of emotions: recriminations, jealousy, passionate devotion, and so on. Despite an interesting idea, the movie suffers from confusing flashbacks that make it difficult to determine the particular time or place. Still, the leads are agreeable and the supporting cast is good.

## The Heartbreak Kid

★★★☆ Fox, 1972, c, 104 min. Dir: Elaine May. SP: Neil Simon, b/o story by Bruce Jay Friedman. Cast: Charles Grodin, Cybill Shepherd, Jeannie Berlin, Eddie Albert, Audra Lindley, William Prince, Augusta Dabney.

Neil Simon's comedy, expertly directed by Elaine May, is wickedly funny, but it also has a streak of cruelty that may alienate some viewers. Charles Grodin is Lenny, an ambitious, manipulative sporting goods salesman who marries the painfully shy and awkward Lila (Berlin). On their honeymoon, he meets Kelly (Shepherd), the golden WASP of his dreams, and becomes determined to win her at all cost. His shabby treatment of his new bride is painful to watch, although it undeniably draws laughs. Grodin is fine as a model of self-absorption and insincerity but Oscar-nominated Berlin (May's real-life daughter) steals the movie as the unfortunate, and ultimately poignant, Lila. Eddie Albert is particularly good as Kelly's skeptical, bigoted father.

## House Calls

★★★☆ Universal, 1978, c, 98 min. Dir: Howard Zieff. SP: Max Shulman, Julius J. Epstein, Alan Mandel, Charles Shyer. Cast: Walter Matthau, Glenda Jackson, Art Carney, Richard Benjamin, Candice Azzara, Dick O'Neill, Thayer David.

Widowed surgeon Charley Nichols (Matthau) returns to L.A.'s Kensington General Hospital, where he finds the same chaos and incompetence under the leadership of senile old Dr. Willoughby (Carney). Charlie also begins a scratchy, then loving relationship with divorcée Ann Atkinson (Jackson), but there's trouble when she demands fidelity from him, instead of his usual womanizing ways. A subplot involves Candice Azzara as a wealthy widow who wants to sue the hospital for hastening her husband's death. Benefiting from an exceptionally sharp screenplay, slouching, rumpled Matthau and briskly British Jackson play well together, but the movie is stolen by Carney as the hilariously out-of-it chief of staff. An enjoyable movie that later became a television series.

## HouseSitter

★★ Universal, 1992, c, 108 min. Dir: Frank Oz. SP: Mark Stein, b/o story by Mark Stein, Brian Glazer. Cast: Goldie Hawn, Steve Martin, Dana Delany, Julie Harris, Donald Moffat, Peter MacNichol, Richard B. Shull, Laurel Cronin, Christopher Durang.

Steve Martin and Goldie Hawn are appealing comic actors, but this comedy, teaming them for the first time, is a mistake. Martin is Newton Davis, an architect who enjoys a one-night stand with Hawn's Gwen, a compulsive liar and spinner of fantasies. Gwen moves into the house Davis built for the girl (Delany) who rejected him, not only furnishing it with his funds but claiming to be his wife! Naturally Davis is aghast but he finds that he cannot escape from her fantasy life and he becomes more deeply involved. Not only does this premise ring false, but Hawn's behavior makes her seem seriously disturbed rather than merely kooky. By the time of the climax—a bogus wedding reception—the movie can only limp to its inevitable conclusion.

## How to Marry a Millionaire

★★★ Fox, 1953, c, 95 min. Dir: Jean Negulesco. SP: Nunnally Johnson, b/o plays by Zoe Akins, Dale Eunson, Katherine Albert. Cast: Betty Grable, Marilyn Monroe, Lauren Bacall, William Powell, David Wayne, Rory Calhoun, Cameron Mitchell.

To show off their new widescreen Cinema-Scope process, Fox dusted off the old idea of three women on the prowl for wealthy husbands and dressed it up in splashy style. The formula shows through, but the movie is genial, lightweight entertainment. The ladies ready for action are Betty Grable, tough, knowing, and determined; Marilyn Monroe, myopic and innocently sexy; and caustic Lauren Bacall, who gets most of the good lines. A touch of class is provided by the unfailing William Powell as Bacall's wryly realistic suitor.

Fox couldn't seem to let go of the three-girls-seeking-rich-husbands plotline—it was used in *Three Blind Mice* (1938), *Moon Over Miami* (1941), and *Three Little Girls in Blue* (1946).

## I.Q.

★★★ Paramount, 1994, c, 95 min. Dir: Fred Schepisi. SP: Andy Breckman, Michael Leeson. Cast: Meg Ryan, Tim Robbins, Walter Matthau, Gene Saks, Lou Jacobi, Stephen Fry, Joseph Maher, Charles Durning. Tony Shalhoub.

The place: Princeton in the Eisenhower years. Ed (Robbins) is a garage mechanic who falls instantly in love with Catherine (Ryan). The problem is, Catherine is a scientist with a brainy but pompous fiancé (Fry) and a disdain for garage mechanics. Also, her uncle happens to be famed scientist Albert Einstein (Matthau). Will Ed's love prevail? Yes, with the help of Einstein and his lovable cronies (Jacobi, Saks, and Maher), who decide to make Ed seem like a genius. The leads are charming and Matthau makes a credible Einstein, but the four scientists together have a terminal case of the "cutes." Still, *I.Q.* is enjoyable, with a more intelligent screenplay than most.

## If Lucy Fell ...

★☆ TriStar, 1996, c, 94 min. Dir and SP: Eric Schaeffer. Cast: Sarah Jessica Parker, Eric Schaeffer, Ben Stiller, Elle Macpherson, James Rebhorn, Robert John Burke, David Thornton, Bill Sage.

Eric Schaeffer produced, wrote, directed, and starred in this lamentable romantic comedy. Sarah Jessica Parker, exuding cuteness to the breaking point, plays Lucy, a psychotherapist whose best friend and roommate is Joe (Schaeffer), a painter. The two agree that if they haven't found true love by age thirty, they will commit suicide jointly. You heard it here. Meanwhile they talk and talk, and Joe has a failed liasion with his gorgeous neighbor (Macpherson). Ben Stiller wins a few laughs (but only a few) as a dreadlocked, off-the-wall painter named Bwick.

## Indiscreet

★★★ Warners, 1958, c, 100 min. Dir: Stanley Donen. SP: Norman Krasna, b/o his play. Cast: Ingrid Bergman, Cary Grant, Phyllis Calvert, Cecil Parker, David Kossoff, Megs Jenkins.

Norman Krasna's play *Kind Sir* was merely a light vehicle for Mary Martin and Charles Boyer. Transferred to the screen by Krasna himself and retitled *Indiscreet,* it is no less of a vehicle for two equally attractive stars. Bergman is a renowned actress who falls for suave banker-diplomat Grant. A confirmed bachelor, he pretends to be married to avoid permanent ties. When Bergman learns the truth, she exclaims, "How *dare* he make love to me and not be a married man!" This glittering but empty bauble seems to have been made only so that Bergman could utter this line. The sets are swank and the stars shine, but the movie is utterly inconsequential. The Bergman-Grant chemistry is much more evident in *Notorious,* made more than a decade earlier.

## It Could Happen to You

★★★ TriStar, 1994, c, 101 min. Dir: Andrew Bergman. SP: Jane Anderson. Cast: Nicolas Cage, Bridget Fonda, Rosie Perez, Red Buttons, Wendell Pierce, Victor Rojas, Seymour Cassel, Stanley Tucci.

The setting: New York City. Charlie (Cage) is a good cop and a great human being—generous, honest, and resourceful. Yvonne (Fonda) is a hard-luck waitress in a coffee shop. When Charlie has no money for a tip, he shares a lottery ticket with Yvonne—and it wins the jackpot! The problem is that Charlie has a wife named Muriel (Perez), a shrill, greedy harridan who wants *all* the winnings. And Yvonne has a sleazy estranged husband (Tucci). You won't be surprised when Charlie and Yvonne continue to meet and soon fall in love. Nasty Muriel stirs up a media uproar that ends in a trial. An engaging romantic New York fable, *It Could Happen to You* has a strictly Capra-corny ending, but Cage and Fonda make a likable couple,

## It Should Happen to You

★★★ Columbia, 1954, 87 min. Dir: George Cukor. SP: Garson Kanin, b/o his story. Cast: Judy Holliday, Jack Lemmon, Peter Lawford, Michael O'Shea, Vaughn Taylor, Connie Gilchrist.

Judy Holliday's abundant charm shines through this amiable—and sometimes satirical—romantic comedy, but she's helped enormously by Jack Lemmon's winning presence in his movie debut. Holliday plays Gladys, a hopeful actress who decides to become "somebody" by placing her name on a billboard in New York's Columbus Circle. With the help of a conniving press agent (O'Shea), she becomes a media celebrity, much to the annoyance of photographer Lemmon, who has come to love her. The movie's spoofing of instant celebrity is rather lame, and Gladys comes across as more dumb than naïve, but the stars make it work reasonably well. Wait for their duet on "Let's Fall in Love."

## It Started with Eve

★★★ Universal, 1941, 90 min. Dir: Henry Koster. SP: Norman Krasna, Leo Townsend. Cast: Deanna Durbin, Charles Laughton, Robert Cummings, Guy Kibbee, Margaret Tallichet, Walter Catlett.

Singer Deanna Durbin is the nominal star of this airy romantic comedy, but it's Charles Laughton, in his Twinkly Old Codger phase, who nearly steals the show. He plays millionaire Jonathan Reynolds, presumably on his deathbed, who asks to meet his son Johnny's fiancée (Tallichet) before he expires. In desperation when she is unavailable, Johnny hires a hatcheck girl and aspiring singer named Anne (Durbin) to play the fiancée. When Reynolds recovers unexpectedly, the complications mount. Durbin is appealing although she is merely competent as an actress, and Laughton (who was only forty at the time) hams his way through his role. Remade in 1964 as *I'd Rather Be Rich*.

## It's My Turn

★★☆ Columbia, 1980, c, 91 min. Dir: Claudia Weill. SP: Eleanor Bergstein. Cast: Jill Clayburgh, Michael Douglas, Charles Grodin, Steven Hill, Beverly Garland, Dianne Wiest, Daniel Stern, Joan Copeland.

At a Chicago university, Kate Gunderson (Clayburgh) is a harassed, vaguely discontented professor of mathematics who lives with Homer (Grodin). Then she travels to New York City for a job interview in management and also to attend the wedding of her father (Hill). At the wedding, she meets and falls in love with Ben Lewin (Douglas), the son of the bride-to-be (Garland). Now she must decide which direction her life should take. Clayburgh gives an expert performance as a complex, difficult, and not entirely likable woman, but the movie is slight and rather sluggish. As usual, Grodin is especially good as an easygoing and somewhat aloof man. Dianne Wiest made her film debut as Kate's cousin.

## Jerry Maguire

★★★☆ TriStar, 1996, 138 min. Dir and SP: Cameron Crowe. Cast: Tom Cruise, Cuba Gooding, Jr., Renée Zellweger, Jay Mohr, Bonnie Hunt, Jonathan Lipnicki, Kelly Preston, Regina King.

Highly entertaining but also too long, *Jerry Maguire* stars Oscar-nominated Tom Cruise in one of his best roles. He's a hotshot sports agent who makes the mistake of writing an earnest "mission statement" for his company. Fired, he is left with only one client, a rambunctious football player named Roy (Gooding in an exuberant, Oscar-winning performance). He also earns the admiration and love of coworker Dorothy (Zellweger), a widow with a young son (Lipnicki). *Jerry Maguire* is an intelligently written, well-performed romantic comedy that deserved its popularity. Zellweger is appealing, and there's a great supporting turn by Bonnie Hunt as her practical-minded sister.

## Joe Versus the Volcano

★★☆ Warners, 1990, c, 102 min. Dir and SP: John Patrick

Shanley. Cast: Tom Hanks, Meg Ryan, Lloyd Bridges, Abe Vigoda, Amanda Plummer, Robert Stack, Dan Hedaya, Ossie Davis, Carol Kane, Nathan Lane.

Tom Hanks and Meg Ryan are talented actors who play well together (*Sleepless in Seattle, You've Got Mail*) but this early teaming is far from their best. A quirky, even goofy comedy, it has Tom as Joe Banks, a pathetic nerd who learns that he has something called a "brain cloud" and only six months to live. At the behest of tycoon Lloyd Bridges, who wants the island's mineral rights, Joe agrees to leap into an active volcano on a Pacific island to appease the natives. Meg Ryan plays three different roles, most conspicuously Bridges's daughter, who accompanies him on his island adventure. (The islanders love orange soda and their songs include "Hava Nagila.") Much silly business and an abrupt ending, suggesting that director-writer Shanley was at a loss for a windup.

## June Bride

★★★ Warners, 1948, 97 min. Dir: Bretaigne Windust. SP: Ranald MacDougal, b/o play by Eileen Tighe, Graeme Lorimer. Cast: Bette Davis, Robert Montgomery, Fay Bainter, Betty Lynn, Tom Tully, Barbara Bates, Jerome Cowan, Mary Wickes.

In *June Bride*, Bette Davis goes after one of her rare comedy roles with the same intensity she gave to her dramatic roles, and here it's a bit unnerving. She plays the editor of *Home Life* magazine—the traditional movie "boss lady"—who travels to Indiana in a wintry March to stage an article on a local June bride. She is accompanied by her star reporter and ex-lover Robert Montgomery who persists in trying to win her back. Davis hits on all cylinders, while Montgomery is painfully arch, but there are some sharply funny lines and a good cast. Look quickly for Debbie Reynolds in her movie debut.

## Kissing a Fool

★☆ Universal, 1998, c, 105 min. Dir: Doug Ellin. SP: James Frey, Doug Ellin. Cast: David Schwimmer, Jason Lee, Mili Avital, Bonnie Hunt, Vanessa Angel, Kari Wuhrer.

There are only two virtues to this quite dreadful romantic comedy: one is the presence of the always watchable Bonnie Hunt; the other, a dubious recommendation, is that David Schwimmer abandons his usual hangdog persona to play Max Abbitt, an obnoxious sportscaster and tireless womanizer. The central situation is ludicrous: Max is about to marry Samantha (Avital), and to test her fidelity, he asks his best friend Jay (Lee) to try to seduce her. Obviously, Jay has always loved "Sam" and just as obviously, Sam will realize that she loves Jay. So why hang around for the inevitable ending? Don't. Hunt, who narrates this inane story, plays the publisher of Jay's novel, and as usual she gives the tired material a refreshing touch of cynicism.

## A Lady Takes a Chance

★★☆ RKO, 1943, 86 min. Dir: William A. Seiter. SP: Robert Ardrey, b/o story by Jo Swerling. Cast: Jean Arthur, John Wayne, Charles Winninger, Phil Silvers, Don Costello, Grant Withers.

A frail, minor comedy given some charm by the piquancy and appealing voice of Jean Arthur. She plays a typical heroine of the period: a repressed girl who kicks up her heels and discovers "life." Her Molly Truesdale goes out west to find adventure and finds love with rodeo cowboy John Wayne. She also learns about cowboy ways in amusing fashion, getting drunk on "cactus milk," watching an all-out brawl, and learning to love the great outdoors. There are some romantic complications before she settles down with the Duke. Charles Winninger shines as Wayne's old traveling companion.

## Legal Eagles

★★★ Universal, 1986, c, 114 min. Dir: Ivan Reitman. SP: Jim Cash, Jack Epps, Jr. Cast: Robert Redford, Debra Winger, Darryl Hannah, Brian Dennehy, Terence Stamp, Steven Hill.

A romantic comedy with thriller aspects, *Legal*

*Eagles* stars Robert Redford as an assistant district attorney and Debra Winger as a top-rated criminal lawyer. The two find themselves on the same team, defending a strange flower child (Hannah), who has been accused of stealing a valuable painting done by her father and then of murder. Not unexpectedly, Redford and Winger bicker, investigate the case, place themselves in jeopardy, and fall in love. Winger gets the best lines and makes the best impression in this lightweight but airily amusing movie.

## Libeled Lady

★★★★ MGM, 1936, 98 min. Dir: Jack Conway. SP: Maurine Watkins, Howard Emmett Rogers, George Oppenheimer, b/o story by Wallace Sullivan. Cast: William Powell, Myrna Loy, Spencer Tracy, Jean Harlow, Walter Connolly, Charley Grapewin, Cora Witherspoon.

One of the best romantic comedies of the thirties, and a surprise considering that it was made by MGM, not exactly noted for its films in that genre. Four stars at the top of their form keep the clever screenplay spinning merrily. When headstrong heiress Myrna Loy is dubbed a home-wrecker by editor Spencer Tracy's newspaper, she files a libel suit against the paper. To make the lie about her a reality, Tracy hires suave William Powell to court her, with his very own fiancée, Harlow, in the role of the maligned "wife." Thus, Loy would be proven a home-wrecker after all. Naturally, his scheme gets out of control, with diverting results. The movie was nominated for an Academy Award as Best Picture. It was remade in 1946 as *Easy to Wed.*

Jean Harlow gets chummy with William Powell, to the dismay of her fiancé, Spencer Tracy, in *Libeled Lady* (1936), one of the best comedies of the thirties.

## The Lonely Guy

★★★ Universal, 1984, c, 90 min. Dir: Arthur Hiller. SP: Stan Daniels, Ed Weinberger, adapted by Neil Simon from book by Bruce Jay Friedman. Cast: Steve Martin, Charles Grodin, Judith Ivey, Robyn Douglass, Steve Lawrence, Merv Griffin, Dr. Joyce Brothers.

Not always successful but amusing comedy with Steve Martin in an uncharacteristic role as nerdlike Larry Hubbard, who has just been dumped by his girlfriend (Douglass). In the park he meets Warren (Grodin), a "lonely guy" who immediately recognizes Larry as another "lonely guy," He introduces Larry to the special world of the lonely guy, but Larry continues to search for his dream woman. When he meets a woman (Ivey) who seems perfect, fate intercedes. Playing in a quieter vein than usual, Martin is effective, but the movie is stolen, not surprisingly, by Grodin, whose portrait of the introverted Warren is on target. Suggested by Bruce Jay Friedman's *The Lonely Guy's Book of Life.*

## Lover Come Back

★★★☆ Universal-International, 1962, c, 107 min. Dir: Delbert Mann. SP: Stanley Shapiro, Paul Henning. Cast: Doris Day, Rock Hudson, Tony Randall, Edie Adams, Jack Kruschen, Ann B. Davis, Joe Flynn, Jack Albertson, Howard St. John.

Amusing and clever, *Lover Come Back* is one of the best of the Doris Day–Rock Hudson romantic comedies of the sixties. Projecting an unforced charm, Day plays an advertising executive at odds with unethical, womanizing Hudson, who works for a rival agency. As usual, he thinks she's undersexed, and she thinks he's oversexed. Plot complications involve an imaginary product called "Vip," and somehow Hudson is obliged to pose as its shy inventor. There are some satirical barbs aimed at advertising, but as in *Pillow Talk,* the movie's true concerns are the couple's sexual maneuverings. Tony Randall is on hand to brighten the movie as the bumbling vice president of Hudson's agency.

## Lovesick

★☆ Warners, 1983, c, 93 min. Dir and SP: Marshall Brickman. Cast: Dudley Moore, Elizabeth McGovern, Alec Guinness, John Huston, Alan King, Ron Silver, Gene Saks, David Strathairn, Wallace Shawn, Renée Taylor.

The idea of a man (usually married) suddenly obsessed with a beautiful woman seems to turn up regularly in Hollywood comedies *(10, The Woman in Red).* But it has seldom received such an abysmal treatment as in this turkey. Dudley Moore plays a married psychiatrist who falls head over heels in love with patient Elizabeth McGovern. His obsession goes so wildly out of control that he begins to behave irrationally, even breaking into her apartment to read her private journal. His behavior alarms everyone, especially his colleagues. The movie's gimmick is that occasionally the shade of Sigmund Freud (Guinness) appears to comment on his predicament. The cast is extraordinary; the movie is wretched.

## Lucky Partners

★★ RKO, 1940, 99 min. Dir: Lewis Milestone. SP: Allan Scott, John Van Druten, b/o story by Sacha Guitry. Cast: Ginger Rogers, Ronald Colman, Jack Carson, Spring Byington, Cecilia Loftus, Harry Davenport.

A romantic comedy that succumbs to an unworkable premise. Ginger Rogers, unbecomingly brunette, is a bookstore clerk who shares a winning sweepstakes ticket with artist Ronald Colman. He proposes to take her on a "strictly impersonal" honeymoon so that she can enjoy life before settling down with insurance salesman Carson. You heard it here. The lady accepts, and the "fun" begins. The entire brouhaha ends up in that favorite locale of thirties comedy, the courtroom. Rogers and Colman seem unhappy in their roles.

## Made for Each Other

★★★ Fox, 1971, c, 107 min. Dir: Robert B. Bean. SP: Renee Taylor, Joseph Bologna. Cast: Renee Taylor, Joseph Bologna, Paul Sorvino, Olympia Dukakis, Louis Zorich, Helen Verbit, Norman Shelly.

She's Pandora (Taylor), a would-be singer and a self-confessed "failure at everything." He's Giggy (Bologna), racked with guilt over all the hearts he has broken over the years. Both in their thirties, they meet at a group encounter session and fall into a stormy relationship that involves falling in love, hurting each other, quarreling bitterly, and ultimately stumbling into marriage. The early lives of these world-class neurotics are shown in flashbacks. Taylor and Bologna also wrote this comedy, which is sometimes right on target about human relationships and other times painfully funny, as when Pandora delivers a nightclub performance. She asks Giggy's opinion, and he minces no words: "It stank. From the beginning to the end."

## Made in America

★★☆ Warners, 1993, c, 110 min. Dir: Richard Benjamin. SP: Holly Goldberg Sloan, b/o story by Marcia Brandwynne, Nadine Schiff, Holly Goldberg Sloan. Cast: Whoopi Goldberg, Ted Danson, Will Smith, Nia Long, Paul Rodriguez, Jennifer Tilly, Peggy Rea.

Sarah Mathews (Goldberg) is happy in her life as the mother of teenage Zora (Long) and the black owner of a store dealing in African artifacts. Then Zora learns that her father came from a sperm bank and decides to track down his identity. He turns out to be Hal Jackson (Danson), a rowdy—and white—pitchman selling trucks on television. All the expected difficulties occur as Hal gets his first fatherly feelings and he also starts falling in love with Sarah, and she with him. The movie is mostly silly and contrived but Will Smith makes an impression as Zora's closest friend.

## The Main Event

★★ First Artists, 1979, c, 112 min. Dir: Howard Zieff. SP: Gail Parent, Andrew Smith. Cast: Barbra Streisand, Ryan O'Neal, Paul Sand, Patti D'Arbanville, Whitman Mayo, James Gregory, Rory Calhoun, Ernie Hudson.

When a crooked accountant walks off with all her money, top business executive Hillary Kramer (Streisand) finds herself with only one possession; the contract to a has-been boxer named Eddie "Kid Natural" Scanlon (O'Neal). Eddie hasn't had a fight in years, and to pay off his debt to her, she forces him to resume fighting and becomes his unlikely manager. (Her advice: "Hit and don't get hit.") Inevitably, they quarrel and then fall in love, until the day of the Big Fight, when everything falls into place. A weak and obvious romantic comedy, with the stars showing little of the rapport they displayed seven years earlier in *What's Up, Doc?*

## Man's Favorite Sport?

★★☆ Universal, 1964, c, 120 min. Dir: Howard Hawks. SP: John Fenton Murray, Steve McNeil, b/o story by Pat Frank. Cast: Rock Hudson, Paula Prentiss, Maria Perschy, Charlene Holt, John McGiver, Roscoe Karns, Norman Alden.

One of the great directors of comedy in the thirties *(Twentieth Century, Bringing Up Baby)*, Howard Hawks fared much less well three decades later, and *Man's Favorite Sport?* is one fairly glum example. Rock Hudson plays a phony fishing expert for Abercrombie & Fitch who is blackmailed by press agent Paula Prentiss into attending a fishing tournament sponsored by the lodge she represents. Of course, he also gets into some romantic entanglements. Hudson's hapless attempt to demonstrate his fishing "skill" is lifted from Jack Conway's *Libeled Lady* (1936).

## Milk Money

★ Paramount, 1994, c, 102 min. Dir: Richard Benjamin. SP: John Mattson. Cast: Melanie Griffith, Ed Harris, Michael Patrick Carter, Malcolm McDowell, Anne Heche, Casey Siemaszko, Philip Bosco.

There is a scene in this dreadful comedy that is so appalling it defies all rational belief. Prostitute Melanie Griffith is brought by twelve-year-old Michael Patrick Carter into his school for a "show-and-tell" demonstration of female anatomy to his classmates, while the frantic teacher tries to get back into her room. Consider that many scenes are almost as bad, and you have the idea. Young Carter meets Griffith, here named Z, on an excursion to the big city with his pals to find a "naked woman." Somehow, Z ends up living in Carter's tree house, with widowed Dad (Harris) thinking she's a math tutor. Carter determines that Z and Dad are meant for each other. And eventually they agree! In a word, poisonous.

## The Mirror Has Two Faces

★★ TriStar, 1997, c, 126 min. Dir: Barbra Streisand. SP: Richard LaGravanese, b/o screenplay by Andre Cayatte, Gerard Oury. Cast: Barbra Streisand, Jeff Bridges, Lauren Bacall, George Segal, Mimi Rogers, Pierce Brosnan, Brenda Vaccaro, Austin Pendleton, Elle Macpherson.

They are both teachers at Columbia University: Rose (Streisand) is the world's most unlikely professor of literature, and supposedly a "meeskite" of the highest order; Gregory (Bridges, woefully miscast) is the world's dullest professor of mathematics and a man who has only bad relationships with women. He decides that he wants to share his life with someone—"without sexual relationships." ("Romance is a myth," and so forth.) Through the machinations of Rose's sister (Rogers), who is married to a cheating sort (Brosnan), Rose and Greg meet and eventually marry. Since she is clearly sexually attracted to him, it is only a matter of time before they are happy between the sheets. The premise is absurd, and some scenes, particularly one climactic fight scene, are embarrassing. The best moments are between Rose and her vain, overbearing mother (Oscar-nominated Bacall).

## Moonstruck

★★★★ MGM, 1987, c, 102 min. Dir: Norman Jewison. SP: John Patrick Shanley. Cast: Cher, Nicolas Cage, Olympia Dukakis, Vincent Gardenia, Danny Aiello, Julie Bovasso, John Mahoney, Louis Guss, Feodor Chaliapin, Anita Gillette.

Cher stars in her Oscar-winning role as a young widow who finds inexplicable romance in this totally enchanting, flavorsome comedy. She's engaged to the dim but decent Aiello when she meets his estranged, hugely eccentric brother (Cage) and finds herself falling in love with him against her better judgment. John Patrick Shanley's Oscar-winning screenplay is filled with diverting characters, most notably Cher's mother (Dukakis), who somehow combines tartness and melancholy. (Dukakis won an Oscar as Best Supporting Actress.) Vincent Gardenia is also fine as Cher's straying but loving father. Virtually everyone in the movie seems to be affected in some way by "la luna," and you may find yourself moonstruck, too.

## The More the Merrier

★★★★ Columbia, 1943, 104 min. Dir: George Stevens. SP: Richard Flournoy, Lewis R. Foster, Robert Russell, Frank Ross, b/o story by Robert Russell, Frank Ross. Cast: Jean Arthur, Joel McCrea, Charles Coburn, Richard Gaines, Bruce Bennett, Ann Savage, Ann Doran.

During World War II, Washington, D.C., was so crowded that it became the target for many jokes and the basis for a number of movies. *The More the Merrier* was one of the best, a genial, sometimes witty comedy that falters only toward the end. The idea: three people—a working-class girl (Arthur), an army sergeant (McCrea), and an elderly but still feisty millionaire, Mr. Dingle (Coburn)—are forced to share a single Washington apartment. Complications are inevitable when the millionaire acts as Cupid for the couple. Best scene: Arthur and McCrea behave amorously on the stoop of their apartment house. They are fine, but Coburn steals the show, winning a Supporting Oscar for his performance. The movie also won a Best Picture nomination, and Arthur was nominated as Best Actress.

## Mr. Wonderful

★★☆ Warners, 1993, c, 98 min. Dir: Anthony Minghella. SP: Amy Schor, Vicki Polon. Cast: Matt Dillon, Annabella Sciorra, Mary-Louise Parker, William Hurt, Vincent D'Onofrio, David Barry Gray, Bruce Kirby, Dan Hedaya, Bruce Altman.

The tangled romantic relationships of a group

of young Italian-Americans is the subject of this occasionally observant but mostly static, juiceless comedy. Financially strapped but anxious to join his coworkers in opening a bowling alley, Gus (Dillon) finally decides that his only hope is to find a new husband for his ex-wife Lee (Sciorra) and avoid paying her alimony. He comes up with a line of suitors, none of whom are even barely acceptable until Dominick (D'Onofrio). In the meantime, he has to cope with his own relationship with Rita (Parker). The good cast is game, but the outcome is predictable from the start and the screenplay lacks color and variation.

## Murphy's Romance

★★★ Columbia, 1985, c, 105 min. Dir: Martin Ritt. SP: Harriet Frank, Jr., Irving Ravetch. Cast: Sally Field, James Garner, Brian Kerwin, Corey Haim, Dennis Burkley, Georgann Johnson, Charles Lane.

James Garner, who has been giving solid performances in many films over the years, won an Oscar nomination for his easygoing performance in this leisurely, uneventful, but somehow pleasing romantic comedy. He's a widowed pharmacist in a small Arizona town who takes an immediate shine to divorcée Sally Field, who has just arrived with her young son (Haim) and is having a hard time making ends meet. It's clear that the two are meant to marry, and the only real complication is the return of Field's rascally ex-husband (Kerwin). Some nice small-town flavor helps, but it's Garner's portrayal of Murphy Jones that makes the movie a small winner.

## My Best Friend's Wedding

★★ TriStar, 1997, c, 112 min. Dir: P. J. Hogan. SP: Ronald Bass. Cast: Julia Roberts, Dermot Mulroney, Cameron Diaz, Rupert Everett, Philip Bosco, Rachel Griffiths.

With her radiant beauty and fetching smile, Julia Roberts is a natural choice to play romantic heroines. But given a role that even veteran actors such as Claudette Colbert and Irene Dunne would find difficult, she is all at sea, and *My Best Friend's Wedding* is a capsized boat. She plays a food critic who learns that her long-time friend (Mulroney) is going to marry a winsome—and wealthy—girl (Diaz). Realizing that she loves Mulroney after all, she decides to break up the affair on the eve of the marriage. Complications ensue, almost all of them forcing Roberts to behave abominably. Diaz is too likable to be a worthy target of Roberts's plotting, and only Rupert Everett gets a chance to shine as Roberts's gay friend, who joins her in the scheming.

## My Man Godfrey

★★★★ Universal, 1936, 95 min. Dir: Gregory La Cava. SP: Morrie Ryskind, Eric Hatch, b/o novel by Eric Hatch. Cast: William Powell, Carole Lombard, Alice Brady, Gail Patrick, Eugene Pallette, Alan Mowbray, Mischa Auer, Franklin Pangborn.

One of the classic screwball comedies, *My Man Godfrey* revolves about the rich Bullocks of Park Avenue, a family of nitwits headed by a grumpy Wall Street tycoon (Pallette). His wife (Brady) is scatterbrained, and his two daughters (Lombard and Patrick) are not much brighter. Into this booby hatch steps Godfrey (Powell), a wry tramp who becomes the Bullock butler when Lombard "wins" him in a scavenger hunt. Of course there's more to Godfrey than meets the eye. The movie mixes romance, social commentary, and giddy farce and comes up with a delicious brew. A dreadful 1957 remake starred June Allyson and David Niven.

## Nine Months

★★☆ Fox, 1995, c, 103 min. Dir and SP: Chris Columbus. Cast: Hugh Grant, Julianne Moore, Jeff Goldblum, Tom Arnold, Joan Cusack, Robin Williams, Ashley Johnson, Emily Yancy, Kristin Davis.

British actor Hugh Grant displays a certain amount of rabbity charm but overworks his stammer and twitch in this highly predictable comedy. He and Julianne Moore are a loving couple in a five-year relationship when Moore announces that she's pregnant. Grant falls apart instantly and completely, until—surprise!—he has a change of heart. Along the way there are some slapstick sequences, some involving Tom Arnold and Joan Cusack as a couple with children, who show a horrified Grant what his life may become. Robin Williams turns up as a Russian obstetrician whose mangled English is supposed to be funny. ("Let's take a look at your volvo.")

## Ninotchka

★★★★ MGM, 1939, 110 min. Dir: Ernst Lubitsch. SP: Billy Wilder, Charles Brackett, Walter Reisch, b/o story by Melchior Lengyel. Cast: Greta Garbo, Melvyn Douglas, Ina Claire, Bela Lugosi, Sig Rumann, Felix Bressart, Alexander Granach.

The enchanting romantic comedy that took Greta Garbo away from the tragic heroines she had played for years at MGM. Garbo is funny as Nina Ivanovna Yakushova, a somber Russian emissary who is sent to Paris on a government mission. She not only falls under the spell of the City of Light but also finds romance with Leon d'Algout (Douglas), the dashing count who begins as her adversary and ends up as her ardent lover. The satirical thrusts at Russia's rigidity under Communism may no longer apply, but nothing can dim the wit and sparkle of the screenplay, nor the charm of the performances. The film was musicalized for the stage as *Silk Stockings,* which was later made into a 1957 movie with Fred Astaire and Cyd Charisse.

## Nobody's Fool

★★☆ Island, 1986, c, 107 min. Dir: Evelyn Purcell. SP: Beth Henley. Cast: Rosanna Arquette, Eric Roberts, Mare Winningham, Jim Youngs, Louise Fletcher, Gwen Welles, Stephen Tobolowsky, Charlie Barnett, J. J. Hardy.

Not to be confused with the 1994 film starring Paul Newman, *Nobody's Fool* centers on Cassie (Arquette), a waitress and an oddball outcast in the Southern town of Buckeye Basin. Deserted by her boyfriend (Youngs), Cassie is miserable and lonely until she meets Riley (Roberts), who works with the theater group passing through town. Based on a screenplay written by Beth Henley before she won fame with *Crimes of the Heart,* this movie also has its share of Henley grotesques, but they are not nearly as fascinating as they would be in her later work. Surprisingly, the chief virtue of *Nobody's Fool* is the reasonably restrained, unmannered performance of Eric Roberts as the hot-headed Riley.

## The Object of My Affection

★★☆ Fox, 1998, c, 110 min. Dir: Nicholas Hytner. SP: Wendy Wasserstein, b/o novel by Stephen McCauley. Cast: Jennifer Aniston, Paul Rudd, Alan Alda, Allison Janney, Nigel Hawthorne, John Pankow, Tim Daly, Steve Zahn, Amo Gulinello.

A sweet-natured, decidedly offbeat, but rather pat romantic comedy, *The Object of My Affection* stars Jennifer Aniston as Nina, a social worker who finds herself pregnant by her current boyfriend, Nick (Pankow). When she decides to live with and have her baby nurtured by her gay teacher-friend, the genial—and recently jilted—George (Rudd), Nick leaves her in anger. Nina falls in love with George, but then he meets another man (Gulinello) and complications ensue. The leading players are appealing, but more interesting roles go to the supporting players: Alan Alda as a hotshot literary agent, Allison Janney as his wife, who is Nina's stepsister, and especially Nigel Hawthorne as an aging, wise drama critic. Charming, to be sure, but not quite believable.

## One Fine Day

★★★ Fox, 1996, c, 105 min. Dir: Michael Hoffman. SP: Terrel Seltzer, Ellen Simon. Cast: Michelle Pfeiffer, George Clooney, Mae Whitman, Alex D. Linz, Robert Klein, Jon Robin Baitz, Charles Durning, Ellen Greene, Pete Hamill.

As contrived and predictable as it may be, *One

# Great Moments from Great Comedies

These comic scenes can still make us laugh every time.

- In *Duck Soup* (1933), Harpo Marx, disguised as Groucho, must pretend to be a mirror image of his brother.

- In *I'm No Angel* (1933), Mae West sues Cary Grant for breach of promise and acts as her own lawyer at the trial. At one point, she saunters past the jury and murmurs, "How'm I doin'?"

- The stateroom scene in *A Night at the Opera* (1935), still regarded as the funniest sequence in sound movies.

- In *It's a Gift* (1934), W. C. Fields, trying to sleep on his porch, is interrupted by a milkman with squeaky shoes, a toppling coconut, and an insurance salesman looking insistently for a man named Karl La Fong.

- Irene Dunne, Cary Grant's ex-wife in *The Awful Truth* (1937), turns up at his new fiancée's house, pretending to be his wild sister Lola.

- In a restaurant in *Ninotchka* (1939), Melvyn Douglas tries to make the somber Greta Garbo laugh by telling her a joke. She remains stone-faced, until he topples off his seat and she finally erupts into laughter.

- Tipsy heiress Katharine Hepburn and reporter Jimmy Stewart share a moonlight rendezvous in *The Philadelphia Story* (1940).

- Jack Lemmon, happy to be with Shirley MacLaine, the girl he loves, strains his spaghetti through a tennis racket in Billy Wilder's *The Apartment* (1960).

- The opening sequence in *Divorce, American Style* (1967): a lawyer with an attaché case walks to a hillside, dons the judicial robe he removes from his case, and begins to conduct the chorus of fury and vituperation emerging from the married couples in the houses below.

- In Mel Brooks's *Young Frankenstein* (1974), Frankenstein (Gene Wilder) and the Monster (Peter Boyle) perform a song-and-dance to "Puttin' on the Ritz."

- Dressed as soap opera actress "Dorothy Michaels" in *Tootsie* (1982), actor Dustin Hoffman confounds and dismays his agent (Sydney Pollack) in a restaurant.

- In *Roxanne* (1987), fire chief Steve Martin uses a dazzling display of verbal pyrotechnics to overwhelm a barroom oaf who has mocked his oversized nose.

*Fine Day* survives and even pleases by way of its attractive stars. Michelle Pfeiffer is Melanie, an architect, and George Clooney is Jack, a newspaper columnist, both stressed-out single parents who meet by chance, then spend one complete day irritating and antagonizing each other, as one disaster follows another. Do they eventually fall in love? Can you doubt it? Pfeiffer is most appealing, even when she is called on to behave in a scatterbrained fashion, and Clooney is a personable leading man. The featherweight story is set against many notable New York backgrounds, which helps considerably in making the time pass pleasantly.

## Only You

★★★ TriStar, 1994, c, 108 min. Dir: Norman Jewison. SP: Diane Drake. Cast: Marisa Tomei, Robert Downey, Jr., Bonnie Hunt, Joaquim De Almeida, Fisher Stevens, Billy Zane, Adam LeFevre, Phyllis Newman.

What can you say about a romantic comedy that boasts stunning Italian scenery, attractive leading players—and an almost totally unworkable premise? See it for the attributes, and forgive it for its silly plotline. For most of her life, Faith (Tomei) has harbored the dream of a perfect soulmate named Damon Bradley. (The Ouija board gave her the name.) On the eve of her wedding to a podiatrist, she receives a call from someone named Damon Bradley, and when the caller disappears, she finds herself compelled to track his whereabouts to Italy. Enter Robert Downey, Jr., an American in Italy who falls for her and claims to be Damon Bradley. Never mind the plot—just relax and enjoy the gorgeous views of Venice and Rome and the likable performers, most notably Bonnie Hunt as Faith's unhappy sister-in-law.

## Overboard

★★★ MGM/UA, 1987, c, 112 min. Dir: Garry Marshall. SP: Leslie Dixon. Cast: Goldie Hawn, Kurt Russell, Edward Herrmann, Katherine Helmond, Michael Hagerty, Roddy McDowall.

This standard but fairly pleasing romantic comedy stars Goldie Hawn as a bitchy society lady with a snobbish husband (Herrmann) and long-suffering butler (McDowall). She insults and mistreats a local carpenter (Russell), and when she falls overboard and gets amnesia, he plots revenge by claiming that she is his long-lost wife who will now run his household and take care of his four sons. Don't be surprised when the lady learns how to be competent, responsible, and loving. Just when she feels that she belongs with this "family," her husband shows up. Hawn is more believable being warm-fuzzy and adorable than bitchy, but she and Russell make an agreeable team.

## The Owl and the Pussycat

★★☆ Columbia, 1970, c, 95 min. Dir: Herbert Ross. SP: Buck Henry, b/o play by Bill Manhoff. Cast: Barbra Streisand, George Segal, Robert Klein, Allen Garfield, Roz Kelly, Jacques Sandulescu, Jack Manning.

If this movie were any thinner, or lighter, it might evaporate entirely. George Segal is Felix, a bookstore clerk and aspiring writer who fancies himself a deep thinker. When he reports his neighbor, a prostitute named Doris (Streisand) to his landlord, she's evicted—and angry. That night, they begin a relationship that has them either bickering noisily or falling into bed. By the time they admit to loving each other, each has stripped away the other's illusions. *The Owl and the Pussycat* has a few good laugh lines but it's much ado about next to nothing. Streisand is shrill as the semi-illiterate hooker, and although Segal is amiable as the would-be writer, his character is strictly in Hollywood's tradition of the pompous intellectual as sitting target.

## The Pallbearer

★★ Miramax, 1996, c, 104 min. Dir: Matt Reeves. SP: Jason Katims, Matt Reeves. Cast: David Schwimmer, Gwyneth Paltrow, Barbara Hershey, Michael Rapaport, Tom Collette, Carol Kane, Michael Vartan, Bitty Schram.

A young man, one year out of college and with no definite future, begins a love affair with an older woman, alienating the girl he really loves. Does this sound familiar? Despite its resemblance to *The Graduate*, *The Pallbearer* is a tepid comedy that fades away even before the final credits. David Schwimmer (of TV's *Friends*) never changes his hangdog expression as he plays hopelessly insecure Tom, who is asked to be a pallbearer and deliver the eulogy at a friend's funeral. The trouble is, he doesn't know the "friend" at all. Instead, he has a sexual liaison with the dead friend's mother (Hershey), distressing his true love (Paltrow), a girl from his past whom he meets at the funeral. Schwimmer's monotonous performance doesn't help.

## Pat and Mike

★★★ MGM, 1952, 95 min. Dir: George Cukor. SP: Garson Kanin, Ruth Gordon. Cast: Katharine Hepburn, Spencer Tracy, Aldo Ray, William Ching, Jim Backus, Sammy White, George Mathews, Loring Smith.

A steadily entertaining entry in the group of Hepburn-Tracy comedies, smoothly directed by George Cukor. Hepburn plays a world-class athlete whose career is taken over by rough-hewn sports promoter Tracy. Unfortunately she has a fiancé whose smugly superior ways inhibit her performances on the tennis courts and golf links. It's only a matter of time, of course, before the two realize that they need and love each other. Aldo Ray wins some laughs as another of Tracy's clients, a punch-drunk boxer. *Pat and Mike* was the team's seventh teaming, and it seems to get better with every airing. Tracy's well-remembered assessment of his leading lady: "Nicely packed, that kid. Not much meat on her, but what's there is *cherce*!" Both actors are, and will always be, "cherce."

## Paternity

★★ Paramount, 1981, c, 94 min. Dir: David Steinberg. SP: Charlie Peters. Cast: Burt Reynolds, Beverly D'Angelo, Norman Fell, Elizabeth Ashley, Paul Dooley, Lauren Hutton, Juanita Moore, Mike Kellin.

One slim premise leads to a predictable outcome in this tired and sometimes embarrassing comedy. The premise: Buddy Evans (Reynolds) is a forty-four-year-old swinging bachelor who decides that he wants to be a father. After several unamusing mishaps with candidates for surrogate motherhood, he settles on waitress and music student Maggie (D'Angelo), who agrees to his proposition. Naturally it's only a matter of time before they realize that they love each other. Meanwhile they go through all the baby routines together and she gets jealous when an old flame (Ashley) surfaces. Actor-comedian Steinberg's inauspicious debut as a director.

## Picture Perfect

★☆ Fox, 1997, c, 105 min. Dir: Glenn Gordon Caron. SP: Arleen Sorkin, Paul Slansky, b/o story by Arleen Sorkin, Paul Slansky, May Quigley. Cast: Jennifer Aniston, Jay Mohr, Kevin Bacon, Olympia Dukakis, Illeana Douglas, Kevin Dunn, Faith Prince.

Burdened with an unsympathetic heroine and an unworkable premise, a romantic comedy scarcely has a chance to succeed. Case in point: *Picture Perfect*. To move ahead in her advertising agency, Kate (Aniston of TV's *Friends*) has to invent a fiancée, ostensibly to prove her stability. The problem is that she has her sights set on a colleague named Sam (Bacon). When she is forced to produce her "fiancé" in person, she settles on Nick (Mohr), a photographer she met casually at a wedding. Will you be surprised when she finally falls for Nick? The movie collapses somewhere at midpoint, with one embarrassing sequence after another.

## Pillow Talk

★★★ Universal-International, 1959, c, 105 min. Dir: Michael Gordon. SP: Stanley Shapiro, Maurice Richlin, b/o story by Russell Rouse, Clarence Greene. Cast: Doris Day, Rock Hudson, Tony Randall, Thelma Ritter, Nick Adams, Julia Meade, Allen Jenkins, Lee Patrick, Marcel Dalio.

This romantic comedy, the first of the Doris Day–Rock Hudson teamings, was once consid-

ered bold in its approach to sexual matters. In light of today's movies, it could not be tamer or more conventional. Day plays a chic interior decorator who shares a party line with womanizing composer Rock Hudson. When she complains about his hogging of the line, he concocts his own kind of revenge: he impersonates a shy Texan whose sweetness and sincerity release Day's long-dormant libido. True love, of course, eventually wins the day. A few of the scenes seemed "adult" at the time, notably one in which the two are seen in a split frame, soaking in their respective bathtubs. How risqué can you get?

## Playing by Heart

★★★☆ Miramax, 1999, c, 121 min. Dir and SP: Willard Carroll. Cast: Gillian Anderson, Ellen Burstyn, Sean Connery, Anthony Edwards, Angelina Jolie, Jay Mohr, Ryan Phillipe, Dennis Quaid, Gena Rowlands, Jon Stewart, Madeline Stowe.

An old Hollywood tradition, scarcely observed these days, is that characters in a romantic comedy can be wittier and more articulate than most people, spouting dialogue that is intelligent but not necessarily realistic. Willard Carroll's comedy-drama *Playing by Heart* honors that tradition. A group of Los Angeles people of various ages seem to have their individual stories of love lost and found (or rediscovered); some are comic and some profoundly sad. A superb cast enacts these stories, and a few of the members should be singled out: Sean Connery and Gena Rowlands as an older couple facing a personal crisis; Angelina Jolie and Ryan Phillipe as a young couple groping toward a relationship. The tricky ending, bringing all the couples together, is more clever than credible, but it doesn't spoil a worthy movie.

Rock Hudson and Doris Day made romantic comedy seem a little bolder with the highly popular *Pillow Talk* (1959). They were teamed again in two more films.

## Pretty Woman

★★★ Touchstone, 1990, c, 117 min. Dir: Garry Marshall. SP: J. F. Lawton. Cast: Richard Gere, Julia Roberts, Ralph Bellamy, Jason Alexander, Laura San Giacomo, Hector Elizondo, Alex Hyde-White, Elinor Donahue.

This romantic comedy would have you believe that a Hollywood hooker with a sad past could be transformed into a stylish, ravishing young woman who radiates warmth and generosity. If you can swallow the premise, you should enjoy this enormously popular movie. Julia Roberts, as Vivian, entrances a wealthy young businessman (Gere), who changes her, Galatea style, into a swan and, after some setbacks, realizes that he has come to love her. Intended as a variation on the Cinderella tale—the hotel personnel who help her turn from prostitute to princess include variations of the fairy godmother and her cohorts—*Pretty Woman* does manage some amusing moments, especially when Vivian invades the posh, snobbish world of Beverly Hills.

## Reality Bites

★★★ Universal, 1994, c, 99 min. Dir: Ben Stiller. SP: Helen Childress. Cast: Winona Ryder, Ethan Hawke, Ben Stiller, Janeane Garofalo, Steve Zahn, Swoosie Kurtz, Joe Don Baker, John Mahoney, David Spade, Renée Zellweger.

A comedy that focuses on the lives—romantic and otherwise—of the postcollegiate generation of the nineties, *Reality Bites* will please viewers in its target market, but not many others. (Virtually everyone in the movie over thirty is a fool.) Basically, the movie concerns a romantic triangle between Lelaina (Ryder), a smart, intense aspiring documentary filmmaker, Troy (Hawke), laid-back, jobless, and proudly contemptuous of society; and Michael (Stiller), an amiable executive with a cable company. Their shifting relationships, and their relationships with friends and others, are covered in scenes that are sometimes satiric and sometimes serious. An interesting but uneven first feature from director Ben Stiller.

## Roman Holiday

★★★☆ Paramount, 1953, 119 min. Dir: William Wyler. SP: Dalton Trumbo, originally credited to Ian McLellan Hunter, John Dighton, b/o story by Dalton Trumbo, also credited to Hunter. Cast: Gregory Peck, Audrey Hepburn, Eddie Albert, Hartley Power, Laura Solari, Harcourt Williams, Tullio Carminati.

When Audrey Hepburn starred in this delightful romantic comedy, she had already appeared in a few British movies and on Broadway in *Gigi.* This movie made her a major star and won her an Oscar as Best Actress. Lithe, elegant, and radiantly beautiful, she played a princess on a state visit to Italy. Bored with the royal routine, she flees anonymously into the heart of Rome, where she finds romance with newspaperman Gregory Peck. Lightweight stuff, to be sure, but director William Wyler wisely focuses on Hepburn and surrounds her with stunning views of Rome—a definite bonus. The Oscar-winning screenplay was actually written by blacklisted writer Dalton Trumbo. There was an unnecessary television version in 1987.

## Roxanne

★★★☆ Columbia, 1987, c, 106 min. Dir: Fred Schepisi. SP: Steve Martin, b/o play by Edmond Rostand. Cast: Steve Martin, Daryl Hannah, Rick Rossovich, Shelley Duvall, John Kapelos, Michael J. Pollard, Damon Wayans.

A sweet-natured romantic comedy, written by and starring Steve Martin as its lovelorn hero. An updating of Edmond Rostand's old warhorse play *Cyrano de Bergerac, Roxanne* has Martin as C. D. Bales, the fire chief in a Washington State ski town. The object of ridicule because of his grotesquely long nose, C. D. secretly adores an astronomy student named Roxanne (Hannah). He uses one of his firemen, a slow-witted hulk (Rossovich) as a surrogate to court his ladylove. Eventually the truth comes out, this time leading to a happier ending than in the play. Martin gives a winning performance that displays his skill at physical comedy—only watch the grace and dexterity with which he demolishes town bullies.

## Rushmore

★★☆ Touchstone, 1998, c, 89 min. Dir: Wes Anderson. Sp: Wes Anderson, Owen Wilson. Cast: Jason Schwartzman, Bill Murray, Olivia Williams, Seymour Cassel, Brian Cox, Mason Gamble, Sara Tanaka, Stephen McCole, Ronnie McCawley, Keith McCawley, Connie Nielsen, Kim Terry.

*Rushmore* has spurts of originality and a refreshingly offbeat point of view, but it's a vastly overpraised comedy. The central character, Max Fischer (Schwartzman) is a fifteen-year-old student at Rushmore Preparatory School, where despite a low academic standing he is enthusiastically involved in every one of the school's activities. (He even invents a few.) Max is befriended by Herman Blume (Murray), a glum millionaire with serious family problems. Trouble ensues when both Max and Herman fall in love with the same woman, Rosemary Cross (Williams), a teacher at the school. Their ensuing war is silly and hardly credible, and the movie strains so hard to be "different" that early on it loses its footing and never regains it.

## Sex and the Single Girl

★★☆ Warners, 1964, c, 114 min. Dir: Richard Quine. SP: Joseph Heller, David R. Schwartz, b/o story by Joseph Hoffman and book by Helen Gurley Brown. Cast: Natalie Wood, Tony Curtis, Henry Fonda, Lauren Bacall, Mel Ferrer, Fran Jeffries, Leslie Parrish, Edward Everett Horton.

Thank goodness for two seasoned professionals named Henry Fonda and Lauren Bacall. As a battling married couple, they provide the only spice and spark in this comedy very loosely suggested by Helen Gurley Brown's best-selling book. Natalie Wood is (believe it or not) a young research psychologist whose specialty is marital and premarital relationships. Tony Curtis is a scandal magazine publisher who scorns her best-selling book and then secretly sets out to show her up by seducing her. It's no secret that they end up in each other's arms. There are some satirical flourishes but wait mostly for the Fonda-Bacall repartee.

## Shakespeare in Love

★★★★ Miramax, 1998, c, 113 min. Dir: John Madden. SP: Marc Norman, Tom Stoppard. Cast: Gwyneth Paltrow, Joseph Fiennes, Geoffrey Rush, Colin Firth, Ben Affleck, Judi Dench, Rupert Everett, Simon Callow, Jim Carter, Imelda Staunton, Tom Wilkinson, Martin Clunes.

Witty, opulent, and romantic, *Shakespeare in Love* is a rare cinematic treat. The movie's conceit: in 1593 London, Will Shakespeare (Fiennes) is suffering not only from writer's block but also from a weakening of his sexual confidence. Enter Viola de Lesseps (Paltrow), a willful beauty who adores the theater and would love to act in it. Although she is pledged to marry the surly Lord Essex (Firth), she disguises herself as a boy to appear as Romeo in Shakespeare's newest play. Romantic sparks fly when Will and Viola meet and fall passionately in love. The Shakespearean in-jokes are funny, the sets and costumes are ravishing, and Paltrow and Fiennes are most attractive leads in a splendid cast. Delightful from first to last. This movie won seven Academy Awards, including Oscars for Best Picture, Best Actress (Paltrow), and Best Supporting Actress (Dench).

## The Shop Around the Corner

★★★★ MGM, 1940, 97 min. Dir: Ernst Lubitsch. SP: Samson Raphaelson, b/o play by Nikolaus Laszlo. Cast: Margaret Sullavan, James Stewart. Frank Morgan, Joseph Schildkraut, Felix Bressart, Sara Haden, Inez Courtney, William Tracy, Charles Smith.

One of the most delightful romantic comedies of Hollywood's "golden" period. The story could not be more slight: in a Budapest shop owned by Frank Morgan, two workers (Sullavan and Stewart) heartily detest each other, unaware that they are really pen pals, sharing their innermost secrets. Of course, they eventually fall in love. The literate screenplay is matched by the cast's exemplary performances, especially by Frank Morgan, who makes a poignant figure of the cuckolded shop owner. Stewart, at his most appealing, and

Sullavan, with her uniquely throaty voice, make a matchless pair of clueless lovers. The movie was turned into a 1949 movie musical called *In the Good Old Summertime* and also into a 1963 stage musical entitled *She Loves Me.* Most recently, the story was updated as the movie *You've Got Mail* (1998).

## Singles

★★★ Warners, 1992, c, 100 min. Dir and SP: Cameron Crowe. Cast: Campbell Scott, Bridget Fonda, Kyra Sedgwick, Matt Dillon, Sheila Kelley, Jim True, Bill Pullman. Writer-director Cameron Crowe proves that his 1989 sleeper *Say Anything . . .* was not a one-time fluke. Here he looks at the lives and the romances of a group of singles in Seattle who are friends and neighbors as well as lovers. His diverting screenplay creates a number of characters who are forever moving in and out of "relationships," particularly Steve (Scott), whose affair with Linda (Sedgwick) moves through many intense phases ("We had good times and bad times, but we had times!"), and also Janet (Fonda), who is involved with self-absorbed rock musician Cliff (Dillon). There are also some funny satirical touches, notably a take-off of dating videos.

## Six Days, Seven Nights

★★☆ Touchstone, 1998, c, 101 min. Dir: Ivan Reitman. SP: Michael Browning. Cast: Harrison Ford, Anne Heche, David Schwimmer, Jacqueline Obrados, Temuera Morrison, Allison Janney, Douglas Weston. Have you heard the one about the rough-hewn loner and the urban sophisticate who are thrown together by chance, bicker, and then fall in love? Many decades ago, the story might have starred Clark Gable and Myrna Loy; some years later, it might have teamed William Holden with Audrey Hepburn. Here, Harrison Ford is a gruff charter pilot who is hired to fly New York editor Anne Heche to a photo shoot in Tahiti. Their plane crash-lands on a remote island where they, yes, bicker and then fall in love. They also cope with hostile pirates, adding some adventure to the romance and comedy. A not-bad movie, but slim and predictable.

## Skin Deep

★★ Morgan Creek, 1989, c, 101 min. Dir and SP: Blake Edwards. Cast: John Ritter, Allyson Reed, Vincent Gardenia, Joel Brooks, Julianne Phillips, Chelsea Field, Michael Kidd, Nina Foch, Denise Crosby. Famed author Zachary Hutton (Ritter) is in terrible shape. He is alcoholic, he is suffering from writer's block, and his many romantic liaisons are going badly. The first scene has him tangling with a current bedmate, an irate mistress, and his even more irate wife (Reed). He tries, but he cannot sustain a permanent relationship. His sexual partners include a body builder who nearly cripples him, a girl who sets fire to his house in a rage, and a girl with a jealous British rocker boyfriend. Blake Edwards crowds all this feverish activity into a witless farce with mostly unpleasant characters. (This is the only movie you are ever likely to see that involves glow-in-the-dark condoms!)

## Sleepless in Seattle

★★★☆ TriStar, 1993, c, 104 min. Dir: Nora Ephron. SP: Jeff Arch, Nora Ephron, David S. Ward, b/o story by Jeff Arch. Cast: Tom Hanks, Meg Ryan, Ross Malinger, Bill Pullman, Rosie O'Donnell, Rob Reiner, Gaby Hoffmann, Victor Garber, Rita Wilson, Cary Lowell, Calvin Trillin, Dana Ivey, David Hyde Pierce. A romantic comedy with a gimmick: the two leading players, clearly destined for each other, do not come face to face until the movie's end. Sam (Hanks) is a Seattle widower with a young son Jonah (Malinger). Unable to assuage his father's grief, Jonah calls a radio station to ask for help for his father. Across the continent, in Baltimore, Annie (Ryan) hears his plea and, although recently engaged, she becomes obsessed with Sam and his plight. The movie conspires to keep Sam and Annie apart until the final scene atop the Empire State Building. Unabashedly romantic, this gossamer movie surely manipulates its audience, but it is so well done, with hugely appealing leads and a firm supporting cast, that it stays in the mind longer than many meatier films.

## Sliding Doors

★★☆ Paramount-Miramax, 1998, c, 105 min. Dir and SP: Peter Howitt. Cast: Gwyneth Paltrow, John Hannah, John Lynch, Jeanne Tripplehorn, Zara Turner, Douglas McFerran.

A romantic comedy with a "Twilight Zone" gimmick. London girl Helen (Paltrow), just fired from her public relations job, is hurrying to catch a subway train. The movie then acts out two alternate possibilities that will change her life. When she catches the train, she meets and begins a romance with a glib stranger named James (Hannah). She also discovers the infidelity of her deceitful live-in lover Gerry (Lynch) with an American girl named Lydia (Tripplehorn). When she just misses the train, she never meets James and only eventually learns about faithless Gerry. *Sliding Doors* carries through each scenario to its conclusion, but neither is particularly interesting or amusing. Nice try at something different, but it doesn't work.

## Speechless

★★★ MGM, 1994, c, 98 min. Dir: Ron Underwood. SP: Robert King. Cast: Michael Keaton, Geena Davis, Christopher Reeve, Bonnie Bedelia, Ernie Hudson, Charles Martin Smith, Ray Baker, Mitchell Ryan.

Michael Keaton and Geena Davis are such ingratiating actors that you may not notice or care that much of this movie is rather shopworn, despite the taken-from-the-headlines premise. At a heated senatorial race in New Mexico, campaign strategist Kevin (Keaton) meets and falls in love with campaign strategist Julia (Davis). They fall in love, not knowing that they are working on opposite sides of the political fence. The situation, of course, resembles the courtship (and eventual marriage) of Democrat James Carville and Republican Mary Matalin, but the screenplay gives the idea a fairly amusing spin on its own. But can they please abandon that tiresome cliché in which a crowd of strangers (this time delegates to a political convention) cheer and applaud the reunited lovers?

## Starting Over

★★★ Paramount, 1979, c, 106 min. Dir: Alan J. Pakula. SP: James L. Brooks, b/o novel by Dan Wakefield. Cast: Burt Reynolds, Jill Clayburgh, Candice Bergen, Charles Durning, Frances Sternhagen, Austin Pendleton, Mary Kay Place.

There are several nice surprises in this enjoyable romantic comedy. One is Burt Reynolds, playing against his usual macho type as a befuddled, recently divorced man who courts a wary, vulnerable nursery-school teacher (Clayburgh). Another is Candice Bergen, who reveals a strong comedic flair as Reynolds's ex-wife, whom he is unable to get entirely out of his system. His confused state of mind leads to a number of complications. James Brooks's screenplay casts a sharp eye on the precarious life of the newly divorced, including the therapy workshops and the dating rituals. Wait for a hilarious scene in Bloomingdale's. Candice Bergen virtually steals the movie as a "liberated" woman who fancies herself a songwriter.

## Sunday in New York

★★ MGM, 1964, c, 105m. Dir: Peter Tewksbury. SP: Norman Krasna, b/o his play. Cast: Jane Fonda, Rod Taylor, Cliff Robertson, Robert Culp, Jo Morrow, Jim Backus.

"It's my firm conviction that I'm the only twenty-two-year-old virgin alive!" Eileen (Fonda) declares, as she barges unexpectedly into the New York pad of her pilot brother (Robertson). Eileen has come to learn all about life and love, and before this silly bit of froth is over, she certainly does. She enjoys an on-again, off-again romance with Mike (Taylor) and also copes with her Albany boyfriend, Russ (Culp), who arrives on the scene. Many tedious misunderstandings later, it all ends well for Eileen and Mike. *Sunday in New York,* adapted by Norman Krasna from his Broadway play, is typical of many sixties comedies, convinced that it's being bold and daring in dealing with sex. Mostly, however, it's just a bore.

## The Sure Thing

★★★ Embassy, 1985, c, 94 min. Dir: Rob Reiner. SP: Stephen Bloom, Jonathan Roberts. Cast: John Cusack, Daphne Zuniga, Anthony Edwards, Boyd Gaines, Tim Robbins, Lisa Jane Persky, Viveca Lindfors, Nicollette Sheridan.

Director Rob Reiner's first film after the hilarious mock-documentary *This Is Spinal Tap* (see page 190) was this utterly predictable but ingratiating romantic comedy. John Cusack plays a recent high school graduate, who is traveling to California at the behest of friend Anthony Edwards, who assures him he will find a "sure thing" in gorgeous Nicollette Sheridan. Cusack's traveling companion is brainy Daphne Zuniga, who is going to meet her boyfriend in California. The two share adventures on the road and inevitably hatred turns to respect and then love. Nothing new but a refreshingly believable screenplay and likable performances combine to make a winning movie.

## Surrender

★★ Warners, 1987, c, 96 min. Dir and SP: Jerry Belson. Cast: Sally Field, Michael Caine, Steve Guttenberg, Peter Boyle, Julie Kavner, Jackie Cooper.

Talk about "meeting cute." Daisy Morgan (Field) is an aspiring artist. Sean Stein (Caine) is a best-selling novelist bitter about his experiences with women and money. A party they are both attending is invaded by terrorists, and they are tied together in the nude. Love blossoms, but he pretends to be a poor unpublished author. Will she love him for himself or will she marry her rich boyfriend, Marty (Guttenberg)? It scarcely matters, since *Surrender* has a pervasively sour and off-putting tone. Good support, however, especially from Julie Kavner as Daisy's perpetually pregnant best friend.

## The Talk of the Town

★★★☆ Columbia, 1942, 118 min. Dir: George Stevens. SP: Irwin Shaw, Sidney Buchman. Cast: Cary Grant, Jean Arthur, Ronald Colman, Edgar Buchanan, Glenda Farrell, Charles Dingle, Rex Ingram, Lloyd Bridges.

A rarity: a literate and full-bodied comedy, with some thought-provoking ideas about the role of law in society. It's also a pleasing showcase for three inimitable stars. Ronald Colman plays a distinguished law professor, a nominee to the Supreme Court, who comes to live temporarily in a house where schoolteacher Jean Arthur is his landlady and housekeeper. Enter Cary Grant, a small-town anarchist who, fleeing from a false charge of murder, hides out in their home. Soon the two men are not only arguing about the law but about their mutual fondness for the lady. There may be too much talk, but the principals acquit themselves with their usual skill. Colman comes off best, with an appealing performance as a man whose convictions about the law are shaken by events.

## Teacher's Pet

★★★ Paramount, 1958, 120 min. Dir: George Seaton. SP: Fay Kanin, Michael Kanin. Cast: Clark Gable, Doris Day, Gig Young, Mamie Van Doren, Nick Adams, Charles Lane.

This moderately enjoyable comedy stars Clark Gable as a crusty newspaper editor who becomes infatuated with an attractive journalism instructor (Day). He enrolls in her class under false pretenses, and gradually, despite their opposite views of journalism and life, they manage to fall in love. The screenplay received an Oscar nomination, and some of the dialogue is indeed bright and amusing. There were many May-December romances in film comedy in the fifties—with stars like Gable holding on to their box-office appeal—and *Teacher's Pet* is one of the better entries in the series.

# 10

★★ Orion, 1979, c, 122 min. Dir and SP: Blake Edwards. Cast: Dudley Moore, Julie Andrews, Bo Derek, Robert Webber, Dee Wallace, Brian Dennehy, Max Showalter, Sam Jones, Nedra Volz.

Poor George (Moore). A middle-aged man who should be happy with his career as a composer, his loving fiancée (Andrews), and his sumptuous beach house, George is, instead, a driven man. The moment he sees luscious Jennie (Derek), he is obsessed with her, to the exclusion of everyone and everything else. The problem is that he discovers Jennie on her wedding day. In trying to get close to his dream girl, George subjects himself to all sorts of physical mishaps and ordeals. When he finally meets Jennie, she is not exactly what he expected. *10* is yet another of Dudley Moore's feeble comedies of the seventies and eighties—as usual, he works very hard to win laughs but Edwards's leering approach to every situation does him in.

## That Touch of Mink

★★☆ Universal, 1962, c, 99 min. Dir: Delbert Mann. SP: Stanley Shapiro, Nate Monaster. Cast: Cary Grant, Doris Day, Gig Young, Audrey Meadows, John Astin.

Doris Day's persistent efforts to protect her virginity in the early sixties never seemed more foolish than in this wafer-thin comedy. She plays a jobless computer operator who gets swept off her feet by a dashing and wealthy business tycoon (Grant, as suave as ever). Against her better judgment, she agrees to accompany him on a trip to Bermuda, where she promptly breaks out in a rash and fortifies herself with liquor. She will settle for nothing less than marriage, of course, and after some

feeble complications she gets her wish. Not much here aside from the attractive stars.

## Theodora Goes Wild

★★★ Columbia, 1936, 94 min. Dir: Richard Boleslawski. SP: Sidney Buchman, b/o story by Mary McCarthy. Cast: Irene Dunne, Melvyn Douglas, Thomas Mitchell, Thurston Hall, Leona Maricle, Spring Byington, Henry Kolker.

In the thirties, it was common for demure movie heroines to break the bounds of propriety and "live" (i.e., enjoy sexual encounters). Irene Dunne's Theodora is one of the more engaging of these heroines: a small-town girl who writes a sexy novel under a pseudonym, becomes thoroughly liberated, and falls for a debonair commercial artist (Douglas) with marital problems. *Theodora Goes Wild* (well, not really) qualifies as a pleasing example of an early feminist comedy. With the stars giving a diverting spin to Sidney Buchman's adroit screenplay, the movie is mostly fun. Dunne's regal persona was one of the ongoing pleasures of moviegoing in the thirties, although there was always something faintly sharklike about that dazzling smile.

## There's Something About Mary

★ Fox, 1998, c, 118 min. Dir: Peter Farrelly, Bobby Farrelly. SP: Ed Decter, John J. Strauss, Peter Farrelly, Bobby Farrelly, b/o story by Ed Decter, John J. Strauss. Cast: Cameron Diaz, Matt Dillon, Ben Stiller, Lee Evans, Chris Elliott, Lin Shaye, Jeffrey Tambor, Markie Post, Keith David, W. Earl Brown.

Here's a movie to test your tolerance of gross-out humor. Do you find the following topics funny? Mental retardation, physical disability, pain inflicted on private parts, serial murder, and masturbation. Are you laughing? Then you might find *Mary* hilarious. Ben Stiller is Ted, an accident-prone, nerdlike high school student who adores a girl named Mary (Diaz). Years later, still obsessed, he tracks her down to Florida, where he is joined by various unappetizing characters. What's offensive about the

The three stars of *The Talk of the Town* (1942): Cary Grant, Jean Arthur, and Ronald Colman. George Stevens's film had a few things to say about the law but it never neglected the romantic triangle.

movie is not the snickering grade-school humor but the almost total lack of anything resembling wit, style, or true comedy. Sadly, many viewers, including some critics, concluded that there was indeed something about *Mary*. The Farrelly brothers made *Dumb and Dumber*. This is *Dumbest*.

## They All Laughed

★★ Moon Pictures, 1981, c, 115 min. Dir and SP: Peter Bogdanovich. Cast: Audrey Hepburn, Ben Gazzara, John Ritter, Dorothy Stratten, Colleen Camp, Blaine Novak, Patti Hansen, George Morfogen, Sean Ferrer.

*They All Laughed* has stunning views of New York City and a pleasing soundtrack with a number of Frank Sinatra standards. End of virtues. A long, incoherent, and mostly boring comedy of sorts, the movie centers on three detectives (Gazzara, Ritter, and Novak) for the Odyssey Detective Agency and their adventures while on the job in the city. They are charged with trailing wives whose husbands suspect them of infidelity. Gazzara falls for Audrey Hepburn (not at her best) and Ritter succumbs to Dorothy Stratten (in the last role before her notorious murder). Other characters include country singer Colleen Camp and a lady taxi driver nicknamed Sam (Hansen). A mistake.

## 'Til There Was You

★★☆ Paramount, 1997, c, 114 min. Dir: Scott Winant. SP: Winnie Holtzman. Cast: Jeanne Tripplehorn, Dylan McDermott, Sarah Jessica Parker, Jennifer Aniston, Craig Bierko, Alice Drummond, Michael Tucker, Nina Foch, Christine Ebersole.

Gwen (Tripplehorn) is a ghostwriter, a born romantic who is constantly being betrayed by lovers, family, and friends. Nick (McDermott) is an architect, a "perfectionist of low self-esteem" with a troubled childhood. Shades of *Sleepless in Seattle*—the two constantly cross paths over the years, but they never meet until the end of the film, when they converge on a

Stop Smoking clinic. Although it was trounced by the critics, *'Til There Was You* is actually not as bad as all that. It has its intermittent charms, mostly contributed by Sarah Jessica Parker as Francesca, a former sitcom star who, like Madonna, keeps reinventing herself and who becomes involved in the lives of Gwen and Nick. Too long, and the plot line is cluttered, but you could do worse.

## Tin Cup

★★★ Warners, 1996, c, 133 min. Dir: Ron Shelton. SP: John Norville, Ron Shelton. Cast: Kevin Costner, Rene Russo, Don Johnson, Cheech Marin, Linda Hart, Rex Linn.

Even if golf is not your favorite sport, you're sure to enjoy this flavorsome romantic comedy. Kevin Costner is Roy McAvoy, nicknamed Tin Cup, once a legendary golf pro but now the owner of a small driving range in West Texas. Enter Molly Griswold (Russo), a psychologist who wants golfing lessons and who turns out to be the current fiancée of Dave Simms (Johnson), Roy's arch rival on and off the links. Soon Roy and Molly are having a steamy affair, and Roy and Dave are confronting each other at the U.S. Open competition. In this climactic game, Roy finally shows his mettle as a man and a golfer. Costner gives a relaxed, funny performance, and Russo is attractive as the woman who comes to love and understand him.

## Tom, Dick and Harry

★★☆ RKO, 1941, 86 min. Dir: Garson Kanin. SP: Paul Jarrico. Cast: Ginger Rogers, Burgess Meredith, George Murphy, Alan Marshal, Phil Silvers, Lenore Lonergan.

What's a girl to do? Young Janie (Rogers) has three suitors: practical car salesman Tom (Murphy), playboy Dick (Marshal), and down-to-earth but eccentric Harry (Meredith). Somehow she gets herself engaged to all three, and now she dreams about what life would be with each suitor. The dreams are cleverly staged, but unfortunately Rogers gives an irritating performance, trying to act at least a decade younger than her chronological age. She also forces her voice into a childish singsong. The movie was well received in its day, but it doesn't hold up.

## A Touch of Class

★★★ Avco Embassy, 1973, c, 105 min. Dir: Melvin Frank. SP: Melvin Frank, Jack Rose. Cast: Glenda Jackson, George Segal, Paul Sorvino, Hildegard Neil, Cec Linder, K. Callan, Mary Barclay.

Glenda Jackson rarely took on comedy roles, but in this airily amusing romantic comedy, she plays a divorcée with two children who has an affair with a married insurance man (Segal) working in London. Her performance won her a Best Actress Oscar. As Vickie Allessio, she falls into a romantic tryst with Steve Blackburn, which begins in Malaga with ardent lovemaking and nearly ends with a furious quarrel that destroys their hotel room. Back in London, Steve's desperate attempt to balance his life between wife and mistress proves too much to handle, and in the end he and Vickie agree to part. The screenplay falters now and again, but the stars work well together, her brittle style meshing nicely with his boyish eagerness to please. The movie received four other Oscar nominations, including one as Best Picture.

## The Truth About Cats and Dogs

★★★ Fox, 1996, c, 97 min. Dir: Michael Lehmann. SP: Audrey Wells. Cast: Uma Thurman, Janeane Garofalo, Ben Chaplin, Jamie Foxx, James McCaffrey.

An extremely talented comic actress, Janeane Garofalo comes into her own in this winsome comedy. In her usual mode of the slightly offbeat, more than slightly caustic woman, she plays Abby, a Los Angeles talk-show host who is loved by a man (Chaplin) who has never met her. Unhappy about her looks (why? she's adorable), she gets a friend, drop-dead gorgeous but scatterbrained Noelle (Thurman), to

impersonate her. It's hard to believe that Chaplin would swallow the hoax, but the two women strike some funny chords in the confusion over their identities. Garofalo has the true comedian's way of making lines sound funnier and sharper than they actually are. Six decades earlier, roles might have been written for her to play.

## Victor/Victoria

★★★ MGM, 1982, c, 133 min. Dir and SP: Blake Edwards. Cast: Julie Andrews, James Garner, Robert Preston, Alex Karras, Lesley Ann Warren, John Rhys-Davies, Graham Stark, Peter Arne.

As Toddy, a wise, gay entertainer in 1934 Paris, Robert Preston walks off with this comedy of sexual identity. Toddy comes upon Victoria Grant (Andrews), a down-on-her-luck singer who needs a job, and he accomodates by turning Victoria into a female impersonator (in other words, a woman pretending to be a man pretending to be a woman!). The ruse works, until King Marchand (Garner), a Chicago nightclub owner with mob connections, comes along and finds himself inexplicably attracted to "Victor." Eventually the premise wears thin but the cast pitches in enthusiastically. Oscar nominations went to Andrews and Preston, and Henry Mancini and Leslie Bricusse won an award for their song score. Julie Andrews repeated her movie role in a 1995 stage musical version.

## Vivacious Lady

★★★ RKO, 1938, 90 min. Dir: George Stevens. SP: P. J. Wolfson, Ernest Pagano, b/o story by I.A.R. Wylie. Cast: Ginger Rogers, James Stewart, Charles Coburn, James Ellison, Beulah Bondi, Frances Mercer, Grady Sutton, Jack Carson, Franklin Pangborn.

Hoping to step out on her own as a serious actress in the late thirties, Ginger Rogers made several films without her famous dancing partner, Fred Astaire. *Vivacious Lady* is one of her better comedies of the period: an amusing tale of a shy young college professor (Stewart) who, on impulse, marries a pert night club singer (Rogers) and brings her home to his college town. Naturally, all sorts of complications ensue. As the tart-tongued heroine, Rogers is refreshingly devoid of her later grande dame manner. But the movie is stolen by Beulah Bondi as Stewart's timid, genteel mother, who finally gets a chance to speak her mind. Viewers are sure to cherish the scene in which she performs the "Big Apple," a dance craze of the day.

## Walk, Don't Run

★★★ Columbia, 1966, c, 114 min. Dir: Charles Walters. SP: Sol Saks, b/o story by Robert Russell, Frank Ross. Cast: Cary Grant, Samantha Eggar, Jim Hutton, John Standing, Miiko Taka, Ted Hartley.

A remake of *The More the Merrier* (1943; see page 102), and Cary Grant's last film, *Walk, Don't Run* is now set in Tokyo during the 1964 Olympics. As in 1943 Washington, there's a housing shortage for the event, and Samantha Eggar agrees to share her tiny flat with businessman Grant and athlete Hutton. With Grant's sly maneuverings as a suave Cupid, he prods Eggar and Hutton into a romance. A highlight of the movie had Grant peeling down to his underwear and joining a cross-city Olympic walkathon in his old debonair style. Tokyo provided a stunning background for the amusing activities.

## The Wedding Singer

★☆ New Line, 1998, c, 93 min. Dir: Frank Coraci. SP: Tim Herlihy. Cast: Adam Sandler, Drew Barrymore, Christine Taylor, Allen Covert, Angela Featherstone, Matthew Glave, Alexis Arquette.

The year is 1985, and Robbie (Sandler) performs at weddings with his small band. He falls to pieces when his airhead fiancée (Featherstone) jilts him just before his own wedding. At the same time, waitress Julia (Barrymore, pert and charming) is on the verge of marrying a boor and a cheat (Glave). It takes a series of dubious misunderstandings before the obvious occurs and Robbie and Julia become a couple. This comedy is wretched in all ways, and Sandler, with his droning voice and unprepossessing appearance, is nobody's idea of a leading man. The climactic scene aboard an airplane is preposterous. Wait, at least, for funny cameos from Steve Buscemi and Jon Lovitz.

## What's Up, Doc?

★★★ Warners, 1972, c, 94 min. Dir: Peter Bogdanovich. SP: Buck Henry, David Newman, Robert Benton. Cast: Barbra Streisand, Ryan O'Neal, Madeline Kahn, Kenneth Mars, Austin Pendleton, Sorrell Booke, Liam Dunn, John Hillerman, Michael Murphy.

Director Peter Bogdanovich's homage to the old screwball comedies (and *Bringing Up Baby* in particular) has a hectic pace and a good number of laughs, and for the most part, it's great fun. Ryan O'Neal is not exactly a born farceur, but he tries hard as an absent-minded professor who arrives in San Francisco with his overbearing fiancée (Kahn) to attend a musicologists's convention. Along comes Barbra Streisand, a one-woman disaster area who sets her cap for O'Neal. With her "help," he's soon involved with jewel thieves, government spies, and assorted lunatics. The movie scarcely pauses to catch its breath as it plunges from one slapstick situation to another, but many of them are funny. Madeline Kahn nearly steals the film as O'Neal's bossy fiancée.

## When Harry Met Sally . . .

★★★ Columbia, 1989, c, 95 min. Dir: Rob Reiner. SP: Nora Ephron. Cast: Billy Crystal, Meg Ryan, Carrie Fisher, Bruno Kirby, Steven Ford, Lisa Jane Persky, Michelle Nicastro, Harley Kozak.

A pleasant, lightweight romantic comedy, no more and no less. The idea is this: Meeting in 1977, Harry (Crystal) and Sally (Ryan) are instantly hostile to each other. But as they meet again at five-year intervals, they are drawn closer together, even as their private lives remain separate. Eventually, they come to realize that they love each other, which doesn't make them happy. The movie strives to emulate Woody Allen's films (the lushly romantic musical score, the shimmering New York photography, Meg Ryan's Diane Keaton–like performance), but it lacks the wit and substance of Allen's best work. The much-talked about restaurant scene provides the movie's funniest line, delivered by the director's mother, Estelle Reiner.

## While You Were Sleeping

★★★ Hollywood, 1994, c, 104 min. Dir: Jon Turteltaub. SP: Daniel G. Sullivan and Fredric Lebow. Cast: Sandra Bullock, Bill Pullman, Jack Warden, Peter Gallagher, Peter Boyle, Glynis Johns, Michael Rispoli, Micole Mercurio.

Lucy (Bullock), a sweet, lonely Chicago girl who works as a subway clerk, finds her life turned upside down when she rescues Peter (Gallagher) from the train tracks where he has been thrown by muggers. Peter, whom she has adored in secret, has a crackpot family who mistake Lucy for Peter's fiancée. Overjoyed at having a "family" for the first time, Lucy goes along with the ruse, while Peter remains in a coma. Then she falls for Peter's brother Jack (Pullman), and trouble begins. A pleasant—and surprisingly popular—romantic comedy, *While You Were Sleeping* was a breakthrough movie for Sandra Bullock, who has charm to spare. The screenplay overdoes the nuttiness of Peter's clan, but a good cast is helpful.

## Without Reservations

★★★ RKO, 1946, 107 min. Dir: Mervyn LeRoy. SP: Andrew Solt, b/o novel by Jane Adams. Cast: Claudette Colbert, John Wayne, Don DeFore, Anne Triola, Frank Puglia, Phil Brown, Thurston Hall, Louella Parsons, Dona Drake.

A breezy romantic comedy, *Without Reservations* stars Claudette Colbert as a novelist who meets Marine John Wayne on a train bound for Hollywood and decides that he would be the perfect choice to play the leading role in a movie adaptation of her book. Circumstances force them to change from the train to an overland route, giving the movie an obvious resemblance to the classic *It Happened One Night*. Before the movie's end, Colbert also decides Wayne would also be the perfect man in her life. Scenes in Hollywood bring in several stars to play themselves, a familiar device in the forties.

## A Woman of Distinction

★★☆ Columbia, 1950, 85 min. Dir: Edward Buzzell. SP: Charles Hoffman, b/o story by Ian McLellan Hunter, Hugo Butler, with additional dialogue by Frank Tashlin. Cast: Rosalind Russell, Ray Milland, Edmund Gwenn, Janis Carter, Mary Jane Saunders, Francis Lederer.

The sort of romantic comedy, heavily laced with slapstick, that prevailed in the thirties and forties but which was becoming obsolete by the fifties. (Doris Day picked up the slack in the sixties.) Rosalind Russell is the dean of a New England women's college who makes the cover of *Time* magazine. Ray Milland is an English astronomy professor touring the United States. Can romance be far behind? Not until the dignified Russell gets involved in a series of comic mishaps and also one not-so-comic scandal involving the real fatherhood of her adopted daughter. By film's end, all is well and she finally surrenders to Milland. Light-headed but fairly enjoyable romp.

## Woman of the Year

★★★☆ MGM, 1942, 112 min. Dir: George Stevens. SP: Ring Lardner, Jr., Michael Kanin. Cast: Katharine Hepburn, Spencer Tracy, Fay Bainter, Dan Tobin, Reginald Owen, Roscoe Karns, William Bendix.

*Woman of the Year* marks the first teaming of Katharine Hepburn and Spencer Tracy, and even though they were to make better films together, it's still hugely entertaining. They play colleagues at the *New York Chronicle*—she's a brittle, brilliant political columnist, and he's a rough-hewn sports writer. They meet, fall in love, and marry, but their lifestyles and attitudes clash, and they separate. Hepburn tries to show him what a housewifely woman she can be, and this, unfortunately, makes for an embarrassing sequence. The rest, however, is cleverly done, and the instant rapport between the stars is a pleasure to behold. The screenplay won an Oscar, and Hepburn was nominated as Best Actress. Lauren Bacall starred in a Broadway musical version in 1981.

## Working Girl

★★★ Fox, 1988, c, 113 min. Dir: Mike Nichols. SP: Kevin Wade. Cast: Melanie Griffith, Harrison Ford, Sigourney Weaver, Alec Baldwin, Joan Cusack, Philip Bosco, Nora Dunn, Oliver Platt, Kevin Spacey, Olympia Dukakis.

Meet Tess (Griffith), a deceptively smart, ambitious secretary who excels at both business and sexual matters. She's the heroine of this light-hearted romantic comedy, directed in deft fashion by Mike Nichols. When Tess's power-hungry boss Katharine (Weaver) breaks her leg in a skiing accident, Tess rises in the ranks by taking over Katharine's job, wardrobe, and even her current lover (Ford). The movie is more of a fanciful fable than a realistic view of the business world, but Griffith makes it work with a shrewdly judged performance that echoes Judy Holliday in her "dumb as a fox" routine. The movie picked up six Academy Award nominations, including Best Picture. Carly Simon's song "Let the River Run" won the Oscar.

## You've Got Mail

★★★☆ Warners, 1998, c, 119 min. Dir: Nora Ephron. SP: Nora Ephron, Delia Ephron, b/o screenplay by Samson Raphaelson and play by Miklos Laszlo. Cast: Tom Hanks, Meg Ryan, Greg Kinnear, Parker Posey, Jean Stapleton, Dabney Coleman, Steve Zahn, David Chappelle.

Both Tom Hanks and Meg Ryan have charm to spare, as they demonstrated in *Sleepless in Seattle,* and here that charm is in full force in a delightful update of the classic romantic comedy *The Shop Around the Corner.* An affectionate valentine to uptown Manhattan

(which never looked better), *You've Got Mail* brings the idea of Ernst Lubitsch's movie into a new age, with Hanks as a corporate heir planning to open a mammoth, commercial book store and Ryan as the owner of a tiny bookshop threatened by his move. Enemies in the work-

place, they are also unwitting—and loving—correspondents on the e-mail network. Totally endearing performances, a sharp screenplay, and a background of great songs make a winning "feel-good" combination.

In *You've Got Mail* (1998) Tom Hanks and Meg Ryan play antagonists who do not know that they are actually ardent e-mail correspondents in this updated remake of *The Shop Around the Corner.*

# Wedded Bliss: Marital Comedies

Let's face it—marriage often produces more blisters than bliss, and movies have found it more profitable to set marital stories in Splitsville than in Seventh Heaven. Since the silent era, cheating husbands, wandering wives, and revenge-minded couples have populated marital comedies, conjuring up an assortment of pranks and schemes to thwart each other, then reuniting for the fadeout. From *The Awful Truth* to *The War of the Roses*, here are the many sides of marriage, movie-style.

## Adam's Rib

★★★☆ MGM, 1949, 100 min. Dir: George Cukor. SP: Ruth Gordon, Garson Kanin. Cast: Katharine Hepburn, Spencer Tracy, Judy Holliday, Tom Ewell, David Wayne, Jean Hagen, Hope Emerson, Polly Moran, Marvin Kaplan.

One of the most enjoyable Tracy-Hepburn pairings, *Adam's Rib* has a few ideas about feminism and the law. When a woman (Holliday) tries to kill her cheating husband (Ewell) and his mistress (Hagen), two happily married lawyers (Hepburn and Tracy) become opponents in the case. She believes Holliday had a woman's inalienable right to defend herself and her family; he sees it as attempted murder. Soon their marriage threatens to collapse under the strain. Tracy and Hepburn are adroit, as usual, but the movie is stolen by Judy Holliday in an endearing performance as the neglected wife, who has her very own way of talking. Tom Ewell as the bewildered husband and David Wayne as an effete songwriting neighbor provide top-notch support.

A classically funny moment from *The Awful Truth* (1937): Irene Dunne tries to conceal an incriminating hat from ex-husband Cary Grant.

# The Awful Truth

★★★★ Columbia, 1937, 92 min. Dir: Leo McCarey. SP: Vina Delmar, b/o play by Arthur Richman. Cast: Irene Dunne, Cary Grant, Ralph Bellamy, Cecil Cunningham, Alexander D'Arcy, Molly Lamont, Esther Dale, Joyce Compton.

Irene Dunne and Cary Grant had a matchless rapport in the thirties and early forties: her tongue-in-cheek wryness complemented his rakish charm. *The Awful Truth* is their best comedy—a hilarious marital mixup that wears well with time. They play Jerry and Lucy Warriner, happily married until Jerry is caught in a lie and Lucy divorces him. Of course they belong together, and Jerry spends the rest of the movie strenuously trying to win Lucy back. Oscar-winning director Leo McCarey keeps things moving briskly, and Dunne and Grant sparkle in their roles. The movie was nominated as Best Picture, and Dunne as Best Actress. There were two earlier versions of the story in 1925 and 1929 and a musical remake called *Let's Do It Again* in 1953.

## Bluebeard's Eighth Wife

★★ Paramount, 1938, 80 min. Dir: Ernest Lubitsch. SP: Billy Wilder, Charles Brackett. Cast: Claudette Colbert, Gary Cooper, David Niven, Edward Everett Horton, Elizabeth Patterson, Herman Bing.

It's hard to imagine how a crackerjack team such as director Lubitsch and writers Wilder and Brackett could have come up with so feeble a jape. After Colbert, the daughter of an impoverished French aristocrat (Horton), meets millionaire Cooper, she learns that he had seven previous wives. She agrees to marry him only if he agrees to pay her $100,000 a year for life if they divorce. Although she ostensibly loves him, she proceeds to drive him into a divorce by firmly insisting on remaining "kissless." Her tactics will have you cringing rather than laughing, as the proven wit of the film's creators inexplicably deserts them. Also filmed in 1923.

## Bob & Carol & Ted & Alice

★★★ Columbia, 1969, c, 104 min. Dir: Paul Mazursky. SP: Paul Mazursky, Larry Tucker. Cast: Natalie Wood, Robert Culp, Dyan Cannon, Elliott Gould, Horst Ebersberg, Donald F. Muhich.

Once considered daring in its approach to marital sexual relationships on screen, *Bob & Carol & Ted & Alice* now seems tame and dated. Still, there are funny moments as two married couples (Wood and Culp, Cannon and Gould) pretend to look for sexual freedom and honesty in their marriages and then, not surprisingly, find themselves in over their heads. The movie's view of a group encounter session earns laughs, as do other spoofs of the "sexual revolution" in full bloom. The acting prize goes to Dyan Cannon as Alice, Ted's repressed wife who is not at all happy with the goings-on. The movie may be an artifact of its times, but it showed the way to depicting marital relations frankly, without resorting to winks and leers.

## Bye Bye, Love

★★☆ Fox, 1995, c, 106 min. Dir: Sam Weisman. SP: Gary David Goldberg, Brad Hall. Cast: Matthew Modine, Randy Quaid, Paul Reiser, Janeane Garofalo, Amy Brenneman, Rob Reiner, Eliza Dushku, Ed Flanders, Jayne Brook, Maria Pitillo, Lindsay Crouse.

The subject is divorce in this uneven but slightly underrated comedy-drama. Three divorced friends (Modine, Quaid, Reiser) try to cope with their special problems: dealing with their ex-wives, finding ways to keep their children happy, coping with the dilemma of dating again. Modine has too many women clamoring for his attention; Reiser still loves his ex-wife (Brook) and has a troubled daughter (Dushku); Quaid is a bitter, angry man. The movie mixes laughter and poignancy in reasonable proportions, but there are too many dry patches. Funniest by far is Janeane Garofalo as Modine's date from hell. Also funny: Rob Reiner as a self-absorbed talk-show host.

## Carnal Knowledge

★★★☆ Avco Embassy, 1971, c, 96 min. Dir: Mike Nichols. SP: Jules Feiffer. Cast: Jack Nicholson, Candice Bergen, Arthur Garfunkel, Ann-Margret, Rita Moreno, Cynthia O'Neal, Carol Kane.

A corrosive, brutally candid comedy from writer-cartoonist Jules Feiffer and director Mike Nichols, *Carnal Knowledge* looks at the sexual hangups of two college roommates (Nicholson and Garfunkel) over several decades. The movie depicts them as perpetually adolescent men who view women as castrating creatures, to be used and discarded like so many Kleenex tissues. Nicholson's marriage to an actress (Ann-Margret) whom he treats cruelly ends in disaster, while Garfunkel's marriage to his college sweetheart (Bergen) also falls apart eventually. Well directed and well acted (especially by Ann-Margret, who won a Supporting Actress Oscar nomination), the film is blistering but also witty and observant.

# A Change of Seasons

★★☆ Fox, 1980, c, 102 min. Dir: Richard Lang. SP: Erich Segal, Ronni Kern, Fred Segal, b/o story by Erich Segal, Philip Lathrop. Cast: Shirley MacLaine, Anthony Hopkins, Bo Derek, Michael Brandon, Mary Beth Hurt, Ed Winter.

Many critics noted that the best part of this marital comedy was the pretitle sequence in which Bo Derek luxuriates in a hot tub. They were right, but the movie is really about Shirley MacLaine and Anthony Hopkins. He's a college professor feeling the symptoms of male menopause; she's his wife of twenty years. When she learns that her husband is having an affair with a voluptuous student (Derek), she begins her own affair with the campus carpenter (Brandon). The actors try, but the movie could use a much wittier screenplay. The centerpiece is a sequence in which the four principals attempt to share the same house on a skiing vacation.

# Diary of a Mad Housewife

★★★☆ Universal, 1970, c, 103 min. Dir: Frank Perry. SP: Eleanor Perry, b/o novel by Sue Kaufman. Cast: Carrie Snodgress, Richard Benjamin, Frank Langella, Lorraine Cullen, Frannie Michel, Lee Addoms.

Pity poor Tina Balser (Snodgress). Married to Jonathan (Benjamin), a maddeningly fastidious, self-important lawyer, saddled with two obnoxious children, she is desperately unhappy and going a little "mad." For a while she finds relief with a writer named George (Langella), who turns out to be as ego-driven and as selfish as her husband. Benjamin and Langella are excellent in difficult roles, skirting possible caricature, but the movie belongs to Carrie Snodgress, who is splendid as a put-upon, striving, clearly intelligent woman trapped in an affluent but unrewarding life. She received a well-deserved Oscar nomination as Best Actress.

# Designing Woman

★★☆ MGM, 1957, c, 118 min. Dir: Vincente Minnelli. SP: George Wells, b/o suggestion by Helen Rose. Cast: Lauren Bacall, Gregory Peck, Dolores Gray, Sam Levene, Tom Helmore, Mickey Shaughnessy, Jesse White, Chuck Connors.

A very loose remake of *Woman of the Year*, but much inferior in every respect. Mike Hagen (Peck) is a sports writer; Marilla Hagen (Bacall) is his wife (after a whirlwind courtship) and also a prominent fashion designer. As in the original, their lifestyles clash, they quarrel, and Mike is soon back trying to avoid the amorous attention of his former girlfriend, musical comedy star Laurie Shannon (Gray). He also becomes involved with some thugs in the sports game, leaving Marilla more bewildered and angry than ever. The movie's decor is lush and Bacall knows her way about a sardonic quip, but Peck, though an able actor, is not very adept at sophisticated comedy. Mickey Shaughnessy is amusing as a punch-drunk fighter who sleeps with his eyes open.

# Divorce American Style

★★★ Columbia, 1967, c, 109 min. Dir: Bud Yorkin. SP: Norman Lear, b/o story by Robert Kaufman. Cast: Debbie Reynolds, Dick Van Dyke, Jason Robards, Jean Simmons, Van Johnson, Joe Flynn, Shelly Berman, Martin Gabel, Lee Grant, Tom Bosley.

An exceptionally good cast and some sharply funny sequences are the best features of this marital comedy. Debbie Reynolds and Dick Van Dyke star as a married couple who split up after fifteen years of marriage. She takes up with a television huckster (Johnson), and he meets Robards, a divorced man anxious to marry off his ex-wife (Simmons) so that he can stop paying alimony. The screenplay runs out of steam in the last reel but along the way there are priceless moments, notably the clever opening and one riotous sequence in which the extended families of divorce come together and try to sort out the various children. Wait also for the early scene in which the married duo vent their spleen without saying a word. The screenplay won an Oscar nomination.

## The First Wives Club

★★★ Paramount, 1996, c, 102 min. Dir: Hugh Wilson. SP: Robert Harling (Paul Rudnick uncredited), b/o novel by Olivia Goldsmith. Cast: Goldie Hawn, Diane Keaton, Bette Midler, Maggie Smith, Dan Hedaya, Victor Garber, Stephen Collins, Stockard Channing, Sarah Jessica Parker, Marcia Gay Harden, Bronson Pinchot, Jennifer Dundas, Eileen Heckart, Philip Bosco.

This enjoyable comedy of revenge stars Goldie Hawn, Bette Midler, and Diane Keaton as college friends who meet again at the funeral of a fourth friend who committed suicide when her husband dumped her. The three join forces to receive payback from their self-centered ex-husbands, which they do in various ingenious ways. The deck, of course, is stacked: the ladies are much brighter and much cleverer than their sleazy, bewildered husbands, but the actresses are clearly having a fine old time stomping all over male egos, and their giddy glee rubs off on the viewer. The movie has an exceptional supporting cast, including Maggie Smith as a society doyenne and Bronson Pinchot as a society decorator.

Dick Van Dyke and Debbie Reynolds head for Splitsville with the aid of lawyer Martin Gabel in *Divorce American Style* (1967).

## For Pete's Sake

★★★ Columbia, 1974, c, 90 min. Dir: Peter Yates. SP: Stanley Shapiro, Maurice Richlin. Cast: Barbra Streisand, Michael Sarrazin, Estelle Parsons, William Redfield, Molly Picon, Louis Zorich, Vivian Bonnell, Richard Ward, Heywood Hale Broun, Joe Maher.

What's a wife to do? When Henry (Streisand) borrows $3,000 from a Mafia loan shark to finance her husband's college education, she begins a chain of events that turns her, for a while, into an inept call-girl and then into a "front" for some contemporary cattle rustlers. As Henry hurtles from one embarrassing situation to another, the movie indulges in all the familiar devices of farce, including outlandish disguises, pratfalls, and wisecracks. Streisand works strenuously but some of the other characters are funnier: Molly Picon as a cheerful Brooklyn madam, Estelle Parsons as Henry's greedy sister-in-law, and Heywood Hale Broun as a libidinous judge.

## For Richer or Poorer

★★☆ Universal, 1998, c, 122 min. Dir: Bryan Spicer. SP: Jana Howington, Steve Lukanic. Cast: Tim Allen, Kirstie Alley, Jay O. Sanders, Michael Lerner, Wayne Knight, Marla Maples, Larry Miller.

Tim Allen and Kirstie Alley are professional actors who have paid their dues on television but they cannot save *For Richer or Poorer* from mediocrity. They play a Manhattan couple—he's a real estate hustler and she's his disgruntled wife—who flee from trouble with the IRS and hide out on an Amish farm in (of course) Intercourse, Pennsylvania. Inevitably, they must cope with Amish customs at the same time they try to foist their urban ways on the simple folk. (She stages a fashion show that uses color instead of black, for example.) Don't be surprised by a sentimental ending that finds them discovering true values while reaffirming their love for each other. The leads are pleasant to watch, but the movie covers familiar ground.

## Forget Paris

★★★☆ Castle Rock, 1995, c, 101 min. Dir: Billy Crystal. SP: Billy Crystal, Lowell Ganz, Babaloo Mandel. Cast: Billy Crystal, Debra Winger, Joe Mantegna, Julie Kavner, Richard Masur, Cynthia Stevenson, William Hickey, Robert Costanzo, John Spencer, Cathy Moriarty.

Billy Crystal co-authored, directed, and starred in this delightful comedy. Studded with funny dialogue and sequences, *Forget Paris* centers on Mickey and Ellen Gordon (Crystal and Winger), whose marriage gradually unravels over the years. Their tale is related by friends gathered at a restaurant, where the estranged couple may—or may not—turn up. Mickey is a basketball coach and Ellen works in Paris for an airline, and after a romantic courtship, their lives grow apart in many ways. Funniest sequences: Ellen and the pigeon, Mickey and the sperm bank. In all, *Forget Paris* is a nice surprise.

## The Four Seasons

★★★☆ Universal, 1981, c, 107 min. Dir and SP: Alan Alda. Cast: Carol Burnett, Alan Alda, Rita Moreno, Jack Weston, Len Cariou, Sandy Dennis, Bess Armstrong.

Alan Alda made his feature directing debut with this movie—he also scripted—and he has yet to top this observant and disarming comedy. The premise: three married couples, longtime friends, have been taking vacations together with every change of season. Then one of their number (Cariou) divorces his wife (Dennis) and marries a much younger woman (Armstrong). The traumatic change affects the other couples, and soon foibles, hangups, and fears are being exposed. There are serious overtones, but Alda keeps it mostly light, extracting fine performances from everyone, especially Jack Weston as a dentist who is apprehensive about everything. (He tells his friends, "You think I don't hurt because I'm quirky, but I'm quirky because I hurt.") As his wife, Rita Moreno registers patience and good cheer, with just a touch of exasperation.

# Full of Life

★★☆ Columbia, 1957, 91 min. Director: Richard Quine. SP: John Fante, b/o his novel. Cast: Judy Holliday, Richard Conte, Salvatore Baccaloni, Esther Minciotti.

Judy Holliday's next-to-last movie before her untimely death is not one of her best, but she is always a pleasure to watch. The movie focuses on the marriage of Nina and Tony Rocco (Holliday and Conte) and the uproar created by two events: Nina's first pregnancy and the arrival of Tony's bombastic Italian father, played by opera basso Salvatore Baccaloni. The screenplay covers the familiar dilemmas of pregnancy but also gives much footage to the antics of the father, who comes across not as a lovable eccentric but as an insensitive boor. Even Holliday's endearing manner could not make *Full of Life* a winner.

# Fun with Dick and Jane

★★★ Columbia, 1977, c, 95 min. Dir: Ted Kotcheff. SP: David Giles, Jerry Belson, Mordecai Richler, b/o novel by Gerald Gaiser. Cast: Jane Fonda, George Segal, Ed McMahon, Dick Gautier, Allan Miller, Hank Garcia.

This marital comedy starts amusingly, then loses its footing, but there are still enough laughs to make it reasonably diverting. George Harper (Segal) is fired from his top executive job and learns all too soon about the wretched life of the unemployed. Wife Jane (Fonda) tries her hand at modeling and causes chaos on her first day. In desperation, the two turn to robbery, haltingly at first (these scenes are funny), then confidently. Finally, they decide to rip off the entire "slush" fund of Dick's corrupt ex-boss (McMahon) in a sequence that makes up the movie's climax. According to this movie, crime pays. In all, not very credible but there are humorous portions, and the leads know how to play comedy.

# Funny About Love

★☆ Paramount, 1990, c, 101 min. Dir: Leonard Nimoy. SP: Norman Steinberg, David Frankel, b/o article by Bob Greene. Cast: Gene Wilder, Christine Lahti, Mary Stuart Masterson, Robert Prosky, Stephen Tobolowsky, Anne Jackson, Susan Ruttan.

The first and possibly the last comedy about infertility. Gene Wilder and Christine Lahti are a married couple—he's a political cartoonist, she's a chef—who are unable to have a baby. Desperately, they try every possible route to conception, until the stress and strain causes them to separate. An able cast, headed by Wilder in his usual manic style, works hard, but there's absolutely nothing funny about *Funny about Love.* More than one sequence has the two arguing noisily in a public place—in a taxicab and in a restaurant—always a sign of the writers' desperation. Add a fertility doctor who cracks jokes and you have a comedy in serious trouble.

# Good Neighbor Sam

★★★ Columbia, 1964, c, 130 min. Dir: David Swift. SP: James Fritzell, Everett Greenbaum, David Swift, b/o novel by Jack Finney. Cast: Jack Lemmon, Edward G. Robinson, Romy Schneider, Dorothy Provine, Michael Connors, Edward Andrews, Louis Nye, Robert Q. Lewis, Joyce Jameson.

Jack Lemmon plays in his best manic style in this lighthearted comedy. He is Sam Bissell, a married advertising man and suburbanite whose life becomes chaos. When his beautiful next-door neighbor (Schneider) needs to have a husband to inherit a huge legacy, Sam volunteers for the role. Big mistake, since his job requires him to maintain a clean, moral life as dictated by boss Robinson (odd casting here). Inevitably, home and work collide in all sorts of farcical ways. The ending is more frantic than funny, which is often the case with comedies of this sort. But there are good moments along the way.

# The Grass Is Greener

★★☆ Universal-International, 1961, c, 105 min. Dir: Stanley Donen. SP: Hugh Williams, Margaret Williams, b/o their play. Cast: Cary Grant, Deborah Kerr, Robert Mitchum, Jean Simmons, Moray Watson.

Four top stars perform amid elegant scenery but the result is not especially entertaining. This talky comedy has Cary Grant and Deborah Kerr as a happily married British couple whose lives are disrupted when the wife suddenly becomes enamored of an American stranger (Mitchum) who wanders into their stately home, which they have opened to paying tourists. Grant finally wins her back, but not before much brittle chatter among the trio, plus some skittish humor from Jean Simmons as a flighty girl who has her eye on Grant. Echoes of Noel Coward (but only echoes) are reinforced by several of Coward's tunes on the soundtrack.

## A Guide for the Married Man

★★★ Fox, 1967, c, 89 min. Dir: Gene Kelly. SP: Frank Tarloff, b/o his book. Cast: Walter Matthau, Inger Stevens, Robert Morse, Sue Ane Langdon, Claire Kelly. Guest stars: Lucille Ball, Jack Benny, Polly Bergen, Sid Caesar, Wally Cox, Jayne Mansfield, Carl Reiner, Phil Silvers, Terry-Thomas, Jeffrey Hunter, others.

Typical of the leering comedies of the sixties, *A Guide for the Married Man* contains some funny, and some not-so-funny, material, plus a bonanza for star-gazers. The premise: Walter Matthau's urge to cheat on wife Inger Stevens leads him to his best friend, Robert Morse, who is only too eager to teach him how to stray. The instruction takes the form of a group of sketches in which a long list of guest stars act out Morse's theories. Jack Benny, for example, shows how to ditch a mistress; Art Carney, teaming with Lucille Ball, demonstrates how a husband can break away from the domestic routine by taking an aggressive stance. On the whole, ribald entertainment.

## I Love You Again

★★★ MGM, 1940, 99 min. Dir: W. S. Van Dyke II. SP: Charles Lederer, George Oppenheimer, Harry Kurnitz, b/o story by Leon Gordon, Maurine Watkins, and novel by Octavus Roy Cohen. Cast: William Powell, Myrna Loy, Frank McHugh, Edmund Lowe, Nella Walker, Donald Douglas.

Another teaming of William Powell and Myrna Loy, and fairly amusing. Powell plays a suave confidence man who discovers that for nine years, suffering from amnesia, he has been living a placid—and dull—life in a small Pennsylvania town. Regaining his true identity after a blow on the head, he decides to walk off with his alter ego's bank account and also his bored wife (Loy). Of course complications get in the way, and he finds himself falling genuinely in love with his bewildered "wife." Powell, who was one of the screen's most expert comic actors, has a field day as a con man suddenly confronted with such unpleasant surprises as a troop of Boy Rangers.

## Irreconcilable Differences

★★★ Warners, 1984, c, 117 min. Dir: Charles Shyer. SP: Nancy Meyers, Charles Shyer. Cast: Shelley Long, Ryan O'Neal, Drew Barrymore, Sharon Stone, Sam Wanamaker, Allen Garfield, David Paymer.

A novel premise is the best feature of this overlong comedy-drama that veers from clever to predictable. Casey (Barrymore), the young daughter of screenwriters Albert and Lucy Brodsky (Long and O'Neal), decides to divorce them after years of vicious, nonstop battling by the couple. We flash back to their lives and to marital roadblocks that seem assembled from previous movies: the bitter professional rivalry between them, Albert's inability to handle success, the devastation wrought by "the other woman" (Stone), and more. There are some nice satirical swipes at Tinseltown ways, and the cast is agreeable. In all, familiar, but no harm done.

## The Last Married Couple in America

★★ Universal, 1980, c, 103 min. Dir: Gilbert Cates. SP: John Herman Shaner. Cast: George Segal, Natalie Wood, Richard Benjamin, Arlene Golonka, Allan Arbus, Marilyn Sokol, Priscilla Barnes, Dom DeLuise, Valerie Harper, Bob Dishy.

Proof positive that even an expert cast cannot guarantee a successful comedy. Some usually impressive players are mixed up in this movie concerning a married couple (Segal and Wood) who become alarmed when their circle of friends begins to split up on a regular basis. The pattern is familiar: they bicker, separate, learn that the sexual revolution is not for them, and finally reunite. The stars are good, but what little fun there is comes from the supporting cast, including Valerie Harper as a swinging divorcée who starts her very own epidemic of venereal disease, Richard Benjamin as Segal's best friend, and Dom DeLuise as a plumber who moonlights in porn films.

## A Letter to Three Wives

★★★★ Fox, 1949, 103 min. Dir: Joseph L. Mankiewicz. SP: Joseph L. Mankiewicz; adapted by Vera Caspary, b/o novel by John Klempner. Cast: Jeanne Crain, Linda Darnell, Ann Sothern, Kirk Douglas, Paul Douglas, Jeffrey Lynn, Thelma Ritter, Connie Gilchrist, Florence Bates.

There's big trouble in marital heaven: on one fateful afternoon, three country-club wives (Crain, Darnell, Sothern) learn that one of their husbands has run off with a friend. But which husband? As the day wanes, each wife reviews her marital status in a flashback. Joseph Mankiewicz's Oscar-winning screenplay may have some dated aspects, but it still sparkles. The Crain-Lynn marriage is the least interesting—she's a fish-out-of-water ninny—and the best by far is the Linda Darnell–Paul Douglas relationship. She's a money-driven girl from the wrong side of the tracks; he's a rough-hewn businessman. She seduces him into an embattled marriage, and the rest is—wait and see. In all, one of the best comedies of the late forties. Mankiewicz also won an Oscar as Best Director.

## The Long, Long Trailer

★★☆ MGM, 1954, c, 103 min. Dir: Vincente Minnelli. SP: Albert Hackett, Frances Goodrich, b/o novel by Clinton Twiss. Cast: Lucille Ball, Desi Arnaz, Marjorie Main, Keenan Wynn, Gladys Hurlbut, Moroni Olsen, Bert Freed.

Lucille Ball and Desi Arnaz took time off from

their *I Love Lucy* television chores to star in this slapstick comedy. They play Tacy and Nicky Collini, a newly married couple who experience all sorts of trouble when they buy a trailer to take them on a cross-country honeymoon. Since the characters they play strongly resemble Lucy and Ricky Ricardo, there is little or no surprise when the situations are not far removed from sitcom land: Nicky learning to drive or clashing with a policeman, Tacy being tossed about in the trailer as it careens down a mountain road, and the like. The only surprise is the director, Vincente Minnelli, who was better known for his elegant musicals.

## Lost and Found

★★☆ Columbia, 1979, c, 112 min. Dir: Melvin Frank. SP: Melvin Frank, Jack Rose. Cast: Glenda Jackson, George Segal, Maureen Stapleton, Hollis McLaren, John Cunningham, Paul Sorvino, Martin Short, John Candy.

Adam (Segal) and Tricia (Jackson) do not meet "cute"—they meet dangerous in this mild marital comedy. After colliding in their cars and then crashing together on the ski slopes, what do they do? They get married, of course, with unhappy results. He's a teacher at a university, and before long there are the expected troubles: he neglects her in his concern about winning tenure, he seems to be dallying with a young researcher (McLaren), and so forth. Unfortunately, Jackson and Segal show little of the rapport they had six years earlier in *A Touch of Class,* and they appear to have no reason to stay together except the whim of the writers. Look for John Candy and Martin Short in small roles.

## Love Crazy

★★☆ MGM, 1941, 99 min. Dir: Jack Conway. SP: William Ludwig, Charles Lederer, David Hertz, b/o story by William Ludwig, David Hertz. Cast: William Powell, Myrna Loy, Gail Patrick, Jack Carson, Florence Bates, Sidney Blackmer, Sig Rumann.

William Powell and Myrna Loy were among the most delightful of movie comedy teams in the thirties and forties, but *Love Crazy* is not one of their best films together. Still, it has some amusing portions, and it is always a pleasure to watch them work together. Here, Powell is a husband divorced by Loy when she finds him in what she wrongly assumes is a compromising situation with neighbor Patrick. His attempts to win her back by pretending to be insane make up most of the movie. As his stratagems become increasingly wild, the movie loses its footing—at one point he has to pass himself off as an elderly matron—but there are some genuine laughs along the way.

## Married to It

★★ Orion, 1993, c, 112 min. Dir: Arthur Hiller. SP: Janet Kovalcik. Cast: Beau Bridges, Stockard Channing, Robert Sean Leonard, Mary Stuart Masterson, Cybil Shepherd, Ron Silver, Don Francks, Donna Vivino.

Made several years before its release date, *Married to It* sinks under the weight of an unworkable premise. Three Manhattan couples meet and, despite being from entirely different backgrounds, become friends who eventually share their secrets and their various crises. Leonard and Masterson are a young couple from Iowa; Bridges and Channing are middle-class strivers with children; Silver is a toy manufacturer whose chic, snobbish second wife (Shepherd) cannot get along with his daughter (Vivino). The friendships are singularly unconvincing, and an uneven screenplay, ranging from perceptive to heavy-handed, does not help.

## The Marrying Kind

★★★☆ Columbia, 1952, 93 min. Dir: George Cukor. SP: Ruth Gordon, Garson Kanin. Cast: Judy Holliday, Aldo Ray, Madge Kennedy, Sheila Bond, John Alexander, Rex Williams, Phyllis Povah, Peggy Cass, Mickey Shaughnessy.

Authors Ruth Gordon and Garson Kanin, whose screenplay for *Adam's Rib* (1949) first brought Judy Holliday to the attention of movie audiences, wrote this deft combination of comedy and drama for the actress. It turned

A bumpy road lies ahead for the just-wedded Aldo Ray and Judy Holliday in George Cukor's *The Marrying Kind* (1952).

out to be one of her best films. She plays the wife of a post-office worker (Ray) who joins with him in recalling their married life as they prepare to divorce. The movie covers the day-to-day but meaningful activities of their marriage, as well as the tragic event that tore them apart. At the end there is a promise of reconciliation. Holliday's special appeal has never been seen to better advantage, and the raspy-voiced Ray is an effective costar.

## The Marrying Man

★☆ Hollywood, 1991, c, 115 min. Dir: Jerry Rees. SP: Neil Simon. Cast: Alec Baldwin, Kim Basinger, Robert Loggia, Elisabeth Shue, Armand Assante, Paul Reiser, Fisher Stevens, Peter Dobson, Gretchen Wyler.

This disaster-plagued comedy is something of a disaster in itself—a serious mistake from author Neil Simon. Alec Baldwin is Charlie Pearl, a wealthy playboy who is engaged to the daughter (Shue) of a studio chief (Loggia). Then, in Las Vegas, he sees and is immediately smitten by lounge singer Vicki Anderson (Basinger), who is mobster Bugsy Siegel's girl. Over the next decade, Charlie and Vicki have a stormy relationship—they marry and divorce several times, and on the third try, they even start a family. All in vain—they cannot break the pattern of coming together and breaking apart, that is, until the movie's ending, when they marry for the fourth time. The striving cast simply cannot overcome Simon's surprisingly witless screenplay.

## Micki & Maude

★☆ Columbia, 1984, c, 118 min. Dir: Blake Edwards. SP: Jonathan Reynolds. Cast: Dudley Moore, Amy Irving, Ann Reinking, Richard Mulligan, George Gaynes, Wallace Shawn, John Pleshette, Lu Leonard, Priscilla Pointer, George Coe.

"I don't want to divorce Micki! I just want to marry Maude!" cries newscaster Rob Salinger (Moore) in this utterly feeble comedy. More of a concept than a movie (and an unworkable concept at that), *Micki & Maude* has Salinger

married to top lawyer Micki (Reinking), and then falling in love with cellist Maude (Irving). Inexplicably, he marries Maude without divorcing Micki, causing unamusing complications. Both of his wives become pregnant and, sure enough, they deliver at the same time, in adjacent rooms, making for a strenuous slapstick climax. Moore's film career never recovered from a string of mostly bad eighties comedies, and this is unquestionably one of them.

## Mr. and Mrs. Smith

★★★ RKO, 1941, 95 min. Dir: Alfred Hitchcock. Sp Norman Krasna. Cast: Carole Lombard, Robert Montgomery, Gene Raymond, Lucile Watson, Philip Merivale, Jack Carson.

The only surprise of this airily amusing comedy is the name of the director: Alfred Hitchcock. "Hitch" decided temporarily to leave his cinematic world of murder and mayhem for the tamer, if not necessarily quieter, world of marriage. It seems that Anne and David Smith (Lombard and Montgomery) discover that they were never legally wed. When David hesitates briefly at the prospect of remarrying Anne, she tosses him out of the house in a fury and falls into the waiting arms of David's law partner (Raymond). Now David has to win her all over again. By the last reel the movie has run out of steam but along the way there are some funny moments, and both Lombard and Montgomery are expert farceurs.

## My Favorite Wife

★★★ RKO, 1940, 88 Min. Dir: Garson Kanin. SP: Samuel Spewack, Bella Spewack. Cast: Irene Dunne, Cary Grant, Gail Patrick, Randolph Scott, Ann Shoemaker, Scotty Beckett, Donald McBride, Granville Bates.

The felicitous teaming of Irene Dunne and Cary Grant in *The Awful Truth* (1937; see page 125) prompted this rematch three years later, and if the comedy is not the equal of its predecessor, it's still enjoyable. Believing that his first wife (Dunne) died in a shipwreck years earlier, Grant remarries on the very day that Dunne returns, alive and well. Now, not only must he cope with *two* wives, but he must also deal with the fact that Dunne spent all that time on a desert island with Randolph Scott. Grant gives one of his best comedy performances, registering shock at seeing his "dead" wife from a moving elevator and sprinting from hotel room to hotel room to the dismay of the clerk (McBride). Watch for Granville Bates's hilarious performance as an addled judge.

## A New Leaf

★★★ Paramount, 1971, c, 102 min. Dir and SP: Elaine May. Cast: Walter Matthau, Elaine May, Jack Weston, George Rose, William Redfield, James Coco, Graham Jarvis, Renee Taylor.

It's hard to determine how this dark comedy might otherwise have fared, since director-writer-star Elaine May insisted on having her name removed from the credits when the studio cut nearly eighty minutes from her original version. The existing movie has its comic moments, with Walter Matthau as a carefree millionaire who spends his way into insolvency and decides to marry a rich woman. He chooses May, a clumsy, myopic heiress, and after disposing of her cheating servants and lawyer, he schemes to murder her for the money. As Chaplin's Monsieur Verdoux could tell him, that isn't always easy. Whatever May intended, she's hilarious as the shunned Henrietta, and the first part of the movie resembles vintage screwball comedy. The rest is intermittently funny.

## A New Life

★★☆ Paramount, 1988, c, 104 min. Dir and SP: Alan Alda. Cast: Alan Alda, Ann-Margret, Veronica Hamel, Hal Linden, John Shea, Mary Kay Place, Bill Irwin.

Life after divorce, and the pressures of a second marriage, are the subjects of this enjoyable but somehow cut-and-dried comedy, written and directed by, and also starring, Alan Alda. Alda plays a stock broker whose marriage to Ann-Margret comes apart. At first all at sea, he falls for and marries a doctor (Hamel), then finds the same noncommitment problems as in his first marriage surfacing again. Ann-Margret takes up with a younger man (Shea), a waiter and part-time sculptor who turns out to be a control freak. Alda's bland and rambling screenplay doesn't help, but the players are agreeable. Alda sports a beard and curly hair.

## The Out of Towners

★ Paramount, 1970, c, 98 min. Dir: Arthur Hiller. SP: Neil Simon. Cast: Jack Lemmon, Sandy Dennis, Sandy Baron, Anne Meara, Robert Nichols, Ann Prentiss, Ron Carey, Graham Jarvis.

If you care to live through more than ninety minutes of a harrowing New York City nightmare, *The Out of Towners* may be just for you, but don't expect to laugh. Neil Simon's relentlessly unfunny screenplay brings Ohio businessman Jack Lemmon to the Big Apple with his wife (Dennis) for an important job interview. Everything goes horribly wrong—they are robbed, scorned, inconvenienced, and insulted on a regular basis. Lemmon reacts by screaming in fury and blaming everyone but his own obnoxious self; Dennis merely whines endlessly, prefacing virtually every sentence with a mournful "George." A microphone appears on the screen about two-thirds of the way through the movie and stays there until the end. Add sloppiness to stupidity, and you get the idea. Remade in 1998.

## Pete 'n' Tillie

★★★ Universal, 1972, c, 100 min. Dir: Martin Ritt. SP: Jules Epstein, b/o novel by Peter de Vries. Cast: Walter Matthau, Carol Burnett, Geraldine Page, Rene Auberjonois, Barry Nelson, Lee H. Montgomery.

An odd combination of frisky comedy and heartbreaking tragedy, *Pete 'n' Tillie* teams Walter Matthau and Carol Burnett as two not-so-young people who meet at a party, exchange barbed quips, and then, to their own amazement, find themselves falling in love. Their happy marriage produces a young son, but tragedy suddenly strikes, leaving them numb and desolate. Considering the comedy expectations of the leads, the switch to drama could have been jolting, but Julius Epstein's Oscar-nominated screenplay makes a smooth transition. There are some laughs contributed by Geraldine Page, also an Oscar nominee as Best Supporting Actress, in one of her over-the-top performances as Carol Burnett's ditsy friend.

## Phffft!

★★★ Columbia, 1954, 91 min. Dir: Mark Robson. SP: George Axelrod. Cast: Judy Holliday, Jack Lemmon, Jack Carson, Kim Novak, Luella Gear, Arny Freeman, Donald Randolph.

After eight years of marriage, Nina (Holliday) and Robert (Lemmon) are divorcing and beginning new lives apart. (She writes television soap operas; he's a lawyer.) Nina takes French lessons and wards off a lecherous suitor (Carson). Robert takes rhumba lessons, buys a flashy sports car, and takes up with a blonde bimbo (Novak). Their paths cross as they compete, quarrel some more, and eventually kiss and make up. Slender and only mildly amusing, *Phffft!* may be a better title than a movie (the ads said, "Don't pronounce it! See it!"), but Holliday and Lemmon are always a pleasure to watch, especially together.

## Ruthless People

★★★ Touchstone, 1986, c, 93 min. Dir: Jim Abrahams, David Zucker, Jerry Zucker. SP: Dale Launer. Cast: Danny DeVito, Bette Midler, Judge Reinhold, Helen Slater, Anita Morris, Bill Pullman, William G. Schilling.

Settle for some pricelessly funny moments and a hilarious performance by Bette Midler, and you'll probably enjoy this hectic comedy. Danny DeVito also gets laughs as a wealthy California businessman who loathes his vulgar wife (Midler) and plots to kill her. Instead she is kidnapped by a bumbling couple (Reinhold and Slater) who have a business grievance against him. Events spin wildly out of control due to a series of mistakes, mishaps, and misunderstandings. DeVito is funny in his usual frenzied mode, but Midler wins the biggest laughs as she drives her captors to distraction, then finally joins with them in a revenge scheme against her husband. Also on hand are Anita Morris as DeVito's greedy mistress and Bill Pullman as her dim-witted boyfriend.

## The Secret Life of an American Wife

★★ Fox, 1968, c, 92 min. Dir and SP: George Axelrod. Cast: Walter Matthau, Anne Jackson, Patrick O'Neal, Edy Williams, Richard Bull, Paul Napier.

Imagine Walter Matthau as a movie star who is also an international sex symbol and "the most physically and sexually attractive man in the world." Of course you are already laughing as you bring to mind the actor's homely, jowly, slouching image. That is the biggest and virtually the only laugh you will find in this tiresome sex comedy. Anne Jackson stars in the title role as a neglected housewife who hires herself out to Matthau as a $100-an-afternoon call girl. An occasional joke works, but most fall flat. Does the lady return happily to her thoughtless husband? Can you doubt it?

## Seems Like Old Times

★★★ Columbia, 1980, c, 102 min. Dir: Jay Sandrich. SP: Neil Simon. Cast: Goldie Hawn, Chevy Chase, Charles Grodin, Robert Guillaume, Harold Gould, George Grizzard, Yvonne Wilder, T. K. Carter.

Neil Simon's original screenplays have veered from abysmal *(The Marrying Man)* to marvelous *(The Goodbye Girl)*. *Seems Like Old Times* falls somewhere in between. Briskly played by a good cast, with more farcical portions than usual, it stars Goldie Hawn as a lawyer who specializes in defending ne'er-do-wells, then bringing them home to do chores when they get suspended sentences. Her second husband (Grodin) is an ambitious district attorney. Then along comes Hawn's ex-husband (Chase), a goofy sort who is being sought by the police for his innocent involvement in a bank robbery. Hawn takes him in and the fun gets under way. The movie's centerpiece is a catastrophic dinner party. The ending is silly, but along the way there are some good Simon one-liners.

## She-Devil

★★ Orion, 1989, c, 99 min. Dir: Susan Seidelman. SP: Barry Strugatz, Mark R. Burns, b/o novel by Fay Weldon. Cast: Meryl Streep, Roseanne Barr, Ed Begley, Jr., Sylvia Miles, Linda Hunt, A Martinez, Elizabeth Peters, Bryan Larkin.

Meryl Streep gives a fine comic performance as Mary Fisher, a glamorous, ego-driven romance novelist, but otherwise this comedy is a shrill, one-note affair. Roseanne Barr plays Ruth Patchett, a plain, unassuming housewife and mother who is dumped by her nasty husband (Begley) for Fisher. Ruth plots an elaborate revenge, depriving her ex-husband of his house, his livelihood, and his freedom. There are some laughs, notably contributed by Sylvia Miles as Mary's vulgar, overbearing mother, but she-devil Ruth wears out her welcome long before the movie ends. Watch it for Streep, if you must.

## She's Having a Baby

★★☆ Paramount, 1988, c, 106 min. Dir and SP: John Hughes. Cast: Kevin Bacon, Elizabeth McGovern, Alec Baldwin, Isabel Lorca, William Windom, Cathryn Damon, James Ray, Holland Taylor.

*She's Having a Baby* was intended to mark writer-director Hughes's first film to move away from his usual teenage world of proms, popularity, and pimples to the adult world of marriage and its problems. Its leading character, however, seems never to have grown up. Jake Briggs (Bacon) is a grumpy sort who apparently married in haste, with little or no regard for his new wife, Kristy (McGovern)— that is, until he learns that he is about to become a father, whereupon he melts into tenderness. Much of the movie's humor stems from their attempts at getting pregnant, but once that's achieved, it settles into sitcom land, with jokes about bra sizes and morning sickness. Not to worry—Jake becomes an adult by the movie's end.

## Something to Talk About

★★★ Warners, 1995, c, 106 min. Dir: Lasse Hallström. SP: Callie Khouri. Cast: Julia Roberts, Dennis Quaid, Gena Rowlands, Robert Duvall, Kyra Sedgwick, Brett Cullen.

Life and love among the Southern horsey set. A pleasant, unexceptional, but reasonably entertaining comedy, *Something to Talk About* centers on Grace (Roberts), who leads a well-to-do, well-ordered life with husband Eddie (Quaid). That is, until she discovers that Eddie is cheating on her regularly. Backed by her acerbic sister-in-law Emma Rae (Sedgwick), Grace begins a campaign of retaliation. At a women's club meeting, she rises to ask, "Has anyone else here slept with my husband?" She feeds Eddie a dinner that makes him ill. And she even tells her mother (Rowlands) about a past indiscretion of her father (Duvall). Everything is resolved—this is, after all, a comedy—but not without some changes. Everyone is competent but Kyra Sedgwick gets the best lines.

## Strange Bedfellows

★★ Universal, 1965, c, 98 min. Dir: Melvin Frank. SP: Melvin Frank, Michael Pertwee, b/o story by Norman Panama, Melvin Frank. Cast: Rock Hudson, Gina Lollobrigida, Gig Young, Edward Judd, Terry-Thomas, Howard St. John, Arthur Haynes.

Nothing remotely as titillating as the title occurs in this lukewarm marital comedy. Rock Hudson is an oil magnate stationed in London and married to Italian Gina Lollobrigida, whose sole interest is avant-garde art. Just when Hudson's big boss arrives, his wife decides to ride through town as Lady Godiva in protest against what she regards as blatant censorship of art. He is embarrassed and things get out of hand, with slapstick and innuendo at every turn. Gig Young plays the "Gig Young" role—cynical, weary, and ready with advice.

## That Old Feeling

★☆ Universal, 1997, c, 105 min. Dir: Carl Reiner. SP: Leslie Dixon. Cast: Bette Midler, Dennis Farina, Paula Marshall, Gail O'Grady, David Rasche, Jamie Denton, Danny Nucci.

Bette Midler is a vibrant comic actress, but she can't save this crude and feeble movie. Every situation is telegraphed in advance, and every tacky attempt at humor produces a groan rather than a laugh. Divorced for fourteen years, Lily (Midler) and Dan (Farina) are thrown together for the wedding of their daughter (Marshall). Their meeting starts as a furious battle and ends unexpectedly with reignited passion, to the dismay of their current mates (O'Grady and Rasche), their daughter, and her priggish new husband (Denton). You can practically feel the strain as each new complication is invented. Best moment: Midler's rendition of a great old song, "Somewhere Along the Way."

## The Thrill of It All

★★★ Universal, 1963, c, 108 min. Dir: Norman Jewison. SP: Carl Reiner, b/o story by Carl Reiner, Larry Gelbart. Cast: Doris Day, James Garner, Arlene Francis, Edward Andrews, Reginald Owen, ZaSu Pitts, Elliott Reid, Alice Pearce.

The contented life of Dr. Gerald Boyer (Garner) and his wife, Beverly (Day), is disrupted when Beverly becomes a national celebrity as the spokesperson for Happy Soap. The good doctor is not pleased to have a working wife, and he does everything he can to change things, including getting her pregnant. Beverly finally returns to home and hearth, proclaiming, "I want to be a doctor's wife again!" This marital comedy pretends to be an early feminist tract, but its heart is clearly on the husband's side. Still, there is some funny material, especially one sequence in which the Boyer house is overrun with suds from Happy Soap. Garner also has a hilarious moment in which he drives his car into a pool he has never seen.

## Two-Faced Woman

★★ MGM, 1941, 94 min. Dir: George Cukor. SP: S. N. Behrman, Salka Viertel, George Oppenheimer. Cast: Greta Garbo, Melvyn Douglas, Constance Bennett, Ruth Gordon, Roland Young, Robert Sterling, Frances Carson.

A sad ending to Greta Garbo's illustrious film career, *Two-Faced Woman* was MGM's abortive attempt to change her image from gloomy tragedienne to sexy siren. A muddled screenplay has Garbo as a ski instructor who marries publisher Melvyn Douglas (her felicitous costar in *Ninotchka*) and then pretends to be her own sexy, animated twin sister when she fears she is losing him to an old rival. Garbo's efforts to seem carefree and effervescent are clearly strained. Some of the situations are vaguely suggestive but apparently they were enough to bring down the wrath of the censors. Constance Bennett steals a movie that is too easily stolen with a hilarious performance as the rival for Douglas's affection.

## Two for the Road

★★★ Fox, 1967, c, 112 min. Dir: Stanley Donen. SP: Frederic Raphael. Cast: Audrey Hepburn, Albert Finney, William Daniels, Eleanor Bron, Claude Dauphin, Nadia Gray, Georges Descrieres, Gabrielle Middleton.

Although you may become irritated with the characters they play, Audrey Hepburn and Albert Finney give assured performances in this offbeat comedy-drama. The movie traces the twelve-year marriage of Joanna (Hepburn) and Mark (Finney), but not in a conventional way. Raphael's adroit screenplay splinters the time sequence, moving back and forth to various points in the marriage, from the ardent, hopeful beginning to what seems to be the bitter ending. Their relationship is disclosed through a series of motor trips they take over the years. Hepburn is captivating, and Finney works hard to make his ill-natured character reasonably appealing. Henry Mancini's romantic musical theme was quite popular.

## The War of the Roses

★★ Fox, 1989, c, 116 min. Dir: Danny DeVito. SP: Michael Leeson, b/o novel by Warren Adler. Cast: Michael Douglas, Kathleen Turner, Danny DeVito, Marianne Sagebrecht, Sean Astin, Heather Fairfield, G. D. Spradlin, Peter Donat.

A jet-black marital comedy, and a forerunner of all the comedies that have stretched the limits of bad taste. When the relatively happy marriage of Oliver and Barbara Rose (Douglas and Turner) crashes in flames, both parties refuse to concede victory in the divorce war that follows. Their mutual thirst for revenge leads to an accelerating series of outrageous and repellent episodes, none of which are worthy of mention here. Their ferocious conflict ends in disaster. Divorce lawyer Gavin D'Amato (DeVito) narrates this sorry tale, which will either have you laughing uproariously or cringing in revulsion. Take your pick, but be warned.

## We're Not Married

★★☆ Fox, 1952, 85 min. Edmund Goulding. SP: Nunnally Johnson. Cast: Ginger Rogers, Fred Allen, Marilyn Monroe, David Wayne, Paul Douglas, Eve Arden, Louis Calhern, Zsa Zsa Gabor, Eddie Bracken, Mitzi Gaynor, Victor Moore.

A genial but fairly labored and obvious multi-part comedy, We're Not Married purports to tell what happens when five married couples learn that Moore, the justice who married them, lacked the authority to do so. The best episode involves radio talk-show hosts Rogers and Allen, who bill and coo on the air but despise each other away from the microphone. In others, voluptuous Monroe, married to Wayne, is named Mrs. Mississippi in a beauty contest; Douglas and Arden barely communicate in their marriage; cheating husband Calhern faces ruin when wife Gabor catches him in an indiscretion. Scattered laughs, but mostly the movie is tame and predictable.

## The Woman in Red

★★★ Orion, 1984, c, 87 min. Dir and SP: Gene Wilder. Cast: Gene Wilder, Charles Grodin, Kelly Le Brock, Joseph Bologna, Judith Ivey, David Huddleston, Gilda Radner.

Triple-threat Gene Wilder starred in, wrote, and directed this often amusing comedy, adapted from the French film *Pardon Mon Affaire*. He plays a happily married advertising executive who suddenly becomes obsessed with a beautiful model (Le Brock). His frantic efforts to meet and seduce this vision of loveliness only get him deeper and deeper into trouble (today he might be labeled a stalker), and he ends up where the movie begins: perched high on a window ledge in a bathrobe. Comically desperate as always, Wilder surrounds himself with some capable actors: Judith Ivey as his clueless wife, Charles Grodin as a friend with his own secret, and Joseph Bologna as another friend with a seriously bumpy marriage.

# Home and Hearth: Family Comedies

Long before the word *dysfunctional* entered the language, families were having their problems, and many of them found their way onto the screen. The problems were not exactly earthshaking: can the Hardy family survive its teenage son Andy? What to name the baby who is *Father's Little Dividend?* Now families in today's comedies must cope with such noncomedic topics as teenage pregnancy, sexual misconduct, and the problems of aging. Is this an improvement? Judge for yourself as you pore over these family comedies.

## The Addams Family

★★☆ Paramount, 1991, c, 102 min. Dir: Barry Sonnenfeld. SP: Caroline Thompson, Larry Wilson, b/o characters created by Charles Addams. Cast: Anjelica Huston, Raul Julia, Christopher Lloyd, Dan Hedaya, Elizabeth Wilson, Judith Malina, Carel Struycken, Christopher Hart, Christina Ricci, Jimmy Workman.

Well, the Addamses *are* a family, aren't they? They're devoted, caring, and . . . well, totally bizarre. Derived largely from the television series (1964–66) that drew on Charles Addams's famous *New Yorker* cartoons, the movie brings to life (life?) that happy couple Gomez (Julia) and Morticia (Huston), their diabolical offspring (Ricci and Workman), and other members of the ghoulish clan. There's a plot of sorts—something involving Gomez's long-lost brother Fester—but most of the movie is made up of jokes about the gleeful perversity of the family's behavior. Huston and Julia are well cast as the loving couple ("Cara mia!"), but the movie is largely for diehard Addams fans. A sequel, *Addams Family Values,* was released in 1993.

## Baby Boom

★★★ MGM/UA, 1987, c, 103 min. Dir: Charles Shyer. SP: Nancy Meyers, Charles Shyer. Cast: Diane Keaton, Sam Shepard, Harold Ramis, Sam Wanamaker, James Spader, Pat Hingle, Britt Leach, Mary Gross, Victoria Jackson, Paxton Whitehead.

More of a Hollywood fable than a treatise on single motherhood, *Baby Boom* stars Diane Keaton as a high-powered business executive who suddenly finds herself overwhelmed by the duties of unexpected motherhood (diapers, nannies, preschooling, and the like) when she inherits the baby of deceased English cousins. When her work suffers and her devotion to the baby grows deeper, she leaves it all to settle in rural Vermont, where she finds happiness with sturdy new boyfriend Sam Shepard and develops a thriving baby food business. The movie advances the dubious notion that women can "have it all," but it's genial entertainment, sparked by Keaton's ingratiating performance.

## Baby's Day Out

★ Fox, 1994, c, 98 min. Dir: Patricia Read Johnson. SP: John Hughes. Cast: Lara Flynn Boyle, Joe Mantegna, Brian Haley, Joe Pantoliano, Cynthia Nixon, Adam Robert Warton, Jacob Joseph Warton.

Another John Hughes variation on *Home Alone,* and hopefully the last. This time three dumbbells (Mantegna, Pantoliano, and Haley) kidnap Baby Bink (the Warton twins) from his home and then try to retrieve him when he escapes from his captors by crawling out a window. With the kidnappers in frantic pursuit, Bink embarks on a series of adventures that prove him to be indestructible. (He also stays amazingly clean.) In the *Home Alone* tradition, the kidnappers are subject to all sorts of physical punishment, from dunkings in cement to blows on the head. Wildly improbable and woefully unfunny.

## Back to School

★★☆ Orion, 1986, c, 94 min. Dir: Alan Metter. SP: Steven Kampmann, Will Porter, Peter Torokvei, Harold Ramis. Cast: Rodney Dangerfield, Sally Kellerman, Keith Gordon, Burt Young, Ned Beatty, Robert Downey, Jr.

Rodney Dangerfield, the burly comedian who gets "no respect," has had a sporadic film career. Here, in one of his better efforts, he plays Thornton Melon, a millionaire clothing manufacturer with an obnoxious wife and a son (Gordon) he adores. When he discovers that his son is neither a fraternity member nor a swimming star but a rather wimpy sort, Melon enrolls in the school after making a sizable donation. In this sort of movie, of course, his down-to-earth approach shows up the college "eggheads," and after some setbacks he becomes a campus hero with a self-assured son. *Back to School* will win no comedy prizes, but Dangerfield is almost likable, with a glint of becoming poignancy in his behavior.

## The Bad News Bears

★★★ Paramount, 1976, c, 102 min. Dir: Michael Ritchie. SP: Bill Lancaster. Cast: Walter Matthau, Tatum O'Neal, Vic Morrow, Joyce Van Patten, Jackie Earle Haley, Alfred W. Lutter.

The first and best of three movies about a Little League team composed of young misfits who enjoy using four-letter words. The team is hopeless until they are whipped into shape by a sloppy, beer-guzzling coach (Matthau) who hires a girl pitcher (O'Neal) with a wicked fast ball. The movie's appeal to young viewers lies in the kids' language, which may be deleted on television, but it's genial fun nonetheless. There were two sequels, *The Bad News Bears in Breaking Training* (1977), with William Devane, and *The Bad News Bears Go to Japan* (1978), with Tony Curtis, plus a TV series.

## Bedtime for Bonzo

★★☆ Universal-International, 1951, 83 min. Dir: Frederick de Cordova. SP: Val Burton, Lou Breslow, b/o story by Raphael David Blau, Ted Berkman. Cast: Ronald Reagan, Diana Lynn, Walter Slezak, Lucille Barkley, Jesse White, Herbert Heyes.

After Ronald Reagan was elected president, *Bedtime for Bonzo* was used as a joking reference for the nadir of his film career. Actually, it's an inoffensive little comedy about a psychology professor (Reagan) who believes that environment is more important than heredity. To prove his case, he takes frisky chimpanzee Bonzo into his house, with just the results you would expect. Before long, Bonzo is behaving like an unruly child, riding a bicycle, jabbering into a telephone, and so forth. And the good professor is having trouble with his haughty fiancée (Barkley), the dean's daughter. Diana Lynn, hired to help with Bonzo's training, is the true love interest. Reagan did not appear in the 1952 sequel.

## Beethoven

★★★ Universal, 1992, c, 87 min. Dir: Brian Levant. SP: Edmond Dantes (John Hughes), Amy Holden Jones. Cast: Charles Grodin, Bonnie Hunt, Dean Jones, Oliver Platt, Stanley Tucci, Nicholle Tom, Christopher Castile, Sarah Rose Karr, David Duchovny, Patricia Heaton.

A good-natured family comedy centering on a huge, slobbering St. Bernard dog named Beethoven. He is taken into the Newton family, where Dad (Grodin) dislikes him and everyone else is overjoyed. After some slapstick mayhem, there's something of a plot when an evil veterinarian (Jones) kidnaps Beethoven and other dogs for unspeakable experiments. Naturally he gets his just desserts by way of the Newtons. The principal joke is that Beethoven seems to understand more than any human. Good fun, and there was a sequel called *Beethoven's 2nd* (1993).

## Betsy's Wedding

★★★ Touchstone, 1990, c, 94 min. Dir and SP: Alan Alda. Cast: Alan Alda, Madeline Kahn, Molly Ringwald, Anthony LaPaglia, Joe Pesci, Ally Sheedy, Catherine O'Hara, Burt Young, Julie Bovasso.

Life is not going well for Eddie Hopper (Alda). It all starts when daughter Betsy (Ringwald) announces that she's engaged to be married. This being Movieland, everything goes comically wrong: the prospective groom's parents are wealthy snobs and control freaks; Betsy has her own way-out ideas about a wedding; and Eddie's corrupt brother-in-law (Pesci) is involving him with all sorts of unsavory types. It's no surprise when the wedding turns into a catastrophe. Alan Alda's comedy is genial and sometimes funny, and it's stolen entirely by Anthony LaPaglia as Stevie, a courtly gangster-in-training who adores Eddie's other daughter Connie (Sheedy), who's a policewoman.

## Big Bully

★★ Warners, 1996, c, 97 min. Dir: Steve Miner. SP: Mark Steven Johnson. Cast: Rick Moranis, Tom Arnold, Julianne Phillips, Carol Kane, Jeffrey Tambor, Curtis Armstrong, Faith Prince, Tony Pierce, Don Knotts, Stuart Pankin.

New novelist David Leary (Moranis) is asked to teach a creative writing course at his old school, where he was once the nerdlike victim of bully Rosco "Fang" Bigger's endless nasty pranks. To his horror, David discovers that Fang (Arnold) is now a shop teacher at the same school and still harbors his sadistic impulses. Fang's assault on David spirals out of control until it turns dangerous. Of course, it ends with sweetness and light all around. Moranis and Arnold go through the motions with their stock roles but the standard nerd-versus-bully formula wears thin quickly.

## Big Night

★★★☆ Goldwyn, 1996, c, 107 min. Dir: Stanley Tucci, Campbell Scott. SP: Joseph Tropiano, Stanley Tucci. Cast: Stanley Tucci, Tony Shalhoub, Isabella Rossellini, Minnie Driver, Ian Holm, Allison Janney, Campbell Scott.

"To eat good food is to be close to God," proclaims Primo (Shalhoub), the brooding, masterful chef in this small but endearing comedy. He and his more pragmatic brother Secondo (Tucci) own a failing restaurant in 1950s Brooklyn. Now, with the seeming help of rival restaurant owner Pascal (Holm), they have one last chance to succeed. Pascal has promised to bring band leader Louis Prima to their restaurant for a glorious meal. What happens in this movie is never earth-shaking, but it is filled with astute observations about life, relationships, and food. (Notice how silence is used to express feelings.) By the time the luscious meal is served, you just might agree with Primo.

## The Birdcage

★★★ United Artists, 1996, c, 117 min. Dir: Mike Nichols. SP: Elaine May, b/o play by Jean Poiret and screenplay by Francis Veber, Edouard Molinaro, Marcello Danon, Jean Poiret. Cast: Robin Williams, Gene Hackman, Nathan Lane, Dianne Wiest, Christine Baranski, Dan Futterman, Calista Flockhart, Hank Azaria.

Yet another reworking of the durable play and movie *La Cage Aux Folles*, *The Birdcage* moves the setting to Miami Beach but keeps the basic story. Armand (Williams) and Albert (Lane) are gay life partners—Armand operates a drag revue and Albert is his star attraction. Their lives are disrupted when Armand's son (Futterman) wants to marry the daughter (Lockhart) of a conservative senator (Hackman) and would like his father to play "straight" when the families meet. Elaine May's funny screenplay and Mike Nichols's lively direction (Nichols and May together again!) combine to make an enjoyable mainstream movie. For the most part, Williams is agreeably restrained, and Lane's over-the-top performance should keep you laughing.

## Blank Check

★★ Buena Vista, 1994, c, 90 min. Dir: Rupert Wainwright. SP: Blake Snyder and Colby Carr. Cast: Brian Bonsall, Karen Duffy, Miguel Ferrer, Tone Loc, Michael Lerner, Rick Ducommun.

Do we really need another variation on *Home Alone*? Yet here it is, and fairly lame too. The concept: Eleven-year-old Preston Waters (Bonsall) strikes it rich when a fleeing crook accidentally runs over Preston's bicycle and hastily gives him a blank check. Preston has his computer type in the sum of a million dollars, and when he takes it to the bank, the corrupt bank president assumes the boy is a courier for the gangster and gives him a million dollars in cash! Preston becomes the millionaire of every boy's dreams. *Blank Check* steals shamelessly from *Home Alone,* but by now it's all very tired. Young children may be amused.

## Breaking Away

★★★☆ Fox, 1979, c, 100 min. Dir: Peter Yates. SP: Steve Tesich. Cast: Dennis Christopher, Dennis Quaid, Daniel Stern, Jackie Earle Haley, Paul Dooley, Barbara Barrie, Robyn Douglass, Amy Wright.

Steve Tesich won an Oscar for his screenplay for this highly appealing comedy. The setting is Bloomington, Indiana, where Dave (Christopher) is one of the working-class young men known as cutters. (Their fathers were once stonecutters.) Dave and his "cutter" pals (Quaid, Stern, and Haley) have one dream: to win the annual bicycle race by defeating the snobbish college kids. Do they win after some setbacks and humiliations? Guess. Dave also has a passion for everything Italian, and for a while he pretends to be an Italian exchange student. Naturally his parents (beautifully played by Dooley and Barrie) are bewildered by his behavior. *Breaking Away* was a sleeper in its year, and deservedly so. A television series based on the movie turned up in 1980.

## The Brothers McMullen

★★★ Fox Searchlight, 1995, c, 97 min. Dir and SP: Edward Burns. Cast: Edward Burns, Jack Mulcahy, Mike McGlone, Connie Britton, Shari Albert, Elizabeth P. McKay, Maxine Bahns, Jennifer Jostyn, Catherine Bolz.

Young filmmaker Edward Burns proved to be a triple threat as director, writer, and star of this winning family comedy. The tribulations of three Irish-American brothers, romantic and otherwise, form the core of the story. Jack (Mulcahy), the eldest, is a high school basketball coach married to a teacher (Britton) who wants children. His eye begins to roam. Middle brother Barry is an aspiring writer who is afraid of settling down until he meets a beautiful model (Bahns). Patrick (McGlone), the youngest, is worried about spending the rest of his life with his Jewish girlfriend (Jostyn). Their conversations are pungent in this modestly made but flavorsome movie.

## Bustin' Loose

★★☆ Universal, 1981, c, 94 min. Dir: Oz Scott. SP: Roger L. Simon, adapted by Lonne Elder III from story by Richard Pryor. Cast: Richard Pryor, Cicely Tyson, Alphonso Alexander, Kia Cooper, Edwin DeLeon, Jimmy Hughes, Edwin Kinter.

It's surprising to see Richard Pryor in a sentimental family comedy, but since he resorts to street language now and again, his fans shouldn't be disappointed. He plays a recent parolee assigned to drive eight displaced children and their guardian (Tyson) to a farm in the state of Washington, where presumably the children will enjoy an untroubled life. During the trip, their bus breaks down, giving Pryor the chance to teach the children strip poker and to keep a little Vietnamese girl from turning prostitute. Once in Washington, there are other problems. Pryor's subversive humor is not much in evidence here, but *Bustin' Loose* is painless.

## Captain Ron

★☆ Touchstone, 1992, c, 100 min. Dir: Thom E. Eberhardt. SP: John Dwyer, Thom E. Eberhardt, b/o story by John Dwyer. Cast: Kurt Russell, Martin Short, Mary Kay Place, Benjamin Salisbury, Meadow Sisto.

When harassed urbanite Martin Short inherits a boat from a deceased uncle, he decides to take the boat from its Caribbean island to Miami, bringing along his wife (Place) and children (Salisbury and Sisto) for a great "adventure." To steer the boat, he hires Captain Ron (Russell), a scruffy, disreputable fellow whose knowledge of seafaring is minimal. All the expected mishaps occur, and a run-in with pirates puts everyone in jeopardy. None of this is the least bit funny, and neither Short nor Russell, who have done better work, can keep the movie from capsizing. Singer Paul Anka (unbilled) plays a boat salesman.

## Clifford

★ Orion, 1994, c, 90 min. Dir: Paul Flaherty. SP: Jay Dee Rock, Bobby Von Hayes. Cast: Charles Grodin, Martin Short, Mary Steenburgen, Dabney Coleman, G. D. Spradlin, Anne Jeffreys, Richard Kind.

The search for good or even adequate film material for the gifted Martin Short received a serious setback with this alleged comedy. Made in 1991 but unreleased until 1994 due to Orion's bankruptcy, *Clifford* is a disaster with a gimmick. Photographed only from the waist up to disguise his height, Short plays a ten-year-old from hell who comes to visit his uncle Martin (Grodin). Martin wants to impress his fiancée (Steenburgen) by pretending to like children, but *nobody* could like the demonically mischievous Clifford. Before long, Martin is behind bars due to his obnoxious nephew. As usual, Grodin gives the material his best, but *Clifford* should have stayed in limbo.

## Cookie

★★★ Warners, 1989, c, 93 min. Dir: Susan Seidelman. Sp Nora Ephron, Alice Arlen. Cast: Peter Falk, Emily Lloyd, Dianne Wiest, Michael V. Gazzo, Brenda Vaccaro, Adrian Pasdar, Lionel Stander, Jerry Lewis, Bob Gunton.

Peter Falk stars in this entertaining comedy as Mario, a Brooklyn Mafia boss who returns home from serving a thirteen-year sentence in Sing Sing, only to find himself the target of both mobsters and the Feds. He's obliged to live with his estranged wife, Bunny (Vaccaro), but he really loves Lenore (Wiest), who is the mother of his teenage daughter, Cookie (Lloyd). Played by young British actress Emily Lloyd with a Brooklyn accent, Cookie is really the movie's center: a gaudy, tough-talking hellion who turns out to be Mario's best driver and a shield against his enemies. The supporting cast includes a few surprises (Jerry Lewis as a mob associate; gravel-voiced Lionel Stander as a godfather).

## Cops and Robbersons

★ TriStar, 1994, c, 93 min. Dir: Michael Ritchie. SP: Bernie Somers. Cast: Chevy Chase, Jack Palance, Dianne Wiest, Robert Davi, David Barry Gray, Jason James Richter, Fay Masterston.

How many times can Chevy Chase play a brain-dead, insufferable paterfamilias before audiences storm the screen in a rage? Here he plays Norman Robberson, a mentally deficient suburbanite who is addicted to television police dramas. When his house is used as a stakeout by veteran cop Jack Palance, Norman causes one disaster after another by his eagerness to "help." At the same time, grumpy Palance learns to be part of a family. Norman's obnoxious personality destroys every grain of humor in the story. It's also painful to watch wonderful actress Dianne Wiest endure the thankless role of his wife.

## Coupe de Ville

★★☆ Morgan Creek, 1990, c, 99 min. Dir: Joe Roth. SP: Mike Binder. Cast: Patrick Dempsey, Arye Gross, Daniel Stern, Alan Arkin, Joseph Bologna, Annabeth Gish, Rita Taggart.

An amiable, low-key "road" movie, centering on three brothers who come together when their father (Arkin) asks them to drive a 1954 Cadillac from Michigan to Florida in time for their mother's fiftieth birthday. A difficult request, since the brothers have quarreled all their lives. The eldest, Marvin (Stern), is an air force sergeant; middle son Buddy (Gross) is a recent college graduate; and the youngest, Bobby (Dempsey) is a rebel in boarding school.

The year is 1963, and it's some time since they've been together. They bicker (most hilariously over the meaning of the song "Louie Louie"), reveal some home truths to each other, and end up as brothers closer to bonding than ever.

## Cousins

★★★ Paramount, 1989, c, 110 min. Dir: Joel Schumacher. SP: Stephen Metcalfe, b/o film by Jean-Charles Tacchella. Cast: Ted Danson, Isabella Rossellini, Sean Young, William Petersen, Lloyd Bridges, Norma Aleandro, George Coe, Keith Coogan, Gina de Angelis.

Adapted from the popular French film *Cousin Cousine, Cousins* has Ted Danson and Isabella Rossellini as married cousins attending a large family wedding. Only they are not married to each other. Danson is wed to sexy second wife Young, and Rossellini's husband (Petersen) is a nasty car salesman with a roving eye. When Danson and Rossellini discover that their respective spouses are sleeping together, they get revenge by pretending to start an affair of their own. Of course the pretense turns into reality as they come to realize that they belong together. Much of the movie's enjoyment comes from the family members, notably Lloyd Bridges as Danson's lusty father and Gina de Angelis as a bitter old relative. Good breezy fun.

## Dennis the Menace

★☆ Warners, 1993, c, 94 min. Dir: Nick Castle. SP: John Hughes, b/o characters created by Hank Ketchum. Cast: Walter Matthau, Joan Plowright, Mason Gamble, Christopher Lloyd, Lea Thompson, Paul Winfield, Robert Stanton, Arnold Stang.

"Why is it that when everyone else feeds on the pleasures of life, I get indigestion?" cries Mr. Wilson (Matthau), the eternal victim of the mischievous behavior of Dennis the Menace (Gamble). This excruciatingly bad adaptation of the long-running comic strip may please small viewers, but everyone else will cringe. There's a plot of sorts—something about Dennis being accused of stealing Mr. Wilson's coin collection and taking on the thief (Lloyd) who did, but there's nothing funny in the series of disasters that befall Wilson, despite Matthau's best efforts. Writer John Hughes fared much better with his *Home Alone* series.

## Down and Out in Beverly Hills

★★★ Touchstone, 1986, c, 103 min. Dir: Paul Mazursky. SP: Paul Mazursky, Leon Capetanos, b/o play by Rene Fauchois. Cast: Nick Nolte, Bette Midler, Richard Dreyfuss, Little Richard, Tracy Nelson, Elizabeth Pena, Evan Richards, Mike the Dog.

As a repressed Beverly Hills matron, Bette Midler has a comic way of walking with her fingers fluttering as if she were continually drying her nails. She gives a hilarious performance in this hectic, occasionally funny farce. Based on Jean Renoir's 1932 French film *Boudou Saved from Drowning,* the movie stars Nick Nolte as Jerry, a scruffy, mysterious bum who invades the home of the affluent Whiteman family after he attempts to drown himself in their pool. Before long, he has changed the life of work-driven Dave Whiteman (Dreyfuss) and stirred up the sexuality of Whiteman's wife (Midler) and daughter (Nelson). Aside from Midler, the movie's best performance is given by Mike the Dog, as the family pet, Matisse.

## Dutch

★★☆ Fox, 1991, c, 105 min. Dir: Peter Faiman. SP: John Hughes. Cast: Ed O'Neill, Ethan Randall, JoBeth Williams, Christopher McDonald, Ari Myers, E. G. Daily, Kathleen Freeman.

Another standard John Hughes comedy, mixing slapstick and sentiment. Ed O'Neill (from TV's "Married . . . With Children") is the title character, a good-hearted working-class guy who vows to bring his girlfriend's obnoxious, estranged son (Randall) home, any way he can. Randall is a snobbish prep-schooler who hates his divorced mother and despises Dutch on sight. Their cross-country journey begins as a battle and becomes an adventure when they are left carless and penniless. If you doubt that the boy will change his attitude drastically and come to love both Mom and Dutch, you have never been to a movie, or at least a John Hughes movie.

## The Egg and I

★★★ Universal-International, 1947, 108 min. Dir: Chester Erskine. SP: Chester Erskine, Fred F. Finklehoffe, b/o book by Betty MacDonald. Cast: Claudette Colbert, Fred MacMurray, Marjorie Main, Percy Kilbride, Louise Allbritton, Richard Long, Billy House, Ida Moore, Donald McBride, Samuel S. Hinds.

A genial adaptation of the best-selling book by Betty MacDonald about her experiences as a city woman turned chicken farmer's wife. Claudette Colbert plays the beleaguered heroine with her usual aplomb, grappling with the perils of farm life, including a stubborn stove and untrustworthy livestock. Not surprisingly, there's also a bit of marital trouble when a local vixen (Allbritton) sets her sights on Bob MacDonald (MacMurray). The movie's single claim to fame is that it introduced Marjorie Main and Percy Kilbride as rambunctious neighbors Ma and Pa Kettle, whose popularity insured them their own series of knockabout farces.

## Family Business

★★ TriStar, 1989, c, 115 min. Dir: Sidney Lumet. SP: Vincent Patrick, b/o his novel. Cast: Sean Connery, Dustin Hoffman, Matthew Broderick, Rosana DeSoto, Janet Carroll, Victoria Jackson, Bill McCutcheon.

Would you believe that Sean Connery, Dustin Hoffman, and Matthew Broderick are members of the same McMullen family? Hardly, although *Family Business* tries to explain it by giving them a mixed Scots-Sicilian-Cherokee-Jewish heritage. Grandfather Jessie (Connery) is a brawler, conman, and retired thief; his son Vito (Hoffman) is a retired, conservative-minded ex-thief and prosperous meat dealer; his grandson Adam (Broderick) is an ace student who wants to drop out of college and join

Grandpa in one last hurrah: a million-dollar heist. Arguments flare while the robbery proceeds, but the three capable actors (Connery is best) cannot make the story convincing or even particularly interesting.

## Father of the Bride

★★★☆ MGM, 1950, 93 min. Dir: Vincente Minnelli. SP: Albert Hackett, Frances Goodrich, b/o novel by Edward Streeter. Cast: Spencer Tracy, Elizabeth Taylor, Joan Bennett, Don Taylor, Billie Burke, Leo G. Carroll, Moroni Olsen, Russ Tamblyn, Melville Cooper.

*Father of the Bride* may offer a never-never-land view of suburban life circa 1950, but it's still a disarmingly funny and likable movie. Oscar-nominated Spencer Tracy stars as Stanley Banks, a gruff but lovable paterfamilias whose daughter (Taylor) suddenly announces her attention to marry. A series of comic catastrophes follows as Banks and his family cope with the wedding. Some of the humor is lightly satirical—there's the expected business about spiraling costs and overbearing caterers—but Tracy's warmth and charm prevail, and Elizabeth Taylor is exquisitely beautiful as the bride-to-be. A sequel, *Father's Little Dividend,* followed in 1951, and Steve Martin starred in a 1991 remake, which had a sequel in 1995.

## Fathers' Day

★ Warners, 1997, c, 98 min. Dir: Ivan Reitman. SP: Lowell Ganz, Babaloo Mandel, b/o screenplay by Francis Veber. Cast: Robin Williams, Billy Crystal, Julia Louis-Dreyfus, Natassja Kinski, Charlie Hofheimer, Bruce Greenwood, Jared Harris.

Lowell Ganz and Babaloo Mandel have written some funny screenplays (*Parenthood,* for example); *Fathers' Day* is not one of them. Jack (Crystal) is a married lawyer, and Dale (Williams) is an unsuccessful, wildly neurotic performance artist. Each is told by Natassja Kinski that he is the father of her teenage son (Harris), who is missing. The two meet and begin a search that brings them eventually to

After the wedding festivities are ended in *Father of the Bride* (1950), father Spencer
Tracy and mother Joan Bennett feel nothing but exhaustion.

the son but also to drug dealers and danger.
The screenplay sounds as if it were made up by
the actors as they moved along, and surprisingly, both Crystal and Williams seem to be all
at sea. Adapted from the French film *Les
Compères*.

## Father's Little Dividend

★★★☆ MGM, 1951, 82 min. Dir: Vincente Minnelli. SP:
Albert Hackett, Frances Goodrich, b/o characters created
by Edward Streeter. Cast: Spencer Tracy, Joan Bennett,
Elizabeth Taylor, Don Taylor, Billie Burke, Moroni Olson,
Russ Tamblyn.

An inevitable sequel to the popular *Father of
the Bride*, and in some ways an improvement
on the original. Spencer Tracy is back as
Stanley Banks, this time disconcerted that he is
going to be a grandfather. He reacts predictably
but amusingly, becoming flustered when there
is a brouhaha over a name for the baby, and

when his pregnant daughter (Taylor) returns to his household after a quarrel with her husband. The hectic climax involves the birth of the baby. Tracy does a smooth repetition of his role, mooring it a bit closer to reality, and Joan Bennett again supplies some nice balance as his wife. The 1995 sequel to Steve Martin's 1991 remake was called *Father of the Bride, Part II*.

## Father Was a Fullback

★★☆ Fox, 1949, 84 min. Dir: John M. Stahl. SP: Aleen Leslie, Casey Robinson, Mary Loos, Richard Sale. Cast: Fred MacMurray, Maureen O'Hara, Betty Lynn, Rudy Vallee, Thelma Ritter, Natalie Wood, Jim Backus, Richard Tyler.

Never much of an actor, Fred MacMurray excelled in good-guy roles (with the notable exception of *Double Indemnity*). Here, he plays George Cooper, a beleaguered husband, father, and coach of the football team. His team is losing every game, his older daughter (Lynn) is being shunned by the boys, and he is being plagued by a stuffy member (Vallee) of the alumni association. These not too earth-shaking problems are solved by the movie's end, with the help of George's patient wife (O'Hara). As usual, Thelma Ritter, as the family servant, gets most of the best lines in this amiable comedy.

## Fatso

★★ Fox, 1980, c, 94 min. Dir and SP: Anne Bancroft. Cast: Dom DeLuise, Anne Bancroft, Ron Carey, Candice Azzara, Michael Lombard, Sal Viscuso, Delia Salvi, Estelle Reiner, Robert Costanzo.

Actress Anne Bancroft wrote, directed, and starred in this comedy, but alas, it's not very good. When the obese cousin of fat man Dominick DiNapoli (DeLuise) dies, Dom vows to lose weight. He chains up the kitchen cupboards, entrusts the keys to his brother (Carey), then chases him around the house with a knife as soon as he gets hungry again. It's a losing game, and Dom's shrewish sister

Antoinette (Bancroft) is no help. Then Dom meets Lydia (Azzara), the girl of his dreams, and for a while he has the incentive to turn his life around. *Fatso* tries to be both raucous and poignant, to little avail.

## Ferris Bueller's Day Off

★★★ Warners, 1986, c, 103 min. Dir and SP: John Hughes. Cast: Matthew Broderick, Alan Ruck, Mia Sara, Jeffrey Jones, Jennifer Grey, Cindy Pickett, Lyman Ward, Edie McClurg.

Ferris Bueller is the world champion teenage con artist. "Life," he tells the audience, "moves pretty fast. If you don't stop and look around once in a while, you'll miss it." So he takes off a day from school, fooling his parents (Pickett and Ward), confounding and humiliating his school's principal (Jones), and enjoying adventures with his best friend (Ruck). There's a great fantasy musical number ("Twist and Shout"), plus some fairly serious business toward the end, but mostly the movie is aimed at the young teen audience that loves Ferris and scoffs at the clueless parents, dull teachers, and stupid principal. Adults, however, may find Ferris devious, selfish, uncaring, and arrogant.

## The Flamingo Kid

★★★ Fox, 1984, c, 100 min. Dir: Garry Marshall. SP: Neal Marshall and Garry Marshall, b/o story by Garry Marshall. Cast: Matt Dillon, Richard Crenna, Hector Elizondo, Molly McCarthy, Martha Gehman, Jessica Walter, Janet Jones, Fisher Stevens, Bronson Pinchot.

In the summer of 1963, ambitious Brooklyn teenager Jeffrey Willis (Dillon) gets a summer job as parking lot attendant at a Long Island cabana club, a garish playground for the newly rich. His father (Elizondo) is angry—he wanted Jeffrey to work at an engineering firm as a practical step toward a career. Jeffrey, however, has other ideas and under the guidance of club member Phil Brody (Crenna), he rises to cabana boy—with dreams of a future in "sales." He also has a romance with a

California girl (Jones). Director and cowriter Marshall captures the sixties Long Island milieu with affection and a shrewd eye, and Dillon is very good as the upwardly mobile Jeffrey. Best sequence: dinner with the Brody bunch.

## Folks!

★ Penta, 1992, c, 107 min. Dir: Ted Kotcheff. SP: Robert Klane. Cast: Tom Selleck, Don Ameche, Anne Jackson, Christine Ebersole, Wendy Crewson, Michael Murphy, Robert Pastorelli.

If this book had a rating lower than one star, *Folks!* would surely qualify. This dreadful movie stars Tom Selleck as a luckless stock broker who travels to Florida to see his parents (Ameche and Jackson), only to learn that his father is rapidly reaching senility. When his father burns their house down, Selleck brings them home to his family, where, sparked by Dippy Daddy, one disaster follows another. Eventually Selleck loses his job, his family, and very nearly his mind, and even goes along with his obnoxious sister (Ebersole), who wants them killed! The awful screenplay will make you cringe and all cast members should have been embarrassed.

## Funny Farm

★★☆ Warners, 1988, 101 min. Dir: George Roy Hill. SP: Jeffrey Boam, b/o book by Jay Cronley. Cast: Chevy Chase, Madolyn Smith, Joseph Maher, Jack Gilpin, Brad Sullivan, MacIntyre Dixon.

A notch or two better than the usual Chevy Chase comedy, which is not saying much. When you know that he's a sportswriter who decides to buy a country home where he can work on his novel in peace and quiet, you know there's nothing but disaster ahead. And sure enough, before long he is coping with various off-the-wall rural types, some of them funny. But then they needed a plot, and the movie has Chase behaving idiotically, and even reprehensibly, when he not only sulks over the fact that his wife (Smith) has sold her own

book but also palms off one of her books as his own! The climactic sequence has to be seen to be disbelieved.

## Garbo Talks

★★★ MGM/UA, 1984, c, 104 min. Dir: Sidney Lumet. SP: Larry Grusin. Cast: Anne Bancroft, Ron Silver, Steven Hill, Carrie Fisher, Catherine Hicks, Steven Hill, Harvey Fierstein, Howard da Silva, Dorothy Loudon, Hermione Gingold, Betty Comden.

This rambling but enjoyable and occasionally poignant comedy-drama stars Ron Silver as Gilbert, a nebbish accountant with a complaining wife (Fisher) and a fierce, constantly embattled mother (Bancroft). When his mother falls fatally ill, her one wish is to meet her lifelong idol, Greta Garbo. In his obsessive search for Garbo, Gilbert not only risks losing his wife and his job but also meets a number of New York eccentrics, including a photographer (da Silva), an agent (Loudon), and an actress (Gingold). Oscar-nominated Bancroft is best, creating an indelible portrait of a feisty, difficult woman as she dances alone in her hospital room or delivers a touching monologue to the visiting Garbo. (Betty Comden plays Garbo in the last scene.)

## Getting Even with Dad

★★☆ MGM, 1994, c, 108 min. Dir: Howard Deutch. SP: Tom S. Parker, Jim Jennewein. Cast: Macaulay Culkin, Ted Danson, Glenne Headley, Saul Rubinek, Gailard Sartain, Hector Elizondo, Sam McMurray.

Ray (Danson) is a cake decorator and ex-convict who joins with two goofy friends (Rubinek and Sartain) in stealing a cache of valuable coins. Then along comes Timmy (Culkin), his resourceful eleven-year-old son, who would like him to go straight. Timmy takes the coins and leads his father and pals on a merry chase that eventually gets him what he wants. Complicating matters is Theresa (Headly), a cop tracking the thieves, who is attracted to Dad. The treatment of the two dumb crooks is very *Home Alone*. The movie was an unsuccessful vehicle for an older Culkin, but it's pleasant enough.

## The Great Outdoors

★★☆ Universal, 1988, c, 90 min. Dir: Howard Deutch. SP: John Hughes. Cast: John Candy, Dan Aykroyd, Stephanie Faracy, Annette Bening, Robert Prosky, Chris Young, Lucy Deakins, Ian Giatti, Hilary Gordon, Rebecca Gordon.

John Hughes (Pretty in Pink, Sixteen Candles) wrote the screenplay for this run-of-the-mill family comedy. John Candy takes his family to a cabin in the Canadian woods for rest and relaxation. Only there's no rest and little relaxation when his overbearing brother-in-law (Aykroyd) descends on them with his family. Candy has to cope not only with Aykroyd but also with familiar vacation disasters: runaway water skiis, giant bears, an onslaught of bats, and more. The late John Candy was such an ingratiating actor that he makes nonsense such as this almost palatable. Almost. Annette Bening's film debut.

## Greedy

★★☆ Universal, 1994, c, 110 min. Dir: Jonathan Lynn. SP: Lowell Ganz, Babaloo Mandel. Cast: Michael J. Fox, Kirk Douglas, Nancy Travis, Phil Hartman, Olivia d'Abo, Ed Begley, Jr., Jere Burns, Colleen Camp, Bob Balaban, Joyce Hyser, Austin Pendleton, Mary Ellen Trainor.

It begins marvelously, with the great Jimmy Durante—in person—singing "Inka Dinka Doo," then moves into a deliciously nasty sequence in which the venal McTeague family members rush to pay homage to their rich old Uncle Joe (Douglas). They want to inherit his fortune, and the plot thickens when they bring in a long-absent nephew (Fox), who is a professional bowler in need of money and a decent sort at heart. At some point the screenplay (by the usually reliable Ganz and Mandel) becomes cluttered and incoherent and, although there are a few surprises, the movie loses its spark and sinks like dead weight. Loosely adapted from Charles Dickens's Martin Chuzzlewit.

## Grumpier Old Men

★★☆ Warners, 1995, c, 105 min. Dir: Howard Deutch. SP: Mark Steven Johnson. Cast: Jack Lemmon, Walter Matthau, Sophia Loren, Ann-Margret, Darryl Hannah, Kevin Pollak, Burgess Meredith, Ann Morgan Guilbert.

A followup to Grumpy Old Men and more of the same, with Jack Lemmon and Walter Matthau as Minnesota neighbors who despise each other and spend much of their time exchanging insults. Now their children (Hannah and Pollak) are about to be married. Also, a new woman (Loren) in town is about to replace their beloved bait shop with a restaurant. The impending marriage runs into some snags, Matthau and Loren enter into a love-hate relationship, and the two old geezers continue their bickering. It's all much ado about very little and only occasionally amusing. Burgess Meredith (in his last role) is back as Lemmon's horny old father and provides the only true fun.

## Grumpy Old Men

★★☆ Warners, 1993, c, 104 min. Dir: Donald Petrie. SP: Mark Steven Johnson. Cast: Jack Lemmon, Walter Matthau, Ann-Margret, Burgess Meredith, Ossie Davis, Darryl Hannah, Kevin Pollak, Buck Henry, Christopher McDonald.

By the nineties, Jack Lemmon and Walter Matthau could probably perform their dual antagonistic-friends routine in their sleep, and in The Odd Couple II (1997), they evidently did. Here, they play mateless neighbors and sworn enemies for half a century, living in snowbound Wisconsin and devising childish pranks to upset each other. Their grown children (Hannah and Pollak) are beginning a long-delayed romance. Then along comes the lushly beautiful Ann-Margret, and the two codgers are locked in a battle to win her favor. Their insults and pranks quickly become tiresome, despite the pair's smooth professionalism. Best: Burgess Meredith as Lemmon's horny old father. Wait for his funny outtakes after the movie ends. Sequel: Grumpier Old Men (1995).

## Guess Who's Coming to Dinner

★★★ Columbia, 1967, c, 108 min. Dir: Stanley Kramer. SP: William Rose, b/o his story. Cast: Spencer Tracy, Katharine Hepburn, Sidney Poitier, Katharine Houghton, Cecil Kellaway, Beah Richards, Roy E. Glenn, Isobel Sanford, Virginia Christine.

A rather decorous combination of drawing-room comedy and social commentary, *Guess Who's Coming to Dinner* marked the final teaming of Spencer Tracy and Katharine Hepburn after twenty-five years as the screen's most memorable acting couple. They play a well-heeled San Francisco couple who are startled to learn that their daughter (Houghton) has married a black man (Poitier). Tracy's liberal beliefs are tested, but not very profoundly, since Poitier makes a handsome, accomplished groom. As Tracy's wife, Hepburn gets to shed some tears and display quiet wisdom, all of which won her the Best Actress Oscar. (William Rose also won an Oscar for his screenplay.) Tracy died several weeks after the movie wrapped.

## Happiness

★★★☆ October, 1998, c, 137 min. Dir and SP: Todd Solondz. Cast: Jane Adams, Dylan Baker, Lara Flynn Boyle, Ben Gazzara, Jared Harris, Philip Seymour Hoffman, Cynthia Stevenson, Elizabeth Ashley, Louise Lasser, Camryn Manheim, Rufus Read.

Can a film both amuse and horrify its audience, sometimes simultaneously? This truly disturbing jet-black comedy by the writer-director of *Welcome to the Dollhouse* offers an affirmative answer. The movie focuses on three sisters (Adams, Boyle, and Stevenson), their families, and their acquaintances, all of whom expose the pain, the nastiness, and the destructive, sometimes dangerous sexual hangups lurking behind the ordinary surface of their lives. The movie is exceptionally graphic: characters include a pederast (Baker) posing as a family man, a forlorn overweight woman (Manheim) with a horrible secret, and a compulsive obscene telephone caller (Hoffman). Grim stuff, to be sure, but there's also laughter at the heedless deceptions, betrayals, and obsessions of these secretly desperate people. There's not much happiness in *Happiness*.

## Home Alone

★★★ Fox, 1990, c, 103 min. Dir: Chris Columbus. SP: John Hughes. Cast: Macaulay Culkin, Joe Pesci, Daniel Stern, John Heard, Roberts Blossom, Catherine O'Hara, John Candy, Angela Goethals, Devin Ratray.

This enormously popular comedy has a sure-fire formula: take one resourceful eight-year-old boy (Culkin) who is shunned or neglected by his family. Arrange events so that he finds himself alone in his house with two totally inept thieves (Pesci and Stern). Have him rig up ingenious booby-traps that inflict comic-book pain on the culprits. Season the story with a sugary subplot involving the boy's strange old neighbor (Blossom). How could it miss? It didn't, as children and their parents flocked to the theaters to see it. Young Culkin is adorable, and Pesci and Stern take their punishment like the troupers they are. The violence quotient is high, but few seemed to care. Two sequels, *Home Alone 2: Lost in New York* (1992) and *Home Alone 3* (1997) merely repeated the formula in another setting.

## Home for the Holidays

★★ Paramount, 1995, c, 103 min. Dir: Jodie Foster. SP: W. D. Richter. Cast: Holly Hunter, Robert Downey, Jr., Anne Bancroft, Charles Durning, Dylan McDermott, Geraldine Chaplin, Cynthia Stevenson, Steve Guttenberg, Claire Danes, Austin Pendleton, David Strathairn.

Meet the Dysfunctional Family of the Year—but only at your own risk. Holly Hunter, a suddenly jobless divorcée with a teenage daughter (Danes), returns home for the Thanksgiving holiday to confront her wildly eccentric family: mother (Bancroft) , father (Durning), obnoxious gay brother (Downey), uptight, humorless sister (Stevenson), dippy aunt (Chaplin), and others, all unappealing. Hunter at least finds the promise of romance with Dylan McDermott, a friend of her brother's, who turns out to be heterosexual and available. The crucial Thanksgiving dinner is designed for laughter but most likely it will make you cringe. Actress-turned-director Jodie Foster tries to make it work, but the odds are against her.

## Houseguest

★★ Hollywood, 1995, c, 109 min. Dir: Randall Miller. SP: Michael J. DiGaetano, Lawrence Gay. Cast: Sinbad, Phil Hartman, Jeffrey Jones, Kim Greist, Stan Shaw, Tony Longo, Paul Ben-Victor, Mason Adams, Ron Glass.

There isn't a believable moment in this hectic farce but Sinbad keeps trying—and failing—to make it funny. He plays hustler Kevin Franklin, a man forever looking for the big score. In heavy debt to a mobster, he tries to flee town but at the airport, he is mistaken for the long-time friend of suburbanite Gary Young (Hartman). Somehow he keeps the ruse going, despite his outrageous behavior. Inevitably he straightens out the messy life of Young and his family, while learning about true friendship. Much yelling and screaming, few laughs, and many plugs for MacDonald's.

## I Love You to Death

★★☆ TriStar, 1990, c, 96 min. Dir: Lawrence Kasdan. SP: John Kostmayer. Cast: Kevin Kline, Tracey Ullman, Joan Plowright, River Phoenix, William Hurt, Keanu Reeves.

Kevin Kline is one of the best comic actors in films, but he falters here with an unconvincing Italian accent. He plays Joey Bocca, the Italian owner of a pizza parlor, who cheats regularly on his wife, Rosalie (Ullman). Her ferocious Yugoslavian mother (Plowright, clearly enjoying herself) urges Rosalie to kill him. Most of the movie is given over to their unsuccessful efforts to send him to that big Pizza Parlor in the sky. When they are finally desperate, they hire two inept hit men (Hurt and Reeves). The good cast works hard, mostly in vain, but there are a few laughs.

## The In-Laws

★★★ Warners, 1979, c, 103 min. Dir: Arthur Hiller. SP: Andrew Bergman. Cast: Peter Falk, Alan Arkin, Nancy Dussault, Richard Libertini, Penny Peyser, Arlene Golonka, Michael Lembeck, Ed Begley, Jr.

"There's no reason to shoot at me! I'm a dentist!" Sheldon Kornpett (Arkin) cries as bullets fly in all directions. Unfortunately, Sheldon has become the patsy for Vince (Falk), the over-the-top lunatic whose son (Lembeck) is about to marry Sheldon's daughter (Peyser). Soon Sheldon is involved with Vince, who claims to be with the CIA, in a wild adventure that takes them from Manhattan to a Central American dictatorship. There are some genuine laughs, and Falk and Arkin make a funny team, but some of the action scenes are staged clumsily, and the comedy veers out of control towards the end. Favorite bit: the song repertoire of the firing squad.

## It Takes Two

★★☆ Warners, 1995, c, 101 min. Dir: Andy Tennant. SP: Deborah Dean Davis. Cast: Kirstie Alley, Steve Guttenberg, Mary-Kate and Ashley Olsen, Jane Sibbett, Philip Bosco, Michelle Grison.

Thin, run-of-the-mill family comedy with the Olsen twins (from television's *Full House*) as identical nine-year-old girls who exchange places. Alyssa (Ashley) is a piano prodigy whose father (Guttenberg), a cell phone millionaire, is about to make a bad marriage to a patently awful woman (Sibbett). Amanda (Mary-Kate) is a foul-mouthed orphan whose best friend is Diane (Alley), a big-hearted social worker. A contrived sitcom ploy has the two girls meet and decide to change places. Their scheme: to get rid of Sibbett and replace her with the more suitable Diane. Echoes of *The Prince and the Pauper* and *The Parent Trap* but only mild fun.

## Jingle All the Way

★☆ Fox, 1996, c, 89 min. Dir: Brian Levant. SP: Randy Kornfield. Cast: Arnold Schwarzenegger, Sinbad, Rita Wilson, Phil Hartman, Jake Lloyd, Robert Conrad, Martin Mull, James Belushi.

Imagine Arnold Schwarzenegger as an overworked Minneapolis father who displeases his wife (Wilson) and neglects his young son (Lloyd). The image doesn't gel, and neither does this hectic farce. The slender premise: to appease his unhappy son, Arnold promises to buy him the wildly popular action toy TurboMan for Christmas. The trouble is that the toy is scarce, and everyone is resorting to desperate measures to find one. Arnold's mad scramble results in slapstick mayhem, rarely if ever funny. He is pursued or attacked by everyone, especially an even more desperate father (Sinbad). The preposterous climax finds Arnold (surprise!) impersonating TurboMan in a giant parade. *Jingle All the Way* is dismal all the way.

## Kotch

★★★ Fox, 1971, c, 113 min. Dir: Jack Lemmon. SP: John Paxton. Cast: Walter Matthau, Deborah Winters, Felicia Farr, Charles Aidman, Larry Linville, Darrell Larson.

As a premier acting team, Jack Lemmon and Walter Matthau have persevered over the years, even though their material is becoming frayed. In this comedy-drama, Lemmon is behind the camera as director and Oscar-nominated Matthau plays the elderly Kotch, who refuses to go quietly into retirement. He proves to be more than a match for his psychologist daughter-in-law (Farr) and others. He also finds new meaning in life by helping a young unwed mother (Winters) through her pregnancy. As always a resourceful actor, Matthau still finds it difficult to be entirely convincing as a feisty seventy-year-old—his white hair, for one, seems patently fake—but he gives the role his best effort under Lemmon's easy-going direction.

## Krippendorf's Tribe

★☆ Touchstone, 1998, c, 94 min. Dir: Todd Holland. SP: Charlie Peters, b/o book by Frank Parkin. Cast: Richard Dreyfuss, Jenna Elfman, Natasha Lyonne, Gregory Smith, Carl Michael Lindner, Stephen Root, Elaine Stritch, Tom Poston, David Ogden Stiers, Doris Belack, Lily Tomlin.

Archaeologist James Krippendorf (Dreyfuss) is on the spot. The grant money he was given to uncover a lost New Guinea tribe has vanished—his life fell apart after his wife's death—and now he must not only lecture on the mythical "tribe" but present visual evidence of its existence. What does he do? He enlists his three children in preparing a fake documentary made in his very backyard! Of course, the scheme spirals out of control as he becomes a media celebrity and even has to impersonate one of the "natives." Jenna Elfman is Krippendorf's colleague, who becomes involved in all the plotting. An unworkable premise makes for an unamusing movie that nobody can save.

## Ladybugs

★ Paramount, 1992, c, 89 min. Dir: Sidney J. Furie. SP: Curtis Burch. Cast: Rodney Dangerfield, Jackee, Jonathan Brandis, Ilene Graff, Valerie Shaw, Tom Parks.

In some movies, Rodney Dangerfield's unabashed vulgarity has won laughs. (See *Back to School,* page 143.) Here, however, he's at a loss in a crude, painfully unfunny comedy. He plays a salesman who, in order to get a promotion and please his boss, agrees to coach an all-girl soccer team. He recruits the young son (Brandis) of his fiancée (Graff) to join the team in drag, and you can guess the rest. Dangerfield fires off some of his patented insults and wisecracks, but *Ladybugs* is dead on arrival.

## Leave It to Beaver

★★☆ Universal, 1997, c, 88 min. Dir: Andy Cadiff. SP: Lon Diamond, Brian Levant. Cast: Christopher McDonald, Janine Turner, Erik von Detten, Cameron Finley, Adam Zolotin, Alan Rachins.

A totally innocuous, mildly pleasing version of the popular television series of the late fifties and early sixties. In the squeaky-clean town of Mayfield, time seems to have stood still for the Cleaver family: father Wade (McDonald), mother June (Turner), teenage Wally (von Detten), and especially young "Beaver"

(Finley). The "Beav" has all the troubles: his bike is stolen, he runs the wrong way at a football game, and he gets himself trapped in a gigantic cup of coffee (don't ask). Children under ten might be amused; baby boomers might experience a small amount of nostalgia for television times gone by. And yes, June Cleaver still vacuums her carpet wearing pearls.

## Look Who's Talking

★★☆ TriStar, 1989, c, 90 min. Dir and SP: Amy Heckerling. Cast: John Travolta, Kirstie Alley, Olympia Dukakis, George Segal, Abe Vigoda, voice of Bruce Willis.

Pregnant by her married lover, Albert (Segal), Molly (Alley) is in a quandary after he deserts her. Then she meets nice-guy taxidriver Jimmy (Travolta)—she goes into labor in his cab—and although they are clearly meant for each other, the movie takes Molly through various dilemmas (including the unexpected return of Albert) before she realizes the truth. There's a gimmick: Molly's baby Mickey expresses his thoughts in the smart-alecky voice of Bruce Willis. (He sees Molly's breasts and shouts, "Lunch!") The movie was popular—it had two sequels—but it's only fair, and the extended chase scene near the end is very silly.

## Love Finds Andy Hardy

★★★ MGM, 1938, 90 min. Dir: George B. Seitz. SP: William Ludwig, b/o stories by Vivien R. Bretherton and characters created by Aurania Rouverol. Cast: Mickey Rooney, Lewis Stone, Judy Garland, Ann Rutherford, Sara Haden, Cecilia Parker, Fay Holden, Gene Reynolds, Don Castle.

One of the best entries in the extremely popular series of Hardy family films of the thirties and forties. Audiences responded to the tribulations, usually romantic, of "typical" teenager Andy Hardy (Rooney). Lewis Stone was his understanding father, Judge Hardy, and the others were mother (Holden), sister (Parker), and aunt (Haden). In several of the movies,

Judy Garland was Betsy, his neighbor and "pal," who usually got to sing. Here, Andy gets mixed up with several girls, one of whom is budding starlet Lana Turner. Dated now and excruciatingly sentimental, the series is a fascinating artifact of its time. A number of the films—there were sixteen in all—are available on videocassette.

## Madhouse

★☆ Orion, 1990, c, 90 min. Dir and SP: Tom Ropelawski. Cast: John Larrouquette, Kirstie Alley, Alison LaPlaca, John Diehl, Jessica Lundy, Bradley Gregg, Dennis Miller, Robert Ginty.

With the right material, John Larroquette and Kirstie Alley are expert comic actors. This is not the right material. A comedy of disasters, *Madhouse* is a disaster in itself, frantic and painfully unfunny. Mark and Jessie Bannister (Larroquette and Alley) are happy homeowners until they are invaded by the house guests from hell: his boorish cousins; her rich-bitch sister, who has been thrown out by her husband; and the next-door neighbor and his kids (their house burns down). By the time everything veers out of control, the Bannisters are having nervous breakdowns. Most of the movie's characters seem to be either terminally stupid or seriously deranged, but they are not amusing. Only funny bit: a parody of *The Night of the Living Dead.*

## Major Payne

★★☆ Universal, 1995, c, 97 min. Dir: Nick Castle. SP: Dean Lorey and Damon Wayans. Cast: Damon Wayans, Orlando Brown, Chris Owen, Karyn Parsons, William Hickey.

A standard comedy, given an added bite by the irreverent style of Damon Wayans. He plays a veteran marine who is mustered out of service and can only find a job as the officer in charge of the junior ROTC cadet training corps at a private school in Virginia. The cadets are the usual mixed bag: the fat one, the egghead, the rebel, and so forth. The humor comes when Payne applies his "killing machine" attitude to these kids. Does he soften by the movie's end? You need only one guess. Vaguely based on *The Private War of Major Benson* (1955).

## Man of the House

★★ Disney, 1995, c, 96 min. Dir: James Orr. SP: James Orr, Jim Cruickshank. Cast: Chevy Chase, Jonathan Taylor Thomas, Farrah Fawcett, George Wendt, David Shiner, Art LaFleur, Richard Portnow.

In this mild, predictable comedy, Chevy Chase is in low gear as Jack, a lawyer who is courting Sandra (Fawcett). Sandra's twelve-year-old son Ben (Thomas of TV's *Home Improvement*) dislikes him on sight and schemes to drive him away by humiliating him. His plot involves joining a youth program called the Indian Guides. There's also a dull subplot involving the mob's attempt to kill Chase. Fawcett is appealing as Ben's mother, trying to do the right thing by her son, and George Wendt (Norm of *Cheers*) wins some laughs as an Indian Guides chief, but most of the humor is lame.

## Max Dugan Returns

★★★ Fox, 1983, c, 98 min. Dir: Herbert Ross. SP: Neil Simon. Cast: Marsha Mason, Jason Robards, Matthew Broderick, Donald Sutherland, Dody Goodman, Sal Viscuso, David Morse, Kiefer Sutherland.

Neil Simon's original screenplay is a lightweight, sentimental comedy-drama with a warm feeling but few surprises. Marsha Mason is a teacher and single parent, struggling to make ends meet for herself and her teenage son (Broderick, in his film debut). Then Max Dugan (Robards), the father who deserted her many years earlier, returns to her life. A shady character wanted by both sides of the law, Max tries to make up for the past by showering daughter and grandson with gifts and other amenities. Not surprisingly, he is also fatally ill. Is there a reconciliation? Guess. Mason and Robards perform so expertly that you may not notice that the material is slight and also frayed. Donald Sutherland appears as a policeman who loves Mason.

## Memories of Me

★★☆ MGM, 1988, c, 105 min. Dir: Henry Winkler. SP: Eric Roth, Billy Crystal. Cast: Billy Crystal, Alan King, JoBeth Williams, Janet Carroll, David Ackroyd, Robert Pastorelli, Sidney Miller.

After surgeon Abbie Polin (Crystal) suffers a mild heart attack, he decides to put his life in order by visiting his long-estranged father Abe (King) in Hollywood. Father is the "King of the Hollywood Extras," rowdy, effusive, and not in tune with family life. They quarrel bitterly, until Abe develops a fatal illness. This comedy-drama, cowritten by Crystal, has its effective moments, and King gets some laughs doing his "schtick" but the movie turns mawkish in its later portions, and the inevitable father-son bonding becomes a bit too much. Still, worth viewing, if you can wade through the heavy sentiment.

## Miami Rhapsody

★★★ Hollywood, 1985, c, 95 min. Dir and SP: David Frankel. Cast: Sarah Jessica Parker, Gil Bellows, Antonio Banderas, Mia Farrow, Paul Mazursky, Kevin Pollak, Barbara Garrick, Carla Gugino.

The movie begins with Louis Armstrong singing "Just One of Those Things." Then Sarah Jessica Parker, as Gwyn Marcus, addresses the camera directly, making caustic remarks about herself and her family. By now there is little doubt that we are in Woody Allen Land, where entangled relationships are the norm. Gwyn, it seems, is happily engaged to Matt (Bellows), but then comes a rude shock: both her parents (Mazursky and Farrow), her brother (Pollak), and her sister (Gugino) are all cheating on their spouses! Questioning her own chance at a happy marriage, Gwyn drifts into an affair with her mother's lover (Banderas). Some sharp dialogue and amusing situations keep the movie on a reasonable course, but in the end *Miami Rhapsody* is marked-down Allen.

## The Money Pit

★★ Universal, 1986, c, 91 min. Dir: Richard Benjamin. SP: David Giler. Cast: Tom Hanks, Shelley Long, Alexander Godunov, Maureen Stapleton, Joe Mantegna, Philip Bosco, Josh Mostel.

Loosely derived from *Mr. Blandings Builds His Dream House* (1947) is a prime example of the diminishing returns of nonstop slapstick. Walter (Hanks) is a lawyer; Anne (Long) is a concert violinist whose ex-husband (Godunov) is the orchestra's conductor. Unmarried but on the verge, Walter and Anne buy a house that turns out to be the world's number one lemon. The main staircase collapses into rubble; an electrical fire destroys the kitchen; all the workers are arrogant and/or inept. And that's just the beginning. One catastrophe follows another, leading to a tense relationship, and when Anne seems to have spent the night with her ex, they part company after a singularly stupid argument in front of the workers. Yes, there's a happy ending, if you can last that long.

## Mother

★★★☆ Paramount, 1996, c, 104 min. Dir and SP: Albert Brooks. Cast: Albert Brooks, Debbie Reynolds, Jeff Morrow, Lisa Kudrow, John P. McGinley, Isabel Glaser, Peter White.

Another highly perceptive comedy from Albert Brooks, with some telling commentary on mother-son relationships. Trying to discover why he has failed at personal relationships, twice-divorced science fiction writer John Henderson (Brooks) decides to return home to his roots and to his seemingly sweet but totally exasperating mother, Beatrice (Reynolds). The movie follows mother and son as they make their way through the minefields of a supermarket, a restaurant, and a clothing store. John uncovers the answer to his problem, but he also learns some surprising things about his mother. Reynolds gives a perfectly tuned, Oscar-nominated performance. (Her refrigerator alone is a source of hilarity with its three-year-old cheese and sherbert that tastes "like an orange foot.") A small gem.

## Moving

★★ Warners, 1988, c, 89 min. Dir: Alan Metter. SP: Andy Breckman. Cast: Richard Pryor, Beverly Todd, Randy Quaid, Dave Thomas, Dana Carvey, Stacey Dash, Gordon Jump, Morris Day, Rodney Dangerfield (unbilled).

Richard Pryor is a gifted comedian, but his gifts do not extend to playing a suburban husband and father whose entire life is one endless disaster. (This is Chevy Chase territory.) In *Moving,* Pryor is Arlo Pear, a transportation engineer who must move from New Jersey to Boise, Idaho, to take a new position. From that point, he is assaulted on all sides by the inhabitants of hell: destructive movers, a car driver (Carvey) with multiple personalities, even a daughter (Dash) who uses nasty forms of sabotage to keep him from selling the New Jersey house. Pear finally turns into a gun-toting commando to set things right. Pryor deserves better than this depressing movie.

## Mr. Blandings Builds His Dream House

★★★ RKO, 1948, 94 min. Dir: H. C. Potter. SP: Norman Panama, Melvin Frank, b/o novel by Eric Hodgins. Cast: Cary Grant, Myrna Loy, Melvyn Douglas, Sharyn Moffett, Connie Marshall, Louise Beavers, Reginald Denny, Lurene Tuttle.

A lightweight but entirely genial comedy. Advertising man Jim Blandings (Grant at his drollest) dreams of living in a spacious, beautiful new Connecticut home with his wife (Loy) and daughters (Moffett and Marshall). Alas, his dream turns into a nightmare of well-digging, price-gouging, dreadful weather conditions, and untrustworthy workmen. Eventually he loses his temper and his patience, but wife Loy tries to remain serene through it all. (This was the actress's specialty.) Melvyn Douglas is pleasantly wry as the family lawyer and friend who arouses Blandings's feelings of jealousy. Loosely remade as *The Money Pit* (see page 158).

## Mr. Hobbs Takes a Vacation

★★★ Fox, 1962, c, 116 min. Dir: Henry Koster. SP: Nunnally Johnson, b/o novel by Edward Streeter. Cast: James Stewart, Maureen O'Hara, Fabian, John Saxon, Marie Wilson, Reginald Gardiner, Lauri Peters, John McGiver, Valerie Varda.

An innocuous but genial family comedy, based on a novel by Edward Streeter, who wrote *Father of the Bride.* The hook: Maureen O'Hara convinces husband Jimmy Stewart to spend a month's vacation in an old house on the Pacific coast. They are joined by assorted family members, including two married daughters, sons-in-law, and grandchildren. Can trouble be far behind? The house is crumbling, the daughters have severe marital problems, and Mr. Hobbs himself must prove that he can handle himself in a sailboat. One dilemma or crisis follows another in the perfect order of a television sitcom, but there's no harm done.

## Mr. Mom

★★ Sherwood, 1983, c, 91 min. Dir: Stan Dragoti. SP: John Hughes. Cast: Michael Keaton, Teri Garr, Martin Mull, Ann Jillian, Jeffrey Tambor, Christopher Lloyd, Frederick Koehler, Taliesin Jaffe, Graham Jarvis.

Michael Keaton is a likable actor, but his second film is overrun by a sitcom sensibility that makes it both silly and predictable. He plays Jack Butler, a family man and engineer who is fired from his job and is forced to become a househusband when his wife (Garr) goes to work. Naturally, his life becomes a disaster (all the workmen arrive on the same day, all the appliances explode), while his wife rises in the ranks and is pursued by her amorous boss (Mull). Jack comes off as clumsy beyond belief, and there's a particularly dumb climax involving the usual misunderstandings. One surprise: why this movie didn't turn into a television series.

## Mrs. Doubtfire

★★★ Fox, 1993, 120 min. Dir: Chris Columbus. S: Randi Mayem Singer, Leslie Dixon, b/o novel by Anne Fine. Cast: Robin Williams, Sally Field, Pierce Brosnan, Harvey Fierstein, Polly Holliday, Lisa Jakub, Matthew Lawrence, Mara Wilson.

Robin Williams brings all of his comic zest and ingenuity to *Mrs. Doubtfire,* but the movie still calls for a huge suspension of disbelief. Thrown out of his house by wife Miranda (Field), sweet-natured but giddily irresponsible actor Dan Hillard (Williams) decides to reenter his family by disguising himself as an ample-bosomed, genteel British nanny named Mrs. Doubtfire. Of course his plan goes seriously awry, leading to all sorts of comic consequences. Williams has fun impersonating Mrs. Doubtfire (watch what he does with a vacuum cleaner), even when he is called upon to make improbably rapid costume changes in a restaurant. Harvey Fierstein has some sharp lines as Hillard's makeup-artist brother.

To be able to see his children, divorced father Robin Williams disguises himself as a dowdy British housekeeper named *Mrs. Doubtfire* (1993). Williams's makeup won an Oscar.

# Neighbors

★ Columbia, 1981, c, 94 min. Dir: John G. Avildsen. SP: Larry Gelbart, b/o novel by Thomas Berger. Cast: John Belushi, Dan Aykroyd, Cathy Moriarty, Kathryn Walker, Lauren-Marie Taylor, Tim Kazurinsky.

Talented writer Larry Gelbart is credited as the author of the screenplay, but it's difficult to believe that he could have written this wretched black comedy. Cast against type (this was his last film), John Belushi plays a mousy suburbanite whose life suddenly becomes a waking nightmare when a weird and possibly dangerous couple (Aykroyd and Moriarty) move in next door. The man is an obnoxious boor; the woman seems to be in a state of perpetual sexual heat. In one night, Belushi's life spins out of control, taking bizarre—and wildly incredible—turns until an ending that defies belief. Is the movie intended as a surrealistic comic nightmare? A satire on suburbia? You may not know, and you certainly will not care. In a word, dreadful.

## Nothing in Common

★★☆ TriStar, 1986, c, 118 min. Dir: Garry Marshall. SP: Rick Podell, Michael Preminger. Cast: Tom Hanks, Jackie Gleason, Eva Marie Saint, Sela Ward, Hector Elizondo, Bess Armstrong, Barry Corbin.

Tom Hanks in his preglory days, before *Philadelphia* and *Forrest Gump.* He plays David Basner, a hotshot advertising man whose good, successful life falls into disarray when his parents (Gleason and Saint) separate after thirty-six years of marriage. As he becomes more deeply involved in their lives, his job suffers and he endangers his position. When his father, an overbearing salesman, falls seriously ill, David finally comes to terms with him. A schizophrenic comedy-drama—one movie is a sharp-edged but overly familiar satire of the advertising game; the other is a domestic drama involving three people at odds with each other. The two movies don't really gel, and the ending is awash in phony sentiment. Jackie Gleason's last movie.

# The Odd Couple II

★★ Paramount, 1998, c, 90 min. Dir: Howard Deutch. SP: Neil Simon. Cast: Jack Lemmon, Walter Matthau, Christine Baranski, Barnard Hughes, Jean Smart, Jonathan Silverman, Lisa Waltz, Jay O. Sanders, Mary Beth Piel, Doris Bellack.

"We mix like oil and frozen yogurt." Sound familiar? Yes, Felix and Oscar are back, those battling buddies in Neil Simon's own sequel to his long-lasting play and television series *The Odd Couple.* Seventeen years after their parting, the two are reunited when Felix's daughter (Waltz) is marrying Oscar's son (Silverman). They meet at Los Angeles airport and when their car is destroyed, they begin an adventurous road trek in which they are sprayed by a crop duster, arrested for transporting illegal aliens, and threatened by the husbands of the two women (Baranksi and Smart) they pick up at a bar. Sadly, none of this is funny, and the jokes are mostly tired and lame. Lemmon-and-Matthau is a cherished acting institution by now, but not here.

## Once Around

★★☆ Universal, 1991, c, 115 min. Dir: Lasse Hallström. SP: Malia Scotch Marmo. Cast: Holly Hunter, Richard Dreyfuss, Danny Aiello, Gena Rowlands, Laura San Giacomo, Roxanne Hart, Danton Stone, Tim Guinee, Greg Germann, Griffin Dunne.

Swedish director Lasse Hallström's first American movie (he directed *My Life as a Dog*) is an uneven comedy-drama with a strong cast. Holly Hunter stars as a Boston waitress from a large, close-knit Italian-American family. On a trip to the Caribbean, she meets and marries wealthy, divorced, and obnoxious time-share salesman Richard Dreyfuss and brings him to meet her family. Bad idea. Brash Dreyfuss is regarded as an interloper and soon enough the air is crackling with conflict. An unexpected development turns the story in the direction of tear-jerking drama. As in *Always* (1989), their previous costarring vehicle, Hunter and Dreyfuss do not make a totally believable couple.

# Parenthood

★★★☆ Universal, 1989, c, 124 min. Dir: Ron Howard. SP: Lowell Ganz, Babaloo Mandel, b/o story by Lowell Ganz, Babaloo Mandel, Ron Howard. Cast: Steve Martin, Mary Steenburgen, Dianne Wiest, Rick Moranis, Jason Robards, Tom Hulce, Martha Plimpton, Keanu Reeves, Harley Kozak, Dennis Dugan, Jasen Fisher, Leaf Phoenix.

A rarity: an intelligent screenplay that is both funny and moving on the subject of parenthood. The movie may be cluttered with plotlines but it is also hugely enjoyable as it focuses on Gil Buckman (Martin), husband of Steenburgen and father of three. He has problems with his young son (Fisher), but all the members of his family (father Robards; sisters Wiest and Kozak; brother Hulce) have their own hangups with being a parent. Martin's fantasies about his son are both funny and unsettling, and the movie is studded with well-observed scenes, among them Martin's blunt conversation with his father and Wiest's half-comical, half-desperate dealings with her children. Wiest won a Supporting Oscar for her marvelous performance as a woman trying to cope with adversity.

# The Parent Trap

★★★ Disney, 1998, c, 124 min. Dir: Nancy Meyers. SP: David Swift, Charles Shyer, Nancy Meyers. Cast: Dennis Quaid, Natasha Richardson, Lindsay Lohan, Polly Holliday, Lisa Ann Walter, Joanna Barnes, Simon Kunz, Elaine Hendrix.

An entirely pleasant, if highly fanciful, retread of the popular 1961 comedy that starred Hayley Mills. It's the same cute story of twins (both played by Lohan) who were separated at birth from their divorced parents and who discover each other at a summer camp more than eleven years later. One girl, Hallie, lives in Napa Valley with her father (Quaid), who owns a vineyard. The other, Annie, lives in London with her mother (Richardson), who designs bridal gowns. The girls decide to switch identities and work at reuniting their parents. Quaid and Richardson are appealing as the parents, even when they remain clueless about their daughters's scheming. Good support from Lisa Ann Walter as Quaid's wise-cracking nanny and housekeeper, and by Simon Kunz as Richardson's butler.

# Passed Away

★★★ Hollywood, 1992, c, 96 min. Dir and SP: Charlie Peters. Cast: Bob Hoskins, Blair Brown, Tim Curry, Frances McDormand, William Petersen, Pamela Reed, Peter Riegert, Maureen Stapleton, Nancy Travis, Jack Warden.

When Jack Scanlan (Warden), the head of a large Irish clan, dies suddenly, his family, normally in disarray, falls to pieces as old wounds return and old scores are settled. His older son (Hoskins) dreams of changing his life as he falls for the woman (Travis) he believes to be his father's mistress. One daughter (McDormand), a militant nun in Guatemala, secretly brings home an illegal alien. Another daughter (Reed), a would-be dancer, has never told her parents that she has been divorced for four years. And so it goes. The family chaos culminates in the wake and funeral. A dark comedy with some funny and some uncertain portions, and the good cast keeps it moving along.

# Paulie

★★★☆ Dreamworks SKG, 1998, c, 92 min. Dir: John Roberts. SP: Laurie Craig. Cast: Gena Rowlands, Tony Shalhoub, Cheech Marin, Bruce Davison, Jay Mohr, Buddy Hackett, Hallie Kate Eisenberg.

Paulie is a parrot with the gift of gab. Caged in the dingy basement of a research laboratory, he sounds like a stand-up comedian with attitude as he relates his story to a Russian immigrant (Shalhoub). He tells how he was parted from the little girl (Eisenberg) who loved him, and how he shuttled from owner to owner, including a kindly old widow (Rowlands), the genial owner of a burrito stand (Marin), and a nasty thief (Mohr, who also supplies Paulie's voice). Finally he falls into the clutches of a glory-seeking scientist (Davison). Not to worry—it all ends happily. Paulie's adventures make for a delightful movie, ideal for young viewers and palatable for adults as well.

# Animals Are Funny, Too

Can you name the comedy movie—or series of movies—in which each of the following animals played a prominent role?

1. A leopard

2. A cat named Pyewacket

3. A parrot

4. A dog named Asta

5. A chimpanzee named Cheetah

6. A dog named Wilby Daniels

7. An ape with a British accent

8. A cat called Cat

9. A calf named Norman

10. A horse named High Hat

## Please Don't Eat the Daisies

★★☆ MGM, 1960, c, 111 min. Dir: Charles Walters. SP: Isobel Lennart, b/o book by Jean Kerr. Cast: Doris Day, David Niven, Janis Paige, Spring Byington, Richard Haydn, Patsy Kelly, Jack Weston, Carmen Phillips.

After being pursued and wooed successfully by Clark Gable and Rock Hudson in the late fifties, Doris Day turned to marriage and domesticity with this very loose adaptation of Jean Kerr's book about life with drama critic Walter Kerr and their children. According to the movie, this life was something of a waking nightmare, with rambunctious children, an English sheepdog, and many daffy visitors. Niven and Day play well together as their marriage becomes divisive over Niven's attentions to musical comedy actress Janis Paige as well as Day's attempts to establish her own identity apart from her husband. Amusing enough, but also too much shouting and frantic activity.

## Postcards from the Edge

★★★☆ Columbia, 1990, c, 101 min. Dir: Mike Nichols. SP: Carrie Fisher, b/o her novel. Cast: Meryl Streep, Shirley MacLaine, Dennis Quaid, Gene Hackman, Richard Dreyfuss, Rob Reiner, Mary Wickes, Annette Bening, Conrad Bain, Simon Callow, Gary Morton.

An impressive cast, headed by Shirley MacLaine and Meryl Streep as mother and daughter, plus a scathingly witty screenplay by Carrie Fisher (from her novel), make *Postcards from the Edge* first-rate entertainment. Streep plays a minor film actress with a bad reputation as a cocaine addict. Her mother (MacLaine) is a fading, alcoholic, but still famous movie star. The movie records their lacerating battles, as well as Streep's relationships with other film people in her life, especially her latest lover (Quaid). Streep gets to sing creditably, and MacLaine gives a brave, no-holds-barred performance as pushy Momma. Cheers to wonderful Mary Wickes as MacLaine's salty mother.

## The Ref

★★★ Touchstone, 1994, c, 93 min. Dir: Ted Demme. SP: Richard LaGravanese, Marie Weiss. Cast: Denis Leary, Kevin Spacey, Judy Davis, Robert J. Steinmiller, Jr., Glynis Johns, Raymond J. Barry, Richard Bright, Christine Baranski.

A variation on O'Henry's story "The Ransom of Red Chief," *The Ref* stars standup comic Denis Leary as a cat burglar who kidnaps an affluent Connecticut couple (Spacey and Davis) after an aborted robbery in another house. He gets much more than he bargained for: the couple not only fight continually but they also have despised relatives who arrive for a holiday supper. Before long the exasperated burglar has become the referee in all-out family war. The one resourceful member is the family's young son (Steinmiller), who sets the events in motion. Until the movie runs out of steam, it has a sharp, sarcastic edge and some amusingly dysfunctional characters.

## Richie Rich

★★★ Warners, 1994, c, 95 min. Dir: Donald Petrie. SP: Tom S. Parker, Jim Jennewein, b/o story by Neil Tolkin. Cast: Macaulay Culkin, Edward Herrmann, Christine Ebersole, John Larroquette, Jonathan Hyde, Michael McShane, Stephi Lineburg, Chelcie Ross.

A rarity: a movie for young viewers that is genuinely entertaining. After a string of failures, young Macaulay Culkin found a suitable vehicle in this fanciful adaptation of the comic strip. He plays Richie Rich, the richest boy in the world, whose doting parents (Herrmann and Ebersole) provide him with a life of utmost luxury, while grooming him for "a life of wealth and responsibility." Naturally, there's a villain lurking in the wings, a nasty character named Van Dough (Larroquette) who schemes to dispense with Richie's parents and take over the fortune. Just as naturally, he's foiled by resourceful Richie, his perfect butler (Hyde), his newly made street friends, and others. The climax goes on for too long but the movie is good fare, especially for preteens.

## Say Anything…

★★★ Fox, 1989, c, 100 min. Dir and SP: Cameron Crowe. Cast: John Cusack, Ione Skye, John Mahoney, Lili Taylor, Amy Brooks, Pamela Segall, Jason Gould, Bebe Neuwirth, Eric Stoltz, Joan Cusack (unbilled).

A small but winning comedy with some serious, surprisingly poignant moments. A recent high school graduate who has never been very popular (he is a compulsive talker), Lloyd (Cusack) is madly in love with the class "brain" Diane (Skye). When she agrees to go the graduation dance with him, he is in seventh heaven, vowing to devote the rest of his life to her. Diane has a deeply loving relationship with her divorced father (Mahoney), and when he is charged with embezzlement, her world collapses. Lloyd, however, remains steadfast in his devotion. The movie captures teenage angst with rare perception, and fine actor John Mahoney is especially good as a father whose devotion to his daughter clouds his reason and judgment.

## She's the One

★★☆ Fox Searchlight, 1996, c, 96 min. Dir and SP: Edward Burns. Cast: Jennifer Aniston, Edward Burns, Cameron Diaz, John Mahoney, Mike McGlone, Maxine Bahns, Anita Gillette, Leslie Mann, Frank Vincent.

Edward Burns's second film (his first was the well-received *The Brothers McMullen*) also has an Irish background. Two Fitzpatrick brothers, Francis (McGlone) and Mickey (Burns), live with their father (Mahoney) on a fishing boat in Brooklyn. Francis is a successful Wall Street investor married to Renée (Aniston) but cheating with Mickey's old girlfriend Heather (Diaz). Taxi-driver Mickey has married Hope (Bahns) only a day after meeting her. Problems arise and to round it all off, Daddy Mahoney has his own troubles with his unseen wife. It's a male-dominated society, but the men seem to be totally clueless about their women. *She's the One* is a tepid comedy but Burns gives the story some flavor and his characters are believable.

## Sibling Rivalry

★★ Castle Rock, 1990, c, 89 min. Dir: Carl Reiner. SP: Martha Goldhirsh. Cast: Kirstie Alley, Bill Pullman, Carrie Fisher, Jami Gertz, Scott Bakula, Frances Sternhagen, John Randolph, Paul Benedict, Bill Macy, Matthew Laurence, Sam Elliott, Ed O'Neill.

As an idea, this black comedy might have seemed hilarious. In reality, it is something of a mess. Exasperated by Harry, her inattentive doctor husband (Bakula), Marjorie (a frenetic Alley) indulges in a one-night stand with a man (Elliott) who dies from a heart attack after intercourse and who—get this—turns out to be a brother-in-law she has never met! (He was returning to home and hearth after many years.) Soon, the situation veers out of hand, sweeping with it a shifty blinds salesman (Pullman), Marjorie's younger sister (Gertz), a cop (O'Neill), and Harry's offensive all-doctors family (Randolph, Sternhagen, Laurence, and Fisher). Hapless Alley carries on in a permanent state of galloping hysteria, but nothing much happens.

## Sitting Pretty

★★★ Fox, 1948, 84 min. Dir: Walter Lang. SP: F. Hugh Herbert, b/o novel by Gwen Davenport. Cast: Robert Young, Maureen O'Hara, Clifton Webb, Richard Haydn, Louise Allbritton, Randy Stewart, Ed Begley.

This lightweight domestic comedy brought new fame to Clifton Webb, a Broadway musical star of the early thirties who had created a sensation on screen four years earlier in *Laura*. Here, as Lynn Belvedere, baby-sitter extraordinary and a man of boundless ego and talent, he arrives at the home of Robert Young and Maureen O'Hara and proceeds to confound, outrage, and ultimately delight the couple and their neighbors. It's all airily amusing, and Webb is fun to watch, except that Richard Haydn nearly steals the movie away from him playing a nosy neighbor with a perennially clogged nose. There were two Belvedere sequels, *Mr. Belvedere Goes to College* (1949) and *Mr. Belvedere Rings the Bell* (1951).

# Sixteen Candles

★★★ Universal, 1984, c, 93 min. Dir and SP: John Hughes. Cast: Molly Ringwald, Anthony Michael Hall, Michael Schoeffling, Paul Dooley, Justin Henry, Gedde Watanabe, Blanche Baker, Carlyn Glynn, Edward Andrews, John Cusack, Joan Cusack.

Molly Ringwald is most engaging in this teen comedy from John Hughes. Confronting her mirror, Samantha (Ringwald) remarks, "You need four inches of bod and a great birthday." But on her sixteenth birthday, nobody remembers to congratulate her, since they are all wrapped up in her older sister's wedding. And worse, Sam is secretly (and agonizingly) in love with Jake Ryan (Schoeffling), never suspecting that he is already attracted to her. John Michael Hall is funny as "the Geek," the would-be swinger who adores Sam. Some portions do not ring true, and the movie skids out of control toward the end, but along the way, there are amusing moments. (Catch the stag line at the dance, looking like a police lineup.)

# Slums of Beverly Hills

★★★ Fox Searchlight, 1998, c, 91 min. Dir and SP: Tamara Jenkins. Cast: Alan Arkin, Natasha Lyonne, Marisa Tomei, Kevin Corrigan, Carl Reiner, Rita Moreno, David Krumholtz, Jessica Walter, Eli Marienthal.

A quirky, often on-target, but uneven comedy-drama about a dysfunctional family at large in Beverly Hills in 1976. Teenage Vivian (Lyonne) is the narrator, describing her nomadic life with her eccentric, overbearing father (Arkin) and her two siblings (Krumholtz and Marienthal) as they move from one tacky apartment to another. Their life is shaken up when they are joined by Arkin's drugged-out, unmanageable niece Rita (Tomei). Lyonne is outstanding as Vivian, blending exasperation and sadness as she tries to cope with her family's crackpot behavior, while also dealing with her own growing sexual awareness. (Her concern with her breast size leads to several funny scenes.) A promising debut for writer-director Tamara Jenkins.

# So Fine

★★☆ Warners, 1981, c, 91 min. Dir and SP: Andrew Bergman. Cast: Ryan O'Neal, Jack Warden, Mariangela Melato, Richard Kiel, Fred Gwynne, Mike Kellin, David Rounds.

Writer Andrew Bergman's first movie as writer-director is a very mixed bag, sometimes funny but more often absurd, yet not in a good way. Ryan O'Neal is a college professor of English and the son of New York City garment manufacturer Jack Warden, who is deeply in debt. O'Neal is forced to join his father's business, where he inadvertently creates the see-through jeans that become a sensation. He also becomes involved with the amorous Italian wife (Melato) of Warden's biggest (in both senses) and most dangerous client (Kiel). *So Fine* has some extraordinarily silly scenes, none more so than the climactic brouhaha at the opera, which even steals from the Marx Brothers.

# Some Kind of Wonderful

★★★ Paramount, 1987, c, 93 min. Dir: Howard Deutch. SP: John Hughes. Cast: Eric Stoltz, Lea Thompson, Mary Stuart Masterson, John Ashton, Craig Sheffer, Elias Koteas, Molly Hagan.

In his eighties films, such as *Sixteen Candles* (1984) and *Prettty in Pink* (1986), producer-writer John Hughes had a way of zeroing in on the day-to-day dilemmas and hangups of teenagers. This time Keith (Stoltz), a high school outsider who would like to be an artist, yearns for Amanda (Thompson), the school's unattainable sexpot. At the same time, tomboy Watts (Masterson), Keith's best pal, has a sizable crush on him. Will the pieces fall into place and will Keith come to realize that Watts is the right girl for him? You can bet on it. Pleasant teen comedy, adroitly directed by Howard Deutch, who also directed *Pretty in Pink.*

# Stuart Saves His Family

★☆ Paramount, 1995, c, 95 min. Dir: Harold Ramis. SP: Al Franken, b/o his book. Cast: Al Franken, Laura San

Giacomo, Vincent D'Onofrio, Shirley Knight, Harris Yulin, Lesley Boone, Julia Sweeney.

An alleged comedy, but where are the laughs? Al Franken recreates the character of Stuart Smiley he plays on "Saturday Night Live": a self-styled guru of "affirmation" whose mantra is "I'm good enough. I'm smart enough. And doggonit, people *like* me!" After he is fired from his cable TV program, ever-smiling Stuart has to cope with his severely dysfunctional family, including alcoholic Dad (Yulin), compliant but desperately unhappy Mom (Knight), overeating sister Jody (Boone), and pot-smoking brother Donny (D'Onofrio). Dreary stuff, but remember, "It is easier to put on slippers than to carpet the whole world."

## The Stupids

★★ New Line, 1996, c, 94 min. Dir: John Landis. SP: Brent Forrester, b/o characters created by Harry Allard, James Marshall. Cast: Tom Arnold, Jessica Lundy, Bug Hall, Alex McKenna, Mark Metcalf, Matt Keeslar, Frankie Faison, Christopher Lee.

A movie whose title practically invites sarcasm, *The Stupids* is based on a series of children's books by Harry Allard and James Marshall. It is built around the adventures of the Stupid family: dad Stanley (Arnold), mom Joan (Lundy), and their two children (Hall and McKenna), all of whom are too dumb to function in the real world. Idiotic Stanley, wondering why his garbage disappears every night, gets involved in a scheme to sell military hardware to some international villains. There's more plot, but it's all in the service of jokes about the Stupids' stupidity. (Stanley cannot even start his car. The family thinks that an elevator is a time machine, and so on and so on). Yes, that is Bob ("Captain Kangaroo") Keeshan in a cameo, and there are other cameos by famed directors.

## Summer Rental

★★☆ Paramount, 1985, c, 87 min. Dir: Carl Reiner. SP: Mark Reisman, Jeremy Stevens. Cast: John Candy, Karen Austin, Richard Crenna, Rip Torn, John Larroquette, Kerri Green, Joey Lawrence, Aubrey Jene.

An entirely predictable but genial comedy starring John Candy as Jack Chester, who brings his wife and three children to a vacation in Citrus Cove, Florida. Not surprisingly, one disaster follows another, as Jack invades the wrong rental house, gets badly sunburned, and arouses the ire of the local bigwig (Crenna). He strikes up a friendship with a crusty boat owner (Torn), who teaches him how to sail. Inevitably, he regains his family's respect and admiration by sailing Torn's boat to victory over Crenna in the all-important regatta. Every situation is telegraphed in advance, but Candy carries it all off with ease. He was a likable comic actor whose ample presence will be missed.

## That's Life!

★★★ Columbia, 1986, c, 102 min. Dir: Blake Edwards. SP: Milton Wexler, Blake Edwards. Cast: Jack Lemmon, Julie Andrews, Sally Kellerman, Robert Loggia, Jennifer Edwards, Rob Knepper, Matt Lattanzi, Chris Lemmon, Cynthia Sykes, Emma Walton, Felicia Farr.

Architect Harvey Fairchild (Lemmon) is turning sixty and falling apart. A neurotic hypochondriac, he is making life miserable for himself and his family, each of whom is beset with his or her own problems. His wife, Gillian (Andrews), a famous singer, is terrified that she may have throat cancer. Harvey's life disintegrates as he seeks help and/or consolation in places that turn out to be either wrong or surprising. An uneven mixture of comedy and drama, *That's Life!* has some telling moments (mainly contributed by Andrews in a perfectly judged performance) but there are trying moments as well. (Lemmon delivering an agonized address on adultery to his church congregation, while he suffers from a badly itching case of crabs, is not hilarious.) For all its lapses, the movie is the best of the Andrews-Edwards collaborations *(S.O.B, 10, Victor/Victoria).*

## This Is My Life

★★★ Fox, 1992, c, 105 min. Dir: Nora Ephron. SP: Nora Ephron, Delia Ephron, b/o novel by Meg Wolitzer. Cast: Julie Kavner, Dan Aykroyd, Samanta Mathis, Gaby Hoffmann, Carrie Fisher, Danny Zorn.

The best thing about this movie is that it gives a starring role to Julie Kavner, the talented actress who played Rhoda's sister Brenda on the long-running sitcom, and who capably supported Woody Allen and others in a number of comedy films. Here Kavner plays Dottie, single mother to two children—teenage Erica (Mathis) and ten-year-old Opal (Hoffmann). Mother is driven to be a stand-up comedian, and when her career takes off, the girls become bitterly resentful. Dottie resolves the problem, but not until after some emotional scenes. *This Is My Life* is a modest comedy-drama, though Julie Kavner infuses it with her own warmth and believability.

## Three Men and a Baby

★★★ Touchstone, 1987, c, 102 min. Dir: Leonard Nimoy, SP: James Orr, Jim Cruikshank, b/o screenplay by Coline Serreau. Cast: Tom Selleck, Ted Danson, Steve Guttenberg, Margaret Colin, Nancy Travis, Celeste Holm, Philip Bosco, Cynthia Harris, Lisa Blair, Michelle Blair.

An amiable but thoroughly contrived comedy, based on the hit French film *Three Men and a Cradle*. Architect Peter (Selleck), actor Jack (Danson), and commercial artist Michael (Guttenberg) are swinging bachelors who are suddenly saddled with an infant that appears to be Jack's by way of Stella (Travis). The problem is that the expected "package" was not the baby at all but a shipment of heroin left for Jack's safekeeping. Soon the men are being badgered by both hoodlums and police, while simultaneously trying to cope with the baby's needs. Surprise! They become sentimentally attached to the baby. The bachelor-and-baby jokes are predictable, but the movie is harmless fun. The sequel was *Three Men and a Little Lady* (1990).

## True Love

★★★ MGM/UA, 1989, c, 104 min. Dir: Nancy Savoca. SP: Nancy Savoca, Richard Guay. Cast: Annabella Sciorra, Ron Eldard, Kelly Cinnante, Star Jasper, Aida Turturro, Roger Rignack, Michael J. Wolfe.

A small film but funny, pungent, and revealing, *True Love* records the brouhaha surrounding an Italian-American marriage, only days before the event. Donna (Sciorra) and Michael (Eldard) are in love, but as friends and family swirl around them, they begin to have severe doubts. Michael, in particular, is unable to separate himself from his friends of long standing, and his feelings create a crisis at the wedding. At the end, the photograph of the bride and groom shows them looking wary and unsettled. A flavorsome comedy, with serious overtones.

## Uncle Buck

★★☆ Universal, 1989, c, 100 min. Dir and SP: John Hughes. Cast: John Candy, Amy Madigan, Jean Louisa Kelly, Gaby Hoffmann, Macaulay Culkin, Elaine Bronka, Garrett M. Brown, Laurie Metcalf.

Meet Buck Russell (Candy), rotund, slovenly, and slightly outrageous. He is not the person one would hire as a baby-sitter, but a family crisis forces him to care for his two nieces and a nephew. Soon he is dealing with his niece's unsavory suitor, dressing down the other niece's vice principal for calling her "a bad egg," and in general taking charge of things in his own way. Eventually, Uncle Buck goes from carefree bachelor to responsible adult. John Candy seldom found a vehicle worthy of his comic style, but his affable persona brightened many movies, including this standard John Hughes entry. Macaulay Culkin plays his nephew, only a year before winning success as the unflappable boy of *Home Alone*.

## A Wedding

★★☆ Fox, 1978, c, 125 min. Dir: Robert Altman. SP: John Considine, Patricia Resnick, Allan Nicholls, Robert Altman, b/o story by Robert Altman, John Considine. Cast: Carol

Burnett, Mia Farrow, Lillian Gish, Nina Van Pallandt, Vittorio Gassman, Desi Arnaz, Jr., Dina Merrill, Pat McCormick, Howard Duff, John Cromwell, Geraldine Chaplin, Lauren Hutton, Viveca Lindfors.

A director with some distinguished credits. A cast of proven talents. Then what went seriously wrong? Another of Robert Altman's "mosaic" movies, in which many small pieces come together to form an overall pattern, this very dark comedy records a nuptial ceremony and the mostly disastrous events and shocking revelations that surround it. Before the afternoon ends, we are given glimpses of nymphomania, drug addiction, lesbianism, infidelity, assault and battery, and more. Everyone works hard, but oddly enough, the actor who fares best is venerable Lillian Gish, who plays the matriarch of the bridegroom's family, lying ill in an upstairs room. She dies long before this hectic movie ends, but hardly anyone seems to notice.

## Welcome to the Dollhouse

★★★☆ Suburban, 1995, c, 87 min. Dir and SP: Todd Solondz. Cast: Heather Matarazzo, Brendan Sexton III, Angela Pietropinto, Daria Kalinina, Matthew Faber, Eric Mabius, Bill Buell.

*Welcome to the Dollhouse* is one of the most savagely funny, perceptive views of early-teen angst you are likely to see. Dawn Wiener (Matarazzo) is a bright but homely seventh-grader whose life is hell. Ignored by her family and treated brutally by her classmates, Dawn agonizes over her lack of popularity, while becoming aware of her budding sexuality. The movie is dead-on accurate in its depiction of preteen misery, losing its footing only toward the end when it introduces a bit of melodrama by having Dawn's younger sister kidnapped. Most memorable scene: Dawn meets with Brandon (Sexton), the boy who has threatened to "rape" her but who in reality is dealing with his own burgeoning feelings of rejection and despair.

## What About Bob?

★★★ Touchstone, 1991, c, 99 min. Dir: Frank Oz. SP: Tom Schulman, b/o story by Alvin Sargent, Laura Ziskin. Cast: Bill Murray, Richard Dreyfuss, Julie Hagerty, Charlie Korsmo, Kathryn Erbe, Tom Aldredge, Susan Willis, Roger Bowen, Doris Belack.

Turned a few notches in another direction, *What About Bob?* might have qualified as a psychological thriller rather than a dark comedy. A world-class neurotic, riddled with every variety of mental ailment, Bob (Murray) latches on to his hapless psychiatrist Dr. Leo Marvin (Dreyfuss) at his vacation home and refuses to leave. Dr. Marvin's family finds Bob endearing, while the doctor becomes increasingly deranged by his unwanted "guest." Eventually, he is plotting Bob's demise. The premise may be disturbing but wisely Dr. Marvin is portrayed as a bit of an egotistical fool so that his comeuppance at the hands of his seriously disturbed patient seems almost deserved. The irritation factor in Bill Murray's performances is carried to the breaking point in this movie.

## Wide Awake

★★☆ Miramax, 1998, c, 90 min. Dir and SP: M. Night Shyamalan. Cast: Denis Leary, Dana Delany, Robert Loggia, Joseph Cross, Camryn Manheim, Dan Lauria, Rosie O'Donnell.

A well-intentioned, sweetly sentimental comedy-drama, *Wide Awake* is no prize winner but it's not as bad as its hostile reviews would indicate. Joshua Beal (Cross) is a sensitive ten-year-old boy living outside Philadelphia. When his beloved grandfather (Loggia) dies, Joshua begins a mission: to find God so that he can learn how Grandpa is faring in heaven. In carrying out his mission, he learns a few home truths about life, death, religion, and football. Joshua is much too articulate for his age, and the movie gets very sticky, especially towards the end, but there are some nice moments. Rosie O'Donnell plays a cheery nun at Joshua's school.

## With Six You Get Eggroll

★★☆ National General, 1968, c, 95 min. Dir: Howard Morris. SP: Gwen Bagni, Paul Dubov, Harvey Bullock, R. S. Allen, b/o story by Gwen Bagni, Paul Dubov. Cast: Doris Day, Brian Keith, Pat Carroll, Barbara Hershey, George Carlin, Alice Ghostley, John Findlater, Jimmy Bracken.

Doris Day's last film to date is a run-of-the-mill family comedy. No longer quite so perky, she plays a middle-aged widow with three sons who marries a middle-aged widower (Keith) with a daughter. If you have seen this situation before in any one of countless films, you know what to expect: the children disrupt their conjugal bliss in innocent and not-so-innocent ways, leaving mom and pop forced to make love in an automobile. By film's end, everything is just fine, thank you. By this time, Day's genuine talent for comedy had been chipped away by too many untaxing roles such as this, and she was probably wise to call it quits.

## Yours, Mine, and Ours

★★☆ United Artists, 1968, c, 111 min. Dir: Melville Shavelson. SP: Melville Shavelson, Mort Lachman, b/o story by Madelyn Davis, Bob Carroll, Jr. Cast: Lucille Ball, Henry Fonda, Van Johnson, Tom Bosley, Tim Matheson, Jennifer Leak, Kevin Burchett.

This domestic comedy should give you either a few laughs or a splitting headache. The situation: naval officer Frank Beardsley (Fonda), a widower with ten children, falls in love with Helen North (Ball), a widow with eight children. After an attenuated period in which they try coyly to keep their progeny a secret, the two marry. Can you guess the rest? The children oppose their parents's union in every way they can, and nobody seems to notice that they are simply obnoxious. Lucille Ball is, of course, an able comic actress (she has a good drunk scene), but even she can't make the material palatable. Henry Fonda is game, trying hard not to look too foolish under the circumstances. Tom Bosley makes a brief, funny appearance as a bewildered doctor.

# Slings and Arrows: Satirical Comedies

Playwright George S. Kaufman was reputed to have said that satire is what closes on Saturday night. If so, movies have ignored his remark by producing a sizable number of spoofs, send-ups, and take-offs that poke malicious fun at various film genres or at the never-ending absurdity of human behavior. Whether you respond to the sheer wackiness of *Airplane!* or the tweaking of media frenzy in *Being There,* satirical comedies are here for your perusal.

## The Adventure of Sherlock Holmes' Smarter Brother

★★★ Fox, 1975, c, 91 min. Dir and SP: Gene Wilder. Cast: Gene Wilder, Madeline Kahn, Marty Feldman, Leo McKern, Dom DeLuise, Roy Kinnear, John LeMesurier.

Gene Wilder's first film as triple threat writer, director, and star obviously emulates Mel Brooks in its broad, hit-and-miss spoof of the Sherlock Holmes movies. Wilder is Sigerson Holmes, the famed detective's younger brother, who gets involved in a case concerning one of those "documents" that threatens the British Empire. The "plot" scarcely matters; the movie is a sometimes funny, sometimes forced series of gags, non sequiturs, slapstick chases, and the like. Walleyed British comedian Marty Feldman gets many of the laughs as Holmes's sidekick, and so does Dom DeLuise as an opera star with the usual boundless ego. And let us not forget the dance called the Kangeroo Hop.

## Airplane!

★★★ Paramount, 1980, c, 96 min. Dir and SP: Jim Abrahams, Jerry Zucker, David Zucker. Cast: Robert Hays, Julie Hagerty, Robert Stack, Lloyd Bridges, Leslie Nielsen, Peter Graves, Kareem Abdul-Jabbar, Lorna Patterson, Stephen Stucker.

Stay with this spoof of in-flight disaster movies, and you'll probably find yourself laughing uproariously, even against your better judgment. The writer-directors are shameless in their use of puns, sight gags, parodies, and wordplays, and surprisingly, many of them work. *Airplane!* was suggested by *Zero Hour,* a serious 1957 movie in which the crew of a plane is felled by food poisoning. Here the poisoning encompasses many of the passengers. Some of the actors have fun spoofing the sort of roles they played in earlier years: Robert Stack as a hotshot pilot with more sunglasses than he needs; Leslie Nielsen as a thick-skulled doctor. Robert Hays is the traumatized ex-pilot who is forced to take over for the poisoned crew. *Airplane II: The Sequel* turned up in 1982.

## An Alan Smithee Film Burn Hollywood Burn

★ Hollywood, 1998, c, 86 min. Dir: Alan Smithee. SP: Joe Eszterhas. Cast: Ryan O'Neal, Eric Idle, Coolio, Chuck D, Richard Jeni, Leslie Stefanson. Guest stars: Whoopi Goldberg, Sylvester Stallone, Jackie Chan.

Try to follow this: "Alan Smithee" is the pseudonym that a studio will use on a film's credits if the original director insists on having his name removed. In the case of this hideous movie, director Arthur Hiller refused to be associated with the product. Ah, but there's more. In the movie, the director (Idle) so loathes what the studio has done to his movie that he steals the print and destroys it. He would have his name deleted, except that his name *is* Alan Smithee! Made as a mock documentary and intended as blistering satire of Hollywood filmmakers, this movie is somewhere beyond awful, an embarrassment to everyone involved, especially its writer, Joe Eszterhas. Many real-life people appear as themselves. Why did they agree to participate?

## The Americanization of Emily

★★★☆ MGM, 1964, 117 min. Dir: Arthur Hiller. SP: Paddy Chayefsky, b/o novel by William Bradford Huie. Cast: James Garner, Julie Andrews, Melvyn Douglas, James Coburn, Joyce Grenfell, Keenan Wynn, Judy Carne, Liz Fraser, Edward Binns, William Windom.

A scathing satirical view of wartime attitudes and behavior, Paddy Chayefsky's screenplay centers on naval officer Charlie Madison (Garner), a wheeler-dealer and self-professed coward who avoids combat by attending to the needs of his admiral (Douglas). Charlie also believes that we "perpetuate war by exalting its sacrifices." Then he meets and falls for war widow Julie Andrews, whose ideas are opposed to his. There are further complications precipitated by the loony admiral. Like Chayefsky's later screenplays *(Network, The Hospital)*, *The Americanization of Emily* is both funny and serious—and also provocative.

## Article 99

★★☆ Orion, 1992, c, 99 min. Dir: Howard Deutch. SP: Ron Cutler. Cast: Ray Liotta, Kiefer Sutherland, Forest Whitaker, Kathy Baker, John Mahoney, Keith David, Eli Wallach, Noble Willingham, Julie Bovasso, Lynn Thigpen, Jeffrey Tambor.

Another well-intentioned but unsuccessful attempt to match the *M\*A\*S\*H* combination of gritty drama and irreverent farce, this one set in a Veterans Administration hospital. As overworked doctors try to treat the war wounded, they are met with meager supplies, corrupt or incompetent superiors, and moun-

tains of red tape. Ray Liotta plays the unofficial head of the beleaguered doctors; Kiefer Sutherland is the new doctor on the scene, and together they wage war against the hostile administration. It all gets out of control in a mostly heavy-handed movie. "Article 99" refers to a fictitious VA regulation that disqualifies veterans for medical benefits if "their diagnosed condition cannot be specifically related to military service."

## The Associate

★★☆ Hollywood, 1996, c, 113 min. Dir: Donald Petrie. SP: Nick Thiel. Cast: Whoopi Goldberg, Dianne Wiest, Eli Wallach, Timothy Daly, Bebe Neuwirth, Austin Pendleton, Lainie Kazan.

Whoopi Goldberg is Laurel Ayres, a highly regarded analyst at a Wall Street corporation. When a conniving rival (Daly) gets the promotion she deserves, she decides to start her own business. And when she learns that the big shots want to deal only with men, she re-creates herself as a powerful partner named Robert S. Cutty—and her business booms. Of course, she eventually has to impersonate the mysterious Cutty. Goldberg is always fun to watch, but the movie deteriorates somewhere at midpoint and never recovers. (In white makeup as Cutty, Goldberg resembles an embalmed cadaver.) Still, it's a pleasure to watch Dianne Wiest as Laurel's frumpy but wise assistant, and her scenes with Goldberg are the best in the movie. A remake of the 1979 French film *L'Associe.*

## Austin Powers: International Man of Mystery

★★ New Line, 1997, c, 95 min. Dir: Jay Roach. SP: Mike Myers. Cast: Mike Myers, Elizabeth Hurley, Michael York, Mimi Rogers, Robert Wagner, Seth Green.

Conceivably there are preteens who will find this spoof of the James Bond films excruciatingly funny; most others will find it merely excruciating. Mike Myers (who also wrote the screenplay) stars as Austin Powers, a flamboyantly garbed secret agent and notorious "swinger" who is cryogenically frozen in 1967 and wakes up to a brand-new world in 1997. His archenemy Dr. Evil (Myers again) has also been frozen and wakes up at the same time with a plan to destroy the world. The joke, of course, is that both men haven't a clue about life in the nineties. The take-off on James Bond gimmickry is occasionally clever, but too much of the humor is of the crude, snickering variety. By the time it's half over, you may grow weary of Austin Powers's smirking face and bad teeth. Sequel: *Austin Powers: The Spy Who Shagged Me* (1999).

## Beat the Devil

★★★ United Artists, 1954, 89 min. Dir: John Huston. SP: Truman Capote, b/o novel by James Helvick. Cast: Humphrey Bogart, Jennifer Jones, Gina Lollobrigida, Robert Morley, Peter Lorre, Edward Underdown, Ivor Bernard, Marco Tulli.

This quirky satire became a cult favorite after its release, but its reputation is not entirely warranted. A sly and sometimes funny take-off on *The Maltese Falcon* and other nest-of-vipers movies, *Beat the Devil* focuses on a group of eccentric thieves who are scheming to gain hold of uranium-rich land in East Africa. Humphrey Bogart is their free-lance partner in crime, and the group is headed by Robert Morley as a falsely jovial fat man not unlike Sydney Greenstreet. Their scheme goes awry when they meet phony British aristocrat Edward Underdown and his wife, Jennifer Jones, who happens to be a compulsive liar. The production is surprisingly awkward, but much of the offbeat dialogue should surprise you into laughter.

## Being There

★★★ United Artists, 1979, c, 130 min. Dir: Hal Ashby. SP: Jerzy Kosinski, b/o his story. Cast: Peter Sellers, Shirley MacLaine, Melvyn Douglas, Jack Warden, Richard Dysart, Richard Basehart, James Noble, David Clennon.

A one-note satirical comedy, but the note is definitely clever, and Peter Sellers is outstanding in his penultimate, Oscar-nominated role. He plays Chance, a retarded gardener who lives in a world of his own where the only things he knows are his job and whatever he sees on television. When his employer dies, Chance is cast into the world of Washington, D.C., where he ends up living in the home of a dying financier (Douglas) and his wife (MacLaine). Soon, Chance's meaningless remarks are interpreted as profoundly wise, and he becomes not only a media celebrity but also a sounding board for policymakers. MacLaine regards him as a chance for sexual fulfillment. *Being There* mocks America's obsession with the media, and the tendency of Americans to take any pronouncement in print or on television as the gospel truth. But once the point has been made, the joke about fool-turned-prophet begins to wear thin. In his final role, Douglas won a Supporting Oscar.

## The Big Picture

★★★ Columbia, 1989, c, 100 min. Dir: Christopher Guest. SP: Christopher Guest, Michael Varhol, Michael McKean, b/o story by Michael Varhol, Christopher Guest. Cast: Kevin Bacon, Emily Longstreth, J. T. Walsh, Jennifer Jason Leigh, Michael McKean, Teri Hatcher, Jason Gould.

An unbilled Martin Short, playing an off-the-wall Hollywood agent, wins the biggest laughs in this satirical comedy. As usual with satire, there are hits and misses, but surprisingly, the movie finds the target much of the time. Kevin Bacon stars as an aspiring young filmmaker whose chance to make a movie gradually disappears as he confronts various odd, self-serving Hollywood types. *The Big Picture* opens with a funny parody of student filmmakers, and there are clever bits in which Bacon fantasizes about his life and work. The late character actor J. T. Walsh excels as a producer who blusters his way in and out of the business. Look for Eddie Albert, Roddy McDowall, Elliott Gould, June Lockhart, and Fran Drescher in unbilled cameo roles.

# The Black Bird

★★ Columbia, 1975, c, 98 min. Dir and SP: David Giler. Cast: George Segal, Stephane Audran, Lionel Stander, Lee Patrick, Elisha Cook, Jr., Felix Silla, Signe Hasso.

The one small pleasure provided by this weak spoof of *The Maltese Falcon* is seeing Lee Patrick and Elisha Cook, Jr., repeating their original roles in the classic film. George Segal stars as a pale shadow of his famous detective-father, Sam Spade. Somehow the original falcon statue is still in the vicinity, and those attempting to seize the black bird include a midget Nazi, four Hawaiian gangsters, and an elegant woman (Audran) who lives in the basement of a church. Very little amusement here, but it's good to see veteran actor Lionel Stander as Andrew Jackson Immelman, a tough yet gentlemanly assistant to Spade, clad in a green plaid suit.

# Bombshell

★★★☆ MGM, 1933, 95 min. Dir: Victor Fleming. SP: Jules Furthman, John Lee Mahin, b/o play by Caroline Francke and Mack Crane. Cast: Jean Harlow, Lee Tracy, Frank Morgan, Franchot Tone, Pat O'Brien, Una Merkel, C. Aubrey Smith, Ted Healy, Ivan Lebedeff.

Good comedies that spoof Hollywood are rare, and *Bombshell* is one of the best: an uproarious take-off on the movie capital's crackpot world in the 1930s. Jean Harlow is clearly having a field day as Lola Burns, a temperamental film star who is constantly being entangled in scandals perpetrated by her agent, Space Hanlon (Tracy). Hanlon thwarts her plans to adopt a baby and also involves her in a bogus romance with an actor (Tone) impersonating a Boston scion. The wisecracks never cease, and many of them are funny. Lola is so steeped in movie illusion that she responds to Tone's ardent lovemaking by exclaiming, "Not even Norma Shearer or Helen Hayes in their nicest pictures were ever spoken to like this!"

# The Brady Bunch Movie

★★★ Paramount, 1992, c, 90 min. Dir: Betty Thomas. SP: Laurice Elehwany, Rick Copp, Bonnie Turner, Terry Turner. Cast: Shelley Long, Gary Cole, Michael McKean, Jean Smart, Henriette Mantel, Christopher Daniel Barnes, Christine Taylor, Paul Sutera, Jennifer Elise Cox, Jesse Lee, Olivia Hack, Reni Santoni.

This is the joke: the Brady bunch, that bland band of two joined families that kept its popularity on television for five years (1969–74), is now living in a time warp. While the rude, crude nineties swirl around them, the Bradys exist in a squeaky-clean, excruciatingly nice world, apparently oblivious to crime, ugliness, or toilets. There's a plot of sorts: the Brady house will be auctioned off unless Mike Brady (Cole) can pay $20,000 in property taxes, and their nasty next-door neighbor (McKean) has plans to raze their neighborhood. But mostly there are mildly satirical jokes aimed at the contrast of the clueless Bradys with the nineties. Innocuous but fairly agreeable entertainment; *A Very Brady Sequel* followed in 1996.

# The 'Burbs

★★ Universal, 1989, c, 103 min. Dir: Joe Dante. SP: Dana Olsen. Cast: Tom Hanks, Carrie Fisher, Bruce Dern, Rick Ducommun, Corey Feldman, Wendy Schaal, Henry Gibson, Brother Theodore, Gale Gordon.

Tom Hanks is indisputably one of the best actors of this generation, but he would do well to delete this film from his list of credits. Presumably a skewered, satirical view of life in suburbia, *The 'Burbs* has Hanks as Ray, a married suburbanite who comes to believe that his strange, secretive next-door neighbors are evil murderers concealing dark and terrible secrets. He is encouraged by neighbors (Dern and Ducommun) who are clearly not playing with a full deck. Their attempts to expose the villains lead inevitably to disaster, but there is a preposterous surprise ending. One prolonged joke does not make a movie.

# Cabin Boy

★ Touchstone, 1994, c, 80 min. Dir: Adam Resnick. SP: Adam Resnick, b/o story by Chris Elliott. Cast: Chris Elliott, Rich Brinkley, James Gammon, Brian Doyle-Murray, Ann Magnuson, Russ Tamblyn, Ricki Lake.

Lee Marvin won an Academy Award for playing a dual role in the Western spoof *Cat Ballou* (1965). Here he's the drunken Kid Sheleen, shaky gun at the ready. Jane Fonda is schoolmarm-turned-outlaw Cat Ballou.

A wretched comedy that might be taken as a spoof of *Captains Courageous,* but then why would anyone want to satirize that old chestnut? The insufferable Chris Elliott stars as Nathanial Mayweather, a rich, obnoxious student at a finishing school for "Fancy Boys" who accidentally finds himself on a grungy fishing boat called *The Filthy Whore* rather than aboard a luxury ship bound for Hawaii. He (and the helpless viewers) must endure various indignities until the boat ventures into a fantasyland called Hell's Bucket, populated with sea monsters and other creatures, all pitifully unconvincing. David Letterman makes an unbilled guest appearance as an old salt in a fishing village.

## Carbon Copy

★★ RKO/Hemdale, 1981, c, 92 min. Dir: Michael Schultz. SP: Stanley Shapiro. Cast: George Segal, Denzel Washington, Jack Warden, Susan Saint James, Dick Martin, Paul Winfield, Tom Poston.

Walter Whitney (Segal), Jewish by birth, has concealed his identity and become a top executive in his father-in-law's company. Then, to his shock and dismay, he learns that he has a black illegitimate son named Roger (Washington, in his film debut). Soon he loses everything: his wife (Saint James), his house, his job, and his dignity, while he is reviled by everyone around him. At the end, he recovers some of his self-esteem. This oddball, very sardonic black comedy works only intermittently, then falls apart completely towards the end. Problem: Walter is depicted as a born victim without a spine, and he loses our sympathy early in the story. A satirical point is being made, but it is lost amid the general silliness.

## Cat Ballou

★★★ Columbia, 1965, c, 96 min. Dir: Elliot Silverstein. SP: Walter Newman , Frank R. Pierson, b/o novel by Roy Chanslor. Cast: Jane Fonda, Lee Marvin, Michael Callan, Dwayne Hickman, Tom Nardini, John Marley, Reginald Denny, Nat King Cole, Stubby Kaye.

Why is pretty young Cat Ballou (Fonda) about to be hung in a Western town? It seems that she came to town as a schoolmarm, but when her rancher father (Marley) was murdered, she became a gun-totin' outlaw to exact revenge. At first she hired a gunslinger but he turned out to be a drunken sot named Kid Sheleen (Marvin), the brother of the nasty gunman Silvernose (Marvin again) who killed her father. Somehow she ends up facing a noose— but only temporarily. This Western spoof is not nearly as funny as it once seemed, but it has a few hilarious moments, contributed mostly by Marvin in his double Oscar-winning role. Leaning against a building in a drunken stupor or dressing to meet his brother in a showdown, Marvin is a treat.

# Catch-22

★★★ Paramount, 1970, c, 121 min. Dir: Mike Nichols. SP: Buck Henry, b/o novel by Joseph Heller. Cast: Alan Arkin, Martin Balsam, Richard Benjamin, Art Garfunkel, Jack Gilford, Bob Newhart, Anthony Perkins, Paula Prentiss, Martin Sheen, Jon Voight, Orson Welles.

An uneven, often mordantly funny adaptation of Joseph Heller's novel depicting war as both charnel house and loony bin. The film's central character is Yossarian (Arkin), a bombardier who, during World War II, becomes convinced that madness reigns and that everyone is determined to see him dead. His memory ranges across the demented characters he has met, including a colonel (Balsam) whose main goal is to be written up in The *Saturday Evening Post* and a general (Welles) who shouts, "Take him out and shoot him!" whenever anyone incurs his displeasure. A fragmented series of sequences—some hilarious, some harrowing—convince Yossarian to desert. Not entirely successful, but fascinating.

# The Cheap Detective

★★★ Columbia, 1978, c, 92 min. Dir: Robert Moore. SP: Neil Simon. Cast: Peter Falk, John Houseman, Nicol Williamson, Fernando Lamas, Madeline Kahn, Dom DeLuise, Marsha Mason, Ann-Margret, Louise Fletcher, Sid Caesar, Stockard Channing.

Neil Simon's often amusing, sometimes obvious spoof of Warners' florid melodramas and thrillers of the forties, including such gems as *Casablanca, The Maltese Falcon,* and *The Big Sleep.* Peter Falk plays the hard-boiled private eye who comes up against parodies of familiar characters from those films, including the *Falcon* fat man (Houseman) and his perfumed crony (DeLuise), overzealous underground fighters from *Casablanca* (Fletcher, Lamas), and a variety of femmes fatales (Ann-Margret, Mason) who find Falk irresistible. As usual, some of the gags work nicely; others fall flat.

# Citizen Ruth

★★★ Miramax, 1996, c, 109 min. Dir and SP: Alexander Payne. Cast: Laura Dern, Swoosie Kurtz, Kurtwood Smith, Mary Kay Place, Kelly Preston, Kenneth Mars, Burt Reynolds, Tippi Hedren.

Laura Dern's brave, warts-and-all, totally unsentimental performance as the title character is easily the highlight of this stinging satire. Her Ruth Stoops is a none-too-bright, unlovable, chemical-sniffing woman whose pregnancy (this is her fifth child) becomes the center of a stormy battle between pro-choice and anti-abortion causes. Ruth really doesn't care—she will go along with whomever will give her the most money—but the forces on both sides want to use her. Nobody comes off sympathetically, which makes Ruth's final action all the more satisfying. The movie will probably offend many people, but it's a funny, biting spoof of fanaticism.

# Clueless

★★★ Paramount, 1995, c, 97 min. Dir and SP: Amy Heckerling. Cast: Alicia Silverstone, Paul Rudd, Stacey Dash, Brittany Murphy, Dan Hedaya, Wallace Shawn, Donald Faison, Breckin Meyer, Jeremy Sisto.

You may need a glossary to understand much of the dialogue, but you will probably enjoy this surprisingly engaging and funny movie. Alicia Silverstone is Cher, the glamorous—and sweetly clueless—teenage queen of Beverly Hills High School, who feels it is her duty to make romantic matches, whether they involve her friends or her teachers. It takes a while -and a few setbacks—for her to discover where her own true love lies. The movie is satirical without being mean-spirited, and the cast is most appealing. Oddly enough, Amy Heckerling derived her screenplay from Jane Austen's novel *Emma,* which was filmed in England in 1996. *Clueless* later became a television series.

# Cold Turkey

★★★ United Artists, 1971, c, 99 min. Dir: Norman Lear. SP: Norman Lear, b/o novel by Margaret Rau, Neil Rau. Cast: Dick Van Dyke, Pippa Scott, Tom Poston, Edward Everett Horton, Bob Elliott, Ray Goulding, Bob Newhart, Vincent Gardenia, Barnard Hughes, Jean Stapleton.

A senile tobacco mogul (Horton, in his last movie) announces that he will give $25 million to any town that can quit smoking for thirty days. Actually, it's only a public relations gimmick perpetrated by PR man Newhart. Van Dyke is a small-town Iowa minister who rallies the townspeople to make the effort to win the money. Most of the humor stems from the desperate efforts to stop smoking. The mayor's wife (Stapleton) goes on a frenzied orgy of eating; Van Dyke's own wife (Scott) is a secret smoker who is gradually losing control, and so on. The satire is fairly toothless, but the overall effect is genial until the contrived ending.

## Critical Care

★★★ Live Entertainment, 1997, c, 107 min. Dir: Sidney Lumet. SP: Steven S. Schwartz, b/o novel by Richard Dooling. Cast: James Spader, Kyra Sedgwick, Albert Brooks, Helen Mirren, Margo Martindale, Philip Bosco, Jeffrey Wright, Wallace Shawn, Anne Bancroft, Edward Herrmann.

An excellent cast and some sharp jabs at medical care in America offset the defects—a verbose screenplay and sluggish pace—of this satirical comedy-drama. James Spader plays a second-year resident doctor who witnesses greedy, corrupt behavior by hospital officials, notably his alcoholic superior (Brooks, almost unrecognizable), whose one concern is profit (is the patient insured?), and a colleague (Bosco) who monitors all his patients on computers. Spader also finds himself in a battle between two sisters (Sedgwick and Martindale) over the issue of whether their dying father should be removed from life support. "Seeing patients is a waste of a doctor's time," says doctor Bosco. Seeing *Critical Care* may not waste your time, but don't watch if you're heading for the hospital.

## Dead Men Don't Wear Plaid

★★☆ Universal, 1982, 89 min. Dir: Carl Reiner. SP: Carl Reiner, George Gipe, Steve Martin. Cast: Steve Martin, Rachel Ward, Rene Santoni, Carl Reiner, George Gaynes, Frank McCarthy.

A mostly silly but sometimes clever "gimmick" movie that spoofs the film noir of the forties. The gimmick: Rigby Reardon (Martin) is a private eye investigating the murder of a big financier. His path crosses dangerously with a host of devious and sinister types, all of whom are well-known stars in scenes excerpted from their movies. And so we see Rigby interacting with the likes of Barbara Stanwyck, Humphrey Bogart, Ray Milland, Lana Turner, Ingrid Bergman, and Kirk Douglas, to name only a few. Movie buffs will enjoy spotting the stars and identifying the movies, but the idea wears thin after a while. The movie is dedicated to acclaimed costume designer Edith Head. (This was her last movie.)

## Dr. Strangelove or How I Learned to Stop Worrying and Love the Bomb

★★★★ United Artists, 1964, 93 min. Dir: Stanley Kubrick. SP: Stanley Kubrick, Terry Southern, Peter George, b/o novel by Peter George. Cast: Peter Sellers, George C. Scott, Sterling Hayden, Keenan Wynn, Slim Pickens, Peter Bull, James Earl Jones.

A wickedly funny black comedy that brings the inanity of the Cold War to its logical, inevitable end. It seems that everything is awry at Burpelson Air Force Base. The demented base commander (Hayden) believes that the Russians have launched a full-scale invasion of America. He orders a squadron of planes to hit strategic Russian targets with atom bombs, unaware that the bombing will set off a cata-strophic "doomsday" device. Caught up in the madness are America's weak-kneed president (Sellers), a belligerent general (Scott), and a sensible British captain (Sellers again). On the sidelines is the very peculiar German scientist Dr. Strangelove (Sellers in a third role), whose mechanical arm insists on giving the Nazi salute. The movie takes aim at the sort of primeval thinking that would spur nationwide protest and alienation in later years. One of the most original films of the sixties.

A meeting in the War Room in *Dr. Strangelove* (1964). Peter Sellers plays the title character (second from left), a German scientist whose mechanical arm cannot help giving the Nazi salute.

## Dragnet

★★☆ Universal, 1987, c, 106 min. Dir: Tom Mankiewicz. SP: Dan Aykroyd, Alan Zweibel, Tom Mankiewicz. Cast: Dan Aykroyd, Tom Hanks, Christopher Plummer, Harry Morgan, Elizabeth Ashley, Alexandra Paul.

A spoof of the hugely popular television program of the fifties and sixties ("Just the facts, ma'am"), *Dragnet* stars Dan Aykroyd as Police Sgt. Joe Friday, the straight-arrow, by-the-rules nephew and namesake of Jack Webb's original Friday. To his dismay, Friday is partnered with free-wheeling Pep Streebek (Hanks), who makes his own rules. Together, the team sets out to rout the wild, destructive group who call themselves PAGANS (People Against Goodness and Normalcy). Aykroyd's on-target imitation of Webb's monotoned, rapid-fire delivery begins amusingly but palls after a while, and the movie, as a whole, is more energetic than funny.

## Fatal Instinct

★★ MGM, 1993, c, 91 min. Dir: Carl Reiner. SP: David O'Malley. Cast: Armand Assante, Sherilyn Fenn, Kate Nelligan, Sean Young, Christopher McDonald, James Remar, Tony Randall.

A hit-and-miss parody of film noir, with many more misses than hits. Poking rather belated fun at such movies as *Basic Instinct* and *Body Heat,* the movie stars Armand Assante as a dim bulb who works as both a cop and a lawyer. He has no clue that his wife (Nelligan) is cheating on him and plotting his demise with her lover (McDonald). Enter a couple of femmes fatales (Fenn and Young) who are hellbent on seducing Assante. (Both ladies also have toilet paper stuck to the soles of their shoes.) Most of the gags are lame or wince-inducing; a few of them work. Where is Leslie Nielsen when you need him?

## George of the Jungle

★★★ Disney, 1997, c, 92 min. Dir: Sam Weisman. SP: Dana Olsen, Audrey Wells, b/o story by Dale Olsen and Jay Ward's sixties animated television series. Cast: Brendan Fraser, Leslie Mann, Thomas Haden Church, Richard Roundtree, Greg Cruttwell, Abraham Benrubi, Holland Taylor.

Aimed squarely at younger viewers, *George of the Jungle* might actually entertain older viewers as well, if they relax and accept it as a broad parody of the Tarzan legend. It's all silly, of course, but it does have a number of laughs. George (Fraser), of course, is the sweet-natured jungle inhabitant, raised by apes. His companions are Shep, an elephant who thinks he's a dog, and Ape, a bespectacled erudite ape who sounds very much like English actor John Cleese. Enter adventurous San Francisco heiress Ursula Stanhope (Mann), who comes upon George in the jungle and ultimately falls for him. Many slapstick gags should have youngsters roaring with laughter and some grown-ups smiling a lot. Favorite section: Ape teaches George how to court Ursula.

## Goodbye, Columbus

★★★ Paramount, 1969, c, 105 min. Dir: Larry Peerce. SP: Arnold Schulman, b/o novella by Philip Roth. Cast: Richard Benjamin, Ali MacGraw, Jack Klugman, Nan Martin, Michael Meyers, Lori Shelle.

Adapted from Philip Roth's novella, *Goodbye, Columbus* is a bitingly satirical look at upwardly mobile Jewish suburban life. Richard Benjamin stars as Neil, a Bronx librarian who falls in love with Brenda Patimkin (MacGraw), a rich, spoiled, and beautiful girl from Westchester. Now he must find a way to cope with her family's wildly materialistic world of overdecorated furniture, overstuffed freezers (the Patimkins *love* fruit), and overelaborate wedding receptions. It's not easy, especially when Brenda's father (Klugman) looks on him with doubt and suspicion. Some of the movie's characters are caricatured, but others are dead-on accurate and funny, especially Brenda's none-too-bright brother, played by Michael Meyers.

## The Great White Hype

★★☆ Fox, 1996, c, 90 min. Dir: Reginald Hudlin. SP: Tony Hendra, Ron Shelton. Cast: Samuel L. Jackson, Jeff

Goldblum, Peter Berg, Damon Wayans, Jon Lovitz, Corbin Bersen, Cheech Marin, Sally Richardson, John Rhys-Davies. A raucous, wicked, but curiously unfinished satire of professional boxing, *The Great White Hype* stars Samuel L. Jackson as the Reverend Fred Sultan, a leading fight promoter and clever fraud who pays James "the Grim Reaper" Roper (Wayans), his champion boxer, in Rolls Royces rather than money. When business drops dangerously, he decides to bring in a white contender who will trigger racial hostility and rake in lots of money. He chooses Terry Conklin (Berg), a naïve boxer who knocked out Roper years earlier. Jeff Goldblum is funny as a ferocious crusader against Sultan who switches sides to become his public relations man. Cynical stuff, but the screenplay could use some fleshing out.

## Hairspray

★★★ New Line, 1988, c, 96 min. Dir and SP: John Waters. Cast: Ricki Lake, Divine, Sonny Bono, Debbie Harry, Ruth Brown, Colleen Fitzpatrick, Michael St. Gerard, Jerry Stiller, Leslie Ann Powers, Shawn Thompson, John Waters, Ric Ocasek.

One of writer-director John Waters's more accessible features, *Hairspray* is his slapdash but often riotous spoof of sixties pop culture. The setting is Baltimore in 1963, and the most popular television program is the dance marathon *The Corny Collins Show.* Economy-size Tracy Turnblad (Lake) is vying for a spot on the show's "council" of influential teenagers but somehow she gets involved with changing the show's "whites only" policy. The movie's real fun lies in the nutty characters: a hilarious Divine as Tracy's mother, Ruth Brown as black disc jockey Motormouth Maybell, Debbie Harry and Sonny Bono as the snooty parents of Tracy's arch rival. Funniest scene: at the Hefty Hideaway House of Fashion.

## H.E.A.L.T.H.

★★★ Fox, 1979, 102 min. Dir: Robert Altman. SP: Frank Barhydt, Robert Altman, Paul Dooley. Cast: Carol Burnett, Glenda Jackson, James Garner, Lauren Bacall, Dick Cavett, Paul Dooley, Donald Moffat, Henry Gibson, Alfre Woodard, Diane Stilwell.

A Florida hotel is the setting for this cluttered but often funny satire from Robert Altman. Scores of guests (many of them bizarre) have gathered, along with television crews, gawkers, and autograph hunters, for a health convention. The boiling issue is who will be the new president of H.E.A.L.T.H (Happiness, Energy, and Longevity Through Health). The two contenders are eighty-three-year-old but amazingly well-preserved Esther Brill (Bacall) and militant Isabella Garnell (Jackson). Swirling around them are a host of characters, each with his or her own agenda. A larger political analogy is clearly intended, but a cast of familiar faces keeps the fun moving briskly if not always coherently. Shelved for two years as "unreleasable," *H.E.A.L.T.H.* actually offers much to enjoy.

## Heaven Can Wait

★★★☆ Fox, 1943, c, 112 min. Dir: Ernst Lubitsch. SP: Samson Raphaelson, b/o play by Lazlo Bus-Fekete. Cast: Don Ameche, Gene Tierney, Charles Coburn, Laird Cregar, Eugene Pallette, Marjorie Main, Allyn Joslyn, Signe Hasso, Dickie Moore.

A delightful comedy, with flashes of fantasy and satire, *Heaven Can Wait* traces the life of New York socialite Henry Van Cleve (Ameche). Arriving in hell after his death, Henry appears before the Devil (Cregar), here called His Excellency, convinced that his many sins deserve punishment. A review of his life, from his earliest days to his last years, proves otherwise. We witness his early flirtations, his mostly happy married life with Martha (Tierney), his coping with his son's roving eye, and finally his serene old age. A witty screenplay, luscious Technicolor photography, and a superb cast combine to make *Heaven Can Wait* a treat. Funniest scene: Martha's midwestern parents (Pallette and Main) argue over the comics at breakfast.

## Hollywood Shuffle

★★★ Goldwyn, 1987, 82 mins. Dir: Robert Townsend. SP: Robert Townsend, Keenan Ivory Wayans. Cast: Robert Townsend, Anne-Marie Johnson, Starletta Dupois, Helen Johnson, Craigus R. Johnson.

A satirical swipe at Hollywood's longstanding concept of blacks, *Hollywood Shuffle* stars director-coauthor Townsend as a black actor in Hollywood who runs into stereotyping at every turn. His daydreams take the form of comedy sketches, some of them amusing. Funny episodes include "Sneakin' in the Movies," a spoof of movie reviewing on television, and a sketch in which an acting school for blacks is staffed by white teachers who instruct the students on how to speak, stand, or walk in black style. Townsend also appears as a black Superman, flying happily over the city.

## Honky Tonk Freeway

★★★ Universal, 1981, c, 107 min. Dir: John Schlesinger. SP: Edward Clinton. Cast: Beau Bridges, Hume Cronyn, Beverly D'Angelo, William Devane, George Dzunda, Teri Garr, Joe Grifasi, Howard Hesseman, Paul Jabara, Geraldine Page, Jessica Tandy, Frances Lee McCain, Deborah Rush, Alice Beardsley.

*Honky Tonk Freeway* is messy, chaotic, and wildly uneven. It's also surprisingly funny. It appears that the town of Ticlaw, Florida, has no exit from or onto the new interstate highway. So the loony residents, led by the mayor (Devane), begin a campaign to raise the necessary money. They paint the town pink, put up billboards advertising their chief attraction, a water-skiing elephant, and give away free food and gas. Nothing works, but meanwhile dozens of equally loony people are about to descend on the town. They include two bank robbers (Dzunda and Grifasi), a girl (D'Angelo) who has slept with three hundred different men in Paducah, Kentucky, and an advertising man (Cronyn) and his alcoholic wife (Tandy), who claims that her husband invented bad breath. Madness reigns in this broadly played farce.

## The Hospital

★★★☆ United Artists, 1971, c, 103 min. Dir: Arthur Hiller. SP: Paddy Chayefsky. Cast: George C. Scott, Diana Rigg, Barnard Hughes, Stephen Elliott, Richard Dysart, Nancy Marchand, Robert Walden, Roberts Blossom, Frances Sternhagen, Lenny Baker.

From writing small-scale television dramas about "real" people and several commendable Broadway plays, Paddy Chayefsky, in his later years, turned to stinging satire. Here he wrote one of his most scathing screenplays, using an incompetent hospital as a metaphor for what he called "the whole wounded madhouse of our times." George C. Scott plays the emotionally drained chief of medicine at a hospital where bungling and pilfering are the norms. Now he must cope with a strike, a riot, and a homicidal maniac on the loose. (He also has a dysfunctional family.) His near-suicidal despair is relieved by a patient's beautiful daughter (Rigg). Chayefsky's screenplay aims at too many targets (money-mad doctors, inept administrators, noisy activists) but it is also abrasively funny.

## Hot Shots!

★★★ Fox, 1991, c, 85 min. Dir: Jim Abrahams. SP: Jim Abrahams, Pat Proft. Cast: Charlie Sheen, Cary Elwes, Valeria Golino, Lloyd Bridges, Kevin Dunn, Jon Cryer, William O'Leary, Kristy Swanson, Efrem Zimbalist, Jr., Bill Irwin.

Created by two of the four people who produced the hilarious *Airplane!, Hot Shots!* is yet another spoof—this one of the "fly-boy" movies from *Only Angels Have Wings* to *Top Gun.* Charlie Sheen plays the son of a pilot who died in disgrace; he now lives in isolation. When he is called back to join a high-level Navy flying mission, he emerges a hero after all. He also falls for the base psychiatrist (Golino). Cary Elwes and Jon Cryer are among his fellow pilots, and Lloyd Bridges is quite funny as an extremely dim admiral. As in *Airplane!* and other similar efforts, the gags come thick and fast, some of them on-target. Sequel: *Hot Shots!: Part Deux* (1993).

## The Hudsucker Proxy

★★★☆ Warners, 1994, c, 111 min. Dir: Joel Coen. SP: Ethan Coen, Joel Coen, Sam Raimi. Cast: Tim Robbins, Jennifer Jason Leigh, Paul Newman, Charles Durning, John Mahoney, Jim True, William Cobbs.

Another offbeat entry from the Coen Brothers, who gave us *Barton Fink* (1991) and would later create the brilliant *Fargo* (1996), among others. This film is a satiric broadside aimed at big business, with Tim Robbins as Norville Barnes, a boob from Muncie, Indiana, who, in the late 1950s, is promoted from mail boy to president of Hudsucker Industries as part of the scheme of power-hungry Sidney Mussbacher (Newman). Norville, however, has an ace up his sleeve called the Hula Hoop ("for kids, you know"). Jennifer Jason Leigh, imitating Katharine Hepburn, is the reporter out to expose him but who falls for him instead. The climax is weak, but the movie works as a latter-day spin on a Frank Capra movie, without the sentiment. Imaginative sets.

## I Love You, Alice B. Toklas!

★★☆ Warners, 1968, c, 93 min. Dir: Hy Averbach. SP: Paul Mazursky, Larry Tucker. Cast: Peter Sellers, Jo Van Fleet, Leigh Taylor-Young, Joyce Van Patten, David Arkin, Herb Edelman.

Peter Sellers had one of his better U.S. roles in this dated but occasionally amusing comedy. He plays Harold Fine, a "square," hard-working lawyer who is about to marry his long-time fiancée, Van Patten. Harold, however, has a "hippie" brother (Arkin) whose disingenuous girlfriend (Taylor-Young) bakes up a batch of brownies in which hashish is a principal ingredient. This transforms Harold into a bearded, beaded "love child" whose life is turned upside down. Eventually he learns that both lifestyles—his old uptight ways and his new free-spirited hippiedom—are shams unworthy of his time or attention. Sellers is fun to watch but three decades later, the satirical material seems stale.

## In the Mood

★★★ Lorimar, 1987, c, 99 min. Dir: Phil Alden Robinson, b/o story by Bob Kosberg, David Simon, Phil Alden Robinson. Cast: Patrick Dempsey, Beverly D'Angelo, Talia Balsam, Michael Constantine, Betty Jinette, Kathleen Freeman, Peter Hobbs, Edith Fellows.

A marvelous score of vintage forties songs is the best feature of this amusing period satire, based on a true story. Patrick Dempsey plays Ellsworth "Sonny" Wisecarver, a gawky fifteen-year-old boy who, in 1944, became known nationwide as "The Woo-Woo Kid" because of his affairs with two older women (Balsam and D'Angelo), one of whom he actually married. There's not much substance, but the details of life in the forties are accurate and funny, and that music will bring back memories to viewers of a certain age. Dempsey is engaging as the bewildered "Woo-Woo Kid."

## Kicking and Screaming

★★★ Trimark, 1995, c, 96 min. Dir and SP: Noah Baumbach. Cast: Josh Hamilton, Olivia d'Abo, Parker Posey, Chris Eigeman, Cara Buono, Eric Stoltz.

The talk in *Kicking and Screaming* is constant and sometimes tiring, but frequently it's also witty and incisive. In a small college town, four friends have just graduated from college, and in the long-standing tradition of movies such as this, they haven't a clue about their future. Instead they exchange cultural or literary references, make plans that never materialize, and chase women who tell them, "You guys all sound alike." (They're right.) The central story involves Grover (Hamilton) and his relationship with Jane (d'Abo), who is leaving him to study abroad in Prague. An interesting if rather self-conscious combination of satire and romantic comedy from writer-director Noah Baumbach.

## The King of Comedy

★★☆ Fox, 1983, c, 109 min. Dir: Martin Scorsese. SP: Paul D. Zimmerman. Cast: Robert De Niro, Jerry Lewis,

Sandra Bernhard, Diahnne Abbott, Shelley Hack, Tony Randall, Ed Herlihy, Fred de Cordova.

A sardonic reflection on America's obsession with celebrity and the sometimes dangerous consequences of this obsession, *The King of Comedy* has its admirers, but not here. Robert De Niro plays obnoxious, self-deluding Rupert Pupkin, who is convinced that he is a master of stand-up comedy. When he is unable to reach his idol, talk-show host Jerry Langford (Lewis), he kidnaps Langford with the help of a crazed fan (Bernhard). There are some effective moments, and Lewis surprises with his non-comedic performance, but asking viewers to spend nearly two hours with Pupkin and his obsession is a serious imposition. The ending is intended as irony, no doubt, but it will leave you feeling glum and incredulous.

## Life with Mikey

★★★ Touchstone, 1993, c, 91 min. Dir: James Lapine. SP: Marc Lawrence. Cast: Michael J. Fox, Christina Vidal, Nathan Lane, Cyndi Lauper, David Krumholtz, David Huddleston, Victor Garber, Tony Hendra, Ruben Blades (unbilled).

A pleasant mixture of satire and sentiment, *Life with Mikey* is at its best when it spoofs the overbearingly wisecracking children on television sitcoms. Michael J. Fox plays Michael Chapman, an ex-television child star who (sort of) runs a children's talent agency with his older brother Ed (Lane). Along comes Angie (Vidal), a tough-talking petty thief and truant who turns out to be the perfect spokesperson for a cookie company. There's hell to play when she moves in with Michael, but of course the two eventually bond as a kind of caring father and daughter. Then her true father (Blades) surfaces, and there are other complications. Best bits: the kiddie auditions.

## Living in Oblivion

★★★ Sony, 1996, c & b/w, 91 min. Dir and SP: Tom DiCillo. Cast: Steve Buscemi, Catherine Keener, Dermot Mulroney, Danielle Von Zerneck, James Le Gros, Rica

Martens, Peter Dinklage, Michael Griffiths.

"Sometimes I wonder what I'm doing in this business!" director Nick Reve (Buscemi) declares in a not-infrequent moment of hopelessness. Directing a very low-budget feature film called, appropriately, *Living in Oblivion,* Nick finds himself continually in a whirlwind of disaster, with malfunctioning equipment and barely functioning actors. A wickedly funny satire of independent filmmaking, this movie is aimed at a special audience that will appreciate all the swollen egos and rampant insecurities on display. Director-writer DiCillo even has a few surprises up his sleeve as the shooting keeps falling apart for various reasons. Buscemi is marvelous in his combination of exuberance and despair. Also fine: James Le Gros as a hunky, brain-dead movie star.

## Lost in America

★★★ Warners, 1985, c, 91 min. Dir: Albert Brooks. SP: Albert Brooks, Monica Johnson. Cast: Albert Brooks, Julie Haggerty, Garry Marshall, Art Frankel, Michael Greene.

David and Linda Howard (Brooks and Haggerty) are the perfect yuppie couple: he's a hotshot advertising man, and she has a good job as a personnel director. But everything unravels when David is passed over for a promotion he expected, and he quits his job in a fury. He decides to follow a lifelong dream and travel across the country with Linda in a mobile home. They will live on his cash for twenty years. Can disaster be far behind? Hardly. On their first stop in Las Vegas, Linda contracts gambling fever and loses all their money. And that's only the beginning. Despite Brooks's often irritating character, *Lost in America* is a sharp, amusing satirical comedy of yuppies out of their natural element, nicely played by the leads.

## The Loved One

★★☆ MGM, 1965, 116 min. Dir: Tony Richardson. SP: Terry Southern, Christopher Isherwood, b/o novel by Evelyn Waugh. Cast: Robert Morse, Jonathan Winters,

Anjanette Comer, Rod Steiger, Ayliene Gibbons, Roddy McDowall, Milton Berle, Margaret Leighton, John Gielgud, Robert Morley, Liberace, James Coburn.

Adapted from Evelyn Waugh's short satirical novel, this deliberately outrageous black comedy savages the American way of death, among other things. Robert Morse stars as Dennis Barlow, a young British poet who comes to Los Angeles to visit his uncle (Gielgud). When his uncle commits suicide, Dennis becomes caught up in the activities at Whispering Glades, an extravagant, bizarre cemetery very much like Forest Lawn. Among the strange creatures he encounters are the effete chief embalmer (Steiger), an oily casket salesman (Liberace), and the Blessed Reverend (Winters), the unctuous founder of Whispering Glades. The movie aims its satirical fire at many targets, but the humor becomes heavy-handed long before the end.

## Mafia!

★★☆ Touchstone, 1998, c, 86 min. Dir: Jim Abrahams. SP: Jim Abrahams, Greg Norberg, Michael McManus. Cast: Jay Mohr, Billy Burke, Christina Applegate, Pamela Gidley, Olympia Dukakis, Lloyd Bridges, Jason Fuchs.

Jim Abrahams, one of the creators of *Airplane!*, directed and coauthored this parody of the Godfather genre, originally entitled *Jane Austen's Mafia*. Once again, the movie scatters its fire in all directions and sometimes hits the target. Jay Mohr, as the Michael Corleone type, narrates the story of his father's youth in Sicily (in the town of Salmonella, "Home of Warm Mayonnaise"), his immigration to America, and his rise to the all-powerful don, played with panache by Lloyd Bridges in his last role. (As he is being riddled with bullets, he seems to be dancing the macarena.) The opening sequence mocks the opening of *Casino*. Some jokes are silly or crude; others are outrageously funny.

## The Man Who Knew Too Little

★ Warners, 1997, c, 94 min. Dir: Jon Amiel. SP: Robert Farrar and Howard Franklin, b/o novel by Robert Farrar. Cast: Bill Murray, Peter Gallagher, Joanne Whalley, Alfred Molina, Geraldine James.

A truly dreadful one-joke movie. The joke is this: dim-witted American tourist Wallace Ritchie (Murray) comes to London to visit his brother (Gallagher). To get rid of him, his brother buys him a ticket to an audience-participation play called "The Theater of Life," which is acted out in the streets. Instead, brain-dead Wallace gets caught up in a real-life spy drama, mistaking every moment of actual skulduggery and violence for the play. Of course everything he says or does is misinterpreted by the scheming participants. Murray is the wrong actor to star in this sort of nonsense—he usually perpetrates the mischief rather than playing the victim—and he seems at a total loss. A laughless misfire.

## The Man with Two Brains

★★★ Warners, 1983, c, 1983. Dir: Carl Reiner. SP: Carl Reiner, Steve Martin, George Gipe. Cast: Steve Martin, Kathleen Turner, George Warner, Paul Benedict, Richard Brestoff, James Cromwell, George Furth, Randi Brooks.

There's a very high silliness quotient in this off-the-wall fantasy-satire, but you will probably find yourself laughing a lot. Steve Martin plays Dr. Michael Hfuhruhurr (don't try to pronounce it), the world's foremost brain surgeon, who marries the venal, murderous Dolores (a very funny Turner), who also turns out to be a terrible tease. No use trying to explain the rest—only know that Dr. Hfuhruhurr falls madly in love with a talking brain in a jar, causing all sorts of madcap and sometimes hilarious complications. The movie is partly a spoof of Frankenstein horror films—we love the castle and laboratory inside a posh hotel. Favorite touch: the brain with hat and wax lips.

## Matinee

★★★ Universal, 1993, c, 98 min. Dir: Joe Dante. SP: Charlie Haas, b/o story by Jerico Stone, Charlie Haas. Cast: John Goodman, Cathy Moriarty, Simon Fenton, Omri Katz,

Kellie Martin, Lisa Jakub, Robert Picardo, David Clennon, Jesse White.

Key West, Florida, November 1962: On the very weekend of the Cuban missile crisis, Lawrence Woolsey (Goodman), "the screen's number one shock expert," is having a matinee showing of his latest horror flick, *Mant*. While he prepares his tacky "special effects," the townspeople teeter at the edge of panic, expecting a missile attack at any minute. Eventually, reality and artifice clash at the showing, as a crowd of hyped-up teenagers react to the gimmicks and things get out of hand. *Matinee* is both ironic and satiric, and the pieces of *Mant* that are shown are an on-target parody of the fifties monster films spawned by atomic fear. Goodman is funny as a character modeled on schlockmeister William Castle.

## Maverick

★★★ Warners, 1994, c, 129 min. Dir: Richard Donner. SP: William Goldman. Cast: Mel Gibson, Jodie Foster, James Garner, James Coburn, Graham Greene, Alfred Molina, Paul Smith, Geoffrey Lewis, Max Perlich, Dub Taylor.

An entertaining screen adaptation of the television series *Maverick*, which ran from 1957 to 1962 with James Garner as dapper card sharp Bret Maverick. The TV series had a sense of humor, which extends to the movie as well, spoofing many Western conventions with unabashed glee. On his way to a high-paying all-night poker tournament aboard a riverboat, Maverick (Gibson) meets con woman Annabelle Bransford (Foster, with a juicy Southern accent), who is also after the big stake. The two join up with retired lawman Zane Cooper (Garner, older and still cagey), and these three take part in a series of rip-roaring—and outlandish—adventures. There's a surprise ending, and Gibson's *Lethal Weapon* costar Danny Glover makes a cameo appearance.

## Movers and Shakers

★★☆ United Artists, 1985, c, 79 min. Dir: William Asher. SP: Charles Grodin. Cast: Walter Matthau, Charles Grodin, Vincent Gardenia, Tyne Daly, Gilda Radner, Bill Macy, Steve Martin, Penny Marshall.

This thin-blooded satire of Hollywood was barely released and scarcely noticed, but it has its moments. Walter Matthau plays a film producer who promises a dying mogul (Gardenia) that he will make a movie out of the best-selling book *Love in Sex*. Charles Grodin, who wrote the screenplay for *Movers and Shakers,* is the unhappy writer hired to adapt the book. The spoofs of Hollywood types—the "yes" men, the shrill wives, the ludicrous has-been star (Martin)—are much too familiar, and the movie ends too abruptly, but Matthau is always fun to watch.

## Movie Movie

★★★ Warners, 1978, c & b/w, 107 min. Dir: Stanley Donen. SP: Larry Gelbart, Sheldon Keller. Cast: George C. Scott, Trish Van Devere, Eli Wallach, Red Buttons, Barbara Harris, Barry Bostwick, Harry Hamlin, Ann Reinking, Rebecca York, Art Carney.

This two-part parody of old movie genres is fairly amusing. The first part, "Dynamite Hands," is the better, an affectionate takeoff of the sort of film that might have starred John Garfield. Harry Hamlin plays the aspiring slum lawyer who turns boxer to save his sister's sight. The plot, the characters, and the sets are all on target, but best is the pseudo-poetic dialogue ("Say the word, baby, and we'll tap dance on a nickel.") George C. Scott is fine as Joey Popchik's big-hearted manager, "Gloves" Malloy. In the second part, "Baxter's Beauties of 1933," a parody of Busby Berkeley musicals, Scott plays "Spats" Baxter, a hard-driving producer putting on his last show. Photographed in color, this mini-feature captures some of Berkeley's Art Deco glitz and brash humor.

## Murder by Death

★★★ Columbia, 1976, c, 94 min. Dir: Robert Moore. SP: Neil Simon. Cast: Peter Sellers, Peter Falk, David Niven, Maggie Smith, James Coco, Alec Guinness, Elsa Lanchester, Eileen Brennan, Nancy Walker, Estelle Winwood, Truman Capote.

You've seen the murder mystery in which a group of people are summoned to appear at a mysterious and sinister locale. (*The Cat and the Canary* and *And Then There Were None* come to mind.) Neil Simon's sometimes funny and sometimes labored spoof of this subgenre brings the world's greatest detectives to a spooky mansion at the behest of an eccentric recluse (author Truman Capote). Among those who confront murder and mayhem are broad takeoffs of Sam Spade (Falk), Charlie Chan (Sellers), Hercule Poirot (Coco), and Nick and Nora Charles (Niven and Smith). Nancy Walker plays a mute cook and Alec Guinness is a blind butler.

## My Favorite Year

★★★ MGM/UA, 1982, c, 92 min. Dir: Richard Benjamin. SP: Norman Steinberg, Dennis Palumbo, b/o story by Dennis Palumbo. Cast: Peter O'Toole, Mark Linn-Baker, Jessica Harper, Joseph Bologna, Bill Macy, Lainie Kazan, Adolph Green, Anne DeSalvo, Lou Jacobi, Selma Diamond, George Wyner, Cameron Mitchell.

Affectionately but with satirical touches, *My Favorite Year* re-creates the golden days of 1950s television, when a program such as *Your Show of Shows* captured audiences with inspired comedy starring Sid Caesar. Mark Linn-Baker plays a fledgling writer for a variety program very much like *Your Show of Shows*, who is assigned to look after the week's guest star, a flamboyant, alcoholic British film actor named Alan Swann. Oscar-nominated Peter O'Toole is extremely funny in this role, reeling from one rowdy incident to another. Joseph Bologna is clearly meant to resemble Sid Caesar as the burly, obstreperous star of the show, and Lainie Kazan wins laughs as Linn-Baker's exuberant mother, a role she repeated ten years later in the failed stage musical version.

## National Lampoon's Loaded Weapon 1

★★ New Line, 1993, c, 83 min. Dir: Gene Quintano. SP: Gene Quintano and Don Holley, b/o story by Don Holley, Tori Tellem. Cast: Emilio Estevez, Samuel L. Jackson, Jon Lovitz, Tim Curry, Kathy Ireland, William Shatner.

Read the title and you don't have to see the movie. A nonstop, helter-skelter spoof of the *Lethal Weapon* series, it stars Emilio Estevez and Samuel L. Jackson as cops who are after a microfilm that contains a formula for turning cookies into cocaine. The chief villain is William Shatner, leaving his *Star Trek* duties behind to play "General Morters." There are take-offs of *Silence of the Lambs* and *Fatal Attraction,* cameos by Whoopi Goldberg, F. Murray Abraham, Joyce Brothers, and others, plus relentless gags, few of them funny. Best bit: the police captain who can't speak without bellowing.

## Nothing Sacred

★★★☆ United Artists, 1937, c, 75 min. Dir: William Wellman. SP: Ben Hecht, b/o story by James H. Street. Cast: Carole Lombard, Fredric March, Charles Winninger, Walter Connolly, Sig Ruman, Frank Fay, Monty Woolley, Margaret Hamilton.

One of Hollywood's best satirical comedies, *Nothing Sacred* takes off on America's obsession with celebrities, a topic that has hardly dated with time. Carole Lombard is Hazel Flagg, a small-town girl who is mistakenly diagnosed with radium poisoning. Although she knows she's perfectly well, she accepts the offer made by newspaper reporter Wally Cook (March) of an all-expenses-paid trip to New York City. Lionized by everyone as the brave heroine smiling through her tragedy, she becomes a top celebrity. Things get complicated when she and Wally fall in love. The movie became a Broadway musical called *Hazel Flagg* in 1953, and a year later Paramount remade the story as *Living It Up,* with Jerry Lewis in the Lombard role.

## Office Space

★★★ Fox, 1999, c, 89 min. Dir and Sp: Mike Judge. Cast: Ron Livingston, Jennifer Aniston, David Herman, Ajay Naidu, Gary Cole, Diedrich Bader, Stephen Root, Richard Riehle.

The first feature film by the creator of *Beavis*

and *Butt-Head* and *King of the Hill, Office Space* is a wickedly amusing satire of corporate office life. If some of it plays like an extended television sketch, there are enough on-target laughs to warrant a viewing. Peter Gibbons (Livingston) is a computer programmer who loathes his dead-end job, so when efficiency experts interview him, he tells the bitter truth and promptly gets promoted. This leads him to concoct an embezzling scheme that would bring him lots of money but only brings him trouble. Stephen Root is funny, if a bit grotesque, as a perpetually terrified, constantly demoted office worker who gets his ultimate revenge. Adapted from a series of animated shorts produced for *Saturday Night Live* in 1993.

## Paris—When It Sizzles

★ Paramount, 1964, c, 110 min. Dir: Richard Quine. SP: George Axelrod. Cast: Audrey Hepburn, William Holden, Noel Coward, Gregoire Aslan.

Proof positive that a movie starring Audrey Hepburn, William Holden, and Noel Coward could be an embarrassment. One must question not only the wisdom but the sanity of the creators in attempting to satirize films and filmmaking and then turning out a satire without teeth and without a reason for existing. Holden is a screenwriter living in Paris who hires typist Hepburn to assist him as he turns out his latest opus. As he keeps changing his storyline—a parody of spy thrillers—the scenes are played out on screen, with Holden and Hepburn as the principals. The movie ends with a lavish but ridiculous climax. *Paris—When It Sizzles,* a candidate for permanent interment, merely fizzles.

## The Princess Bride

★★☆ Fox, 1987, c, 98 min. Dir: Rob Reiner. SP: William Goldman, b/o his book. Cast: Cary Elwes, Mandy Patinkin, Chris Sarandon, Christopher Guest, Robin Wright, Wallace Shawn, Andre the Giant, Peter Falk, Fred Savage, Peter Cook, Billy Crystal, Carol Kane.

Is it possible to mix a straightforward fantasy-adventure and a spoof of fantasy-adventure in the same movie? Judging by *The Princess Bride,* the answer is: only occasionally. On one level, the film is a fanciful tale of a beautiful princess (Wright) who loves a farm boy (Elwes) but is abducted by a nasty prince (Sarandon) with a secret agenda. She is rescued after a series of trials and tribulations. On another level, the film is a sly parody of the subgenre, with some characters straight out of Mel Brooks. (Most conspicuous: Billy Crystal as "Miracle Max," who appears to have wandered into the film from Miami Beach.) Some laughs but also some surprisingly dull, talky sections as well. Favorite character: Wallace Shawn as Vizzini, a self-described "genius."

## Ready to Wear (Prêt-à-Porter)

★ Miramax, 1994, c, 133 min. Dir: Robert Altman. SP: Robert Altman, Barbara Shulgasser. Cast: Sophia Loren, Marcello Mastroianni, Julia Roberts, Tim Robbins, Kim Basinger, Lauren Bacall, Danny Aiello, Teri Garr, Forest Whitaker, Linda Hunt, Sally Kellerman, Tracey Ullman, Anouk Aimee, Stephen Rea.

A satirical look at the fashion industry, starring an impressive cast of international actors under the direction of Robert Altman. The possibilities are intriguing; the result is catastrophic. A vitriolic spoof of the industry, *Ready to Wear* assembles a group of designers, models, photographers, and reporters in Paris for the big spring fashion event. Their lives intersect as they fake kinship, spew venom, and cross swords. Among the attendees are rival magazine editors (Hunt, Kellerman, Ullman) and clashing reporters (Robbins, Roberts) who are forced to share the same hotel room. Sophia Loren and Marcello Mastroianni are best as reunited Italian lovers. But they are only one part of a tedious, ill-calculated movie.

## Risky Business

★★★ Warners, 1983, c, 96 min. Dir and SP: Paul Brickman. Cast: Tom Cruise, Rebecca De Mornay, Curtis Armstrong, Bronson Pinchot, Nicholas Pryor, Janet Carroll, Richard Masur, Kevin Anderson.

Teenage Tom Cruise's star took on a new luster when he danced alone in his underwear near the beginning of this movie. Yet *Risky Business* has a darkly satirical edge absent from most teenage comedies. Tom plays Joel, your average decent, horny teenager, who finds himself alone in his house, weighed down by the rules of his clueless parents. A friend hires a prostitute named Lana (De Mornay) for Joel, but she turns out to have an unexpected business sense, and after several mishaps, Joel finds himself running a prostitution ring in his home, at least while his folks are away. The final shot of a smirking Joel, eyes hidden behind dark glasses, suggests the end of innocence.

## Roxie Hart

★★★ Fox, 1942, 75 min. Dir: William A. Wellman. SP: Nunnally Johnson, b/o play by Maurine Watkins. Cast: Ginger Rogers, Adolphe Menjou, George Montgomery, Lynne Overman, Nigel Bruce, Spring Byington, William Frawley, Sara Allgood, Iris Adrian.

This fast-paced satire on morality in Chicago of the twenties was based on the stage play *Chicago,* which was first filmed in 1927. When gum-chewing flapper Ginger Rogers shoots her lover, she hires "a simple barefoot mouthpiece" (Menjou), who turns her into a media celebrity. Roxie rides the case to fame with a press that is more than happy to accommodate her. Although not in a class with Wellman's best work, the movie is sardonic fun, much of which comes from the expert timing of Menjou and Lynne Overman as a cynical reporter. In 1975, the movie was turned into the stage musical *Chicago,* which was revived successfully in 1996.

## The Russians Are Coming! The Russians Are Coming!

★★☆ United Artists, 1966, c, 126 min. Dir: Norman Jewison. SP: William Rose, b/o novel by Nathaniel Benchley. Cast: Carl Reiner, Eva Marie Saint, Alan Arkin, Brian Keith, Jonathan Winters, Paul Ford, Theodore Bikel, John Philip Law, Tessie O'Shea, Ben Blue, Doro Merande, Parker Fennelly.

A hectic spoof of cold war paranoia that doesn't come off, despite an expert cast of comedy performers. On Gloucester Island off the New England coast, a Russian submarine is grounded by its captain (Bikel). As the Russian sailors come ashore, the islanders become convinced that a full-scale Soviet invasion is taking place. Soon comic chaos reigns, involving, among others, a visiting writer (Reiner) and his family. Most of the characters behave like fools, which is no guarantee of laughs. Alan Arkin, in his feature debut, is genuinely funny as a Russian sailor, and some of the veterans in the cast, particularly Doro Merande as the island's hapless postmistress, are still a pleasure to watch. But the movie loses steam long before the end.

## S.O.B.

★★☆ Lorimar, 1981, c, 121 min. Dir and SP: Blake Edwards. Cast: Julie Andrews, William Holden, Robert Preston, Richard Mulligan, Robert Vaughn, Loretta Swit, Shelley Winters, Larry Hagman, Stuart Margolin, Craig Stevens, Gene Nelson., Marisa Berinson, Robert Loggia.

Ostensibly bitter about his treatment by the film capital in the early seventies, Blake Edwards wrote and directed this caustic satire. Treacherous, cynical, and heartless behavior is rampant in Hollywood after producer Felix Farmer (Mulligan) cracks up when his latest mega-movie fails ignominiously. Swirling around him are such characters as his movie-star wife (Andrews), a cheerfully debauched director (Holden, in his last movie), a "feel-good" doctor (Preston), a gossip ogre (Swit), and many others. The cast is well seasoned, and the story moves fairly effortlessly between slapstick and satire, but the tone is so unrelentingly sour that many viewers might check out before the movie ends.

## The Secret of My Success

★★☆ Universal, 1987, c, 109 min. Dir: Herbert Ross. SP: Jim Cash, Jack Epps, Jr., A. J. Carothers, b/o story by A. J.

Carothers. Cast: Michael J. Fox, Helen Slater, Margaret Whitton, Richard Jordan, John Pankow, Fred Gwynne, Christopher Murney.

A sort of nonmusical *How to Succeed in Business Without Really Trying*, *The Secret of My Success* stars Michael J. Fox as an eager young man from Kansas who aspires to be a top-ranking business executive. Joining the corporation of his Uncle Howard (Jordan), he starts in the mail room, then commandeers an empty office where he sets himself up as an executive. He has an affair with a predatory woman (Whitton) who turns out to be his aunt and also falls for a fellow executive (Slater), who is trying to end an affair with Uncle Howard. All these amorous maneuverings are mixed in with some satirical reflections on big business, and the result is pleasant but hardly memorable.

## Serial Mom

★★ Savoy, 1994, c, 93 min. Dir and SP: John Waters. Cast: Kathleen Turner, Sam Waterston, Ricki Lake, Matthew Lillard, Mink Stole, Suzanne Somers.

Another attempt by director John Waters to go mainstream, this black comedy seems to have found an audience but its satire is very heavy-handed. Kathleen Turner plays Beverly Sutphin, a cheerful Baltimore housewife who has one serious flaw: she murders anyone who displeases her. This includes her son's teacher, her thoughtless neighbor, and a hapless woman who makes the fashion mistake of wearing white shoes after Labor Day. Beverly's killing spree makes her a media celebrity. Much of Waters's humor is gross indeed, and after a while the single idea becomes tiresome, but some viewers laughed appreciatively.

## Shampoo

★★★ Columbia, 1975, c, 109 min. Dir: Hal Ashby. SP: Robert Towne, Warren Beatty. Cast: Warren Beatty, Julie Christie, Goldie Hawn, Lee Grant, Jack Warden, Carrie Fisher, Tony Bill.

The date: November 4, 1968, on the eve of Richard Nixon's election. Beverly Hills hairdresser George Roundy (Beatty) does not have politics on his mind—he is too busy juggling his women: pert Jill (Hawn), married Felicia (Grant), and ex-lover Jackie (Christie). To complicate matters, Felicia is married to Lester (Warden), whose current mistress is Jackie. *Shampoo*, however, is much more than a sexual roundelay—it is also a biting commentary on the high life of the late sixties, when many people seemed to be morally and emotionally bankrupt. For all of his sexual prowess ("It makes me feel like I'm going to live forever!"), George ends up alone, deserted by everyone. *Shampoo* sometimes presses too hard to make its points, but it is definitely worth a look.

## Smile

★★★☆ United Artists, 1975, c, 113 min. Dir: Michael Ritchie. SP: Jerry Belson. Cast: Bruce Dern, Barbara Feldon, Michael Kidd, Geoffrey Lewis, Nicholas Pryor, Colleen Camp, Joan Prather, Annette O'Toole, Maria O'Brien, Denise Nickerson, Eric Shea.

A true gem, and one of the neglected films of the seventies, *Smile* takes a satirical, and highly perceptive, look at a teenage beauty pageant held in Santa Rosa, California. As adolescent girls compete for the coveted title of beauty queen, a hectic atmosphere of merchandising, boosterism, and backstage politics swirls around them. Characters include Bruce Dern as the contest's chief judge, a local mobile-home dealer; Barbara Feldon as the girls's mother hen who fails to see her own marital problems; and Michael Kidd as the pageant's choreographer, whose career is fading. The movie may lack the sharp teeth of true satire—it really is fond of its beleaguered people—but it wins laughs. A worthy stage musical version had a brief Broadway run in 1986.

## Soapdish

★★★ Paramount, 1991, c, 92 min. Dir: Michael Hoffman. SP: Robert Harling, Andrew Bergman. Cast: Sally Field, Kevin Kline, Robert Downey, Jr., Cathy Moriarty, Whoopi

Goldberg, Elisabeth Shue, Carrie Fisher, Garry Marshall, Teri Hatcher.

What goes on behind the scenes of a soap opera? This hectic but sometimes uproarious spoof would have you believe that the daily activities include rivalry, treachery, and hanky-panky. The plot of the soap opera being performed defies belief, but the offstage carryings-on are not much more credible. Sally Field is the temperamental soap-opera queen who is being conspired against by the show's producer (Downey) and a predatory blonde (Moriarty). Kevin Kline plays a down-on-his luck actor and an ex-lover of Field's who is brought back into the cast. Many in-jokes at the expense of television make *Soapdish* rowdy fun.

## Support Your Local Sheriff

★★★ United Artists, 1969, c, 93 min. Dir: Burt Kennedy. SP: William Bowers. Cast: James Garner, Joan Hackett, Walter Brennan, Bruce Dern, Jack Elam, Harry Morgan, Henry Jones, Walter Burke.

James Garner in his trademark style—bemused, cagey, self-protective, and funny—stars in this diverting Western spoof. He plays Jason McCullogh, who takes a job as sheriff to a wild Western town controlled by nasty Pa Denby (Brennan, in a takeoff of his Old Man Clanton character in *My Darling Clementine*). Jason also finds himself saddled with a hopelessly inept deputy (Elam) and romantically involved with the mayor's feisty but clumsy daughter Purdy (Hackett). ("Puberty hit her hard," her father admits.) The movie sends up many Western clichés in cheerful style. Some of the players, including Garner, and the director returned for a similar movie, not a sequel, called *Support Your Local Gunfighter* (1971).

## Sweet Liberty

★★☆ Universal, 1986, c, 107 min. Dir and SP: Alan Alda. Cast: Alan Alda, Michael Caine, Michelle Pfeiffer, Bob Hoskins, Lillian Gish, Lise Hilboldt, Saul Rubinek, Lois Chiles.

Alan Alda wrote and directed this mildly satiric comedy, which is not among his best. He also plays Michael Burgess, a college professor whose historical novel set during the American Revolution is being filmed. A movie company descends on Michael's small college town to shoot the movie version of his book. Among them are the film's leading man (Caine), screenwriter (Hoskins), and director (Rubinek). Michael is dismayed to learn that his book is being turned into a lusty Revolutionary War comedy. He also becomes involved with the movie's sexy leading lady (Pfeiffer). An attractive cast, but the movie never has the bite it needs to spoof adequately the chaos of movie-making on location. Lillian Gish appears in a small role as Alda's dotty old mother.

## Swimming with Sharks

★★☆ Trimark, 1994, 101 min. Dir and SP: George Huang. Cast: Kevin Spacey, Frank Whaley, Michelle Forbes, Benicio Del Toro, Jerry Levine, Roy Dotrice.

Buddy Ackerman (Spacey) is an authentic monster. As Vice President of Production for a major Hollywood studio, he delights in berating, abusing, and humiliating everyone he can. His latest victim is Guy (Whaley), who has ambitions for making it big in the movie business. Guy endures Buddy's sadistic treatment but only up to a point, when he turns the tables in ruthless fashion. Michelle Forbes is a woman who uses Guy to get "access" to Buddy. George Huang's movie offers some razor-sharp satire in the early portions, but turns dank and sour later on. Fine actor Spacey is riveting as Buddy.

## Swingers

★★★ Miramax, 1996, c, 97 min. Dir: Doug Liman. SP: Jon Favreau. Cast: Jon Favreau, Vince Vaughn, Ron Livingston, Patrick Van Horn, Alex Desert.

Surprise: here's a genial, frequently funny film that actually has something to say about the single life of men in Los Angeles. Mike (Favreau, who also wrote the screenplay) is an aspiring comedian from Queens who feigns savoir-faire while striking out continually with women. He and friend Trent (Vaughn) travel to Las Vegas, where their luck is not much better. Back in Los Angeles, Mike continues to offend the locals in his very own clueless ways. (He wears a Queens College T-shirt while playing golf badly.) *Swingers* does an expert job of capturing the bravura and the deceptions of Mike and his friends.

## Taking Off

★★★☆ Universal, 1971, c, 93 min. Dir: Milos Forman. SP: Milos Forman, John Guare, Jean-Claude Carriere, and John Klein. Cast: Lynn Carlin, Buck Henry, Linnea Heacock, Georgia Engel, Tony Harvey, Audra Lindley, Paul Benedict, Vincent Schiavelli.

A favorite theme of the late sixties and early seventies was the clash between conservative parents and their anti-establishment children. *Taking Off* takes off amusingly on this theme, dealing with a suburban couple (Carlin and Henry) whose impressionable daughter (Heacock) vanishes into the dropout culture of New York City's East Village. The couple's search for their daughter takes them into a startling new world that releases their own inhibitions. Much of the movie's satire revolves about the Society for Parents of Fugitive Children, where (in the funniest sequence) members smoke pot at a black-tie banquet or play strip poker with their newly acquired friends. Milos Forman's first American movie.

## Teachers

★★☆ MGM, 1984, c, 106 min. Dir: Arthur Hiller. SP: W. P. McKinney. Cast: Nick Nolte, JoBeth Williams, Judd Hirsch, Ralph Macchio, Lee Grant, Allen Garfield, Laura Dern, Richard Mulligan, Morgan Freeeman, Crispin Glover.

This comedy-drama would like to be to teachers what *The Hospital* (1971; see page 180) was to doctors (both films even have the same director), but it's much too strident and its mixture of blistering satire and serious drama doesn't gel. The setting is John F. Kennedy High School, where the teachers are incompetent, indifferent, or boring, and the students are sometimes out of control. Amidst all the chaos, one ex-student is suing the school for allowing him to graduate without learning how to read or write. Nick Nolte plays a burned-out social studies teacher who recovers pride in his profession while falling for the lawyer (Williams) involved in the lawsuit. There are a few pungent scenes and an over-the-top Frank Capra–like climax that strains credulity.

## This Is Spinal Tap

★★★☆ Embassy, 1984, c, 82 min. Dir: Rob Reiner. SP: Christopher Guest, Michael McKean, Harry Shearer, Rob Reiner. Cast: Rob Reiner, Christopher Guest, Michael McKean, Harry Shearer, Tony Hendra, June Chadwick, R. J. Parnell.

A funny—and wickedly accurate—mock-documentary, Rob Reiner's *This Is Spinal Tap* purports to be a film about a British rock band called Spinal Tap and their whirlwind tour of America. The band is, in fact, not only fictional but also dreadful, and the movie exposes their precipitous descent to near-oblivion. A documentary filmmaker named Martin DiBergi (Reiner himself) records their dwindling audiences, their quarrels among themselves, and their truly inane lyrics. ("The looser the waistband, the deeper the quicksand.") Reiner uses all the familiar documentary techniques to reveal Spinal Tap's fatuousness and abysmal lack of talent. *This Is Spinal Tap* eventually became a justified cult success.

## ¡Three Amigos!

★★ Orion, 1986, c, 105 min. Dir: John Landis. SP: Steve Martin, Lorne Michaels, Randy Newman. Cast: Chevy Chase, Steve Martin, Martin Short, Joe Mantegna, Patrice Martinez, Alfonso Arau, Jon Lovitz.

It's 1916, and three silent movie heroes (Chase, Martin, and Short) are suddenly out of work, tossed out by the studio that made them stars. Of course they are, in fact, inept fools one and all. Summoned to Mexico by peons who believe their publicity and want them to rid their town of tyrants, the Three Amigos (as they call themselves) find big trouble in the form of a bandit chieftain called El Guapo (Arau) and his cohorts, as well as some nasty German types who would like to see them dead. Despite their bumbling attempts at heroism, the Amigos prevail. Virtually every joke is telegraphed or stale, but there are a few amusing songs by Randy Newman. (For one "sunny" tune, the animals of the area gather in reverent attention.).

## To Be or Not To Be

★★★☆ United Artists, 1942, 99 min. Dir: Ernst Lubitsch. SP: Edwin Justus Mayer, b/o story by Ernst Lubitsch, Melchior Lengyel. Cast: Jack Benny, Carole Lombard, Robert Stack, Felix Bressart, Sig Ruman, Lionel Atwill, Stanley Ridges.

At the height of World War II, Director Ernst Lubitsch provoked some controversy with this satirical view of the spreading Nazi insanity. Jack Benny temporarily left his popular radio show to play Joseph Tura, the ego-driven half of a famous Polish acting team. Carole Lombard, in her last film, is Irene, the alluring other half. When the Nazis take over Poland, the couple manages to outwit the invaders, but not before many plot complications. Lubitsch was accused of trivializing the plight of occupied Poland, but the movie's mixture of satire, melodrama, and a touch of poignancy stamps it as an original of the period. Mel Brooks's 1983 remake was merely adequate.

## To Die For

★★★ Columbia, 1995, c, 103 min. Dir: Gus Van Sant. SP: Buck Henry, b/o novel by Joyce Maynard. Cast: Nicole Kidman, Matt Dillon, Joaquin Phoenix, Illeana Douglas, Casey Affleck, Dan Hedaya, Alison Folland, Kurtwood Smith.

Say hello to Suzanne Stone (Kidman). Stunning in face and figure, Suzanne is also sweetly homicidal. Totally obsessed with becoming a television celebrity, she decides to eliminate her gentle husband (Dillon) when he wants her to forget her search for TV stardom and settle down to home and children. And so she seduces an impressionable teenager (Phoenix) into killing her husband, with the help of several equally clueless friends. The murder makes her the celebrity she always wanted to be. Although it doesn't always work, To Die For is a wickedly funny spin on the American lust for fame at any cost, and Nicole Kidman makes a fetching psychopath. Best performance: Illeana Douglas as Suzanne's knowing sister-in-law.

## Vampire's Kiss

★★ Hemdale, 1988, c, 96 min. Dir: Robert Bierman. SP: Joseph Minion. Cast: Nicolas Cage, Maria Conchita Alonso, Jennifer Beals, Elizabeth Ashley, Kasi Lemmons, Bob Lujan, Jennifer Lundy.

Take your pick: Is Vampire's Kiss a horror film or a spoof of a horror film? Is Nicolas Cage's performance a tour-de-force, or simply the Worst Performance by an Actor in a Leading Role? He plays a hotshot literary agent by day and a tireless womanizer by night. One unlucky night he is bitten in the jugular by a fanged woman (Beals). Soon he is convinced that he is a vampire, chomping on insects and live pigeons, smashing mirrors, and gorging on the neck of a disco patron. Cage is outrageously over the top in a snarling, eye-popping, demented display that may have you laughing rather than screaming. Funniest bit: Cage and his makeshift coffin.

## Wagons East!

★ Tri-Star, 1994, c, 106 min. Dir: Peter Markle. SP: Matthew Carlson, b/o story by Jerry Abrahamson. Cast: John Candy, Richard Lewis, Ellen Greene, John C. McGinley, Robert Picardo, Ed Lauter, Rodney A. Grant, William Sanderson.

John Candy's last film, and sadly, a poor one. Drawing on little of his amiable persona, this would-be spoof of Western films has him playing James Harlow, a bewhiskered souse who signs on as wagonmaster to a group of pioneers who are sick of the wild West and want to return home. Harlow is inept but game as the wagon train confronts Indians, an outlaw named Slade (who is pursued like the Road Runner), and even the U.S. Cavalry in an absurd climax. Richard Lewis, usually trading on his doom-laden comic style, gets few opportunities to win laughs as the doctor who organizes the journey. *Wagons East!* is so bad it makes Mel Brooks's *Blazing Saddles* look like a masterpiece.

## Wholly Moses

★★ Columbia, 1980, c, 109 min. Dir: Gary Weis. SP: Guy Thomas. Cast: Dudley Moore, Laraine Newman, James Coco, Paul Sand, Jack Gilford, Dom DeLuise, Richard Pryor, Madeline Kahn, John Houseman, David L. Lander, John Ritter.

*Wholly Moses* is clearly intended as a spoof of Biblical epics in the Mel Brooks style, but most of it simply doesn't come off. Dudley Moore plays Herschel, who comes to believe that he and not Moses is the savior who will free the Israelites from bondage in Egypt. (Moses is his brother-in-law.) His hapless adventures bring him into contact with a variety of characters, including his one true love (Newman), a lone stranger in the desert (DeLuise in a funny cameo), an archangel (Houseman) holding secret meetings in Sodom, and the Pharaoh himself (a very modern-day Pryor). An expert cast, but too often the movie merely plods along, dispensing feeble gags.

## Will Success Spoil Rock Hunter?

★★☆ Fox, 1957, c, 94 min. Dir and SP: Frank Tashlin, b/o play by George Axelrod. Cast: Tony Randall, Jayne Mansfield, Betsy Drake, Joan Blondell, Henry Jones, John Williams, Mickey Hargitay.

Frank Tashlin used George Axelrod's Broadway play as a springboard for a wild-and-woolly farce with splashes of satire, and it now seems more like an artifact of the period than an authentically entertaining movie. Tony Randall plays Rockwell Hunter, an advertising man who strives to save his job and his agency by getting the endorsement of movie glamor queen Rita Marlowe (Mansfield in the role she played on stage) for his client's lipstick. Instead he becomes her "lover boy" and a media sensation. The movie has a few unusual touches, notably a mid-movie spoof of television, but it's more frenetic than funny.

## Without a Clue

★★ Orion, 1988, c, 106 min. Dir: Thom Eberhardt. SP: Gary Murphy, Larry Strawther. Cast: Michael Caine, Ben Kingsley, Jeffrey Jones, Lysette Anthony, Paul Freeman, Nigel Davenport, Peter Cook.

A one-joke satire, but not a particularly good joke. The movie advances the idea that Sherlock Holmes (Caine) was actually a sodden, stupid actor who merely impersonated the famed detective and that the true deductive genius was his friend Dr. John Watson (Kingsley). The two are brought into a case in which the economic future of Great Britain is in jeopardy when the original engravings for the hundred-pound note are stolen. The thief, of course, is Holmes's perennial nemesis, Dr. Moriarty (Freeman). A handsome production is offset by a tepid screenplay that milks the one joke repeatedly and sparks little interest in the case at hand. Caine and Kingsley do all they can with the weak material.

## The World's Greatest Lover

★★★ Fox, 1977, c, 89 min. Dir and SP: Gene Wilder. Cast: Gene Wilder, Carol Kane, Dom DeLuise, Fritz Feld, Ronny Graham, Hannah Dean, Candice Azzara, Carl Ballantine.

An all-Gene Wilder production, with Wilder co-producing, writing, directing, and starring in an occasionally funny comedy satire. He plays Rudy Valentine, a neurotic Milwaukee butcher who, in 1926, sets out for Hollywood to become the new Rudolph Valentino. Undeterred by the fact he in no way resembles the star, Valentine is accompanied by his daffy wife, Annie (Kane), who has a crush on the real

Valentino. It's no surprise that the movie resembles a Mel Brooks comedy, but on his own Wilder extracts some real laughs from Dom DeLuise as a manic studio chief and Ronny Graham as a harried movie director. Inspired by Fellini's 1950 comedy, *The White Sheik*.

## Wrongfully Accused

★★ Warners, 1998, c, 85 min. Dir and SP: Pat Proft. Cast: Leslie Nielsen, Richard Crenna, Kelly Le Brock, Sandra Bernhard, Michael York, Melinda McGraw.

Pat Proft, one of the writers on the *Naked Gun* films, strikes out on his own in this parody of *The Fugitive,* and on the whole, he strikes out. Leslie Nielsen, by now the uncrowned King of Spoofs, stars as Ryan Harrison, who is found holding a gun and lying next to the dead body of tycoon Hibbing Goodhue (York). Harrison claims that the murder was committed by a one-armed, one-legged, one-eyed terrorist but of course nobody believes him, and he is soon convicted of murder. He escapes, and spends the rest of the movie trying to prove his innocence. The constant barrage of gags includes references to Hong Kong action movies, *Titanic, North by Northwest,* and the *E.R.* television series, among many others. A few laughs, but not much more.

## Zorro the Gay Blade

★★☆ Fox, 1981, c, 93 min. Dir: Peter Medak. SP: Hal Dresner, b/o character created by Johnston M. McCulley. Cast: George Hamilton, Lauren Hutton, Brenda Vaccaro, Ron Leibman, Donovan Scott, James Booth, Helen Burns, Clive Revill.

George Hamilton shows an unexpected flair for comedy in this broad, highly uneven spoof of the dashing swashbucklers about the legendary bandit Zorro. Here, Hamilton plays a dual role, both as Don Diego Vega, the nineteenth-century Spanish-American aristocrat who disguises himself as the masked and caped Zorro and rides around the countryside "helping the helpless and defeating the defeatless," and as Don Diego's foppish, effeminate brother Bunny Wigglesworth. When Don Diego is felled by a broken ankle, guess who takes over. Ron Leibman does little more than scream and shout as Zorro's overbearing enemy, but Brenda Vaccaro is funny as his sex-hungry wife.

# Across the Footlights: Comedies from the Stage

The theater has long been a prolific source of material for motion pictures; one of the earliest movies had stage star Sarah Bernhardt repeating her role as England's Queen Elizabeth I for the camera. If something is occasionally lost in transition (humor can flatten out on its way to the screen), we can at least appreciate the wit, the charm, and the tweaking of humankind's foibles that made theater audiences laugh.

## Ah, Wilderness!

★★★ MGM, 1935, c, 101 min. Dir: Clarence Brown. SP: Albert Hackett, Frances Goodrich, b/o play by Eugene O'Neill. Cast: Wallace Beery, Lionel Barrymore, Eric Linden, Aline MacMahon, Cecilia Parker, Mickey Rooney, Spring Byington, Charley Grapewin, Bonita Granville.

Often revived and even musicalized for the screen (*Summer Holiday,* 1948) and the stage (*Take Me Along,* 1959), Eugene O'Neill's gentle, affectionate play receives a competent MGM treatment in this film. Far removed from O'Neill's somber dramas, it centers on young Richard Miller (Linden), whose churning adolescence leads him mildly astray. Barrymore plays his understanding father and Beery is his boisterous, alcoholic uncle. Since both actors were congenitally incapable of underplaying any role, the movie loses some of its quiet charm, but there is enough flavorsome Americana to make the film genial entertainment.

## Any Wednesday

★★☆ Warners, 1966, c, 108 min. Dir: Robert Ellis Miller. SP: Julius J. Epstein, b/o play by Muriel Resnik. Cast: Jane Fonda, Jason Robards, Dean Jones, Rosemary Murphy, Ann Prentiss, Jack Fletcher.

A comedy hit on Broadway in 1964, *Any Wednesday* comes to the screen with the basic idea intact and probably the same number of laughs, but it's much ado about very little. Jane Fonda plays Ellen, a thirty-year-old woman who is being kept by John Cleves (Robards), her well-to do and married lover, in a tax-exempt executive suite. Robards plays the rather philandering Cleves with his usual brusque authority, and Fonda, as she was in her early acting years, is extremely frisky and animated. The choice performance, however, is given by Rosemary Murphy, repeating her stage role as Cleves's wife, Dorothy. Dean Jones is on hand to win Fonda in the end.

## Auntie Mame

★★★☆ Warners, 1958, c, 143 min. Dir: Morton DaCosta. SP: Betty Comden, Adolph Green, b/o novel by Patrick Dennis and play by Jerome Lawrence, Robert E. Lee. Cast: Rosalind Russell, Forrest Tucker, Coral Browne, Peggy Cass, Fred Clark, Roger Smith, Jan Handzlik.

The story of irrepressible Mame Dennis had a long career in books, movies, and theater. This is the movie version without music, starring Rosalind Russell, who originated the role. The movie is more of a series of blackout sketches than a coherent narrative, but it covers the high points in entertaining style as Mame's fortunes rise and fall over the years. Always the center of her attention—and the true love of her life—is her nephew (Handzlik as a boy, Smith as an adult), whom she teaches all about bigotry, individuality, and life itself. Russell is delightful, but the movie is stolen by Peggy Cass as Mame's dowdy secretary Agnes Gooch, who really learns how to "live." Cass, Russell, and the movie won Oscar nominations.

## Barefoot in the Park

★★★ Warners, 1967, c, 105 min. Dir: Gene Saks. SP: Neil Simon, b/o his play. Cast: Jane Fonda, Robert Redford, Charles Boyer, Mildred Natwick, Herb Edelman.

A lighthearted film version of Neil Simon's Broadway success, *Barefoot in the Park* centers on the Bratters (Redford and Fonda), a newly married young couple who move into a top-floor apartment of a walk-up building in New York City. He's an aspiring lawyer, and she's an adorable free spirit, and inevitably there are problems, resulting in quarrels and a brief separation. More fun than these two are Charles Boyer as a rakish, eccentric neighbor and Mildred Natwick as Fonda's wry, sensible mother who unwinds under Boyer's influence. Far too much is made of the steep climb to the Bratters' apartment, which leaves everyone breathless. Neil Simon would do better work in later years, but *Barefoot in the Park* is likable entertainment.

## Bell, Book and Candle

★★★ Columbia, 1958, c, 103 min. Dir: Richard Quine. SP: Daniel Taradash, b/o play by John Van Druten. Cast: James Stewart, Kim Novak, Jack Lemmon, Hermione Gingold, Elsa Lanchester, Ernie Kovacs, Janice Rule.

Considering the subject matter, it would be nice to say that this romantic comedy, an adaptation of a John Van Druten play, is "bewitching," but it's not. It is, however, a moderately entertaining film, with a good cast and an attractive physical production. Kim Novak plays a beautiful modern-day witch, the owner of a shop selling primitive art, who places the publisher (Stewart) she covets under a romantic spell, only to make the unwitchlike mistake of falling in love with him. Stewart and Novak are adequate but hardly up to their stage equivalents, Rex Harrison and Lilli Palmer. The supporting cast is best, especially Jack Lemmon as Novak's mischievous brother and Elsa Lanchester as her dotty aunt.

## Biloxi Blues

★★★ Rastar. 1988, c, 106 min. Dir: Mike Nichols. SP: Neil Simon, b/o his play. Cast: Matthew Broderick, Christopher Walken, Matt Mulhern, Corey Parker, Markus Flanagan, Penelope Ann Miller, Casey Siemaszko, Park Overall, Michael Dolan.

This second entry in Neil Simon's stage trilogy on the adventures of Brooklynite Eugene Jerome has its share of serious moments, but mostly it's an enjoyable movie , a notch or two better than the standard military comedy. Now Eugene has been drafted into the army near the end of World War II, and he must contend with the standard-issue tough sergeant (Walken). He is also inaugurated into sex (by way of prostitute Overall) and enjoys a brief romance with a local belle (Miller). Unlike the old service comedies with Bob Hope or Abbott and Costello, *Biloxi Blues* touches on such subjects as anti-Semitism and homosexuality. Matthew Broderick is amiable in his stage role of the endlessly wisecracking Eugene.

## Born Yesterday

★★★ Columbia, 1950, 103 min. Dir: George Cukor. SP: Albert Mannheimer, b/o play by Garson Kanin. Cast: Judy Holliday, William Holden, Broderick Crawford, Howard St. John, Frank Otto, Larry Oliver, Barbara Brown.

Judy Holliday always invested her dumb-as-a-fox roles with a singular warmth and appeal. Here she repeated her famous stage role and won an Oscar for her effort. She plays Billie Dawn, the none-too-bright mistress of powerful junk dealer Harry Brock (Crawford), who has come to Washington to form an illegal cartel. Harry makes the mistake of hiring reporter Paul Verrall (Holden) to give Billie some polish. She turns out to be a fast learner who not only recognizes Harry's corrupt ways but who also starts a romance with Paul. Holliday is wonderful, but Holden is miscast and Crawford plays Harry as a bellowing blunderbuss without a shred of likability. Except for a few shots of the nation's capital, the movie has something of the static quality of a filmed play. A weak 1993 remake starred Melanie Griffith and John Goodman.

## Boy Meets Girl

★★★ Warners, 1938, 86 min. Dir: Lloyd Bacon. SP: Bella Spewack, Samuel Spewack, b/o their play. Cast: James Cagney, Pat O'Brien, Marie Wilson, Ralph Bellamy, Dick Foran, Penny Singleton, Frank McHugh, Ronald Reagan.

A helter-skelter spoof of Hollywood ways, derived by Bella and Samuel Spewack from their Broadway play. James Cagney and Pat O'Brien play manic writers who take a pregnant waitress (Wilson) under their protective wing. The baby, known as "Happy," becomes a movie star. The movie extracted some of the teeth from the stage satire, but there was enough fun in seeing the familiar Cagney-O'Brien team cutting capers. Amusing characters included the numbskull producer (Bellamy) and the idiot Western star (Foran). Look for Ronald Reagan's brief appearance as a radio announcer.

## Bus Stop

★★★ Fox, 1956, c, 96 min. Dir: Joshua Logan. SP: George Axelrod, b/o play by William Inge. Cast: Marilyn Monroe, Don Murray, Arthur O'Connell, Betty Field, Eileen Heckart, Robert Bray, Hope Lange, Hans Conried, Casey Adams.

Marilyn Monroe proved that she could give an effective, even touching performance in this very good adaptation of the hit Broadway play. She's Cherie, the none-too-bright, sweet-natured girl who is ardently pursued by Beau (Murray, in his film debut), a wild young cowboy who is determined to marry her. The setting is an Arizona bus stop where a winter storm has kept the passengers (including Cherie and Beau) from continuing on their

In *Born Yesterday* (1950), junk dealer Broderick Crawford (center) hires William Holden to smarten up his girlfriend Judy Holliday. Holliday repeated her stage performance and won an Oscar.

way. There is interaction among the characters, but the heart of this comedy-drama is the ever-changing, volatile relationship of Cherie and Beau, and especially Cherie's efforts to find a measure of dignity and happiness in a hostile world. Highlight: Monroe's "performance" of "That Old Black Magic."

## Butterflies Are Free

★★☆ Columbia, 1972, c, 109 min. Dir: Milton Katselas. SP: Leonard Gershe, b/o his play. Cast: Goldie Hawn, Edward Albert, Eileen Heckart, Michael Glaser, Mike Warren.

Leonard Gershe's mild adaptation of his equally mild Broadway play, *Butterflies Are Free* gave Goldie Hawn another opportunity to transfer her "kooky" *Laugh-In* persona to the screen. (Her 1969 debut in *Cactus Flower* won her an Academy Award.) Here she plays the light-headed neighbor to blind young Edward Albert, with whom she starts a tentative romance. Trouble looms with Albert's overprotective suburban mother, played with Oscar-winning finesse by fine actress Eileen Heckart. (In many stage productions, the mother became the leading role.) You won't be surprised when Mother abandons her selfish ways for the happy ending. Hawn is winsome and adorably dumb, which is all the role requires.

## Cactus Flower

★★ Columbia, 1969, c, 103 min. Dir: Gene Saks. SP: I.A.L. Diamond, b/o play by Abe Burrows, adapted from play by Barillet and Gredy. Cast: Walter Matthau, Ingrid Bergman, Goldie Hawn, Jack Weston, Rick Lenz, Vito Scotti, Irene Hervey.

It's difficult to fathom why Ingrid Bergman, after an absence of twenty years, would return to Hollywood to star in this dismal adaptation of the Broadway play. There is scarcely a shred of wit in this tale of an amorous dentist (Matthau) and his long-time nurse (Bergman). Matthau has told his latest girlfriend (Hawn) that he has a wife, and when the scatterbrained Hawn demands to meet her, he asks Bergman to play the role. Bergman, who has loved him in silence all these years, agrees, and complications mount. As the efficient nurse, Bergman is called on eventually to unbend, cavort, and dance to a disco beat; as usual, when Hollywood asks its regal stars to shed their dignity, it's an embarrassing mistake. Inexplicably, Hawn won the Best Supporting Actress Oscar.

## California Suite

★★★ Columbia, 1978, c, 103 min. Dir: Herbert Ross. SP: Neil Simon, b/o his play. Cast: Jane Fonda, Alan Alda, Michael Caine, Maggie Smith, Bill Cosby, Richard Pryor, Walter Matthau, Elaine May, Herb Edelman.

On the stage, Neil Simon's play offered four sketches involving various guests of the Beverly Hills Hotel. Translated to the screen, the four stories were interwoven to create a fitfully amusing film. The stories involved Jane Fonda and Alan Alda as a divorced couple exchanging barbs; Walter Matthau as the victim of a prank that entangles him in a seeming indiscretion; Bill Cosby and Richard Pryor as vacationers caught up in slapstick mishaps; and Maggie Smith and Michael Caine as an estranged, bickering British couple attending the Academy Award ceremonies (she is a nominee). The last segment was much the best, sharply written and expertly played by Caine and Smith. In a case of life imitating art, Smith won that year's Best Supporting Actress Oscar.

## The Cemetery Club

★★☆ Buena Vista, 1993, c, 100 min. Dir: Bill Duke. SP: Ivan Menchell, b/o his play. Cast: Ellen Burstyn, Olympia Dukakis, Diane Ladd, Danny Aiello, Lainie Kazan, Jeff Howell, Christina Ricci, Bernie Casey, Alan Manson.

In this adaptation of the Broadway play, three Jewish widows strive to find meaning in their lives after their bereavement. Esther (Burstyn) was happily married for thirty-nine years. Doris (Dukakis) has never stopped grieving, and to her, visiting her husband's grave site is a religious calling. Lucille (Ladd) is an ever-hopeful widow with an unhappy secret. Their friendly relationship is threatened when Esther becomes involved with a retired policeman (Aiello) who drives a cab. *The Cemetery Club* mixes humor and sentiment, with perhaps more emphasis on the sentiment, but a good cast cannot bring it to life. In the great tradition of cemetery scenes, each of the ladies takes a turn talking to her husband's tombstone.

## Come Blow Your Horn

★ Paramount, 1963, c, 112 min. Dir: Bud Yorkin. SP: Norman Lear, b/o play by Neil Simon. Cast: Frank Sinatra, Molly Picon, Lee J. Cobb, Tony Bill, Barbara Rush, Jill St. John, Dan Blocker.

Adapted from Neil Simon's first Broadway success, *Come Blow Your Horn* is a movie of stupefying awfulness. Frank Sinatra stars as Alan Baker, a playboy with wall-to-wall girlfriends, a posh New York pad, and an indifference to work. Along comes his kid brother (Bill), free at last from their overpowering parents and eager to learn about life and love from Big Brother. The big troublemakers are Mom and Dad, portrayed as grotesque parodies of Jewish parenthood: Mom (Picon) has a doctorate in Guilt Inducement and Dad (Cobb) never stops bellowing. They are a depressing pair. Here it is at last: a comedy without a single redeeming quality.

## Dinner at Eight

★★★★ MGM, 1933, 133 min. Dir: George Cukor. SP: Frances Marion, Herman J. Mankiewicz, Donald Ogden Stewart, b/o play by George S. Kaufman, Edna Ferber. Cast: Marie Dressler, John Barrymore, Wallace Beery, Jean Harlow, Lionel Barrymore, Billie Burke, Lee Tracy, Edmund Lowe, Madge Evans.

*Dinner at Eight* is one of two MGM blockbusters of the thirties that represent the apex of the studio's glittering, all-star approach to moviemaking. (*Grand Hotel* is the other.) An entertaining mixture of comedy and drama, the film revolves around the party to be given by shipping tycoon Lionel Barrymore and wife Billie Burke. Among the guests are a washed-up movie idol (John Barrymore), an aging actress (Dressler), and a boorish wheeler-dealer (Beery) who is about to sink his host's business. Beery's wife is a hilariously vulgar Jean Harlow, who walks off with the movie. There are various plot complications, but the movie's lasting appeal rests in the full-steam-ahead performances of the cast. Dressler's last line to Harlow at the movie's end is a classic.

## Don't Drink the Water

★★ Avco Embassy, 1969, c, 100 min. Dir: Howard Morris. SP: R. S. Allen, Harvey Bullock, b/o play by Woody Allen. Cast: Jackie Gleason, Estelle Parsons, Ted Bessell, Joan Delaney, Michael Constantine, Howard St. John, Danny Meehan, Richard Libertini.

A mostly clumsy film version of Woody Allen's Broadway play, *Don't Drink the Water* stars Jackie Gleason as a Newark caterer who finds himself trapped with his family behind the Iron Curtain, where they seek sanctuary in the American embassy. In very little time, they are suspected of espionage. The wisecracks and the sight gags arrive on schedule but most of them collapse limply on the screen. As the hapless Walter Hollander, Jackie Gleason can do little but bluster through his lines, although Estelle Parsons as his wife at least tries for a characterization. A television version, with Woody Allen himself as the beleaguered caterer, turned up in 1994, but it was not much better.

## Enter Laughing

★☆ Columbia, 1967, c, 112 min. Dir: Carl Reiner. SP: Joseph Stein, Carl Reiner, b/o play by Joseph Stein and novel by Carl Reiner. Cast: Reni Santoni, José Ferrer, Shelley Winters, Elaine May, Jack Gilford, Janet Margolin, Michael J. Pollard, David Opatoshu, Don Rickles.

Shelley Winters wins the Most Obnoxious Jewish Mother Award, hands down, in this dreary film version of the novel and play. Her son is David Kolowitz (Santoni), an aspiring but talent-free actor who would like to escape from the clutches of possessive, guilt-inducing Mama. (You cringe whenever she appears.) He joins a tacky theater company headed by Harrison

Marlowe (Ferrer) where the play is so bad it's miles beyond camp. Despite opposition from all sides, David persists in his hopeless quest to be an actor. Ferrer and May (as his actress-daughter) win a few laughs, but everyone else is defeated by the awful material. Even wonderful Jack Gilford is embarrassing as David's boss.

## First Monday in October

★★★ Paramount, 1981, c, 98 min. Dir: Ronald Neame. SP: Jerome Lawrence, Robert E. Lee, b/o their play. Cast: Walter Matthau, Jill Clayburgh, Barnard Hughes, Jan Sterling, James Stephens, Joshua Bryant.

A Spencer Tracy–Katharine Hepburn comedy without Tracy and Hepburn, *First Monday in October* adapts the Broadway play into a talky but fairly literate movie. Walter Matthau plays Dan Snow, the most liberal (and probably the crustiest) Justice on the Supreme Court. Jill Clayburgh is Ruth Loomis, a firm-minded, conservative, and widowed judge who is the newest appointee to the Court. The two are diametrically opposed in their views—he calls her "positively dangerous" and she says he is "an arrogant, self-centered male chauvinist pig!"—but of course they come to respect each other, with a hint of more than respect. The movie ends abruptly, but the leads make it reasonably palatable until then.

## 40 Carats

★★ Columbia, 1973, c, 110 min. Dir: Milton Katselas. SP: Leonard Gershe, b/o play by Barillet and Grédy, as adapted by Jay Allen. Cast: Liv Ullmann, Gene Kelly, Edward Albert, Binnie Barnes, Deborah Raffin, Nancy Walker, Rosemary Murphy, Don Porter.

A mild, only marginally entertaining adaptation of a hit Broadway comedy, which in itself was adapted from a French farce. Liv Ullmann (somewhat miscast) plays a forty-year-old divorcée who has a brief romantic fling with a twenty-two-year-old American (Albert) during a vacation in Greece. When he shows up back in New York City, still pursuing her amorously and now eager to marry, she agonizes over her

May-September situation until the inevitable conclusion. Gene Kelly helps as Ullmann's jaunty ex-husband, a movie actor, and the always welcome Binnie Barnes contributes a few bright notes as Ullmann's light-headed mother. But it's all much ado about very little.

## George Washington Slept Here

★★☆ Warners, 1942, 93 min. Dir: William Keighley. SP: Everett Freeman, b/o play by George S. Kaufman, Moss Hart. Cast: Jack Benny, Ann Sheridan, Charles Coburn, Percy Kilbride, Hattie McDaniel, Charles Dingle, Joyce Reynolds.

In the forties, Warner Bros. was fond of buying successful (or moderately successful) stage comedies and then beating them with a sledge hammer for the silver screen. *George Washington Slept Here* is a case in point. The Kaufman-Hart play about a Manhattan couple who buy a house in Bucks County, Pennsylvania, was not exactly subtle but it was never as heavy-handed as the movie. Jack Benny gets all the acerbic wisecracks and Ann Sheridan just looks harassed and beautiful as things go from bad to worse. As a hilariously laconic caretaker, Percy Kilbride repeats his stage performance and steals the show. A forerunner of all the Houses from Hell movies such as *Mr. Blandings Builds His Dream House*, *Funny Farm*, *The Money Pit*, and the like.

## Harvey

★★★ Universal-International, 1950, 104 min. Dir: Henry Koster. SP: Mary Chase, Oscar Brodney, b/o play by Mary Chase. Cast: James Stewart, Josephine Hull, Peggy Dow, Charles Drake, Victoria Horne, Cecil Kellaway, Jesse White, Wallace Ford, Nana Bryant.

The prize performance in this amiable comedy is given by Josephine Hull, who is totally endearing as Veta, the bewildered sister of cheerful drunkard Elwood P. Dowd (Stewart). Elwood, it seems, spends most of his time in a bar chatting with his best friend, a six-foot-three-and-a-half-foot invisible rabbit named Harvey. Complications ensue when Veta tries to have her brother committed to an asylum.

Adapted from the long-running, prize-winning Broadway comedy, *Harvey* is rather drably made, but Stewart is delightful as the blissful souse, and he and Ms. Hull, repeating her stage role, make it worthwhile viewing. Stewart played the role on Broadway in 1947 and then again in 1970, with Helen Hayes as Veta.

## Having Wonderful Time

★★☆ RKO, 1938, 71 min. Dir: Alfred Santell. SP: Arthur Kober, b/o his play. Cast: Ginger Rogers, Douglas Fairbanks, Jr., Peggy Conklin, Lucille Ball, Lee Bowman, Richard (Red) Skelton, Jack Carson, Donald Meek.

A great cast, but Arthur Kober did a disservice to his own play about a Jewish summer camp in the Catskills by removing all the ethnic flavor and color. The amusing play became a standard romantic comedy, with Ginger Rogers as a guest who eventually finds romance with Douglas Fairbanks, Jr. as the world's most unlikely waiter. It's good to see such reliable performers as Lucille Ball, Jack Carson, and Red Skelton (in his feature film debut), but they fail to add very much to the bland proceedings. The property was later musicalized for the stage as *Wish You Were Here* (1953), with the ethnic flavor restored.

## His Girl Friday

★★★★ Columbia, 1940, 92 min. Dir: Howard Hawks. SP: Charles Lederer, Ben Hecht (uncredited), b/o play by Ben Hecht, Charles MacArthur. Cast: Rosalind Russell, Cary Grant, Ralph Bellamy, Gene Lockhart, Helen Mack, Ernest Truex, Clarence Kolb, John Qualen, Porter Hall, Billy Gilbert.

Hilarious—and fast, fast, fast are the key words for this classic comedy based on the Hecht-MacArthur play *The Front Page*. The play had wily newspaper editor Walter Burns at war with his star reporter, Hildy Johnson. Hildy wants to quit the paper and get married, but Walter has other ideas. The movie has the inspired idea of turning Hildy into a woman and making her Walter's ex-wife as well. The embattled pair become involved with an escaped convict (Qualen) on the eve of his execution for murder. The dialogue and action move at a dizzying pace, and both Grant and Russell savor every quip and wisecrack. *The Front Page* was originally filmed in 1931 and remade by Billy Wilder in 1974. *Switching Channels* was a loose 1988 version of the story.

## Holiday

★★★☆ Columbia, 1938, 93 min. Dir: George Cukor. SP: Sidney Buchman, Donald Ogden Stewart, b/o play by Philip Barry. Cast: Katharine Hepburn, Cary Grant, Lew Ayres, Doris Nolan, Edward Everett Horton, Henry Kolker, Binnie Barnes, Jean Dixon, Henry Daniell.

There is the faint whiff of mothballs about this adaptation of Philip Barry's stage play, but the wit and charm still shine through. Katharine Hepburn plays a discontented rich girl who finds herself falling for Cary Grant, her haughty sister's fiancé. Grant has no use for the family's millions—he wants to earn a lot of money quickly, then take an extended "holiday." Naturally this plan upsets the stuffed shirts but enchants Hepburn, who wins him in the end. The movie has the thirties attitude about rich people being basically unhappy in their single-minded quest for wealth, but Hepburn and Grant keep the material buoyant. Also filmed in 1930.

## I Ought to Be in Pictures

★★ Fox, 1982, c, 107 min. Dir: Herbert Ross. SP: Neil Simon, b/o his play. Cast: Walter Matthau, Dinah Manoff, Ann-Margret, Lance Guest, Lewis Smith, Martin Ferrero, David Faustino.

Dinah Manoff (daughter of actress Lee Grant, whom she resembles) repeats her Broadway role in Neil Simon's feeble adaptation of his play. She is Libby Tucker, a nineteen-year-old Brooklynite who travels to Los Angeles to see her father, Herb (Matthau), who deserted her and her mother many years earlier. Daddy is a sometime screenwriter who drinks and gambles heavily, and their relationship at first is antagonistic. In time they come to love and understand each other, but their big emotional confrontation near the end is fraudulent and rather embarrassing. Ann-Margret has the thankless role of Matthau's girlfriend.

## I'm Not Rappaport

★★☆ Gramercy, 1996, c, 136 min. Dir and SP: Herb Gardner, b/o his play. Cast: Walter Matthau, Ossie Davis, Amy Irving, Craig T. Nelson, Martha Plimpton, Guillermo Diaz, Boyd Gaines, Ron Rifkin, Irwin Corey.

Herb Gardner wrote and directed this adaptation of his Tony Award–winning Broadway comedy, and despite his best efforts to "open up" the play, the stage origins are glaringly evident. Walter Matthau and Ossie Davis play two codgers, both about eighty, who sit on a bench and ruminate about their lives and what they have learned. This was the heart of the play, but now Gardner has added "plot": Matthau has a daughter (Irving) who wants to put him in an old folks' home. A sinister drug dealer (Nelson) lurks in the neighborhood, abusing the lonely girl (Plimpton) who wants to get off drugs. And there's even more, too much more for the slender story to handle. However, Matthau and Davis are just fine, and they are worth watching.

## Jeffrey

★★★ Orion, 1997, c, 92 min. Dir: Christopher Ashley. SP: Paul Rudnick, b/o his play. Cast: Steven Weber, Michael T. Weiss, Patrick Stewart, Bryan Batt, Sigourney Weaver, Nathan Lane, Olympia Dukakis, Christine Baranski, Robert Klein, Kathy Najimy.

Jeffrey (Weber) is a gay thirtyish New York actor-waiter who decides to give up sex out of fear of the AIDS epidemic. Then he meets Steve (Weiss), the man of his dreams, and he has difficulty resisting him. By the time he changes his mind, Steve has his own misgivings. Paul Rudnick adapted his off-Broadway hit into a movie that is sometimes satirically funny and touching but also more of a series of revue sketches than a coherent narrative. There are bursts of fantasy, addresses directly to the viewers, and even one musical number. Various noted actors turn up: Sigourney Weaver as an evangelist; Nathan Lane as a gay

priest; Christine Baranski as the hostess at a society "hoedown" for AIDS research. Patrick Stewart stands out as Sterling, a gay decorator whose lover is dying of AIDS.

## Last of the Red Hot Lovers

★ Paramount, 1972, c, 98 min. Dir: Gene Saks. SP: Neil Simon, b/o his play. Cast: Alan Arkin, Sally Kellerman, Paula Prentiss, Renee Taylor.

Neil Simon's plays often fare badly when adapted to the screen, but *Last of the Red Hot Lovers* hits rock bottom. All of the actors have proven themselves in other roles, but here they are at a loss. Alan Arkin is Barney Cashman, an ostensibly doting husband and father and the owner of a successful restaurant. When he concludes that life has not offered him any illicit pleasures, he makes assignations with three different women in his mother's Manhattan apartment. Each assignation, of course, is doomed to failure. The three women have only one thing in common: they are not at all funny. What might have been amusing on stage comes across as deadweight on the screen.

## Life with Father

★★★ Warners, 1947, c, 118 min. Dir: Michael Curtiz. SP: Donald Ogden Stewart, b/o play by Howard Lindsay, Russel Crouse and writings of Clarence Day. Cast: William Powell, Irene Dunne, Edmund Gwenn, ZaSu Pitts, Elizabeth Taylor, Jimmy Lydon, Martin Milner.

Derived by Howard Lindsay and Russel Crouse from Clarence Day's memoirs about his family in New York City of the late 1880s, the long-running Broadway play was turned into this handsomely produced and pleasantly diverting movie. William Powell fits comfortably into the role of irascible, bellowing paterfamilias Clarence Day, whose confession that he has never been baptized sparks the slender plot. Irene Dunne is Vinnie, his seemingly flighty but actually level-headed wife—her brief illness also figures in the plot—and the most prominent of his red-headed sons are played by Jimmy Lydon and Martin Milner. Lydon, the eldest son, gets to swoon over bewitching young Elizabeth Taylor, on loan from MGM and cast as a visiting cousin.

## Love! Valour! Compassion!

★★★ Fine Line, 1997, c, 115 min. Dir: Joe Mantello. SP: Terrence McNally, b/o his play. Cast: Jason Alexander, Stephen Bogardus, John Glover, John Benjamin Hickey, Stephen Spinella, Randy Becker, Justin Kirk.

A mixture of viperish humor and tearjerking sentiment, this version of Terrence McNally's Broadway play (adapted by the author) works reasonably well on the screen. A group of gay men share three country weekends one summer in upstate New York, and as time passes, they expose their fears and longings, to the accompaniment of some witty dialogue. The host is Gregory (Bogardus), an aging dancer and choreographer whose lover is blind Bobby (Kirk). The tour-de-force performance is given by John Glover, who plays identical twins John and James, one of whom is dying of AIDS. The funniest role goes to Jason Alexander (replacing the stage's Nathan Lane) as flamboyant Buzz. The closing, with the cast in ballerina costumes for a rehearsal of "Swan Lake," is especially moving as it reveals the fate of each man.

## Luv

★ Columbia, 1967, c, 95 min. Dir: Clive Donner. SP: Elliott Baker, b/o play by Murray Schisgal. Cast: Jack Lemmon, Peter Falk, Elaine May, Nina Wayne, Eddie Mayehoff, Paul Hartman, Severn Darden.

On Broadway, Murray Schisgal's three-character comedy was a moderate hit, but transferred to the screen, it fails miserably. Brought up close and flattened on the screen, Schisgal's musings on human absurdity, especially in matters of love, are merely silly and tedious. Milt (Falk) meets old friend Harry (Lemmon), just as wretched Harry is about to leap off a bridge. Milt brings Harry home to his wife, Ellen (May), but his heart is with another woman, Linda (Wayne). Soon all four are engaged in a game of marital musical chairs that need not be described here. The characters come across as figures in a cartoon strip rather than real people, and the intended humor falls flat.

## The Male Animal

★★★ Warners, 1942, 101 min. Dir: Elliott Nugent. SP: Julius J. Epstein, Philip G. Epstein, Stephen Morehouse Avery, b/o play by James Thurber, Elliott Nugent. Cast: Henry Fonda, Olivia de Havilland, Joan Leslie, Jack Carson, Eugene Pallette, Don De Fore, Herbert Anderson.

Clearly dated but also entertaining, *The Male Animal* is derived from the Broadway play concerning midwestern English professor Tommy Turner (Fonda), who gets into hot water over his reading of a "controversial" letter by anarchist Bartolomeo Vanzetti to his class. Other complications involve his wife, Ellen (de Havilland), and her overbearing ex-beau (Carson), once the school's leading football hero. The fuss over the Vanzetti letter now seems quaintly innocent, but some of the dialogue still sparkles, in spite of Warners' usual tendency to broaden its adapted comedies. Fonda makes a convincing embattled academic but de Havilland is somewhat too arch as his loyal wife.

## The Man Who Came to Dinner

★★★☆ Warners, 1941, 112 min. Dir: William Keighley. SP: Julius J. Epstein, Philip G. Epstein, b/o play by George S. Kaufman, Moss Hart. Cast: Bette Davis, Monty Woolley, Ann Sheridan, Jimmy Durante, Reginald Gardiner, Billie Burke, Richard Travis, Grant Mitchell, Mary Wickes, Elisabeth Fraser.

The 1939 Broadway comedy gets the Warners treatment and although the studio, as usual, hits every comic point with an anvil, much of the play's biting wit survives. Monty Woolley is marvelous in his stage role as irascible Sheridan Whiteside (modeled on eccentric author and raconteur Alexander Woollcott), who descends on an Ohio family after he breaks his hip on their doorstep and proceeds to disrupt everyone's life. He also welcomes visits from his celebrity friends, including flamboyant actress Ann Sheridan (read Gertrude Lawrence), madcap Jimmy Durante (actually

Harpo Marx), and effete author Reginald Gardiner (modeled on Noel Coward). As Whiteside's secretary, Bette Davis plays with unusual—and becoming—restraint.

## Mary, Mary

★★ Warners, 1963, c, 126 min. Dir: Mervyn LeRoy. SP: Richard L. Breen, b/o play by Jean Kerr. Cast: Debbie Reynolds, Barry Nelson, Michael Rennie, Hiram Sherman, Diane McBain.

Any play or movie with characters named Tiffany and Dirk should be immediately suspect, and *Mary, Mary* is no exception. This stagebound, talky, and overlong version of the hit Broadway comedy has little to recommend it. Publisher Barry Nelson is about to remarry (the girl is named Tiffany) when his ex-wife Mary (Reynolds) returns, as adorable and blunt-speaking as ever. (With her, says Nelson, "life was like going into a telephone booth with an open umbrella.") It's only a matter of time before the two are happily reconciled. Nelson and Rennie (as actor Dirk Winston) repeat their stage roles and Reynolds gives a reasonable impersonation of the original stage star, Barbara Bel Geddes.

## The Matchmaker

★★★ Paramount, 1958, 101 min. Dir: Joseph Anthony. SP: John Michael Hayes, b/o play by Thornton Wilder. Cast: Shirley Booth, Shirley MacLaine, Anthony Perkins, Paul Ford, Robert Morse, Wallace Ford.

This engaging if somewhat muted version of Thornton Wilder's play *The Merchant of Yonkers* was later turned into the blockbuster stage musical *Hello, Dolly!* Without the music, it still dispenses a good deal of charm, especially with the presence of the inimitable Shirley Booth. As Dolly Levi, the turn-of-the-century matchmaker who has her eye on merchant Horace Vandergelder (Ford), she outclasses virtually every other Dolly with her warmth and firm resolve. Paul Ford as the blustery Vandergelder, Anthony Perkins as his adventure-seeking clerk, and Shirley MacLaine

as an amorous milliner are all fine in support of Ms. Booth. But where was the needed color?

## Miss Firecracker

★★★☆ Corsair, 1989, c, 102 min. Dir: Thomas Schlamme. SP: Beth Henley, b/o her play. Cast: Holly Hunter, Scott Glenn, Mary Steenburgen, Tim Robbins, Alfre Woodard, Trey Wilson, Bert Remsen, Ann Wedgeworth, Amy Wright.

Beth Henley assembles more of her Southern eccentrics for this entertaining adaptation of her hit off-Broadway play. Holly Hunter, excellent in a repeat of her stage performance, is Carnelle Scott, known for years in Yazoo City, Mississippi, as "Hot Tamale." Now seeking respectability, she enters as a contestant in the annual Miss Firecracker Contest. Arriving at her home are her cousins Elain (Steenburgen), a previous Miss Firecracker ("I have deeply enjoyed my life as a beauty!") and Elain's violently inclined brother Delmount (Robbins). Alfre Woodard is outstanding as Carnelle's friend Popeye Jackson, who helps her prepare for the pageant. The first-rate cast does an effective job with Henley's floridly comic dialogue.

## Mister Roberts

★★★☆ Warners, 1955, c, 123 min. Dir: John Ford, Mervyn LeRoy. SP: Frank Nugent, Joshua Logan, b/o play by Joshua Logan, Thomas Heggen. Cast: Henry Fonda, James Cagney, William Powell, Jack Lemmon, Betsy Palmer, Ward Bond, Nick Adams, Harry Carey, Jr.

Splendid performances by an expert cast highlight this adaptation of the long-running Broadway play. In the Pacific during World War II, the ship U.S.S. *Reluctant* is stuck "between the islands of Tedium and Ennui," charged with delivering toothpaste and toilet paper to other ships. Henry Fonda (repeating his stage role) is the well-loved Lieutenant (j.g.) Roberts, who defies the tyrannical captain (Cagney, not well cast), while longing for combat duty. Powell is his usual suave self as the ship's doctor, but it is Jack Lemmon as the mischievous Ensign Pulver who nearly steals the movie with an Oscar-winning performance. During the production,

Mervyn LeRoy replaced John Ford as director. After the film was completed, Joshua Logan refilmed two key scenes.

## The Moon Is Blue

★★☆ United Artists, 1953, 95 min. Dir: Otto Preminger. SP: F. Hugh Herbert, b/o his play. Cast: William Holden, David Niven, Maggie McNamara, Tom Tully, Dawn Addams, Fortunio Bonanova.

Imagine: a movie comedy, adapted from a successful Broadway play, that dares to use such words as "virgin" and "pregnant." Can you believe that this lapse in morality was denounced by the movie censors and condemned by the Catholic Legion of Decency? Yet this is what happened when *The Moon Is Blue* opened in 1953. Actually, it turned out to be a mildly amusing trifle concerning a militantly virginal actress (McNamara), a marriage-shy bachelor (Holden), and a lecherous neighbor (Niven). There's no surprise when the bachelor, worn down by the girl's relentless purity, proposes marriage. All the publicity turned the movie into a hit, but it now seems laughably tame.

## My Sister Eileen

★★★ Columbia, 1942, 96 min. Dir: Alexander Hall. SP: Jerome Fields, Joseph Chodorov, b/o their play and on stories by Ruth McKinney. Cast: Rosalind Russell, Brian Aherne, Janet Blair, George Tobias, Allyn Joslyn, June Havoc, Gordon Jones, Jeff Donnell.

Rosalind Russell is a treat in her role as wry, sensible Ruth Sherwood in this merry adaptation of the Broadway play. Ruth and Eileen Sherwood are Ohio sisters who move into a ramshackle apartment in New York City's Greenwich Village, where they cross paths with all sorts of eccentric people. Naïve, aspiring actress Eileen attracts many men while aspiring writer Ruth merely looks on until editor Bob Baker (Aherne) comes into her life. Funniest sequence: covering a newspaper story, Ruth is pursued back to the Village by an enthusiastic group of Portuguese mariners who speak no English. In 1953 Russell repeated her role in *Wonderful Town,* a stage musical version of the story, and in 1955, the story was remade as a musical under its original title, with Betty Garrett as Ruth.

## Noises Off

★★☆ Touchstone, 1992, c, 104 min. Dir: Peter Bogdanovich. SP: Michael Frayn and Marty Kaplan, b/o play by Michael Frayn. Cast: Michael Caine, Carol Burnett, Denholm Elliott, Julie Hagerty, Marilu Henner, Mark Linn-Baker, Christopher Reeve, John Ritter, Nicollette Sheridan.

Knockabout farces on the stage seldom work when transferred to the screen, and *Noises Off* is no exception. A frantic farce revolving about a touring theater company, it works strenuously to draw laughter but comes up short, despite a stellar cast. Michael Caine is the despairing director of the company, which is staging a door-slamming bedroom farce. As they move from one disastrous engagement to another, in-fighting as well as hanky-panky among the actors and the director causes all sorts of predicaments. Carol Burnett is funny as a character actress who has onstage difficulties with a can of sardines. But *Noises Off* doesn't come off.

## The Odd Couple

★★★☆ Paramount, 1968, c, 105 min. Dir: Gene Saks. SP: Neil Simon, b/o his play. Cast: Jack Lemmon, Walter Matthau, Herb Edelman, John Fiedler, David Sheiner, Larry Haines, Monica Evans, Carol Shelley.

Let's face it: sloppy sportswriter Oscar Madison (Matthau) and fussy, hypochondriacal photographer Felix Unger (Lemmon) are practically indestructible. Brought together by playwright Neil Simon in his hit Broadway play, the two have intimidated, tortured, and forgiven each other for three decades. Divorced men who live together, they find that they still have the same problems they shared with their ex-mates. Matthau squeezes every drop of comic juice out of his role as rumpled Oscar, but Lemmon is somewhat less successful, playing Felix glumly and too realistically. The actors became a virtual franchise after this, starring together in many movies, most recently *The Odd Couple II*. The television version, with Tony Randall and Jack Klugman, ran from 1970 to 1975, and these two actors starred on Broadway in a 1997 revival.

## Only When I Laugh

★★★ Columbia, 1981, c, 120 min. Dir: Glenn Jordan. SP: Neil Simon, b/o his play. Cast: Marsha Mason, Kristy McNichol, James Coco, Joan Hackett, David Dukes, John Bennett Perry, Kevin Bacon.

Marsha Mason gives a bravura performance as alcoholic actress Georgia Hines in Neil Simon's loose adaptation of his 1970 Broadway play, *The Gingerbread Lady*. Racked for years by her need to drink and by her bad relationships with men, Georgia returns from a successful bout with drying out. But now she must deal with a teenage daughter (McNichol) who is wise beyond her years, as well as with a former lover (Dukes) who has written an unsparing play about their tormented relationship. All this, plus her basic insecurity, brings her back to the breaking point. Mason is superb, and James Coco is good as a loyal friend who is also a failed actor. Joan Hackett shines as an aging socialite obsessed with her appearance.

## Other People's Money

★★☆ Warners, 1991, c, 101 min. Dir: Norman Jewison SP: Alvin Sargent, b/o play by Jerry Sterner. Cast: Danny DeVito, Gregory Peck, Penelope Ann Miller, Piper Laurie, Dean Jones, A. D. Call, Mo Gaffney.

"I love money! I love money more than the things it can buy!" So proclaims Larry Garfield (DeVito), known as Larry the Liquidator, who enjoys buying and then liquidating companies. Now he's after New England Wire and Cable Company, headed by lovable, benign old Andrew Jorgenson (Peck). However, Larry doesn't count on the input of Kate (Miller), a chic, sharp lawyer, who is also the daughter of "Jorgy's" companion and assistant (Laurie). The movie cuts away some of the sharp edges of the hit off-Broadway play and also makes a futile effort to work up some sexual tension between Larry and Kate, but it all adds up to rather mild material. DeVito's Larry is boorish, arrogant, and not at all endearing—or amusing, for that matter.

## The Philadelphia Story

★★★★ MGM, 1940, 112 min. Dir: George Cukor. SP: Donald Ogden Stewart, b/o play by Philip Barry. Cast: Katharine Hepburn, Cary Grant, James Stewart, Ruth Hussey, Roland Young, John Howard, John Halliday, Virginia Weidler, Mary Nash, Henry Daniell.

Adapted from the hit Broadway play, *The Philadelphia Story* is silken entertainment, blessed with sterling performances by a marvelous cast. In the role fashioned for her from the beginning, Katharine Hepburn plays Tracy Lord, a haughty rich girl intolerant of human weakness. On the eve of her remarriage, various people arrive to upset her apple cart and teach her humility, principally her dapper ex-husband (Grant) and a reporter for *Spy* Magazine (Stewart). Hepburn is a delight, but so are her leading men—surprisingly, Stewart won an Oscar. There were four other Oscar nominations, including one for Best Picture. The movie was remade as the Cole Porter musical *High Society*. A stage musical version, with the same title and songs from Porter's repertoire, surfaced in 1998.

## Plaza Suite

★★★ Paramount, 1971, c, 115 min. Dir: Arthur Hiller. SP: Neil Simon, b/o his play. Cast: Walter Matthau, Maureen Stapleton, Barbara Harris, Lee Grant, Louise Sorel.

Walter Matthau stars in all three parts of Neil Simon's adaptation of his Broadway play, all set in a suite of New York City's Plaza Hotel. In the first, he plays a straying middle-aged husband who finally confronts the widening gap in his twenty-four year marriage to Maureen Stapleton. There are some home truths—plus an undercurrent of anger and melancholy—in this segment. In the second, Matthau is a famous movie director who tries to seduce an old schoolmate (Harris), In the final part, Matthau and Lee Grant play harrassed parents of a bride who has locked herself in the suite bathroom on her wedding day. Some good farcical moments conceal the play's basically sour tone.

## Prelude to a Kiss

★★ Fox, 1992, c, 106 min. Dir: Norman René. SP: Craig Lucas, b/o his play. Cast: Meg Ryan, Alec Baldwin, Kathy Bates, Ned Beatty, Patty Duke, Sydney Walker, Stanley Tucci, Richard Riehle, Annie Golden.

On Broadway, Craig Lucas's play was a modest hit; adapted for the screen, it hardly works at all. Alec Baldwin (repeating his stage role) and Meg Ryan meet at a party and fall in love quickly. Both have their personality quirks, but they marry. At the ceremony, an old well-wisher (Walker) kisses Ryan, and nothing is ever the same again. It seems that Ryan and the old man have exchanged souls in some mysterious transference. By the time all is right again (at

least with the couple; the old man is dying), everyone has learned a few cosmic—and banal—truths about the sanctity of life, the futility of judging people by outward appearances, and so forth. Tedious stuff.

## The Prisoner of Second Avenue

★★★ Warners, 1975, c, 105 min. Dir: Melvin Frank. SP: Neil Simon, b/o his play. Cast: Jack Lemmon, Anne Bancroft, Gene Saks, Elizabeth Wilson, Florence Stanley, M. Emmet Walsh.

In the sixties and seventies, Jack Lemmon virtually built his acting career on playing men at the end of their rope (*The Odd Couple, The Out-of-Towners, Save the Tiger,* others). In *The Prisoner of Second Avenue,* adapted by Neil Simon from his stage play, he is almost ready to hang himself with that rope. As Mel, a once-happy city dweller suddenly down on his luck, he is badgered at every turn by neighbors, relatives, and the daily trauma of urban life in the

Jack Lemmon is Mel, the city dweller who considers himself *The Prisoner of Second Avenue* (1975). Anne Bancroft is his wife in Neil Simon's adaptation of his Broadway play.

mid-seventies. His on-screen nervous breakdown is not exactly hilarious, but Lemmon gives the character a core of strength and tenacity that makes him endurable if not likable. Anne Bancroft is fine as his sensible wife.

## Romantic Comedy

★★ MGM/UA, 1983, c, 103 min. Dir: Arthur Hiller. SP: Bernard Slade, b/o his play. Cast: Dudley Moore, Mary Steenburgen, Ron Leibman, Frances Sternhagen, Janet Eilber, Robyn Douglass.

This adaptation of the Broadway play is not quite as bad as many of Dudley Moore's films in the eighties, but it's emaciated and lacks genuine wit and humor. Moore is Jason Carmichael, a successful but difficult playwright who takes on Phoebe Craddock (Steenburgen) as his new writing partner. It's clear early on that the two are in love, but it takes the entire movie for them to figure this out. In the meantime, both marry unsuccessfully (no surprise there), while skirting around the truth of their relationship. Both leads are expert in their roles (Steenburgen is an exceptionally charming actress), but the movie evaporates before long.

## Same Time, Next Year

★★★ Universal, 1978, c, 119 min. Dir: Robert Mulligan. SP: Bernard Slade, b/o his play. Cast: Ellen Burstyn, Alan Alda.

The stage origin of this comedy-drama is obvious, but the expert acting of the stars and the funny, touching aspects of Bernard Slade's play and screenplay make it palatable. George (Alda), a New Jersey accountant, and Doris (Burstyn), an Oakland housewife, both married, begin an odd adulterous affair in which they meet once every year. Beginning their assignations in 1951, they meet for the next twenty-six years. They change with the times—George takes on a new lifestyle, becomes a piano player, and endures a personal tragedy. Doris goes from hippie to businesswoman to grandmother. The story seems more like a calculated gimmick than a realistic view of two people but it's pleasing if you can suspend disbelief. Burstyn and author Slade were nominated for Oscars.

## Send Me No Flowers

★★☆ Universal, 1964, c, 99 min. Dir: Norman Jewison. SP: Julius Epstein, b/o play by Norman Barasch, Carroll Moore. Cast: Doris Day, Rock Hudson, Tony Randall, Clint Walker, Paul Lynde, Hal March, Edward Andrews, Patricia Barry.

If you can accept Rock Hudson as a whining hypochondriac, you might enjoy this marital comedy derived from a modest 1960 Broadway play. Hudson is George, husband to Judy (Day), who mistakenly believes that he is dying of heart trouble. (He overheard his doctor talking about a much older patient's fatal condition.) With the help of friend Arnold (Randall), he sets about making sure his wife will be properly taken care of, then searches for a second mate for her. The third and last Day-Hudson teaming, *Send Me No Flowers* is fairly silly but it never lapses into poor taste. Funniest: Paul Lynde as a salesman of cemetery plots.

## A Shot in the Dark

★★★☆ United Artists, 1964, c, 101 min. Dir: Blake Edwards. SP: Blake Edwards, William Peter Blatty, b/o plays by Harry Kurnitz, Marcel Archard. Cast: Peter Sellers, Elke Sommer, George Sanders, Herbert Lom, Tracy Reed, Graham Stark.

Writer-director Blake Edwards took a play by Harry Kurnitz (adapted from a French play) that had a run on Broadway in 1961 and turned it into the second and by far the funniest of the "Inspector Clouseau" comedies. As embodied peerlessly by Peter Sellers, Inspector Jacques Clouseau is the dumbest and clumsiest of detectives, and here he investigates the murder of a chauffeur at the chateau of wealthy M. Ballon (Sanders). The maid Maria (Sommer) is the likeliest suspect, but Clouseau is smitten by her and insists that she is innocent. A few more murders occur as the idiotic Clouseau continues to drive his Chief Inspector Dreyfus (Lom) to near-madness. A scene in a nudist colony should have you howling with laughter.

## The Sunshine Boys

★★★ MGM, 1975, c, 111 min. Dir: Herbert Ross. SP: Neil Simon, b/o his play. Cast: Walter Matthau, George Burns, Richard Benjamin, Lee Meredith, Carol Arthur, Howard Hesseman, Ron Rifkin, Fritz Feld, F. Murray Abraham.

Do you remember the vaudeville team of Al Lewis (Burns) and Willie Clark (Matthau)? For many years they performed their hilarious sketches across the country. Now television wants to reunite them for the first time in eleven years. One problem: they despise each other. Neil Simon's adaptation of his own Broadway play gets full comic mileage out of the situation, and Matthau and Oscar-winner Burns give zesty, all-out performances as the adversaries. The play consists essentially of variations on the explosive Lewis and Clark relationship, with some not unexpected touches of sentiment toward the end. A 1998 stage revival starred television's *Odd Couple* Tony Randall and Jack Klugman.

## Switching Channels

★★★ TriStar, 1988, c, 105 min. Dir: Ted Kotcheff. SP: Jonathan Reynolds, b/o play by Ben Hecht, Charles MacArthur. Cast: Burt Reynolds, Kathleen Turner, Christopher Reeve, Ned Beatty, Henry Gibson, George Newbern, Al Waxman, Joe Silver, Fiona Reid, Ken James, Charles Kimbrough.

Another reworking of the durable Hecht-MacArthur play *The Front Page,* this time set in the world of broadcast news. Burt Reynolds is the cheerfully unscrupulous manager of a TV news station, and Kathleen Turner is his star anchorwoman and ex-wife. Now she's quitting to marry wealthy Christopher Reeve, and Reynolds is determined to stop her and win her back. Some of the plotline has been altered to suit the times, but the pace is still frantic and much of the material is still funny. The movie is not up to Howard Hawks's classic 1940 version, *His Girl Friday* (who could match Cary Grant and Rosalind Russell?), but much better than Billy Wilder's 1974 remake.

## The Teahouse of the August Moon

★★☆ MGM, 1956, c, 123 min. Dir: Daniel Mann. SP: John Patrick, b/o his play and novel by Vern J. Sneider. Cast: Marlon Brando, Glenn Ford, Machiko Kyo, Eddie Albert, Paul Ford, Jun Negami, Nijiko Kiyokawa.

Broadened from its long-running Pulitzer Prize–winning Broadway version (by the author himself), *The Teahouse of the August Moon* has a few diverting moments but not nearly enough. Glenn Ford plays (actually overplays) the American captain who becomes involved in turning an Okinawan village into a bastion of workable democracy, while Marlon Brando (in a surprise casting) is Sakini, the Okinawan rogue who slyly confuses and subverts the captain's intention at every turn. Brando makes a game try at the role, but the actor's artifice shows through the shiny black wig and the broken English. Paul Ford, as yet another bombastic army officer, could probably play the role in his sleep.

## A Thousand Clowns

★★☆ United Artists, 1965, 118 min. Dir: Fred Coe. SP: Herb Gardner, b/o his play. Cast: Jason Robards, Barbara Harris, Martin Balsam, Barry Gordon, Gene Saks, William Daniels.

Jason Robards repeats his stage role as Murray Burns, a world-class nonconformist, in this faithful adaptation of the play by its author. Murray doesn't believe in working, and he insists on raising his young nephew Nick (Gordon, also from the play) as another unencumbered spirit. Nick, however, is a sober and serious sort. Along come welfare workers Sandra (Harris) and Albert (Daniels), who would like to take Nick away. Irresolute Sandra falls for Murray, causing complications. Murray's carefree attitude once seemed amusing; now it comes across as an irritating affectation. Compensations: Gene Saks as a hypertense television clown called Chuckles the Chipmunk and Martin Balsam in an Oscar-winning performance as Murray's sensible brother.

## Tunnel of Love

★★ MGM, 1958, 98 min. Dir: Gene Kelly. SP: Joseph Fields, b/o play by Joseph Fields and novel by Peter De Vries. Cast: Doris Day, Richard Widmark, Gia Scala, Elisabeth Fraser, Elizabeth Wilson, Vikkie Dougan.

Gene Kelly directed this heavy-handed comedy built around a single joke: after an infertile couple (Day and Widmark) contact a child-adoption agency, the husband comes to believe that he has somehow impregnated the woman (Scala) who is investigating the couple as prospective parents. Reduced to a dithering idiot when he learns that the baby they will receive from the agency may well be his own, the husband tries to keep the secret from his adoring wife. On this misunderstanding, the movie comes up with a series of farcical situations that lack taste, humor, and style. The sight of Doris Day grappling with temperature charts is depressing.

## Twentieth Century

★★★★ Columbia, 1934, 91 min. Dir: Howard Hawks. SP: Ben Hecht, Charles MacArthur, b/o their play. Cast: John Barrymore, Carole Lombard, Walter Connolly, Roscoe Karns, Etienne Girardot, Charles Lane, Edgar Kennedy.

A treat from first frame to last, *Twentieth Century* should have you roaring with laughter. John Barrymore, in his hammiest mode, plays flamboyant theatrical producer Oscar Jaffe, who is determined to win back Lily Garland (Lombard), the temperamental stage star he created single-handedly out of plain Mildred Plotka. Now Oscar and Lily are both riding the 20th Century Limited from New York to California, and they alternate between adoring and wanting to destroy each other. Hecht and MacArthur adapted their own hit Broadway play, and they preserved every witty line and crackpot moment. Howard Hawks directed it all at a fast, fast clip. A stage musical adaptation turned up on Broadway in 1978.

## Two for the Seesaw

★★☆ United Artists, 1962, 120 min. Dir: Robert Wise. SP: Isobel Lennart, b/o play by William Gibson. Cast: Robert

John Barrymore is flamboyant Broadway producer Oscar Jaffe and Carole Lombard is Lily Garland, his headstrong star, in the hilarious *Twentieth Century* (1934).

Mitchum, Shirley MacLaine, Edmond Ryan, Elisabeth Fraser, Eddie Firestone, Billy Gray.

Jerry Ryan (Mitchum) is a withdrawn, newly divorced lawyer from Nebraska who begins a tentative New York romance with Gittel Mosca (MacLaine), an energetic Jewish girl from the Bronx. If you already suspect that something is wrong with the casting, you are right. This film version of William Gibson's long-running, two-character Broadway play cannot pass muster with these two ordinarily capable actors in the only major roles. Jerry and Gittel meet, and they talk a lot, but their affair never takes on the breath of life it may have had on the stage, even when a jealous Jerry begins to behave more like Robert Mitchum and slaps Gittel around. The stars strive to make it all real and even touching at times, but they are seldom convincing.

## Under the Yum Yum Tree

★ Columbia, 1963, c, 110 min. Dir: David Swift. SP: Lawrence Roman, David Swift, b/o play by David Swift. Cast: Jack Lemmon, Carol Lynley, Dean Jones, Edie Adams, Paul Lynde, Imogene Coca, Robert Lansing.

In the early sixties, filmmakers delighted in turning out leering sex farces that exceeded what was previously permissible on the screen. Few of these "aren't-we-devils" movies were any good, and Under the Yum Yum Tree, derived from a Broadway play, is one of the worst. Jack Lemmon plays the lecherous landlord of an apartment house who takes pride in seducing his female tenants. Carol Lynley and boyfriend Dean Jones move into one of the apartments with the absurd intention of testing their compatibility for marriage by avoiding sex altogether. Lemmon's attempt to add Lynley to his string of conquests makes for the movie's unfunny complications.

## Without Love

★★★ MGM, 1945, 111 min. Dir: Harold S. Bucquet. SP: Donald Ogden Stewart, b/o play by Philip Barry. Cast: Spencer Tracy, Katharine Hepburn, Lucille Ball, Keenan Wynn, Patricia Morison, Felix Bressart, Gloria Grahame, Carl Esmond.

Not the best of the Tracy-Hepburn teamings, Without Love is still fairly diverting entertainment. Tracy is a research scientist who enters into a special arrangement with young widow Hepburn. They will marry on a purely platonic basis ("without love") so that she can help him with his research. It will not surprise you when they fall in love, but the screenplay (adapted from the Broadway play in which Hepburn appeared) has its share of amusing lines and situations. Tracy's penchant for sleepwalking triggers one of the funniest scenes. Perhaps even better than the leads are Lucille Ball and Keenan Wynn in supporting roles—she as a real estate agent and he as Hepburn's cousin. If you get restless, you might count the number of times Hepburn exclaims, "By gum!"

## The Women

★★★☆ MGM, 1939, 132 min. Dir: George Cukor. SP: Anita Loos, Jane Murfin, b/o play by Clare Boothe. Cast: Norma Shearer, Joan Crawford, Rosalind Russell, Paulette Goddard, Mary Boland, Joan Fontaine, Marjorie Main, Virginia Weidler, Lucile Watson, Phyllis Povah, Mary Nash, Ruth Hussey, Dennie Moore.

Clare Boothe's poisonously witty Broadway comedy came to the screen all dressed up with a top-drawer MGM production and a stellar cast headed by the studio's two reigning queens, Norma Shearer and Joan Crawford. Some of the play's jaundiced view was extracted but audiences lapped it up. The movie is a wicked but funny view of women (not a man in sight), taking them from beauty parlors to dude ranches, from dressing rooms to powder rooms, all the while revealing their obsession with men. Shearer is the wronged, noble wife, Crawford is her hard-as-nails nemesis, and Russell (in an over-the-top performance) is Shearer's shrill, deceitful "friend." Note the clever opening credits. Remade badly in 1956 as a musical entitled The Opposite Sex.

# Flights of Fancy: Comedy Fantasies

Angels with their own agenda. Witches bent on mischief or revenge. Veterinarians who can talk to their patients. Friendly ghosts and not-so-friendly ghosts. The movies have always been pleased to offer up fantasies in every genre, including comedy, and state-of-the-art special effects have made them more popular than ever. Welcome to the comedy-fantasy world where anything can happen, and usually does.

## All of Me

★★★ Universal, 1984, c, 93 min. Dir: Carl Reiner. SP: Ed Davis, Phil Alden Robinson. Cast: Steve Martin, Lily Tomlin, Victoria Tennant, Madolyn Smith, Richard Libertini, Dana Elcar, Jason Bernard, Selma Diamond.

Steve Martin's tour-de-force performance is the principal reason to see this clever comedy-fantasy. He plays a lawyer named Roger Cobb, who gets caught up in a bizarre scheme initiated by dying heiress Edwina Cutwater (Tomlin). With the help of a guru (Libertini), Edwina has arranged to exchange souls after her death with her stableman's beautiful daughter (Tennant). By accident, however, she enters the body of Roger. With both Edwina and Roger inhabiting the same body, chaos reigns and Roger loses his job, his fiancée, and nearly his mind. The plot not only thickens but also curdles—still, Martin is so hilarious and inventive in his peculiar plight that he makes *All of Me* worth viewing.

## Angels in the Outfield

★★★ MGM, 1951, 102 min. Dir: Clarence Brown. SP: Dorothy Kingsley, George Wells. Cast: Paul Douglas, Janet Leigh, Donna Corcoran, Keenan Wynn, Spring Byington, Ellen Corby, Jeff Richards, Lewis Stone, Marvin Kaplan.

Pity the Pittsburgh Pirates. The players are not only in last place in the National League but they have to put up with their explosive, foul-mouthed manager, Paul Douglas. Then one day a celestial messenger tells Douglas that his team can win the pennant if he promises to stop his blasphemous language and behave better toward his fellow human beings. It works until an orphaned girl (Corcoran) claims that she sees an "angel" standing behind each Pittsburgh player, and the media takes over. A pleasant comedy-fantasy, with Douglas in one of his best roles as the profane manager. Remade in 1994.

## Back to the Future

★★★ Universal, 1985, c, 116 min. Dir: Robert Zemeckis. SP: Robert Zemeckis, Bob Gale. Cast: Michael J. Fox, Christopher Lloyd, Lea Thompson, Crispin Glover, Thomas F. Wilson, Wendie Jo Sperber, Marc McClure, Claudia Wells, James Tolkan.

This popular comedy-fantasy stars Michael J. Fox as teenager Marty McFly. It's 1985, and Marty has a crackpot inventor friend, Doc Brown (Lloyd), who has built a time machine from an old DeLorean car. Somehow Marty gets into the machine and finds himself projected back to 1955. Now he must not only get back to 1985 but must also make sure that his parents (Thompson and Glover) fall in love and marry. (Otherwise, he doesn't exist). Oh, yes, he must also keep Doc Brown from dying in 1985 at the hands of Libyan terrorists. (Can you follow this?) The early portions of the movie are paced slowly, but back in 1955 the pace accelerates and the jokes are clever. There were two sequels, *Back to the Future Part II* (1989) and *Back to the Future Part III* (1990).

# Big

★★★☆ Fox, 1988, c, 102 min. Dir: Penny Marshall. SP: Gary Ross, Anne Spielberg. Cast: Tom Hanks, Elizabeth Perkins, John Heard, Robert Loggia, Jared Rushton, Mercedes Ruehl, Jon Lovitz, David Moscow.

A delightful comedy-fantasy, sparked by an engaging performance by Tom Hanks. The premise: Josh Baskin (Moscow), aged thirteen, would like to be "big"—an adult without a kid's dependency or hangups. He tells his wish to a mysterious figure in an amusement park, and the next morning he wakes up in the body of a thirty-year-old man (Hanks). Behaving like a child in a man's body, he has to cope with the business world—he rises in the ranks of a toy company—and with the confusion of a sexual relationship with a coworker (Perkins). The screenplay is inventive, Penny Marshall's direction is on-target, and Tom Hanks exudes ample charm and comic timing in his boy-man role. He received a well-deserved Oscar nomination.

# Buffy the Vampire Slayer

★★☆ Fox, 1992, c, 86 min. Dir: Fran Rubel Kuzui. SP: Joss Whedon. Cast: Kristy Swanson, Donald Sutherland, Paul Reubens, Rutger Hauer, Luke Perry, Michele Abrams, Hilary Swank, Paris Vaughan, David Arquette, Candy Clark, Randal Batinkoff.

Southern California cheerleader Kristy Swanson has one ambition: "to graduate high school, go to Europe, marry Christian Slater, and die." Then she learns from her bearded mentor Donald Sutherland that she is one of the "chosen ones," slated to seek out and kill roaming vampires. Her ultimate goal is to destroy top vampire Rutger Hauer. For a time the movie has satirical fun with the culture clash of Southern California versus Transylvania. (Sitting at the edge of a grave, she asks Sutherland, "Do you have any gum?") But ultimately the movie wears down to a disappointing climax. Paul

Reubens (the former Pee-Wee Herman) plays Hauer's sidekick. Later a TV series.

# Casper

★ Paramount, 1995, c, 100 min. Dir: Brad Silbering. SP: Sherri Stoner, Deanna Oliver. Cast: Bill Pullman, Christina Ricci, Cathy Moriarty, Eric Idle, Amy Brenneman, Ben Stein, Don Novello.

What *were* they thinking? Casper, the Friendly Ghost, was an animated fixture on television, a sweet apparition always looking for someone to play with. This dreadful movie turns him into the ghost of a dead boy (!) who is haunting a dilapidated mansion named Whipstaff Manor. His only companions are his uncles Stretch, Fatso, and Stinkie. Whipstaff owner Cathy Moriarty hires "ghost therapist" Bill Pullman to rid her house of the spooky inhabitants. Pullman arrives with daughter Ricci, who becomes the love of Casper's life. Why go on? The computer-generated special effects are not much, nor is there much humor in the proceedings. Cameos by some stars do not help at all.

# Chances Are

★★★ TriStar, 1989, c, 108 min. Dir: Emile Ardolino. SP: Perry Howze, Randy Howze. Cast: Cybill Shepherd, Robert Downey, Jr., Ryan O'Neal, Mary Stuart Masterson, Christopher McDonald, Josef Sommer, Henderson Forsythe.

A widow for many years, Corinne Jeffries (Shepard) still mourns her late husband, while raising her daughter, Miranda (Masterson). Then, by a heavenly fluke, her husband is reincarnated as Alex (Downey), a student at Yale, which Miranda also attends. Alex begins dating Miranda, but when he meets Corinne, he realizes that she is his wife! At that point things become even more complicated. The situation could easily turn tricky and/or unpalatable (man dating his own daughter?) but surprisingly, *Chances Are* plays it all out with some degree of wit and feeling. Downey is exceptionally good as the reincarnated husband.

# Clean Slate

★★ MGM, 1994, c, 107 min. Dir: Mick Jackson. SP: Robert King. Cast: Dana Carvey, Valeria Golino, James Earl Jones, Kevin Pollak, Michael Murphy, Michael Gambon, Olivia D'Abo, Phil Leeds.

Here's a movie in which a sight-impaired dog named Barkley draws the only real laughs. Dana Carvey plays Maurice Pogue, a private detective who is working as a bodyguard. One day he sustains injuries that afflict him with a rare kind of amnesia in which each day seems like the first day of his life. He witnesses a crime, causing him to tangle with the mob while also coping with his odd situation. Amusing on television, Carvey seems never to have found the right starring role in films, and this clone of *Groundhog Day* (see page 218) is not the one.

# Cocoon

★★★ Fox, 1985, c, 116 min. Dir: Ron Howard. SP: Tom Benedek, b/o novel by David Saperstein. Cast: Don Ameche, Wilford Brimley, Hume Cronyn, Brian Dennehy, Jack Gilford, Steve Guttenberg, Maureen Stapleton, Jessica Tandy, Gwen Verdon, Herta Ware, Tahnee Welch, Tyrone Power, Jr.

Watching a group of marvelous veteran actors at work is the main pleasure of this popular comedy-fantasy. An alien spaceship lands on earth bent on retrieving some of the alien creatures that were left behind eons ago and who are now encased in cocoons hidden in a deserted Florida pool. Only the pool is not deserted—elderly male residents of a nearby retirement home are using it and becoming physically and sexually revitalized by the force generated by the cocoons. Soon the aliens and the oldsters are interacting in unexpected ways. The cast is superb—Don Ameche won a Supporting Oscar—but the movie takes a rather patronizing view of old age, and its ending makes a dubious assumption. A 1988 sequel, *Cocoon: The Return,* was not successful.

# Coneheads

★☆ Paramount, 1993, c, 88 min. Dir: Steve Barron. SP: Dan Aykroyd, Tom Davis, Bonnie Turner, Terry Turner. Cast: Dan Aykroyd, Jane Curtin, Michelle Burke, Michael McKean, Chris Farley, Jason Alexander, Lisa Jane Persky, David Spade, Phil Hartman, Dave Thomas.

A mostly dull expansion of the *Saturday Night Live* sketches about the outer-space family known as the Coneheads. On a mission to destroy Earth, Beldar and Prymaat Conehead (Aykroyd and Curtin) take a wrong turn and land in the East River. Claiming to have come from France, they settle in New Jersey with daughter Connie (Burke), where their strange appearance and ways seem to go unnoticed. That is, until a zealous immigration official (McKean) suspects they are illegal aliens. The movie consists mostly of verbal and sight gags about Conehead reactions to—and interpretations of—earthly matters, but this wears thin in about fifteen minutes. Best watched while "consuming mass quantities" of popcorn.

# Death Becomes Her

★★ Universal, 1992, c, 104 min. Dir: Robert Zemeckis. SP: Martin Donovan, David Koepp. Cast: Meryl Streep, Goldie Hawn, Bruce Willis, Isabella Rossellini, Ian Ogilvy, Adam Storke, Jonathan Silverman, Nancy Fish, Mimi Kennedy.

It's good to see Meryl Streep playing a glamorous musical star instead of her usual angst-ridden heroine, but this black comedy-fantasy is more grotesque than amusing. Streep is Madeline Ashton, who steals away Ernest Menville (Willis, cast wildly against type), the fiancé of her over-the-years arch rival Helen Sharp (Hawn). Years later, when Helen transforms herself into a slim, successful sexpot determined to win Ernest back, Madeline goes to extreme lengths to stay young. The movie veers into fantasy involving swiveling heads, gaping but nonfatal body wounds, and other Oscar-winning visual effects. The intention is to offer a savage satire of youth-obsessed American women, but despite the cast's strenuous efforts, it all becomes tedious long before the end.

# Defending Your Life

★★★ Warners, 1991, c, 111 min. Dir and SP: Albert Brooks. Cast: Albert Brooks, Meryl Streep, Rip Torn, Lee Grant, Buck Henry.

An intriguing comedy-fantasy, with problems. Albert Brooks and Meryl Streep die on earth and meet in Judgment City, a postdeath waystation resembling southern California without the smog. In Judgment City your past life is examined, and you are either recycled back to earth (bad), or move on to a better place (good). The movie shuttles between Brooks's trial and his developing romance with the uninhibited Streep. The first half of *Defending Your Life* is funny and clever, but then Brooks the writer runs out of plot, and the film becomes repetitive. Brooks the actor, ranging in expression from smug-happy to smug-unhappy, is not much help, but Streep is delightful as a woman of frank sensuality. On balance, *Defending Your Life* is amusing and even thought-provoking.

# Doctor Dolittle

★★☆ Fox, 1998, c, 85 min. Dir: Betty Thomas. SP: Nat Mauldin, Larry Levin. Cast: Eddie Murphy, Ossie Davis, Oliver Platt, Peter Boyle, Richard Schiff, Kristen Wilson, Jeffrey Tambor, Kyla Pratt.

Hugh Lofting, the author of the beloved *Doctor Dolittle* books, may be spinning in his grave at the very thought of this latter-day version. Preteenagers, however, might find some fun in the idea of wisecracking animals and birds. Dr. John Dolittle (Murphy) regains his singular ability to communicate with animals, but most of the communication is done by the animals—the dogs, rats, pigs, geese, and such (voiced by Chris Rock, Ellen DeGeneres, Albert Brooks, and others), all of whom have a snappish, disdainful attitude toward humans. Most of the time Murphy merely reacts to the animals, which is a waste of his talent. At least this doctor doesn't have to sing to a forlorn seal, as Rex Harrison was obliged to do in the 1967 musical version.

# 18 Again!

★★☆ New World, 1988, c, 100 min. Dir: Paul Flaherty. SP: Josh Goldstein, Jonathan Prince. Cast: George Burns, Charlie Schlatter, Tony Roberts, Anita Morris, Red Buttons, Miriam Flynn, Jennifer Runyon.

Another in the cluster of "switched identities" comedies of the late eighties, *18 Again!* at least has the virtue of starring irrepressible George Burns as the codger who, in a car accident, suddenly changes identities with his grandson (Schlatter). While the grandson, in the body of Burns, lies in a coma, the revitalized, seemingly eighteen-year-old Burns touches all the bases, learning more about his son (Roberts), dealing with his sexy but false-hearted companion (Morris), and even getting to court his grandson's would-be girlfriend (Runyon). No surprises here, but Schlatter is appealing in the movie's largest role, and Burns is twinkly, as usual.

# Flubber

★★ Disney, 1997, c, 93 min. Dir: Les Mayfield. SP: John Hughes, Bill Walsh. Cast: Robin Williams, Marcia Gay Harden, Christopher McDonald, Raymond J. Barry, Wil Wheaton, Clancy Brown, Ted Levine, Scott Michael Campbell, Edie McClurg.

A feeble remake of the popular 1961 comedy-fantasy *The Absent-Minded Professor, Flubber* stars Robin Williams in the Fred MacMurray role as Phillip Brainard, a professor who is absent-minded to the point of stupidity. In his laboratory chock full of Rube Goldberg–like gadgets, the professor inadvertently invents flubber (flying rubber), a hyperkinetic substance that makes inanimate objects fly. He runs into opposition from a scheming colleague (McDonald) and from a nasty tycoon (Barry) whose stupid son (Wheaton) is getting a failing grade from Brainard. Somehow Brainard manages to save his college, his job, and his long-standing romance with Marcia Gay Harden. The special effects are sometimes clever, but the movie simply rehashes old ideas without adding anything fresh or particularly amusing.

## Freaky Friday

★ Disney, 1977, c, 97 min. Dir: Gary Nelson. SP: Mary Rodgers, b/o her book. Cast: Barbara Harris, Jodie Foster, John Astin, Patsy Kelly, Sorrell Booke, Dick Van Patten, Marie Windsor, Kaye Ballard, Ruth Buzzi, Marvin Kaplan.

A precursor of the "switched-identities" plot that surfaced a decade later with such movies as *Like Father, Like Son* (1987) and *Vice Versa* (1988), and pretty awful, despite the best efforts of Barbara Harris and Jodie Foster. Mother (Harris) and daughter (Foster), simply switch identities for a day, and of course every possible catastrophe occurs. It's hard to decide which sequence is more excruciating: "mother" (really daughter) acting kittenish with the boy next door or "daughter" (really mother) reacting to her husband's sexy secretary. The only fun is spotting such veteran actors as Patsy Kelly, Kaye Ballard, Ruth Buzzi, and Marvin Kaplan in small roles. Remade for television in 1995.

## Ghost

★★★ Paramount, 1990, c, 122 min. Dir: Jerry Zucker. SP: Bruce Joel Rubin. Cast: Patrick Swayze, Demi Moore, Whoopi Goldberg, Tony Goldwyn, Vincent Schiavelli, Rick Aviles, Gail Boggs, Armelia McQueen, Phil Leeds.

A movie with something for everyone, *Ghost* is a cluttered mixture of romance, fantasy, melo-drama, and comedy, topped by a reassuring view of life after death. Patrick Swayze is a young stockbroker who is murdered and then, as an agile ghost, must warn his grieving wife (Moore) of the threat to her life. Along comes Whoopi Goldberg as a fake spiritualist who is amazed to discover that she has genuine pow-ers. Reluctantly, she helps the ghostly Swayze protect his wife and dispense with the culprits. Goldberg's Oscar-winning performance is a treat—she makes something hilarious and endearing of her rowdy character. Bruce Joel Rubin's screenplay also won a statuette.

## Ghostbusters

★★★ Columbia, 1984, c, 107 min. Dir: Ivan Reitman. SP: Dan Aykroyd, Harold Ramis. Cast: Bill Murray, Dan Aykroyd, Sigourney Weaver, Rick Moranis, Harold Ramis, William Atherton, Ernie Hudson, Annie Potts.

This elaborate, extremely popular fright come-dy should please prepubescents who like slimy and scary things, as well as adults who can enjoy the special effects. Aykroyd, Murray, and Ramis, later joined by Hudson, are self-described "ghostbusters" who find themselves suddenly battling all sorts of ghostly—and ghastly—creatures at large in New York City. It seems that the creatures are determined to destroy not only the city but also the world in an apocalyptic judgment day. Sigourney Weaver is the beauty whose apartment house is the central station for all the ghouls. (She becomes one of their agents.) The storyline veers out of control but many of the special effects are impressive. A sequel, *Ghostbusters II*, was released in 1989.

## The Golden Child

★★ Paramount, 1986, c, 96 min. Dir: Michael Ritchie. SP: Dennis Feldman. Cast: Eddie Murphy, Charlotte Lewis, Charles Dance, Victor Wong, Randall "Tex" Cobb, James Hong, J. L. Reate.

A mixture of comedy, fantasy, and adventure, *The Golden Child* is Eddie Murphy's take on *Raiders of the Lost Ark* and one of his weakest films. He plays Chandler, a professional searcher for lost children who is chosen to recover a holy child from Tibet, who has been kidnapped by evil Sardo (Dance) and his min-ions. If this Golden Child dies, the world will apparently become hell. Now Chandler must find a magic dagger, defeat Sardo's henchmen, and survive a series of trials by fire, all with the help of a beautiful girl (Lewis) who has a talent for karate. Murphy gets very few chances to be funny, and after a while all the special effects become simply boring.

## Groundhog Day

★★★ Columbia, 1993, c, 103 min. Dir: Harold Ramis. SP: Danny Rubin, Harold Ramis. Cast: Bill Murray, Andie MacDowell, Chris Elliott, Stephen Tobolowsky, Brian Doyle-Murray, Marita Geraghty, Angela Paton, Rick Ducommun, Robin Duke.

Bill Murray is ideally cast in this clever comedy-fantasy. Once again the curmudgeon who sees the light, he plays Phil Connors, a Pittsburgh weatherman who comes to Punxsutawney, Pennsylvania, to cover Groundhog Day. Cynical and obnoxious ("people are morons"), he is startled to learn that he is doomed to relive every moment of Groundhog Day indefinitely. Disbelief gives way to recklessness and despair (and some manipulation of events) until he begins to fall for Rita, his lovely producer (MacDowell). By the film's end, when his life goes back to normal, he is a new man who has captured Rita's heart. The screenplay manages to come up with amusing variations on Phil's plight, and while the movie goes on too long, it is almost always watchable.

## Harry and the Hendersons

★★☆ Columbia, 1987, c, 110 min. Dir: William Dear. SP: William Dear, William E. Martin, Ezra D. Davenport. Cast: John Lithgow, Melinda Dillon, Margaret Langrick, Joshua Rudoy, Kevin Peter Hall, David Suchet, Lainie Kazan, Don Ameche, M. Emmet Walsh.

A mild ripoff of *E.T.* While driving back to Seattle, the Henderson family, headed by George (Lithgow), runs over Bigfoot (Hall), the

In *Groundhog Day* (1993), weatherman Bill Murray (right) finds himself trapped in a time warp, forced to relive the same day over and over again. Here he converses with coworkers Andie MacDowell and Chris Elliott.

huge, hairy half-man, half-beast that stalks the mountains of the Pacific Northwest. They take him home, where they nurse him back to health and try to keep him a secret. Harry (as they name him) smells bad, and he's so big that he almost destroys the house. He's also apparently a sentimental sort, prone to weeping even at television commercials. When his presence becomes known, everyone in town is out to snare him and take the credit. The movie is a little too cute and soggy, but nothing could stop the *E.T.* clones.

## Hello Again

★★ Buena Vista, 1987, c, 96 min. Dir: Frank Perry. SP: Susan Isaacs. Cast: Shelley Long, Judith Ivey, Gabriel Byrne, Corbin Bernsen, Sela Ward, Austin Pendleton, Carrie Nye, Robert Lewis.

Lucy Chadman (Long) is an accident-prone Long Island housewife who dies after choking on a "South Korean chicken ball" at a party. A year later she is brought back to life by her eccentric sister Zelda (Ivey), who is an amateur occultist. Now Lucy must cope with husband Jason (Bernsen), his new wife Kim (Ward), who was once her best friend, and most of all, with her newfound celebrity. She also begins a new romance with Kevin Scanlon (Byrne), the emergency-room doctor who tried to save her life. Despite strenuous effort, nothing can really save this dim comedy.

## Here Comes Mr. Jordan

★★★☆ Columbia, 1941, 93 min. Dir: Alexander Hall. SP: Sidney Buchman, Seton I. Miller, b/o play by Harry Segall. Cast: Robert Montgomery, Evelyn Keyes, Claude Rains, James Gleason, Edward Everett Horton, Rita Johnson, John Emery.

Hugely popular in its day, this comedy-fantasy still entertains, although it is a bit worn about the edges. The premise is this: boxer Joe Pendleton (Montgomery) dies in a plane crash fifty years before his time. Since it's Joe's destiny to become the next world heavyweight champion, heavenly bookkeeper Mr. Jordan

(Rains) sends him back to earth to take up residence in another man's body. The problem is that Joe's new body belongs to a man freshly murdered by his wife (Johnson) and her lover (Emery). James Gleason is wonderful as Max Corkle, Joe Pendleton's utterly bewildered manager. Buchman and Miller won Oscars for their screenplay, and nominations went to the movie and to Montgomery. The 1978 remake was entitled *Heaven Can Wait.*

## Honey, I Shrunk the Kids

★★★ Buena Vista, 1989, c, 93 min. Dir: Joe Johnston. SP: Ed Naha, Tom Schulman, b/o story by Stuart Gordon, Brian Yuzna, Ed Naha. Cast: Rick Moranis, Matt Frewer, Marcia Strassman, Kristine Sutherland, Thomas Brown, Jared Rushton, Amy O'Neill, Robert Oliveri.

An amiable comedy-fantasy, with some expert special effects. What happens is this: Wayne Szalinski (Moranis) loves to tinker with his elaborate gadgets in the cellar, but his tinkering gets out of hand when he accidentally zaps his and the neighbors' children down to a quarter-inch size. When the kids get thrown out with the trash, they have to cope with giant-size terrors—the backyard becomes a jungle, a bee becomes a threatening monster, and even a bowl of cereal turns into a menace. An ant is friendly, but not much else. Neatly handled and popular, the movie warranted a 1992 sequel, *Honey, I Blew Up the Kid.* This time Dad turns his two-year-old into a lumbering giant.

## I Married a Witch

★★★ United Artists, 1942, 76 min. Dir: René Clair. SP: Robert Pirosh, Marc Connelly, b/o story by Thorne Smith, completed by Norman Matson. Cast: Fredric March, Veronica Lake, Robert Benchley, Susan Hayward, Cecil Kellaway, Elizabeth Patterson.

A French director renowned for his stylish wit, René Clair fared less well with his American films. *I Married a Witch,* his second effort, is a moderately amusing comedy-fantasy concerning a comely witch (Lake) who returns in human form to torment March, the descendant of the Puritan who burned her in colonial days. A smug New Englander who is running for governor, March finds himself suddenly bewitched by Lake, despite his engagement to the sour, jealous Hayward. Needless to say, a true romance develops between the witch and her victim, leading to an odd marriage and some clever special effects. Neither March nor Lake is a capable farceur, but they manage to keep it all reasonably light.

## The Incredible Mr. Limpet

★★☆ Warners, 1964, c, 102 min. Dir: Arthur Lubin. SP: Jameson Brewer, John C. Rose, b/o novel by Theodore Pratt. Cast: Don Knotts, Carole Cook, Jack Weston, Andrew Duggan, Larry Keating, Elizabeth McRae.

During World War II, Henry Limpet (Knotts) is a mild-mannered, bespectacled Brooklyn bookkeeper with a wife (Cook) who objects to his love for fish. Then one day he falls into the ocean and begins a new life—as a dolphin. Now an animated fish with Don Knotts's voice, the newly revitalized Mr. Limpet becomes a submarine detector for the Navy and, in the movie's climax, becomes a hero by outwitting an enemy onslaught. He even falls in love with another fish. A pleasant, partially animated fantasy for children.

## The Incredible Shrinking Woman

★★ Universal, 1981, c, 88 min. Dir: Joel Schumacher. SP: Jane Wagner, suggested by a novel by Richard Matheson. Cast: Lily Tomlin, Charles Grodin, Ned Beatty, Henry Gibson, Elizabeth Wilson, Mark Blankfield, Maria Smith. Richard A. Baker.

The extraordinary trouble that rampant consumerism can cause is given a comic spin in this variation on *The Incredible Shrinking Man.* Lily Tomlin is Pat Kramer, a complacent, harried housewife and mother, who, after being inundated with a houseful of products, suddenly begins shrinking, to the dismay of her husband (Grodin). All the expected consequences of being Tiny Pat are shown, until a plot takes over in which Pat is kidnapped by power-mad

scientists and aided by an ape named Sidney (Baker, giving the funniest performance). This second part of the movie is just plain silly, and even a game Tomlin cannot save it.

## Innerspace

★★★ Warners, 1987, c, 120 min. Dir: Joe Dante. SP: Chip Proser, Jeffrey Boam, b/o story by Chip Proser. Cast: Dennis Quaid, Martin Short, Meg Ryan, Kevin McCarthy, Fiona Lewis, Vernon Wells, Robert Picardo, Wendy Schaal, Henry Gibson, Orson Bean, William Schallert.

Remember *Fantastic Voyage,* in which a team of medical experts were miniaturized and injected into the body of a dying scientist? *Innerspace* is an entertaining comic variation on the theme. As a scientific experiment, a loutish Navy test pilot named Tuck Pendelton (Quaid) is slated to be miniaturized and injected into the body of a rabbit. Instead, he is accidentally injected into the body of a hopelessly neurotic supermarket checker named Jack Putter (Short). With a tiny Tuck directing his every move, Jack becomes the target of insidious villains who want to steal the miniaturization process. Quaid is one of the most likable actors in films, but the movie belongs to Short, who is often hilarious as a hysteric-turned-action hero. Oscar winner for Best Special Effects.

## Junior

★★★ Universal, 1994, c, 110 min. Dir: Ivan Reitman. SP: Kevin Wade and Chris Conrad. Cast: Arnold Schwarzenegger, Emma Thompson, Danny DeVito, Frank Langella, Pamela Reed, Aida Turturro, Judy Collins, James Eckhouse.

*Junior* has some comical moments and some strained moments, but on the whole, it's fun. Arnold Schwarzenegger is an Austrian scientist partnered with fertility doctor Danny DeVito in creating an experimental new fertility drug. Secretly, they test the drug by using Arnold as the guinea pig, and lo! he not only becomes pregnant but insists on carrying the baby to term. (Don't ask for sense or reason.) You won't be surprised when he learns what it means to be a childbearing woman. Emma Thompson is charming as the endearingly clumsy scientist who inadvertently supplies the fertilized egg for Arnold's baby and who inevitably falls for him.

## Kiss Me Goodbye

★ Fox, 1982, c, 101 min. Dir: Robert Mulligan. SP: Charlie Peters. Cast: Sally Field, James Caan, Jeff Bridges, Paul Dooley, Claire Trevor, Stephen Elliott, Dorothy Fielding, William Prince.

An exceptionally good cast labors mightily to bring some fun to this comedy-fantasy, but the movie, derived from the Brazilian film *Dona Flora and Her Two Husbands,* is an embarrassment. Sally Field is a widow of three years who is about to marry Jeff Bridges, when suddenly the antic ghost of James Caan, her first husband, appears in the house they once shared and causes mischief and confusion. The main problem is that the dead husband is supposed to be a charming rogue but instead he's something of a nuisance. One objectionable or silly scene follows another, until the movie collapses. Sole saving grace: the always reliable Claire Trevor as Field's mother.

## Like Father, Like Son

★ TriStar, 1987, c, 98 min. Dir: Rod Daniel. SP: Lorne Cameron, Steven L. Bloom. Cast: Dudley Moore, Kirk Cameron, Margaret Colin, Catherine Hicks, Patrick O'Neal, Sean Astin.

Draw the veil on this disastrous comedy-fantasy, one of several late-eighties films with a similar switched-identities premise. This time it's Doctor Dudley Moore, a respected surgeon, who, through some mysterious voodoo involving a "brain transference" potion, exchanges bodies with his teenage son, Kirk Cameron. It's all wildly predictable and painfully unfunny, with Moore having to behave like a shy teenager and Cameron forced to deal with his father's surgical duties. One sequence is more embarrassing than the next, although it would be hard to top the one in which young Cameron, in his father's body, makes the hospital rounds with his staff.

## Love at First Bite

★★★ Orion, 1979, c, 96 min. Dir: Stan Dragoti. SP: Robert Kaufman. Cast: George Hamilton, Susan St. James, Richard Benjamin, Dick Shawn, Arte Johnson, Sherman Hemsley, Isabel Sanford, Barry Gordon, Ronnie Schell.

George Hamilton is surprisingly funny as a displaced Dracula in this rather ramshackle but enjoyable comedy. Thrown out of his Transylvanian home (they need his castle as a training center for gymnasts), the Count travels to New York, where he takes up residence with his servant (Johnson). The trouble is, nobody is frightened by the Count anymore, and worse, he has fallen in love with a famous model (St. James). Her current boyfriend, psychiatrist Benjamin, is not too pleased and he sets about warning New Yorkers that a vampire is among them. Do they care? Hardly. Hamilton shows a flair for broad comedy, even when some of the jokes backfire.

## The Love Bug

★★★ Buena Vista, 1969, c, 107 min. Dir: Robert Stevenson. SP: Bill Walsh, Don Da Gradi, b/o story by Gordon Buford. Cast: Dean Jones, Michele Lee, David Tomlinson, Buddy Hackett, Joe Flynn, Benson Fong, Joe E. Ross, Barry Kelley, Iris Adrian.

Meet Herbie, the Volkswagen with a mind of his own, in the first of the popular Disney fantasy comedies that turned up regularly for several years. Herbie is acquired by Jim (Jones), a has-been racing driver who finds himself winning races due to the car's gumption and determination. Buddy Hackett plays Jim's friend Tennessee, who recognizes Herbie's special human qualities, and David Tomlinson is the villainous car dealer and racing driver who opposes Jim and Herbie until the last big race. Good special effects in an amiable comedy-fantasy that should please young viewers. Three sequels followed.

## Maid to Order

★★☆ Vista, 1987, c, 96 min. Dir: Amy Jones. SP: Amy Jones, Perry Howze, Randy Howze. Cast: Ally Sheedy,

Michael Ontkean, Beverly D'Angelo, Dick Shawn, Valerine Perrine, Tom Skerritt, Merry Clayton.

A sweet Cinderella-in-reverse tale with one big surprise, *Maid to Order* stars Ally Sheedy as a rich, irresponsible teenager whose privileged life is turned upside down when her disgruntled father (Skerritt) wishes that she was never born. He is granted his wish, and Sheedy finds herself toiling as a maid in the garish home of music agent Dick Shawn and wife Valerie Perrine. Of course Sheedy learns about the work ethic and humility, and she even finds romance with chauffeur-composer Ontkean. The movie's surprise is a singer named Merry Clayton, who delivers two powerhouse musical numbers that have little relation to the story.

## Making Mr. Right

★★☆ Orion, 1987, c, 95 min. Dir: Susan Seidelman. SP: Floyd Byars, Laurie Frank. Cast: John Malkovich, Ann Magnuson, Glenne Headly, Ben Masters, Laurie Metcalf, Polly Bergen, Harsh Nayyar, Hart Bochner, Polly Draper.

Susan Seidelman, who directed *Desperately Seeking Susan* two years earlier, failed to duplicate that success with this mildly amusing fantasy-comedy. John Malkovich, who is not known for his comedy roles, plays a people-hating scientist who creates an android named Ulysses in his own image. Public relations expert Ann Magnuson (an "image consultant") is assigned to humanize Ulysses for the public. All the expected things occur when the scientist and Ulysses are mistaken for each other, especially when Ulysses roams free and falls for Magnuson. A skilled comic actor, Magnuson deserves better roles than this.

## Mannequin

★ Gladden, 1987, c, 89 min. Dir: Michael Gottlieb. SP: Edward Rugoff, Michael Gottlieb. Cast: Andrew McCarthy, Kim Cattrall, James Spader, Meshach Taylor, G. W. Bailey, Estelle Getty, Carole Davis.

This thoroughly silly comedy-fantasy stars Andrew McCarthy as Jonathan Switcher, a department store window dresser who falls in love with Emmy (Cattrall), one of his mannequins, who is really an ancient Egyptian princess. When she comes to life only for his eyes, there are many slapstick complications, with Jonathan finding opposition from the store's treacherous supervisor (Spader), an overzealous security chief (Bailey), and his ex-girlfriend (Davis). Meshach Taylor is a bundle of stereotypes as Hollywood, Jonathan's giddy, flagrantly gay friend and fellow window dresser. Followed by a sequel in 1991. Why?

## Matilda

★★★ TriStar, 1996, c, 93 min. Dir: Danny DeVito. SP: Nicholas Kazan, Robin Swicord, b/o book by Roald Dahl. Cast: Danny DeVito, Rhea Perlman, Mara Wilson, Embeth Davidtz, Pam Ferris, Paul Reubens, Tracey Walter.

A very dark comedy-fantasy, much too dark for young children but one that older children should enjoy. Matilda (Wilson) is a luckless girl with repulsive, abusive parents (DeVito and Perlman), and when she is sent to a private school, the headmistress Miss Trunchbull (Ferris) turns out to be a sadistic monster who could make the Wicked Witch seem like Mary Poppins. Luckily, Matilda discovers she has telekinetic powers—she can move objects with her eyes—and eventually all is set right. Miss Trunchbull is perhaps too frightening a character, but the special effects are clever, and little Ms. Wilson is an appealing actress.

## Maxie

★★ Orion, 1985, c, 90 min. Dir: Paul Aaron. SP: Patricia Resnick, b/o novel by Jack Finney. Cast: Glenn Close, Mandy Patinkin, Ruth Gordon, Barnard Hughes, Valerie Curtin, Googy Gress.

It's nice to see Glenn Close in a rare comedy role, but *Maxie* is a fantasy-comedy sadly short of wit or magic. Close is Jan, a San Francisco secretary who is assistant to a bishop (Hughes) and who is married to Nick (Patinkin). On one fateful day, her body is taken over by Maxie Malone, a brash twenties flapper who died at a young age in a car crash. Soon Jan is behaving outrageously, creating embarrassing situations and causing Nick to lose his job. Finally, Maxie consents to leave if she can have one last chance to achieve the stardom that eluded her. Close appears to be enjoying herself as the uninhibited Maxie, but the screenplay gives her little support. As her neighbor, and a long-ago friend of Maxie's, Ruth Gordon gives her usual performance as Ruth Gordon.

# Michael

★★★ Warners, 1997, c, 105 min. Dir Nora Ephron. SP: Delia Ephron, Nora Ephron, Pete Dexter, Jim Quinlan, b/o story by Pete Dexter, Jim Quinlan. Cast: John Travolta, William Hurt, Andie MacDowell, Bob Hoskins, Robert Pastorelli, Jean Stapleton, Teri Garr.

John Travolta exudes a great deal of charm in this engaging comedy-fantasy, which, with some modifications, might have been made by Frank Capra six decades ago. He plays Michael, an earthbound angel—but not your usual angel. He's raunchy rather than asexual, loves to dance and fight, and is also rather grungy in his appearance. Two cynical tabloid reporters (Hurt and MacDowell) visit Michael in Iowa, and it's only a matter of time before they fall under his uncommon spell and fall in love with each other. But like E.T., Michael's time on earth is running out. There is not an abundance of plot in *Michael*, but Travolta's charismatic performance makes it worth viewing.

# Monkey Business

★★★ Fox, 1952, 97 min. Dir: Howard Hawks. SP: Ben Hecht, Charles Lederer, I.A.L. Diamond. Cast: Cary Grant, Ginger Rogers, Charles Coburn, Marilyn Monroe, Hugh Marlowe, Henri Letondal, Larry Keating, Esther Dale, George Winslow.

A hectic but often amusing comedy-fantasy starring Cary Grant as an absent-minded, bespectacled professor (shades of his role in Hawks's *Bringing up Baby)* whose sole preoc-cupation is the invention of a rejuvenation serum. When the serum gets into the water supply at his laboratory, courtesy of a lab chim-panzee, many are affected, including Barnaby, wife Edwina (Rogers), and his boss (Coburn). The premise is not believable (as Hawks later admitted), but there are laughs watching Grant and Rogers behave like juveniles. Classic line: Coburn to his voluptuous secretary, Marilyn Monroe: "Find someone to type this."

# Multiplicity

★★☆ Columbia, 1996, c, 117 min. Dir: Harold Ramis. SP: Chris Miller, Mary Hale, Lowell Ganz, Babaloo Mandell. Cast: Michael Keaton, Andie MacDowell, Harris Yulin, Richard Masur, Eugene Levy, Ann Cusack, Brian Doyle-Murray.

Doug Kinney (Keaton) is a harried man, unable to cope with the demands of his job, wife (MacDowell), and children. He finds an unusu-al solution with an odd company called the Gemini Institute, which clones people. At first it all works beautifully with Doug and his clone sharing responsibilities. But everything starts unraveling, especially when two more clones appear on the scene, causing confusion and havoc. Eventually, Doug loses his family and his job, until he gets his life together. Keaton is an amiable comic actor, but the premise is shaky from the start, and the details of Doug's plight with his clones are not worked out sat-isfactorily. A good try but a strikeout.

# My Stepmother Is an Alien

★ Columbia, 1988, c, 108 min. Dir: Richard Benjamin. SP: Jerico Weingrod, Herschel Weingrod, Timothy Harris, Jonathan Reynolds. Cast: Dan Aykroyd, Kim Basinger, Jon Lovitz, Alyson Hannigan, Joseph Maher, Seth Green, voice of Ann Prentiss.

This may be the only movie in which comedi-an Jimmy Durante figures in the plotline. Otherwise, *My Stepmother Is an Alien* is sim-ply an embarrassment. Dan Aykroyd stars as a widowed astrophysicist whose experiment in outer space reaches another galaxy. Along comes Celeste (Basinger), a gorgeous extrater-restrial who comes to earth to learn his research so that she can save her planet. Celeste has no knowledge of human activities, including sex, and thrives on such items as battery acid, but Aykroyd is enchanted and marries her. The consequences are not amusing.

## Oh, God!

★★★ Warners, 1977, c, 104 min. Dir: Carl Reiner. SP: Larry Gelbart, b/o novel by Avery Corman. Cast: George Burns, John Denver, Teri Garr, Paul Sorvino, George Furth, Ralph Bellamy, Barnard Hughes, David Ogden Stiers.

A fanciful idea that translates into a surprisingly winning comedy, largely due to the warmth and charm of veteran comedian George Burns. He plays the title role, personified as a cigar-smoking codger who has come to earth to tell people that he is alive and well. He appears to supermarket manager John Denver, a decent sort who is properly astonished at being selected and then does a good job at conveying God's messages. (These messages are standard clichés—be nicer to each other and so on—but no matter.) The cast works adequately, but the show belongs to Burns, as his God muses about mistakes and misconceptions. There were two sequels, *Oh, God! Book II* (1980) and *Oh, God! You Devil* (1984).

## Pleasantville

★★★★ New Line, 1998, c, 116 min. Dir and SP: Gary Ross. Cast: Tobey Maguire, Reese Witherspoon, Jeff Daniels, Joan Allen, William H. Macy, J. T. Walsh, Don Knotts, Marley Shelton, Jane Kaczmarek.

Here is a rarity: a comedy that makes you think and a fantasy that gives you something to chew on. David (Maguire) and Jennifer (Witherspoon) are teenagers of the nineties, children of a broken marriage. David is obsessed with a

Jeff Daniels and Joan Allen, characters in the perfect sitcom world of *Pleasantville* (1998), develop a poignant relationship in Gary Ross's comedy-fantasy.

long-running fifties television series called *Pleasantville* in which life is completely sanitized. A mysterious TV repair man (Knotts) transports the siblings to the town, where they gradually disrupt the serene life, introducing the black-and-white people to such things as color, toilets, rainstorms, art, and sex. Witty and cleverly wrought, *Pleasantville* is a parable that skewers the kind of conformity that leads to ignorance and bigotry and also asserts that a life without diversity or challenges or passion is scarcely a life at all.

# Rabbit Test

★ Avco-Embassy, 1978, c, 86 min. Dir: Joan Rivers. SP: Joan Rivers, Jay Redack. Cast: Billy Crystal, Alex Rocco, Joan Prather, Doris Roberts, George Gobel, Imogene Coca, Paul Lynde.

How to develop a splitting headache: watch any fifteen minutes of Joan Rivers's *Rabbit Test*. A kind of Mel Brooks movie gone fatally amuck, the film has a premise that must have struck her as hilarious: a world-class nerd named Lionel Carpenter (Crystal) has a one-time sexual encounter that results in his becoming pregnant. At first he is lionized, particularly by the lunatic family of the girl (Prather) he comes to love. But then he becomes an object of wrath to everyone, including the president (Gobel). Atrocious, with any number of tasteless gags. Many cameos by such actors as Roddy McDowall, Sheree North, Norman Fell, and Rivers herself.

# The Santa Clause

★★☆ Disney/Hollywood, 1994, c, 97 min. Dir: John Pasquin. SP: Leo Benvenuti, Steve Rudnick. Cast: Tim Allen, Wendy Crewson, Judge Reinhold, Eric Lloyd, David Krumholtz, Peter Boyle, Mary Gross, Larry Brandenberg.

Young viewers may well enjoy this comedy-fantasy; others may gag on the heavy sentiment. Still, *The Santa Clause* does a decent job of introducing television star Tim Allen to the big screen. He plays Scott Calvin, marketing executive for a toy manufacturer, who accidentally kills Santa Claus on Christmas eve. (Yes, you heard it right.) By virtue of the "Santa Clause," he *becomes* Santa, traveling to the North Pole with his delighted son Charlie (Lloyd). Of course everyone else, including his ex-wife (Crewson), thinks he's deranged. There are some nice fantasy touches at the Pole, including the modern-day gimmicks for Santa and his elves. The climax, however, is impossibly hokey.

# The Shaggy Dog

★★☆ Buena Vista, 1959, 104 min. Dir: Charles Barton. SP: Bill Walsh, Lillie Hayward, suggested by a story by Felix Salten. Cast: Fred MacMurray, Jean Hagen, Tommy Kirk, Kevin Corcoran, Tim Considine, Annette Funicello, Cecil Kellaway, Alexander Scourby, Roberta Shore, James Westerfield.

The Disney studio's first foray into slapstick comedy, *The Shaggy Dog* scored a hit with young audiences, but it's really lukewarm entertainment. The idea is this: young Wilby Daniels (Kirk) utters some magic words from the inscription on an ancient ring and turns into a shaggy dog. Mom and Dad (MacMurray and Hagen) are alarmed, to put it mildly, and so are Wilby's friends and neighbors. It all leads to a preposterous climax in which our shaggy hero foils a nest of sinister foreign spies. There were several sequels, including one for television in 1994.

# A Simple Wish

★★☆ Universal, 1997, c, 95 min. Dir: Michael Ritchie. SP: Jeff Rothberg. Cast: Martin Short, Mara Wilson, Kathleen Turner, Robert Pastorelli, Amanda Plummer, Francis Capra, Ruby Dee, Teri Garr, Alan Campbell, Jonathan Hadary.

Martin Short is a talented actor-comedian who has yet to find the breakthrough role he deserves. His role in this comedy-fantasy gives him some delightful moments, but the screenplay is mostly unmagical. He plays Murray, an inept fairy godmother (the only male in his class), who appears to eight-year-old Anabel (Wilson). Her one wish is to have her actor-father win the leading role in a musical version of *A Tale of Two Cities*. Murray and Anabel get into all sorts of trouble due to Murray's clumsy magic, and they are also opposed by wicked godmother-turned-witch Claudia (Kathleen Turner, camping it up gleefully). The movie has some nice special effects, but it wears out its welcome much too soon.

## Splash

★★★ Buena Vista, 1984, c, 111 min. Dir: Ron Howard. SP: Lowell Ganz, Babaloo Mandel, Bruce Jay Friedman. Cast: Tom Hanks, Daryl Hannah, John Candy, Eugene Levy, Dody Goodman, Richard B. Shull, Shecky Greene, Howard Morris.

An engaging, sweet-natured comedy fantasy in which Tom Hanks fully revealed the abundant charm that would make him a major star in a few years. He plays Alan, a lonely New York bachelor who is rescued from drowning in Cape Cod waters by a beautiful mermaid. When she follows him to the city in human form, he falls for this strange, bewitching creature, unaware that she reverts to being a mermaid when wet. Lapses in logic are fully covered by funny moments: the mermaid at large in Bloomingdale's, or consuming a lobster shell in a restaurant. As Alan's lecherous brother, John Candy steals every scene in which he appears. A 1988 television sequel was unnecessary.

## Switch

★★ HBO, 1991, c, 104 min. Dir and SP: Blake Edwards. Cast: Ellen Barkin, Jimmy Smits, JoBeth Williams, Lorraine Bracco, Tony Roberts, Perry King, Bruce Martyn Payne.

Ellen Barkin works hard to breathe some life into this comedy-fantasy, but the movie is dead on arrival. *Switch* is yet another gender-bender tale: arrogant womanizer Steve Brooks (King) is murdered by three women he's treated badly. Whether he goes to heaven or hell depends on his returning to earth and finding one woman who liked him. Here's the joke: he is given the eye-filling shape of a woman named Amanda (Barkin), who confounds everyone with her "macho" behavior, especially Steve's best friend Walter (Smits). After all the standard male-female jokes, the movie turns queasily sentimental toward the end as Steve really learns what it means to be a woman.

## Topper

★★★ MGM, 1937, 97 min. Dir: Norman Z. McLeod. SP: Jack Jevne, Eric Hatch, Eddie Moran, b/o novel by Thorne Smith. Cast: Cary Grant, Constance Bennett, Roland Young, Billie Burke, Alan Mowbray, Eugene Pallette, Arthur Lake, Hedda Hopper.

The movie that started a modest trend in comedy-fantasy, *Topper* is still lighthearted fun, although a little frayed around the edges. Cosmo Topper (Young) is a staid, respectable banker whose life is taken over by two friends, George and Marion Kerby (Grant and Bennett). The Kerbys just happen to be ghosts of a couple killed in an automobile accident. Playful and irresponsible rich folk, they turn Topper's life upside down with their invisible trickery. They also teach him how to break out of his shell and live freely and happily. Grant and Bennett are clearly having a good time, but the comic heart of the film is Roland Young, who adds touches of whimsy and even poignancy to his role. There were two sequels, a television series, and a television remake in 1979.

## Topper Returns

★★☆ United Artists, 1941, 88 min. Dir: Roy Del Ruth. SP: Jonathan Latimer, Gordon Douglas, b/o characters conceived by Thorne Smith. Cast: Joan Blondell, Roland Young, Carole Landis, Billie Burke, Dennis O'Keefe, Patsy Kelly, Eddie "Rochester" Anderson.

A good cast gives a bit of a spark to this third and last in the "Topper" film series. This entry has Cosmo Topper (Young) goaded by ghost Gail Richards (Blondell) into tracking down the person who stabbed her to death in a spooky old mansion. The plot involves the usual quota of misunderstandings concerning Mrs. Topper (Burke), their chauffeur (Anderson), and various strange types at the mansion. The movie makes little sense but it manages a bright moment or two, mostly because of Joan Blondell's expert way with a quip, even a poor one.

## Vampire in Brooklyn

★★ Paramount, 1995, c, 103 min. Dir: Wes Craven. SP: Charles Murphy, Michael Lucker, Christopher Parker. Cast: Eddie Murphy, Angela Bassett, Allen Payne, Kadeem Hardison, John Witherspoon, Zakes Mokae, Joanna Cassidy. A distinct change of pace for Eddie Murphy, but why? He plays Maximilian, the last member of a legendary breed of vampires, who comes to America in search of the half-vampire Rita (Bassett). Maximilian hopes to seduce her into a dance that would make her his soulmate forever. Rita happens to be a police officer whose partner, Justice (Payne), is secretly in love with her. The movie tries to combine comedy and horror but succeeds at neither, and oddly, Murphy's role keeps him sleek and sinister throughout, without a trace of his street-smart charm. Most of the humor falls to John Witherspoon as a gruff night watchman and to Kadeem Hardison as a hustler who becomes Maximilian's servant.

# Dress Right: Military Comedies

Any military man—or woman—will tell you: the martial life is no bed of roses, especially when the bed is hard, cold, or a trench in the middle of nowhere. Still, from the silent years to the present day, the movies have found comedy gold in the humiliating predicaments of soldiers, sailors, and other servicemen. Laugh along with Capt. "Hawkeye" Pierce, Private Benjamin, Sgt. Bilko, and all their military friends.

## Captain Newman, M.D.

★★★ Universal, 1964, c, 126 min. Dir: David Miller. SP: Richard L. Breen, Phoebe Ephron, Henry Ephron, b/o novel by Leo Rosten. Cast: Gregory Peck, Tony Curtis, Angie Dickinson, Eddie Albert, Bobby Darin, James Gregory, Bethel Leslie, Robert Duvall, Jane Withers, Dick Sargent, Larry Storch, Robert F. Simon.

You will be glad to meet Captain Josiah Newman, M.D. As chief of the neuropsychiatric section of an army base hospital in Arizona in the waning years of World War II, Captain Newman is a miracle worker: compassionate, wise, patient, and all things wonderful. During the course of this long but intelligent comedy-drama, he takes on the cases of a schizophrenic colonel (Albert), a guilt-ridden corporal (Darin), and a deeply withdrawn captain (Duvall). The good captain even finds time for a bit of flirtation with his adoring nurse (Dickinson). Tony Curtis is on hand to provide comic relief as an irrepressible corporal.

## Down Periscope

★★☆ Fox, 1996, c, 92 min. Dir: David S. Ward. SP: Hugh Wilson, Andrew Kurtzman, Eliot Wald, b/o story by Hugh Wilson. Cast: Kelsey Grammer, Lauren Holly, Rob Schneider, Rip Torn, Bruce Dern, William H. Macy, Harry Dean Stanton.

A passable service comedy, predictable from first to last, but with some laughs. Kelsey Grammer is Lt. Commander Tom Dodge, a maverick officer who is assigned to command a broken-down submarine with a crew from hell. (He dubs it the U.S.S. *Rustoleum*.) Dodge's assignment: to participate in war games in which his sub attempts to penetrate U.S. naval forces in Norfolk harbor and sink a dummy ship. Nasty admiral Bruce Dern is determined to thwart him. If you've seen similar movies, can you doubt that Dodge will triumph in the end? Rob Schneider is over the top as Dodge's first officer, and Lauren Holly causes a few flurries as the only girl on board.

## Good Morning, Vietnam

★★★ Touchstone, 1987, c, 120 min. Dir: Barry Levinson. SP: Mitch Markowitz. Cast: Robin Williams, Forest Whitaker, Bruno Kirby, Chintara Sukapatana, Robert Wuhl, Tung Thanh Tran.

Robin Williams's manic, motor-mouth comedy routines can be either brilliant or off-putting, depending on your inclination. He puts his stand-up style to work in this movie, in which he plays the real-life Adrian Cronauer, an irreverent, rapid-fire disc jockey for Armed Forces Radio during the Vietnam War. Inevitably, he tangles gleefully with the uptight, humorless military types, but he also has his serious involvement, mostly with a young Vietnamese boy (Tung Thanh Tran) and his sister (Sukapatana). The material may occasionally become heavy-handed but Williams dazzles with his flights of free association. Incidentally, the real Adrian Cronauer claimed that he was not at all like the character played by Robin Williams.

## I Was a Male War Bride

★★★ Fox, 1949, 105 min. Dir: Howard Hawks. SP: Charles Lederer, Leonard Spigelgass, Hagar Wilde, b/o story by Henri Rochard. Cast: Cary Grant, Ann Sheridan, William Neff, Eugene Gericke, Marion Marshall, Randy Stuart.

Suave, dapper, debonair. These adjectives eminently suited Cary Grant, probably the screen's foremost comic actor. So it was always great fun to see him lose his aplomb and savoir faire in slapstick situations. (See *Bringing up Baby,* page 86, for example.) Howard Hawks's lively farce is a case in point: as a French (!) officer who marries a WAC and is then forced to disguise himself as a female officer to be near her, Grant must endure any number of humiliations. He dozes in the driver's seat of a runaway motorcycle, gets himself wound up in an awning as he exits a window, and ultimately dresses in drag. Ann Sheridan has little to do but display her talent for wry, sarcastic humor.

## The Last Detail

★★★☆ Columbia, 1973, c, 105 min. Dir: Hal Ashby. SP: Robert Towne, b/o novel by Darryl Ponicsan. Cast: Jack Nicholson, Otis Young, Randy Quaid, Clifton James, Michael Moriarty, Carol Kane, Nancy Allen.

You'll find one of Jack Nicholson's best early performances in this raucously funny yet oddly melancholy comedy. He plays Billy "Bad Ass" Buddusky, a sailor who, along with buddy Mulhall (Young), is assigned to transport naïve young Meadows (Quaid) to naval prison, where he is to serve eight years for theft. Their trip to the prison turns into one long movable party of drinking and brawling, with stop-offs in many cities. All the time their pity and affection for Meadows grows, until turning him over to the authorities becomes extreme*ly*

painful. Despite all the ribald, good-time activity, the feeling persists that these men can never express their true emotions. Jack Nicholson's Oscar-nominated performance beautifully conveys this ambiguity.

## M*A*S*H

★★★★ Fox, 1970, c, 116 min. Dir: Robert Altman. SP: Ring Lardner, Jr., b/o novel by Richard Hooker. Cast: Elliott Gould, Donald Sutherland, Sally Kellerman, Robert Duvall, Tom Skerritt, René Auberjonois, Gary Burghoff, Jo Ann Pflug, John Schuck, Roger Bowen.

Robert Altman's blistering black comedy uses the Korean "police action" of the fifites to skewer the futility, stupidity, and brutality of all wars. Alternating scenes of bloody carnage with brashly farcical sequences, the movie centers on a M*A*S*H (Mobile Army Surgical Hospital) unit in Korea and particularly on the antics of Captains "Hawkeye" Pierce (Sutherland) and "Trapper John" McIntyre (Gould), two brilliant surgeons who, when they are not up to their armpits in blood and gore, enjoy carrying on like ribald teenagers. A one-of-a-kind movie—a farce with deadly serious intentions—*M*A*S*H* won an Oscar for its writer, Ring Lardner, Jr., and became an enormously popular television program that lasted for many seasons.

## McHale's Navy

★★☆ Universal, 1997, c, 108 min. Dir: Bryan Spicer. SP: Peter Crabbe, Andy Rose; b/o story by Andy Rose. Cast: Tom Arnold, David Alan Grier, Dean Stockwell, Debra Messing, Tim Curry, Bruce Campbell, Henry Cho, Tommy Chong, Ernest Borgnine.

A loose adaptation of the popular TV series that ran from 1962 to 1966, *McHale's Navy* is a passable action-comedy with a few laughs and no surprises. Lt. Commander Quinton McHale (Arnold) is now retired and living on his own Caribbean island. He is called back into service to thwart "the second best terrorist in the world" (Curry) in his sinister plan to establish a New World Order. Reunited with his old buddies, McHale ultimately wins the day. Dean Stockwell is miscast as the idiot officer who is the butt of many of the jokes. Ernest Borgnine, the original McHale, appears as an admiral.

## Never Wave at a WAC

★★☆ RKO, 1952, 87 min. Dir: Norman Z. McLeod. SP: Ken Englund, b/o story by Frederick Kohner, Fred Brady. Cast: Rosalind Russell, Paul Douglas, Marie Wilson, William Ching, Arleen Whelan, Leif Ericson, Charles Dingle, Hillary Brooke, Lurene Tuttle, Frieda Inescort, Louise Beavers.

A standard, breezy service comedy starring Rosalind Russell as a divorced society hostess who joins the WACs to be near her current boyfriend (Ching). She finds, instead, that she is the lowliest of privates, and also a guinea pig in a scientific experiment conducted by her former but still loving husband (Douglas). The star moves briskly and gamely through the sometimes slapstick proceedings, making the transition from lofty lady to just-one-of-the-WACs exactly as expected. Marie Wilson is fun in her usual dim-bulb role, this time as the least likely candidate for the Intelligence branch of the service.

## No Time for Sergeants

★★★ Warners, 1958, c, 119 min. Dir: Mervyn LeRoy. SP: John Lee Mahin, b/o novel by Mac Hyman and play by Ira Levin. Cast: Andy Griffith, Myron McCormick, Nick Adams, Murray Hamilton, Don Knotts.

First a novel by Mac Hyman, then a television play by Ira Levin, and then a Broadway hit by Levin, *No Time for Sergeants* had the good sense to bring Andy Griffith's Broadway role to the screen. He plays Will Stockdale, a naïve and likable Georgia farm boy who enters the service and innocently creates chaos. Myron McCormick also repeated his Broadway role as the sergeant tested almost beyond endurance by Griffith. Don Knotts has a small role as a noncommissioned officer, and look quickly for an actor named Jameel Farah, who later became Jamie Farr of the *M\*A\*S\*H* series. In

1964, *No Time for Sergeants* was turned into a television series that lasted one season.

## Operation Mad Ball

★★★ Columbia, 1957, 105 min. Dir: Richard Quine. SP: Arthur Carter, Jed Harris, Blake Edwards, b/o play by Arthur Carter. Cast: Jack Lemmon, Ernie Kovacs, Kathryn Grant, Mickey Rooney, Dick York, Arthur O'Connell, Roger Smith, James Darren.

A service comedy with a higher quota of laughs than many others. The situation is simple: at an army base in postwar Normandy, a group of bored soldiers, led by Private Al Hogan (Lemmon) decides to stage "the maddest mad ball in the history of the United States Army." Needless to say, everything goes hilariously wrong as Hogan and his cohorts tangle with the nasty, up-tight officer-in-charge

In *Operation Mad Ball* (1957), Dick York, Mickey Rooney, and Jack Lemmon play soldiers who plan "the maddest mad ball in the history of the United States Army."

# Other Clowns of Comedy

The performances of these gifted comedians have brightened our lives over the years. Not all of their films are available on tape, but many can be found with a little perseverance.

## Lucille Ball

Yes, she was the Queen of Television Comedy, but Lucille Ball also had an amazingly long and varied career both before and after Lucy Ricardo. As early as 1933, she could be spotted as a chorus girl in Samuel Goldwyn's *Roman Scandals,* then played featured roles in such RKO movies as *Stage Door* (1937), *Joy of Living* (1938), and *Having a Wonderful Time* (1938). She went from leading roles in MGM musicals (*DuBarry Was a Lady, Best Foot Forward,* both 1943) to playing Bob Hope's leading lady in such comedies as *Sorrowful Jones* (1949) and *Fancy Pants* (1950). After achieving television fame with husband Desi Arnaz, Ball starred with him in two MGM comedies, *The Long, Long Trailer* (1954) and *Forever, Darling* (1956). No comic actor was ever more adept at slapstick while keeping her lovable qualities fully intact.

## George Burns and Gracie Allen

Burns and Allen came out of vaudeville and entered radio and movies to become one of the best-loved teams in America's entertainment history. George Burns played the sly, artful straight man to wife Gracie's endearing dumbness. They were usually the best feature of the movies in which they appeared, including such musicals as *We're Not Dressing* (1934), *A Damsel in Distress* (1937), and *College Swing* (1938). Later, a widowed Burns enjoyed a whole new career as a twinkly oldster in such films as *The Sunshine Boys* (1975), *Oh, God* (1977), and *Going in Style* (1979).

(Kovacs). Back in the scheming-serviceman mode that made him famous in *Mister Roberts,* Jack Lemmon is at the top of his form and brings many of the normally staid cast members along with him. Some of the situations border on bad taste (one involves a misplaced corpse) but you may be laughing too hard to notice.

## Operation Petticoat

★★★ Universal-International, 1959, c, 124 min. Dir: Blake Edwards. SP: Stanley Shapiro, Maurice Richlin, b/o story by Paul King, Joseph Stone. Cast: Cary Grant, Tony Curtis, Joan O'Brien, Dina Merrill, Arthur O'Connell, Gene Evans, Dick Sargent, Virginia Gregg.

In the early weeks of World War II, a Navy sub-marine is trying to make its way from the Philippines to Australia. The ship's commander (Grant) is asked to take aboard five nurses, and you can guess the problems that arise in this breezy service comedy. Where do they sleep? How do they use the bathroom facilities? How can commander Grant keep his crew's minds on their work? And especially what should he do about his mischievous, scrounging junior officer, played by Tony Curtis? (Ensign Pulver, Luther Billis, move over.) An easy-to-take movie, especially with Grant at the helm.

## Private Benjamin

★★★ Warners, 1980, c, 110 min. Dir: Howard Zieff. SP: Nancy Meyers, Charles Shyer, Harvey Miller. Cast: Goldie

## Eddie Cantor

Eddie Cantor's extraordinarily long career involved him in every major area of the performing arts. He was a star of Florenz Ziegfeld's opulent revues, a beloved icon of "old-time" radio, top man in a number of musical movies, and a tireless television performer. His rolling, bulging eyes, his flapping arms, and his busy feet can be found in *Whoopee* (1930), *Roman Scandals* (1933), *Kid Millions* (1934), and *Show Business* (1944).

## Joan Davis

It's too bad that Joan Davis is largely remembered only as the star of her television comedy series, *I Married Joan*. She was much funnier in featured roles in movies of the thirties and forties, playing goofy but amiable characters. She can be spotted in such Fox musical films as *Just Around the Corner* (1938), *My Lucky Star* (1938), and *Sun Valley Serenade* (1941). Twice she costarred with Eddie Cantor, in *Show Business* (1944) and *If You Knew Susie* (1948), and she appeared opposite "Tin Man" Jack Haley in *George White's Scandals* (1945).

## Martha Raye

Like Joe E. Brown, Martha Raye was often teased for her wide mouth, but it was her brashly funny personality and gift for slapstick that kept her successfully in the public eye on stage, in films, and on television. She was happily featured in a number of Paramount musicals in the thirties, including *Rhythm on the Range* (1938), *Waikiki Wedding* (1937), and *The Big Broadcast of 1938* (1938). Many years later, she made an ingratiating foil for Jimmy Durante in *Billy Rose's Jumbo* (1962).

Hawn, Eileen Brennan, Armand Assante, Robert Webber, Sam Wanamaker, Barbara Barrie, Mary Kay Place, Albert Brooks, Harry Dean Stanton, P. J. Soles, Sally Kirkland, Craig T. Nelson.

A pampered Jewish-American princess with a record of two disastrous marriages (the second lasted six hours), Judy Benjamin is at a loss about what to do with her life. ("I'm twenty-nine years old and trained to do nothing.") So what does she do? She joins the army, and by the time this enjoyable comedy has ended, Judy has "found" herself. There are few surprises here, but Goldie Hawn is so engaging in the role that her saga is very easy to follow. She's helped by an excellent supporting cast, notably Eileen Brennan as a spit-and-polish offi-

cer. A television series from 1981 to 1983 had Brennan repeating her movie role.

## Renaissance Man

★★ Touchstone, 1994, c, 124 min. Dir: Penny Marshall. SP: Jim Burnstein. Cast: Danny DeVito, Gregory Hines, James Remar, Ed Begley, Jr., Kadeem Hardison, Lillo Brancato, Jr., Mark Wahlberg.

An uneasy mixture of raucous comedy and tear-jerking sentiment, *Renaissance Man* stars Danny DeVito as Bill Rago, a failed copywriter who takes the only job he can get: teaching remedial English to army recruits. The recruits are young and rowdy, but many of them turn out to bear hidden scars from their mean lives. In time, Rago moves from contempt for his pupils to teaching them Shakespeare's *Hamlet* as a springboard for instilling pride of accomplishment. This device may have seemed a good idea for a funny, heartwarming movie but it doesn't work: none of the ways Rago uses *Hamlet* has an ounce of believability. By the time the boys are behaving like members of the chorus in a musical comedy, the concept has collapsed entirely.

## Sgt. Bilko

★★ Universal, 1996, c, 92 min. Dir: Jonathan Lynn. SP: Andy Breckman. Cast: Steve Martin, Dan Aykroyd, Phil Hartman, Glenne Headly, Daryl Mitchell, Max Casella.

From 1955 to 1959, comedian Phil Silvers starred as Sgt. Ernie Bilko, head of the motor pool at mythical Fort Baxter, where his outrageous money-making schemes were the joy of his platoon and the bane of his commander, Colonel Hall, played by Paul Ford. Silvers's brash style won many laughs, and some of the episodes are legendary to fans of old-time television. Gifted comic actor Steve Martin stars in this updated remake, and it just doesn't work. Martin is wrong for the role—he seems to be standing outside the character in the wearisome style of Chevy Chase, and he's not funny. There is much noisy slapstick as Bilko takes on his adversary, nasty Col. Thorn (Hartman), but the best episodes of the crude old television show had much more spark than this.

## Stripes

★★☆ Columbia, 1981, c, 102 min. Dir: Ivan Reitman. SP: Harold Ramis, Len Bloom, Daniel Goldberg. Cast: Bill Murray, Harold Ramis, Warren Oates, P. J. Soles, John Larroquette, John Candy, Sean Young, John Diehl, Judge Reinhold.

Bill Murray's movie persona, at least in the eighties, is that of a scruffy, unruly, mocking loser and perennial put-on who somehow succeeds in winning the day. In this very popular but predictable service comedy, he plays John, a taxi driver who joins the army with his pal Russell (Ramis). He finds the standard assortment of characters: witless recruits (John Candy, as Ox, is one), a bellowing top sergeant (Oates), and an off-the-wall company commander (Larroquette). Of course, John and his cohorts get into all sorts of trouble, and when the platoon is sent overseas, guess who rescues the platoon when it is held prisoner by the Russians in East Germany? Right. Noisy, frenetic, and fun for those who enjoy this sort of movie.

## The Wackiest Ship in the Army

★★★ Columbia, 1960, c, 99 min. Dir: Richard Murphy. SP: Richard Murphy, b/o story by Herbert Margolis, William Raynor. Cast: Jack Lemmon, Ricky Nelson, John Lund, Chips Rafferty, Tom Tully, Joby Baker, Warren Berlinger, Patricia Driscoll, Mike Kellin, Alvy Moore.

A fast-paced service farce, with Jack Lemmon as a hapless Navy lieutenant who, during World War II, is placed in charge of a rusty old schooner manned by butter-fingered incompetents. His mission: to sail the boat from Australia to New Guinea. Not surprisingly, this leads to a series of slapstick capers, at least until midpoint when the ship is used as a decoy to put an Australian coast-watcher (Rafferty) behind enemy lines. A burst of action toward the end turns the bumbling crew into heroes. Lemmon acquits himself well as the bewildered but game skipper.

# Cut to the Chase: Comedy and Crime

Crime doesn't pay (we are told), but at movie box offices, it can certainly keep the cash flowing. Nasty killers are not much fun, but according to movie lore, policemen, detectives, gangsters, and thieves can be a steady source of humor, and under the right circumstances, even homicide can provoke some laughter. Here is ample proof that mixing crime and comedy has its occasional rewards.

## After the Thin Man

★★★☆ MGM, 1936, 113 min. Dir: W. S. Van Dyke II. SP: Frances Goodrich, Albert Hackett, b/o story by Dashiell Hammett. Cast: William Powell, Myrna Loy, Jessie Ralph, Sam Levene, Joseph Calleia, Elissa Landi, James Stewart, Dorothy McNulty (Penny Singleton).

The unexpected success of *The Thin Man* persuaded MGM to make a sequel, using the same writers and director. Surprisingly, the result was somewhat better than the original, with a nicely convoluted plot, an able cast, and a goodly batch of Nick-and-Nora quips. The plot, involving the murder of the shiftless husband of Nora's cousin (Landi), brings in the usual collection of colorful suspects, one of whom is a very young Jimmy Stewart. Once again Nick and Nora Charles provide the main pleasure as they temper their obvious love for each other with the slightest edge of mockery. At one point in the midst of the mayhem, Nick asks her, "Having a good time, Mrs. Charles?" "Couldn't be better," she replies. And who could blame her?

## Amos & Andrew

★★ Columbia, 1993, c, 94 min. Dir and SP: E. Max Frye. Cast: Nicolas Cage, Samuel L. Jackson, Dabney Coleman, Michael Lerner, Margaret Colin, Brad Dourif, Giancarlo Esposito, Bob Balaban.

This hectic farce with satirical overtones runs out of steam long before the conclusion. When neighbors of black Pulitzer Prize–winner Andrew Sinclair (Jackson) suspect that he is a burglar in his own brand-new home, they tell the politically ambitious police chief (Coleman), who starts his own volatile police action. When he realizes his bad mistake, he tries to cover his stupidity by using career criminal Amos O'Dell (Cage) as a foil who will get him off the hook. But Amos has his own agenda, and soon the area is swarming with police, reporters, a hostage negotiator, and black activists. Much frantic activity, very little amusement.

## Analyze This

★★★ Warners, 1999, c, 110 min. Dir: Harold Ramis. Sp: Peter Tolan, Harold Ramis, Kenneth Lonergan. Cast: Robert De Niro, Billy Crystal, Lisa Kudrow, Joe Viterelli, Chazz Palminteri, Leo Rossi, Richard Castellano, Molly Shannon, Max Casella.

For years Robert De Niro has coasted on his reputation, giving perfunctory performances in essentially supporting roles. Here, as Paul Vitti, a top mobster with psychological hangups, he gives a full-blown comic performance, and the result is exhilarating. The premise: confronted with embarrassing panic attacks, Vitti turns to psychiatrist Ben Sobel (Crystal) for help, then makes Sobel's life a living hell, upsetting his impending wedding and involving him in criminal activities. De Niro and Crystal make a funny team, and much of the movie, especially the sections spoofing gangster films, is on target. Like so many comedies, however, *Analyze This* runs its good idea into the ground, ending with a contrived climax. But De Niro is fun to watch.

# Armed and Dangerous

★★ Columbia, 1986, c, 88 min. Dir: Mark L. Lester. SP: Harold Ramis, Peter Torokvei, b/o story by Brian Grazer, Harold Ramis, James Keach. Cast: John Candy, Eugene Levy, Robert Loggia, Kenneth McMillan, Meg Ryan.

John Candy is a clumsy cop, and Eugene Levy is an inept lawyer. When they are both fired from their jobs, they join the Guard Dog Security Company as guards. After studying the use of firearms for two whole hours, the two set off on a series of bungled cases, until they realize that their company is in league with the security union's mobster president (Loggia). They go undercover, ending with a wild chase that turns a million-dollar heist into a free-for-all. Meg Ryan, not yet a star, provides some romantic interest in this standard-issue farce.

# Beverly Hills Cop

★★★ Paramount, 1984, c, 105 min. Dir: Martin Brest. SP: Daniel Petrie, Jr., b/o story by Danilo Bach, Daniel Petrie, Jr. Cast: Eddie Murphy, Lisa Eilbacher, Judge Reinhold, Steven Berkoff, Ronny Cox, Stephen Elliott, Paul Reiser, Bronson Pinchot, James Russo.

A fast, violent action comedy with Eddie Murphy at his sly, funny best. He plays Axel Foley, a Detroit cop who comes to Beverly Hills to track down the killer of his friend. He stays to break up a major drug ring. The movie's overriding joke is that Foley is sharper, more resourceful, and more effective than all the by-the-numbers policemen in Los Angeles. One scene after another has him blustering his way to success in posh locales, including a fancy hotel and an exclusive club. Murphy is clearly enjoying himself and the movie was so successful that it spawned two (inferior) sequels, in 1987 and 1994.

# The Big Lebowski

★★★ Gramercy, 1998, c, 117 min. Dir: Joel Coen. SP: Joel Coen, Ethan Coen. Cast: Jeff Bridges, John Goodman, Julianne Moore, Steve Buscemi, David Huddleston, John Turturro, Philip Seymour Hoffman, David Thewlis, Sam Elliott, Ben Gazzara.

Just when you thought that the Coen brothers, Joel and Ethan, had discovered a measure of discipline with the excellent *Fargo* (1996), they returned with this wildly offbeat comedy-thriller. Don't try to sort out the pieces of the plot—just enjoy Jeff Bridges as the Dude, a scruffy, laid-back dropout from the seventies, who is mistaken for a millionaire (Huddleston) with the same name. Before long he is being threatened, drugged, arrested, and in mortal danger as various eccentric characters swirl around him. Whenever the Dude is knocked unconscious, the movie veers into a kind of hallucinatory fantasy, including one deranged Busby Berkeley-like musical number. *The Big Lebowski* is not in a class with other Coen efforts, but relax and you might have a good time.

# Breaking In

★★★ Goldwyn, 1989, c, 91 min. Dir: Bill Forsyth. SP: John Sayles. Cast: Burt Reynolds, Casey Siemaszko, Sheila Kelley, Lorraine Toussaint, Albert Salmi, Harry Carey, Maury Chaykin, Steve Tobolowsky, David Frishberg.

In the many cop and good ol' boy roles he played for years, Burt Reynolds's acting skills were seldom tested. *Starting Over* (see page 113) gave him the first role in which he played a rounded, vulnerable character. A decade later, he gave a strong performance in this offbeat crime comedy as a mature, worldly wise safecracker. He plays Ernie, an aging career criminal who takes in Mike (Siemaszko), a free-wheeling youngster who needs to learn not only about the "art" and painstaking skill of safecracking but also about life. *Breaking In* has neither highs nor lows, but in its quiet way, it's pleasing entertainment.

# Brother Orchid

★★★ Warners, 1940, 91 min. Dir: Lloyd Bacon. Dir: Lloyd Bacon. SP: Earl Baldwin, b/o story by Richard Connell. Cast: Edward G. Robinson, Ann Sothern, Humphrey Bogart, Ralph Bellamy, Donald Crisp, Allen Jenkins, Cecil Kellaway, Morgan Conway.

Jeff Bridges is the Dude, Steve Buscemi is Donny, and John Goodman is Walter, in the Coen Brothers' oddball movie *The Big Lebowski* (1998).

Edward G. Robinson's snarling gangsters were turning softer by the end of the thirties, due to the movie industry's Production Code. Here he plays Little John Sarto, who suddenly gets a yen for "culture." When he returns from a trip to Europe he finds that his life is in danger, and he hides out in a monastery. The monks have no idea of his identity and as time passes, Little John begins to enjoy his life of contemplation. He takes time off to eliminate his rival (Bogart), then returns to the monastery for good. Ann Sothern shines as Little John's moll, and the Warners stock company of players helps out.

## Cadillac Man

★★☆ Orion, 1990, c, 95 min. Dir: Roger Donaldson. SP: Ken Friedman. Cast: Robin Williams, Tim Robbins, Annabella Sciorra, Pamela Reed, Zack Norman, Fran Drescher, Lori Petty.

A curious, lopsided comedy that works on occasion and falls flat on others. In the movie's first part, Robin Williams plays a car salesman with serious women and job problems. He has a married mistress (Drescher) and a hostile ex-wife (Reed), and he needs to sell a dozen cars at a big upcoming sale. Then coworker Sciorra's violently jealous husband (Robbins), suspecting his wife of cheating with one of the salesmen, comes crashing into the dealership, threatening to kill everyone, and the movie becomes a cat-and-mouse game between Williams and Robbins. Williams gives his usual energetic spin to his performance, but the movie gives off sparks only intermittently.

## Compromising Positions

★★★ Paramount, 1985, c, 98 min. Dir: Frank Perry. SP: Susan Isaacs, b/o her novel. Cast: Susan Sarandon, Raul Julia, Judith Ivey, Edward Herrmann, Mary Beth Hurt, Joe Mantegna, Josh Mostel, Deborah Rush, Joan Allen, Anne De Salvo.

A Long Island dentist named Bruce Fleckstein (Mantegna) has been murdered, and now many of the women with whom he had sexual relations are very nervous suspects. Enter Judith Singer (Sarandon), housewife, Fleckstein patient, and former newspaper reporter, who decides to reenter journalism by solving the mystery. Surrounding her are her stodgy husband (Herrmann), her wisecracking best friend (Ivey, in a scene-stealing performance), and an investigating police lieutenant (Julia) whose relationship with Judith becomes somewhat more than professional. An enjoyable comedy-mystery with some bright dialogue.

## Cops and Robbers

★★★ United Artists, 1973, c, 89 min. Dir: Aram Avakian. SP: Donald E. Westlake. Cast: Cliff Gorman, Joseph Bologna, Dick Ward, Shepperd Strudwick, Ellen Holly, John P. Ryan, Nino Ruggeri, Gayle Gorman.

Author Donald E. Westlake, whose novels provided the basis for such films as *The Hot Rock* and *Bank Shot,* wrote the screenplay for this enjoyable caper movie. Tom (Gorman) and Joe (Bologna) are two only slightly corrupt policemen with pregnant wives and a devout wish to obtain the better things in life. And so they plan to steal a fortune in bearer bonds on the day New York City is staging a ticker-tape parade for the first astronauts to land on the moon. Of course everything goes comically wrong. There's a funny chase sequence near the end, and both Gorman and Bologna are fine as enterprising cops.

## Disorganized Crime

★★ Touchstone, 1989, c, 98 min. Dir and SP: Jim Kouf. Cast: Corbin Bernsen, Hoyt Axton, Ruben Blades, Fred Gwynne, Ed O'Neill, Lou Diamond Phillips, Daniel Roebuck, William Russ, Marie Butler Kouf.

Career criminal Corbin Bernsen invites four men, all ex-cons, to join him in robbing the bank in a small Montana town. But before he can meet them, he is arrested by two inept New Jersey detectives. The four crooks plan the robbery without Bernsen, who escapes on the way to the airport. Now Bernsen, the crooks, and the cops are all on separate courses, hoping to find each other somewhere along the way. It's certainly disorganized crime, but *Disorganized Crime* is no better than routine, with only scattered laughs. The comic highlight is intended to occur when the gang hitches a ride in the back of a truck that happens to be full of manure. No further comment necessary.

## Fletch

★★☆ Universal, 1985, c, 96 min. Dir: Michael Ritchie. SP: Andrew Bergman, b/o novel by Gregory McDonald. Cast: Chevy Chase, Joe Don Baker, Dana Wheeler-Nicholson, Richard Libertini, Tim Matheson, M. Emmet Walsh, George Wendt, Kenneth Mars, Geena Davis.

On the beach, investigative reporter Fletch (Chase) is mistaken for a beach bum by an aviation executive, who offers him $50,000 if Fletch will kill him for insurance purposes. Fletch smells a rat, and his investigation eventually leads him to uncover a connection between some Los Angeles cops and the drug business. Fletch's gimmick is that he enjoys assuming disguises, and here he plays a doctor, an insurance salesman, and a black basketball player. Okay mystery-comedy if you like Chevy. Sequel: *Fletch Lives* (1989).

## Foul Play

★★★ Paramount, 1978, c, 116 min. Dir and SP: Colin Higgins. Cast: Goldie Hawn, Chevy Chase, Dudley Moore, Rachel Roberts, Burgess Meredith, Eugene Roche, Marilyn Sokol, Billy Barty.

An entertaining comedy-mystery that introduced Chevy Chase in his first leading-man role, *Foul Play* has a Hitchcock-like plot that gets out of hand, but enough laughs and suspense to hold viewer interest. Goldie Hawn is the damsel in distress—a rather light-headed San Francisco librarian who stumbles on a plot to assassinate visiting Pope Pius XIII. Chase is the bumbling detective who comes to believe that her life is in danger. There's the inevitable—and in this case, funny—car chase across the hills of San Francisco, plus a theater climax that obviously echoes Hitchcock. Look for good comic support from Dudley Moore as a way-out swinger who happens to be an orchestra conductor and Burgess Meredith as a helpful neighbor with a snake for a pet.

## Fuzz

★★☆ Filmways, 1972, c, 92 min. Dir: Richard A. Colla. SP: Evan Hunter (Ed McBain), b/o his novel. Cast: Burt Reynolds, Raquel Welch, Yul Brynner, Jack Weston, Tom Skerritt, James McEachin, Peter Bonerz.

Obviously, *Fuzz* would like to do for the police what *M*A*S*H* did for the military but its mixture of raucous comedy and violent action doesn't quite make it. The movie takes place at a Boston precinct, where four plain-clothes detectives, headed by Burt Reynolds, continue to botch their stakeouts while searching for criminals. (One has Reynolds, moustache and all, dressed as a nun.) Their principal target is a mysterious bomber (Brynner, a long distance from Siam), who keeps killing local officials. Hunter based the screenplay on one of his "87th Precinct" stories written as Ed McBain.

## Get Shorty

★★★☆ MGM/UA, 1995, c, 105 min. Dir: Barry Sonnenfeld. SP: Scott Frank, b/o novel by Elmore Leonard. Cast: John Travolta, Gene Hackman, Rene Russo, Danny DeVito, Dennis Farina, Delroy Lindo, James Gandolfini, David Paymer, Bette Midler (unbilled), Harvey Keitel (unbilled).

In recent years, novelist Elmore Leonard's combination of comedy and gunplay has finally been given proper treatment on the screen. (Check out the excellent *Out of Sight.*) *Get Shorty* also gets it right in a story that spoofs the ways of Hollywood while shedding some blood. John Travolta heads a fine cast as Chili Palmer, an enterprising Miami loan shark who comes to the movie capital to collect on a few outstanding bets and stays on to play a part in the film business. He gets involved with a seedy producer (Hackman), an actress (Russo), and an ego-driven film star (DeVito), with whom he shares the movie's funniest scene. There's also some violent activity when he tangles with criminal types. Much pungent dialogue in a crackling movie.

## Grosse Pointe Blank

★★☆ Hollywood, 1997, c, 106 min. Dir: George Armitage. SP: Tom Jankiewicz, D. V. DeVincentis, Steve Pink, John Cusack. Cast: John Cusack, Minnie Driver, Dan Aykroyd, Alan Arkin, Joan Cusack, Jeremy Piven, Hank Azaria, Barbara Harris.

If you can accept the idea of a young professional hit man as the romantic lead, you might enjoy this quirky combination of comedy and gangster film. John Cusack plays Martin Q. Blank, a killer-for-hire who botches an assassination attempt and decides to flee to Grosse Pointe, Michigan, for his high school's tenth-anniversary reunion. His real goal is Debi (Driver), the girl he ditched at the senior prom ten years earlier. Unfortunately, he is pursued to Grosse Pointe by four assassins bent on killing him, especially a top rival hood named Grocer (Aykroyd). The relentlessly oddball dialogue and situations become tiresome after a while and the bloodletting, particularly in a jumbled climax at the reunion, is not conducive to laughter. A near-miss.

## Hanky Panky

★☆ Columbia, 1982, c, 110 min. Dir: Sidney Poitier. SP: Henry Rosenbaum, David Taylor III. Cast: Gene Wilder, Gilda Radner, Richard Widmark, Kathleen Quinlan, Robert Prosky, Josef Sommer, Johnny Sekka.

Gene Wilder is a funny actor with largely one string to his bow: comic hysteria. In this dreadful Hitchcock "wannabe," he practically blows a gasket as he sprints about New York City in danger from assassins, cops, and shadowy government figures. He plays innocent-at-large Michael Jordan, who quickly becomes involved with a woman (Quinlan) desperately in need of his help. When she is murdered, guess who is the chief suspect. Gilda Radner is Kate, a girl who seems to want to help Michael but who also has her own secret agenda. Richard Widmark is the chief villain. There's scarcely an amusing or suspenseful moment in this botched story, and very little of it makes sense.

## Hopscotch

★★★ Avco Embassy, 1980, c, 104 min. Dir: Ronald Neame. SP: Bryan Forbes and Brian Garfield, b/o novel by Brian Garfield. Cast: Walter Matthau, Glenda Jackson, Sam Waterston, Ned Beatty, Herbert Lom.

"He's a class act!" says CIA agent Cutter (Waterston) about his longtime colleague Miles Kendig (Matthau). But Kendig is in big trouble: demoted by Myerson (Beatty), his stupid boss, Kendig has decided to get even by writing his memoirs, telling the nasty truth about CIA operations. Now a fugitive, he leads Myerson and the agency on a merry, teasing chase, with the help of Isobel (Jackson), a former operative and former flame. An enjoyable comedy-melodrama, *Hopscotch* makes good use of Matthau's slouching, rumpled persona, and as usual, he's fun to watch. Glenda Jackson helps in what is essentially a supporting role.

## The Hot Rock

★★★ Fox, 1972, c, 105 min. Dir: Peter Yates. SP: William Goldman, b/o novel by Donald E. Westlake. Cast: Robert Redford, George Segal, Ron Leibman, Paul Sand, Zero Mostel, Moses Gunn, William Redfield, Charlotte Rae.

Just out of prison, career thief John Dortmunder (Redford) decides to steal a precious diamond called the Sahara Stone. His big mistake is to ally himself with some less than reliable confederates: his brother-in-law (Segal) and two inept others (Leibman, Sand). They keep failing in their mission as the diamond moves from one locale to another, ending up hidden in a police station, which the four men attempt to raid by helicopter. (At one point, they land on the wrong roof.) A light, amusing caper comedy, *The Hot Rock* manages to pull off a few surprising if unlikely twists. Zero Mostel is very funny in a small role as Sand's blatantly corrupt lawyer-father.

## Mad Dog and Glory

★★★ Universal, 1993, c, 96 min. Dir: John McNaughton. SP: Richard Price. Cast: Robert De Niro, Bill Murray, Uma Thurman, David Caruso, Mike Starr, Kathy Baker.

Here's a bit of reverse casting: in this comedy-melodrama, Robert De Niro is a mild-mannered crime photographer for the Chicago police. (His ironic nickname is "Mad Dog.") Bill Murray is a top hood who moonlights as a comedian in his own nightclub. When De Niro saves Murray's life in an attempted robbery, Murray rewards him by giving him an unusual thank-you gift for a week: bartender Uma Thurman. De Niro and Thurman fall in love, and there's big trouble ahead for both of them. De Niro and Murray acquit themselves reasonably well in this entertaining movie.

## Married to the Mob

★★★ Orion, 1988, c, 103 min. Dir: Jonathan Demme. SP: Barry Strugatz, Mark Burns. Cast: Michelle Pfeiffer, Matthew Modine, Dean Stockwell, Mercedes Ruehl, Alec Baldwin, Joan Cusack, Trey Wilson.

What's a poor mob widow to do? When her

hood husband is murdered, Michelle Pfeiffer tries to escape her connection with the mob—to no avail. The mob boss (Stockwell) who killed her husband lusts for her, and an eager, clumsy young FBI man (Modine) is following her, hoping to nail the boss. One misunderstanding leads to another, until the hectic climax. The movie is breezy and sometimes hilarious, but its most memorable feature is the decor, especially the wildly garish homes and hotel rooms inhabited by the wealthy Mafia "families." Michelle Pfeiffer is appealing as the hapless widow, but Mercedes Ruehl is even better as a fiercely jealous mob wife.

## My Blue Heaven

★★☆ Warners, 1990, c, 95 min. Dir: Herbert Ross. SP: Nora Ephron. Cast: Steve Martin, Rick Moranis, Joan Cusack, Carol Kane, Daniel Stern, Bill Irwin.

Steve Martin stars as a middle-level New York hoodlum who is assigned to the witness protection program in California as a witness in a major underworld trial. Nerdy FBI agent Rick Moranis is assigned to watch over him, and his life becomes a nightmare as Martin keeps returning to his criminal instincts. Joan Cusack plays the local assistant district attorney, also a divorcée and a mother of two, who becomes involved in the proceedings. *My Blue Heaven* is an occasionally amusing though often forced comedy with a good cast, but this time Martin seems uneasy in a role that might have been better played by someone like Anthony LaPaglia.

## My Cousin Vinny

★★★ Fox, 1992, c, 119 min. Dir: Jonathan Lynn. SP: Dale Launer. Cast: Joe Pesci, Marisa Tomei, Ralph Macchio, Mitchell Whitfield, Fred Gwynne, Lane Smith, Austin Pendleton, Bruce McGill.

This overlong, easygoing, highly popular comedy stars Joe Pesci in a tailor-made role as Vinny Gambini, a Brooklyn lawyer without experience but with tons of chutzpah. Accompanied by street-smart girlfriend Mona Lisa Vito (Tomei, in her Oscar-winning role), Vinny travels to Alabama to defend his young cousin Bill (Macchio) and Bill's friend Stan (Whitfield) against a charge of murdering a local store owner. Vinny's defense almost sends the boys to the electric chair, until Mona Lisa takes over. The movie is conventional and unsurprising, but Pesci gives the material his own pungent flavor and Tomei extracts every laugh. Fred Gwynne is very funny as the sorely tried trial judge.

## Nothing to Lose

★★☆ Touchstone, 1998, c, 97 min. Dir and SP: Steve Oedekerk. Cast: Tim Robbins, Martin Lawrence, John C. McGinley, Giancarlo Esposito, Michael McKean, Kelly Preston, Susan Barnes.

There's hardly a believable moment in this hectic, fitfully amusing comedy. When advertising man Nick Beam (Robbins) discovers that his wife is cheating on him with his boss, he goes all to pieces. So when thief T. Paul (Lawrence) tries to hold him up, Nick turns the tables by taking a startled T. along with him on a crime spree that culminates in robbing his boss's office. (T., it turns out, is really a desperate, jobless family man.) Soon Nick and T. are involved not only with the police but also with two nasty look-alike thieves (McGinley and Esposito). The movie doesn't make much sense, but the leads work hard to win laughs. Director Oedekerk has one great scene as a nighttime security guard who cannot restrain his impulse to dance.

## Opportunity Knocks

★★☆ Imagine Films, 1990, c, 105 min. Dir: Donald Petrie. SP: Nat Bernstein, Mitchel Katlin. Cast: Dana Carvey, Robert Loggia, Todd Graff, Julia Campbell, Doris Belack, Milo O'Shea, James Tolkan, Sally Gracie.

On the television series *Saturday Night Live*, slight, pixieish Dana Carvey proved to have a genuine gift for mimicry. Here, in his first starring role in a feature film, he seems amiable but too mild for major stardom. He plays

Eddie, a Chicago con man who is fleeing from the mob boss he offended. Hiding out, he assumes the identity of a young financial wizard and is taken under the wing of a business tycoon (Loggia) who believes he is his son's best friend. Eddie also falls for the tycoon's doctor-daughter (Campbell). Carvey works hard, perhaps too hard, to demonstrate his comic skills, but he comes across as lightweight.

## Out Cold

★★★ Hemdale, 1988, c, 92 min. Dir: Malcolm Mowbray. SP: Leonard Glasser, George Malko, b/o novel by Leonard Glasser. Cast: John Lithgow, Teri Garr, Randy Quaid, Bruce McGill, Lisa Blount, Alan Blumenfeld.

An offbeat, amusing black comedy set largely in a butcher shop, *Out Cold* stars Teri Garr (in an expert performance) as Sunny, the wife of a nasty butcher named Ernie (McGill). Fed up with his womanizing, Sunny seizes the chance to lock him in his freezer, where his dead body is discovered by his shy, fussy partner Dave (Lithgow). Dave has always loved Sunny, and together they try to dispose of Ernie's body. Enter Lester (Quaid), a dull-witted detective whose investigation causes comic misunderstandings. Malcolm Mowbray directed the British comedy *A Private Function* (about a purloined pig) in 1985, and *Out Cold* might just as easily have been set in England as in California.

## Out of Sight

★★★☆ Universal, 1998, c, 122 min. Dir: Steven Soderbergh. SP: Scott Frank, b/o novel by Elmore Leonard. Cast: George Clooney, Jennifer Lopez, Ving Rhames, Don Cheadle, Dennis Farina, Albert Brooks, Steve Zahn, Luis Guzman.

Sly, sassy, and very funny, *Out of Sight* is a genuine original. George Clooney finally seems star-worthy as a seasoned bank robber who botches his latest heist, goes to prison, and in an attempted breakout, finds himself locked in the trunk of a car with sexy federal agent Jennifer Lopez. But that's only the beginning as

the plot spins in various directions (including flashbacks) to reveal a group of mostly disreputable characters, all surprisingly well realized in Scott Frank's screenplay. They include Don Cheadle as a shrewd, violent con man, Ving Rhames as Clooney's pal, and Albert Brooks as a Wall Street billionaire imprisoned for insider trading. Top-notch entertainment.

## Outrageous Fortune

★★☆ Touchstone, 1987, c, 105 min. Dir: Arthur Hiller. SP: Leslie Dixon. Cast: Shelley Long, Bette Midler, Peter Coyote, Robert Prosky, John Schuck, Anthony Heald, George Carlin.

There's scarcely a believable moment in this hectic chase comedy, this time involving women rather than men as the principals. Lauren (Long in her prissy "Cheers" mode) and Sandy (Midler, brassy as usual) are aspiring actresses who discover, to their mortification, that they are both having an affair with the same man (Coyote). Only the man turns out to be not a teacher but a corrupt former government agent who has stolen a secret and potentially deadly formula. Soon the two women are running for their lives, while CIA men and KGB operatives are falling over each other in an effort to save them or kill them. The script plays up the obvious differences between the women—they go from rivals to buddies—but it's all rather silly and not much fun.

## The Pink Panther

★★★ United Artists, 1964, c, 113 min. Dir: Blake Edwards. SP: Maurice Richlin, Blake Edwards. Cast: David Niven, Peter Sellers, Capucine, Robert Wagner. Claudia Cardinale, Brenda De Banzie, Fran Jeffries.

The movie that introduced Inspector Jacques Clouseau to the world, *The Pink Panther* has a few moments of inspired farce but it is only moderately entertaining. When the inept, extraordinarily stupid Clouseau comes to the Riviera with his wife (Capucine), he is blithely unaware that skulduggery is afoot. A notorious jewel thief (Niven), pretending to be a debonair Englishman on holiday, is after the fabulous diamond called the Pink Panther, owned by a beautiful princess (Cardinale). What's more, Niven's confederate in the robbery is Clouseau's wife! Gags abound, some of them funny, others not, but Sellers's idiot inspector clearly hit America's funnybone, and more Clouseau movies followed in the years ahead.

## The Pink Panther Strikes Again

★★★ MGM/UA, 1976, c, 103 min. Dir: Blake Edwards. SP: Frank Waldman, Blake Edwards. Cast: Peter Sellers, Herbert Lom, Lesley-Anne Down, Colin Blakely, Herbert Rossiter, Burt Kwouk.

This fifth entry in the Inspector Clouseau series has its share of both funny and flat gags and situations. By this time, dim bulb Clouseau (Sellers) has driven Chief Inspector Dreyfuss (Lom) insane, and now the deranged man has acquired a Doomsday machine with which he threatens to destroy the world unless Clouseau is eliminated within seven days. Some of the material is predictable—Dreyfuss brings together the world's greatest assassins and of course they destroy each other. Sellers gamely goes through several of his idiotic Clouseau disguises, including a Quasimodo whose "hump" inflates and causes him to float over Paris into the Seine.

## Prizzi's Honor

★★★☆ Fox, 1985, c, 129 min. Dir: John Huston, SP: Richard Condon, Janet Roach, b/o novel by Richard Condon. Cast: Jack Nicholson, Kathleen Turner, Anjelica Huston, Robert Loggia, William Hickey, John Randolph, Lee Richardson.

A brilliant comedy-melodrama, black as night and extremely funny, Prizzi's Honor sends up the gangster subgenre with glee and more than a little violence. Jack Nicholson gives one of his best performances as Charlie Partanna, a not overly bright hit man for a powerful Mafia family, who falls for Irene Walker (Turner), only to learn that she is a hit woman with her own agenda. Anjelica Huston, in an Oscar-winning performance, walks off with the movie as Maerose Prizzi, a scorned Mafia daughter who sets in motion her own plan of revenge. The results of her scheming are startling, with a final encounter that will stun you. Director Huston keeps it all moving swiftly and expertly.

## Rush Hour

★★★ New Line, 1998, c, 98 min. Dir: Brett Ratner. SP: Jim Kouf, Ross LaManna, b/o story by Ross LaManna. Cast: Jackie Chan, Chris Tucker, Tom Wilkinson, Elizabeth Pena, Julia Hsu, Philip Baker Hall, Mark Rolston, Tzi Ma.

Jackie Chan, the undisputed king of Asian action comedy, gets his best American workout to date in Rush Hour. He plays Inspector Lee, a Hong Kong detective who is sent to the U.S. to help find the Chinese consul's kidnapped eleven-year-old daughter (Hsu). He is teamed with a motor-mouthed, rule-breaking cop named James Carter (Tucker). True to form, they quarrel and then bond, as they rip their way through a series of carefully choreographed action sequences. Chan's flipping, swiveling, and kicking routines get their full due, but so do Tucker's nonstop profane wisecracks. Most fun: the two become buddies by exchanging cultural ideas. Wait around for the outtakes.

## Quick Change

★★★ Warners, 1990, c, 88 min. Dirs: Howard Franklin and Bill Murray. SP: Howard Franklin. Cast: Bill Murray, Geena Davis, Jason Robards, Randy Quaid, Philip Bosco, Phil Hartman, Bob Elliott, Tony Shalhoub, Stanley Tucci.

Dressed as a clown, Grimm (Murray) robs a New York City bank of a million dollars, using two confederates, girlfriend Phyllis (Davis) and infantile pal Loomis (Quaid), to carry out his clever plan. But there's a big problem: how do you get out of a city cluttered with boobytraps of all kinds? In one night, with police chief Robards on their tail, they confront a helpful man who turns out be a thief himself, a cab driver who knows no English, a gang of mobsters, and more. The climax at the airport gets out of hand, but *Quick Change* is lively, funny, and easy to take.

## Raising Arizona

★★★☆ Fox, 1987, c, 92 min. Dir: Joel Coen. SP: Ethan Coen, Joel Coen. Cast: Nicolas Cage, Holly Hunter, John Goodman, Trey Wilson, William Forsythe, Sam McMurray, Frances McDormand, Randall "Tex" Cobb.

The Coen brothers, Joel and Ethan, have won a reputation for making quirky, offbeat films unlike any other: usually surprising combinations of black comedy and melodrama. *Raising Arizona,* their second movie, is no exception. Slapstick and melodrama combine when career thief Hi (Cage) and his ex-policewoman wife, Ed (Hunter), learn that their marriage is going to be childless. To please his distraught wife, Cage kidnaps one of the brand-new quintuplets of furniture mogul Nathan Arizona. Unforeseen consequences lead to wildly comic sequences involving, among others, Cage's disreputable convict pals (Goodman and Forsythe). Cage and Hunter are perfectly cast as the not-too-bright but endearing couple.

## A Shock to the System

★★☆ Corsair, 1990, c, 88 min. Dir: Jan Egleson. SP: Andrew Klavan, b/o novel by Simon Brett. Cast: Michael Caine, Elizabeth McGovern, Peter Riegert, Swoosie Kurtz, Will Patton, John McMartin, Barbara Baxley, Jenny Wright.

What would you do if you were burdened with a nagging wife (Kurtz) and a job that was going nowhere? (You lose a top promotion to a hated rival.) Executive Graham Marshall (Caine) finds a solution, first by accident, then by design. You simply kill those who stand in your way! Happiness and success are yours if you find ingenious ways to commit murder. For a while, this black comedy has a nice edge of satire, especially when it spoofs corporate greed, but then it slides into improbability and loses that edge. Finally, it just leaves a sour taste. Caine, however, appears to be enjoying himself in his homicidal role.

## Silver Streak

★★★ Fox, 1976, c, 113 min. Dir: Arthur Hiller. SP: Colin Higgins. Cast: Gene Wilder, Jill Clayburgh, Richard Pryor, Patrick McGoohan, Ned Beatty, Clifton James, Ray Walston, Richard Kiel.

Quickly, how many thrillers, comic or otherwise, can you name that were set aboard a speeding train? Here's another, and it's frantic, jumbled, and occasionally diverting. Gene Wilder, strictly in his hysterical mode, plays a hapless editor aboard the Silver Streak who becomes involved (innocently, of course) in skulduggery and murder. The villain is nefarious art dealer McGoohan, whose assistant (Clayburgh) turns out to be a lady in distress. Midway through the movie Richard Pryor enters as a resourceful thief and teams up with Wilder (as he would several times again) for a few hilarious sequences. The truly spectacular climax involves a runaway train.

## Sneakers

★★★ Universal, 1992, c, 125 min. Dir: Phil Alden Robinson. SP: Lawrence Lasker, Walter F. Parkes, Phil Alden Robinson. Cast: Robert Redford, Sidney Poitier, Dan Aykroyd, River Phoenix, Ben Kingsley, Mary McDonnell, David Strathairn, George Hearn, Timothy Busfield.

With such a high-powered cast, *Sneakers* should have been better, but it will suffice as a lively if convoluted comedy-thriller. Robert Redford stars as a once-notorious computer hacker who now runs a company that tests computer systems. His colleagues all have shady pasts but they are experts in their fields. They all become embroiled in high-level intrigue involving a black box that can break absolutely any existing computer code. Before long there are a series of break-ins, narrow escapes, and near-fatal encounters, often tinged with a sense of humor. The movie is sometimes difficult to follow, but stay alert and you should be entertained.

## Stakeout

★★★ Touchstone, 1987, c, 115 min. Dir: John Badham. SP: Jim Kouf. Cast: Richard Dreyfuss, Emilio Estevez,

In *Silver Streak* (1976), con man Richard Pryor and editor Gene Wilder become entangled in skulduggery and murder. The movie was their first as a team.

Madeleine Stowe, Aidan Quinn, Dan Lauria, Forest Whitaker, Ian Tracy.

*Stakeout* mixes comedy and melodrama with agreeable results, although it hardly offers anything new. Richard Dreyfuss and Emilio Estevez are Seattle cops and partners who could not be less alike. Dreyfuss is a loose cannon, totally unpredictable, and Estevez is a stable family man. They get into trouble when they are ordered to guard the girlfriend (Stowe) of an escaped convict and Dreyfuss falls in love with her. The ingredients for another buddy-cop movie are all here: sardonic banter between the cops, shootouts, and the like. A sequel, logically called *Another Stakeout,* appeared in 1993.

## The Sting

★★★☆ Universal, 1973, c, 129 min. Dir: George Roy Hill. SP: David S. Ward. Cast: Paul Newman, Robert Redford, Robert Shaw, Charles Durning, Ray Walston, Harold Gould, Dana Elcar, Eileen Brennan, Robert Earl Jones.

Everybody's favorite comedy-caper movie, *The Sting* surprised Hollywood by winning seven Oscars. In mid-thirties Chicago, street-smart Robert Redford joins with aging boozer Paul Newman and other pals to revenge the murder of a friend by mobster Robert Shaw. They devise an ingenious plan to take Shaw to the cleaners. The scheme works but there's a surprise twist at the end. Everything is first-rate—the deft direction by George Roy Hill, Marvin

Hamlisch's adaptations of Scott Joplin's ragtime music, and the top-notch performances by the entire cast. A feeble sequel turned up in 1983.

## Stir Crazy

★★★ Columbia, 1980, c, 111 min. Dir: Sidney Poitier. SP: Bruce Jay Friedman. Cast: Gene Wilder, Richard Pryor, Georg Stanford Brown, JoBeth Williams, Miquelangel Suarez, Craig T. Nelson, Barry Corbin.

Accept the extremely unlikely premise and you might enjoy this raucous comedy. Gene Wilder and Richard Pryor play two hapless friends who are mistaken for bank robbers and sentenced to 125 years in prison. As Wilder tries to be reasonable and friendly and Pryor tries desperately to be inconspicuous, their lives turn into a comic nightmare. Wilder's prowess with a mechanical bull gets him into the prison rodeo and a chance for them both to escape. Nothing much is believable but as in *Silver Streak,* the two stars play well together. Later, their partnership wore thin due to bad material and Pryor's all-too-visible illness.

## Taking Care of Business

★★☆ Hollywood, 1990, c, 107 min. Dir: Arthur Hiller. SP: Jeffrey Abrams, Jill Mazursky. Cast: James Belushi, Charles Grodin, Anne DeSalvo, Loryn Locklin, Stephen Elliott, Hector Elizondo, Veronica Hamel, Mako.

Another switched-identity comedy, this one rather tired despite the presence of that highly skilled comic actor, Charles Grodin. Jim Belushi plays a convicted car thief and a rabid Chicago Cubs fan who steals away from his minimum-security prison to cheer on his team at the World Series. Grodin is an uptight workaholic, a wealthy advertising executive with a house in Las Vegas. By a purely contrived plot device, the two men switch identities, causing many complications. Belushi gets a taste of the good life; Grodin, left to his own devices, loosens up and learns how to "live." In the end, the two men become great friends. (Sure.) Amusing enough, but nothing new in the formula.

## The Thin Man

★★★☆ MGM, 1934, 93 min. Dir: W. S. Van Dyke II. SP: Albert Hackett and Frances Goodrich, b/o novel by Dashiell Hammett. Cast: William Powell, Myrna Loy, Maureen O'Sullivan, Nat Pendleton, Minna Gombell, Cesar Romero, Natalie Moorhead, Edward Ellis, Porter Hall.

By this time virtually everyone knows that the "thin man" refers not to suave detective Nick Charles but to a character played by Edward Ellis. No matter. When tippling Nick (Powell) and his smart, sassy wife Nora (Loy) exchanged loving quips, nobody really cared who murdered whom, or why. What mattered was the refreshing new view of married bliss and the candid sexual sparks that passed between the Charleses. Their warm regard for each other was tempered by an amused awareness of each other's weaknesses, mostly for martinis. Adapted from a popular mystery novel by Dashiell Hammett, the movie had a modest budget and MGM considered it a routine entry, but audiences loved it, and it was a huge hit that prompted five sequels and many imitations.

## Tough Guys

★★☆ Touchstone, 1986, c, 104 min. Dir: Jeff Kanew. SP: James Orr, Jim Cruickshank. Cast: Burt Lancaster, Kirk Douglas, Alexis Smith, Eli Wallach, Dana Carvey, Charles Durning, Billy Barty.

It must have seemed a good idea at the time to reunite seasoned professionals Burt Lancaster and Kirk Douglas for this senior-citizen caper, but the result is only lukewarm. They play once-notorious bank robbers released from prison after serving thirty years. They are bewildered by such new-age things as yogurt and gay bars, and before long they are plotting to return to their old business of robbing a bank. As you might guess, everything goes comically wrong. Lancaster and Douglas do their best with stale material, but at least the supporting cast includes some welcome faces.

## Turner & Hooch

★★ Touchstone, 1989, c, 97 min. Dir: Roger Spottiswoode. SP: Dennis Shryack, Michael Blodgett, b/o story by Dennis Shryack. Cast: Tom Hanks, Mare Winningham, Craig T. Nelson, Reginald VelJohnson, Scott Paulin, J. C. Quinn, John McIntyre, Beasley.

Long before Tom Hanks became everyone's favorite actor, he made this mediocre cop-and-comedy film about a man and a dog. Fastidious detective Turner (Hanks) is reluctantly saddled with a huge, slobbering dog named Hooch (Beasley). The dog's eccentric master was murdered, and Hooch was the only witness. Now the dog must help Turner capture the culprits. At first Turner cannot tolerate Hooch's leaking mouth, gas attacks, and bad breath, but he learns to love him. Unfortunately, the ending is a total downer. Mare Winningham plays the veterinarian who captures Turner's heart.

## Undercover Blues

★★☆ MGM, 1993, c, 89 min. Dir: Herbert Ross. SP: Ian Abrams. Cast: Dennis Quaid, Kathleen Turner, Fiona Shaw, Stanley Tucci, Larry Miller, Obba Babatunde, Tom Arnold, Park Overall, Saul Rubinek.

An unsuccessful try at the sort of airy comedy-thriller that used to star William Powell and Myrna Loy in "The Thin Man" series. Dennis Quaid and Kathleen Turner are Jeff and Jane Blue, retired secret agents who are on a sabbatical now that they have a baby. Sure enough, they are dragged back into a case involving a sexy Communist woman (Shaw) who is buying top-secret explosives from a traitorous chemist in New Orleans. Soon the Blues are sprinting about the city's scenery, tangling with villains. Also involved are a pair of cops (Miller and Babatunde) and a tourist couple (Arnold and Overall). Stanley Tucci earns some laughs as a luckless mugger named Muerte.

## Who Is Killing the Great Chefs of Europe?

★★★ Warners, 1978, c, 112 min. Dir: Ted Kotcheff. SP: Peter Stone, b/o novel by Nan Lyons, Ivan Lyons. Cast: Jacqueline Bisset, George Segal, Robert Morley, Jean-Pierre Cassel, Philippe Noiret, Jean Rochefort, Madge Ryan.

In virtually all of his films, British actor Robert Morley succeeded in stealing scenes from everyone, which, in his case, was grand larceny. He does it again in this clever, lighthearted comedy mystery. He plays a magazine editor who not only rates restaurant dishes but also eats and enjoys them with rare gusto. Now he is involved in a puzzling mystery in which Europe's leading chefs are being murdered, one by one. Heroine Jacqueline Bissett is a pastry chef who seems to be next in line. The movie is no more than light entertainment, but like a nice soufflé, it goes down easily.

# Hats in the Ring: Political Comedies

At a time when real-life politics and politicians are funnier and more improbable than any screenplay could devise, it is well to remember that political comedy has long found a place in the archives of film. Where else can you find such a tasty collection of charlatans, blowhards, and self-serving schemers? Here is a small but select group of political comedies that may warrant your attention.

## Blaze

★★★ Touchstone, 1989, c, 119 min. Dir: Ron Shelton. SP: Ron Shelton, b/o book by Blaze Starr, Huey Perry. Cast: Paul Newman, Lolita Davidovich, Jerry Hardin, Robert Wuhl, Gailard Sartain, Jeffrey DeMunn, Richard Jenkins.

Paul Newman gives a full-bodied performance as Earl K. Long, the bawdy, hot-tempered, tough-minded governor of Louisiana in the 1950s. Partly fictionalized, the movie traces Long's relationship with Blaze Starr (Davidovich), the stripper who was his lover and faithful companion for a number of years. The screenplay also touches on Long's surprising passion for civil rights for blacks, which earned him the bitter enmity of many and forced him into a mental hospital. The movie's color and vigor begin to fade somewhere at midpoint, but Newman keeps his character in sharp focus. Best line: Long, after viewing Blaze's strip act: "Powerful expression of basic human needs."

## The Best Man

★★★ United Artists, 1964, 102 min. Dir: Franklin Schaffner. SP: Gore Vidal, b/o his play. Cast: Henry Fonda, Cliff Robertson, Lee Tracy, Edie Adams, Margaret Leighton, Ann Sothern, Gene Raymond, Kevin McCarthy, Shelley Berman, John Henry Faulk, Richard Arlen.

Adapted by Gore Vidal from his 1960 Broadway play, *The Best Man* shows why politics can be an entertaining sport. It centers on two men who come to their party's presidential convention, seeking the nomination: Henry Fonda is the cerebral, liberal Secretary of State and Cliff Robertson is his archrival, a ruthless conservative Senator. Each man tries to repudiate the other with "dirty" secrets. Razor-sharp dialogue prevails throughout in this intelligent comedy-drama. The best performance is given by Oscar-nominated Lee Tracy, a veteran star of the thirties, as an ex-president who knows the score.

## Bob Roberts

★★★ Paramount, 1992, c, 102 min. Dir and SP: Tim Robbins. Cast: Tim Robbins, Susan Sarandon, Giancarlo Esposito, Gore Vidal, Allan Rickman, Ray Wise, Rebecca Jenkins.

Meet Bob Roberts (Robbins), senatorial candidate from Pennsylvania. He's an affable, down-home, guitar-strumming man with a well-oiled political machine and a huge public following. He's also an archconservative millionaire with a potentially dangerous agenda. Tim Robbins wrote, directed, and starred in this wickedly funny—and also sobering—political satire filmed in the form of a mock-documentary. Television commercials, rallies, and debates show the candidate as he wants to be seen, but the camera cannot conceal the real Roberts. The movie turns preachy toward the end, but on the whole it is cleverly made, with some vivid scenes. Many familiar faces appear in cameo roles.

# Bulworth

★★★ Fox, 1998, c, 130 min. Dir: Warren Beatty. SP: Warren Beatty, Jeremy Pikser (Aaron Sorkin, uncredited), b/o story by Warren Beatty. Cast: Warren Beatty, Halle Berry, Oliver Platt, Don Cheadle, Christine Baranski, Jack Warden, Isaiah Washington, Laurie Metcalf, Paul Sorvino, Joshua Malina, Richard Sarafian, Amiri Baraka.

What on earth has happened to Senator Jay Billington Bulworth (Beatty)? On the eve of the 1996 California primary, the once-liberal, now conservative senator has become completely unstrung, no longer believing in his own speeches or his party platform. Worst of all, he does the unthinkable: he starts speaking the truth! Soon he has immersed himself in black urban life, talking in rhyming rap cadences. In despair, he also arranges for a hit man to take his life. Warren Beatty's political satire is a pungent original for the first hour, then falls to confusion in the later portions, with sequences that defy credibility. (Bulworth's obscenity-laced climactic television appearance would have barely lasted thirty seconds.) Best performance: Oliver Platt as the senator's frazzled aide. The screenplay won an Oscar nomination.

# The Candidate

★★★☆ Warners, 1972, c, 110 min. Dir: Michael Ritchie. SP: Jeremy Larner. Cast: Robert Redford, Melvyn Douglas, Peter Boyle, Don Porter, Allen Garfield, Karen Carlson, Quinn Redeker, Michael Lerner, Kenneth Tobey.

A probing, satirical look at the political process, *The Candidate* won an Oscar for its screenwriter, Jeremy Larner. Robert Redford excels as Bill McKay, a liberal, idealistic young Democrat from California who starts his run for the Senate as a fighter for the good causes and ends up, not corrupted, but sadly neutralized and defused. (His last line after an unexpected outcome is "What do we do now?") The movie covers the political rituals, from fundraising dinners to handshaking tours, with a keen eye. Redford gets firm support from Melvyn Douglas as his realistic father, Peter Boyle as his wily campaign manager, and Don Porter as his opponent in the race.

# Dave

★★★ Warners, 1993, c, 105 min. Dir: Ivan Reitman. SP: Gary Ross. Cast: Kevin Kline, Sigourney Weaver, Frank Langella, Charles Grodin, Kevin Dunn, Ving Rhames, Ben Kingsley, Faith Prince, Laura Linney, Bonnie Hunt, Anna Deavere Smith.

If you can accept the rather preposterous premise, or if you can think of the film as a political fantasy, you should enjoy this amusing comedy. Dave Kovic (Kline) is the amiable, laid-back owner of a temporary employment agency in Washington, D.C. He's also a dead ringer for the current president Bill Mitchell (also Kline), and when the president suffers a near-fatal stroke, Dave is asked to take his place in secret, temporarily. The "new" Mitchell pleases everyone, including a baffled First Lady (Weaver), with the conspicuous exception of Bob Alexander (Langella), the scheming, ambitious Chief of Staff. The movie turns silly at times, but it all ends satisfactorily. Kline proves once again that he is one of the screen's most skillful comedy actors.

# The Distinguished Gentleman

★★★ Hollywood, 1992, c, 112 min. Dir: Jonathan Lynn. SP: Marty Kaplan, b/o story by Marty Kaplan, Jonathan Reynolds. Cast: Eddie Murphy, Lane Smith, Sheryl Lee Ralph, Joe Don Baker, Victoria Rowell, Grant Shaud, Charles S. Dutton, Kevin McCarthy.

Eddie Murphy is at his best when he is pitting his street-smart persona against pretentious, hypocritical people of society's upper strata. In *The Distinguished Gentleman,* he gets a role that allows him to do just that, and the result is amusing, once you get past the far-fetched premise. He plays a seasoned con man who decides to use his special skills to get elected to the House of Representatives. You have to believe that he not only wins a seat but also changes from cheerful corruption to good deeds once he finds a true love (Rowell).

In *Dave* (1993), Dave Kovic (Kevin Kline) is the "temporary" U.S. president, with a White House aide (Kevin Dunn, left) and the shifty chief of staff (Frank Langella, right).

Murphy's easy charm, shark's smile, and put-on style are in full bloom here, even when the story makes no sense.

## The Farmer's Daughter

★★★ RKO, 1947, 97 min. Dir: H. C. Potter. SP: Allen Rivkin and Laura Kerr, b/o play by Juhni Tervataa. Cast: Loretta Young, Joseph Cotten, Ethel Barrymore, Charles Bickford, Rose Hobart, Rhys Williams, Harry Davenport, Tom Powers, Lex Barker, William Harrigan.

An exceptionally beautiful, competent actress for many years, Loretta Young finally came into her own and won an Oscar for her performance in this pleasing comedy. She plays a Minnesota farm girl who goes to work as a maid in the home of a congressman (Cotten) and ends up not only running for Congress herself but winning the heart of her charmed employer. The screenplay has a few things to say about politics and government, but mostly the movie is a lighthearted fairytale that most viewers should enjoy. Ethel Barrymore lends her dignity to the role of Cotten's wise mother, and Charles Bickford is the household's somewhat informal butler. *The Farmer's Daughter* became a television series that ran from 1963 to 1966.

## Moon over Parador

★★☆ Universal, 1988, c, 104 min. Dir: Paul Mazursky. SP: Leon Capetanos, Paul Mazursky, b/o story by Charles G. Booth. Cast: Richard Dreyfuss, Sonia Braga, Raul Julia, Jonathan Winters, Fernando Rey, Polly Holliday, Sammy Davis, Jr., Charo, Michael Greene.

In *Moon over Parador,* Richard Dreyfuss has fun playing another ego-driven actor as in *The*

*Goodbye Girl* but his material here is only passable. He's Jack Noah, working on location in the Latin American country of Parador. A dead ringer for Parador's dictator, Jack is kidnapped and forced to impersonate the leader, who has expired of a heart attack. Anger and confusion turn to pleasure when he starts to enjoy the role, until he learns about the insidious agenda of the chief of the secret police (Julia) and the oppression of Parador's people. Sonia Braga plays the dictator's sexy mistress, who recognizes the ruse and helps Jack to do the right thing. The movie is intended as political satire but it doesn't come off due to faulty writing and a sluggish pace.

## My Fellow Americans

★★★ Warners, 1996, c, 102 min. Dir: Peter Segal. Sp: E. Jack Kaplan, Richard Chapman, Peter Tolan. Cast: Jack Lemmon, James Garner, Dan Aykroyd, John Heard, Lauren Bacall, Sela Ward, Wilford Brimley, Bradley Whitford.

Sometimes funny and sometimes strained, *My Fellow Americans* offers the fanciful notion that two ex-presidents, Democrat Matt Douglas (Garner) and Republican Russell P. Kramer (Lemmon), archenemies over many years, are forced to flee together for their lives when Kramer becomes innocently involved in a kickback scandal perpetrated by the current president (Aykroyd). Never mind the plot; the movie is really an excuse for the two men to exchange barbed remarks as they sprint across the country, meeting all sorts of odd types. Somehow they end up on horseback in the environs of the White House. Silly stuff, but Lemmon and Garner are seasoned professionals who make it palatable.

## Primary Colors

★★★☆ Universal, 1998, c, 144 min. Dir: Mike Nichols. SP: Elaine May, b/o novel by "Anonymous" (Joe Klein). Cast: John Travolta, Emma Thompson, Billy Bob Thornton, Kathy Bates, Adrian Lester, Maura Tierney, Larry Hagman, Diane Ladd, Mykelti Williamson, Rebecca Walker, Rob Reiner.

A razor-sharp, intelligent screenplay and first-rate performances (especially by John Travolta and Kathy Bates) are the principal virtues of this riveting, too-close-for-comfort political comedy-drama. Based on the best-selling novel by "Anonymous" (later revealed to be Joe Klein), the film centers on the presidential campaign of Jack Stanton, a charismatic if somewhat slippery Southern governor who continually tests the loyalty and dedication of his followers with his philandering ways. Travolta excels in his Clinton-like portrayal of a man with deep convictions and equally deep personal flaws, and Emma Thompson is superb as his clear-eyed wife, but it is Kathy Bates who rivets our attention as Stanton's boisterous, idealistic, but inwardly tormented campaign consultant.

## Protocol

★★☆ Warners, 1984, c, 96 min. Dir: Herbert Ross. SP: Buck Henry, b/o story by Charles Shyer, Nancy Meyers, Harvey Miller. Cast: Goldie Hawn, Chris Sarandon, Richard Benjamin, Andre Gregory, Gail Strickland, Cliff De Young, Kenneth Mars, Ed Begley, Jr.

There's a dab or two of satire and some scattered laughs in this made-to-order comedy for Goldie Hawn. She plays Sunny, a pert Washington cocktail waitress who becomes a national heroine through a series of comic accidents. To her bewilderment, she is made a protocol official for the State Department, not knowing that she is a pawn in the department's plan concerning a fictitious Middle Eastern country. The result is comic chaos, especially when Sunny takes the country's emir for a night on the town. There are some funny swipes at the crackpot ways of Washington, D.C., and Hawn goes dutifully through her patented dumb-as-a-fox routine.

## The Senator Was Indiscreet

★★★ Universal-International, 1947, 74 min. Dir: George S. Kaufman. SP: Charles MacArthur, b/o story by Edwin Lanham. Cast: William Powell, Ella Raines, Arleen Whelan,

Peter Lind Hayes, Ray Collins, Allen Jenkins, Hans Conried, Whit Bissell.

The satirical target of this movie is not new—the U.S. Senate has been cheerfully mocked for decades—but with Charles MacArthur (*The Front Page* and others) writing the screenplay, and witty playwright George S. Kaufman directing his first (and only) film, *The Senator Was Indiscreet* is a good deal of fun. William Powell is Senator Melvin Ashton, a white-haired fool who aspires to be president. Unfortunately, he has kept a diary that records all of his party's skulduggery over thirty-odd years. When the diary is stolen, it naturally becomes the center of furious contention. The jokes come thick and fast, and if many are dated, many others hit their targets, and probably would even today. Powell discards his usual suavity to play the dim-witted senator, with obvious relish.

## State of the Union

★★★☆ MGM, 1948, 124 min. Dir: Frank Capra. SP: Anthony Veiller, Myles Connolly, b/o play by Howard Lindsay, Russel Crouse. Cast: Spencer Tracy, Katharine Hepburn, Van Johnson, Angela Lansbury, Adolphe Menjou, Lewis Stone, Raymond Walburn.

Katharine Hepburn replaced Claudette Colbert as the wife of Spencer Tracy in this adaptation of the Broadway play, and if she isn't ideally cast, she succeeds in holding her own in a cast of heavyweight MGM actors. Tracy plays a Republican presidential candidate who is nearly crushed by the powerful political machine headed by Adolphe Menjou. Hepburn is his conscience who forces him to remember his long-standing commitment to "principle, integrity, honesty." Frank Capra manages to include some of his usual theme about good people versus corrupt politicians, but it doesn't detract from the sharp, often witty dialogue. Angela Lansbury, only in her early twenties at the time, plays a tough, influential newspaper publisher.

## Wag the Dog

★★★☆ New Line, 1997, c, 96 min. Dir: Barry Levinson. SP: Hilary Henkin, David Mamet. Cast: Dustin Hoffman, Robert De Niro, Anne Heche, Denis Leary, Willie Nelson, Andrea Martin, Kirsten Dunst, William H. Macy, Craig T. Nelson, Woody Harrelson.

A wickedly funny—and also eerily prescient—spoof of the sometimes unholy alliance between presidential politics and public relations. When the U.S. president is accused of sexually molesting a Firefly Girl in the Oval Office, top "spin" doctor Conrad Bream (De Niro) is called upon to think up a diversion from this scandal. Bream asks top Hollywood producer Stanley Motss (Hoffman) to create the "appearance" of a war with Albania, using fake commercials and a "patriotic" song performed by a fervent chorus to fire up the populace. So carried away is Motss by his efforts that he is compelled to go on even further, with ultimately deadly consequences. *Wag the Dog* is sharply etched satire, acted to a fine turn by everyone.

# Nose-Thumbing: Rude and Raucous Farces

How far should movies go in "pushing the envelope" of what's possible to show on screen? When does bad taste turn into execrable taste? How hilarious is rampant stupidity? You may want to think about these questions if you view some of the recent films in this category. On the other hand, you may want to give more of your attention to movies that pay homage to the honorable art of slapstick, sometimes successfully and sometimes not.

## Airheads

★★☆ Fox, 1994, c, 91 min. Dir: Michael Lehmann. SP: Rich Wilkes. Cast: Brendan Fraser, Steve Buscemi, Adam Sandler, Chris Farley, Michael McKean, Joe Mantegna, Judd Nelson, Ernie Hudson, Amy Locane, Michael Richards.

The simple premise for this frantic but passable farce is this: three clueless, self-deceiving members of a rock band (Fraser, Buscemi, Sandler) have only one goal: to play their demo record for a radio station. (They call themselves the Lone Rangers.) When the station's disc jockey (Mantegna) and manager (McKean) treat them with contempt, the three take over the station with toy guns. The resulting furor involves the station's employees, the police, and a crowd of rock fans. Lots of noisy slapstick and even a few laughs for easy-to-please viewers.

## Another You

★ TriStar, 1991, c, 98 min. Dir: Maurice Phillips. SP: Ziggy Sternberg. Cast: Gene Wilder, Richard Pryor, Mercedes Ruehl, Stephen Lang, Vanessa Williams.

A sad reunion of Gene Wilder and Richard Pryor, *Another You* stars Wilder as a pathological liar who is discharged from a mental hospital after three years. Pryor, looking unwell, plays the con man who is sentenced to community service and whose first assignment is to help Wilder make his transition to civilian life. Soon after their meeting, the two are caught up in an elaborate scam in which Wilder is mistaken for a missing millionaire beer manufacturer. Never mind; the situations are never amusing, and the stars, often so funny together, are at a loss.

## Bachelor Party

★★☆ Fox, 1984, c, 106 min. Dir: Neal Israel. SP: Neal Israel, Pat Proft, b/o story by Bob Israel. Cast: Tom Hanks, Adrian Zmed, Tawny Kitaen, George Grizzard, Barry Diamond, William Tepper, Robert Prescott, Michael Dudikoff.

This raucous farce marked Tom Hanks's first starring role in a feature film, many years before the fame and the Oscars. He plays Rick, who interrupts the freewheeling life of his friends to announce that he is marrying Debbie (Kitaen). So begins the night of Rick's wild bachelor party, which veers out of control with a spiraling series of mishaps, mistakes, and miscalculations. Involved in the fracas are hookers; Debbie's friends, who are giving her a shower; Debbie's straight-arrow father (Grizzard); and many others. Toward the end the movie tries to top one tasteless gag with another and it starts falling apart. But there are laughs along the way.

## BASEketball

★★ Paramount, 1998, c, 98 min. Dir: David Zucker. SP: David Zucker, Robert LoCash, Lewis Friedman, Jeff Wright. Cast: Trey Parker, Matt Stone, Yasmine Bleeth, Jenny McCarthy, Robert Vaughn, Ernest Borgnine.

Hey, dudes, here's another gross-out teenager comedy, directly from the creators of television's *South Park.* Parker and Stone play high school friends who invent baseketball, a game combining baseball, basketball, and volleyball. (Apparently it's an actual game, invented by director Zucker.) The movie begins as a spoof of pro sports (say hello to the Preparation H Arena), but quickly turns into just another of the breed: noisily and proudly offensive. There are some complications—a nasty entrepreneur (Vaughn) tries to gain control of the profitable sport; the two goofballs quarrel over their mutual attraction to Yasmine Bleeth—but it all ends with a long, juicy, nonerotic kiss between Parker and Stone. Incidentally, yet another movie in which a desperately ill child is the target of jokes. Enough.

## The Beverly Hillbillies

★ Fox, 1993, c, 103 min. Dir: Penelope Spheeris. SP: Lawrence Konner, Mark Rosenthal, Jim Fisher, Jim Staahl, b/o TV series created by Paul Henning. Cast: Jim Varney, Cloris Leachman, Dabney Coleman, Lily Tomlin, Erica Eleniak, Diedrich Bader, Rob Schneider, Lea Thompson.

The unfortunate trend of turning popular television sitcoms into feature films continued with this dismal version of the long-running *Beverly Hillbillies.* The movie retains the simple-minded humor and basic story of the original: the hillbilly Clampetts strike oil on their Arkansas farm and move to Beverly Hills as millionaires. While banker Coleman and his assistant Tomlin try to ingratiate themselves with the family, Coleman's treacherous employee Schneider and partner-in-crime Thompson scheme to take over the Clampett fortune. Watch the television reruns, if you must.

## Big Business

★★☆ Touchstone, 1988, c, 94 min. Dir: Jim Abrahams. SP: Dori Pierson, Marc Reid Rubel. Cast: Bette Midler, Lily Tomlin, Fred Ward, Edward Hermann, Michele Placido, Daniel Gerroll, Barry Primus.

Try to follow this. Two sets of identical twins are accidentally split up by a myopic nurse. Rose and Sadie Shelton (Midler) are the offspring of wealthy New Yorkers. Rose and Sadie Ratliff (Tomlin) are born to a slow-witted couple from Jupiter Hollow. Years later, Rose Shelton is the cut-throat CEO of a conglomerate, and her sister Sadie is a hapless nonentity. Rose Ratliff is a feisty, hard-headed woman, while her sister Sadie is a kittenish dreamer. Never mind. Through plot manipulations, the two sets of twins come together in New York City and of course are mistaken for each other by almost everyone. Midler is boisterous fun and the trick photography is clever, but virtually every situation is telegraphed in advance. A disappointment from the director of *Airplane!*

## Billy Madison

★ Universal, 1995, c, 90 min. Dir: Tamra Davis. SP: Tim Herlihy and Adam Sandler. Cast: Adam Sandler, Darren McGavin, Bradley Whitford, Bridgette Wilson, Norm MacDonald, Theresa Merritt, Chris Farley.

Of all the *Saturday Night Live* alumni, Adam Sandler must be the most actively annoying. His pose of crude, relentless stupidity makes many of the other SNL players seem like comedy icons by comparison. In the title role of *Billy Madison,* he is the rich, terminally weird son of hotel magnate McGavin, who will lose his inheritance of the hotel chain to a nasty vice president (Whitford) unless he manages to complete his entire education—first to twelfth grade—in only two weeks. We are asked to laugh at grown-up (only in size) Billy attending classes with elementary school children, but Sandler is so obnoxious that the only true response is nausea. Depressing from beginning to end.

## Black Sheep

★☆ Paramount, 1996, c, 87 min. Dir: Penelope Spheeris. SP: Fred Wolf. Cast: Chris Farley, David Spade, Tim Matheson, Gary Busey, Christine Ebersole, Grant Heslov, Timothy Carhart, Bruce McGill.

"He's like Roger Clinton, Billy Carter, and Ronald Reagan's whole family rolled into one!" somebody comments about Mike (Farley), the well-meaning but oafish younger brother of gubernatorial candidate Matheson. To keep Mike out of trouble, campaign worker Steve (Spade) is assigned to watch over him. Sure enough, one disaster follows another, with Mike taking the brunt of the pain, slapstick style. At one point, he is mistaken for his brother and, in a stoned state, addresses a rock concert organized to get out the vote. A follow up to *Tommy Boy* (1995), with the same stars and the same brain-dead approach to comedy.

# Brain Donors

★★ Paramount, 1992, c, 80 min. Dir: Dennis Dugan. SP: Pat Proft. Cast: John Turturro, Bob Nelson, Mel Smith, Nancy Marchand, John Savident, George de la Pena, Juli Donald, Spike Alexander.

Well, they tried. Some of the people involved with the hilarious *Airplane!*—writer Pat Proft, producers David and Jerry Zucker—attempted a duplication of a Marx Brothers movie, specifically *A Night at the Opera,* and came up severely short. Here, John Turturro, Bob Nelson, and Mel Smith emulate the immortal Brothers and invade a ballet company, turning it upside down with a barrage of nonstop slapstick and gags. The matches to *Opera* characters are evident, such as Nancy Marchand in the Margaret Dumont role and John Savident in the Sig Ruman role. Turturro is an able actor but he can't duplicate the inspired zaniness of Groucho.

# Caddyshack

★★☆ Orion, 1980, c, 99 min. Dir: Harold Ramis. SP: Brian Doyle-Murray, Harold Ramis, Douglas Kenney. Cast: Michael O'Keefe, Chevy Chase, Rodney Dangerfield, Ted Knight, Bill Murray, Cindy Morgan, Sarah Holcomb, Scott Colomby, Brian Doyle-Murray.

Life is hectic at the Bushwood Country Club. The owner (Knight) is in a permanent state of fury. The caddies are rowdy and irreverent. And the greenskeeper (Murray) is a dim-witted slob whose only goal in life is destroying the gopher who is chewing up the grounds. The club members include rich golf wizard Ty Webb (Chase) and most conspicuously, the loud, vulgar Czervik (Dangerfield). Watching it all is Danny (O'Keefe), the caddy with one eye on the caddy scholarship and the other on a club waitress (Holcomb). Dangerfield wins most of the laughs in this noisy, hectic, and very popular farce. Best moment: the caddy ballet. Worst moment: the Butterfinger in the pool. *Caddyshack II* was a 1988 sequel in name only.

# The Cannonball Run

★★ Fox, 1981, c, 95 min. Dir: Hal Needham. SP: Brock Yates. Cast: Burt Reynolds, Roger Moore, Farrah Fawcett, Dom DeLuise, Dean Martin, Sammy Davis, Jr., Jack Elam, Adrienne Barbeau, Terry Bradshaw.

More car-race nonsense from the director of *Smokey and the Bandit* and its sequel. Burt Reynolds and many of his friends appear in this frantic farce about the Cannonball Run, a car race from Connecticut to Southern California. No surprises here, just spectacular car crashes, dizzying pursuits, sudden breakdowns, and a score to shatter eardrums. As in *Smokey,* Reynolds is a king among drivers, and others are cast in unlikely roles: Martin and Davis as hard-drinking hustlers disguised as Catholic priests, and Moore as the wealthy heir to a girdle-manufacturing fortune, who keeps insisting he's Roger Moore. *Cannnonball Run II* came out in 1984.

# Car Wash

★★☆ Universal, 1976, c, 97 min. Dir: Michael Shultz. SP: Joel Schumacher. Cast: Richard Pryor, Franklin Ajaye, Sully Boyar, Richard Brestoff, Ivan Dixon, Bill Duke, George Carlin, Irwin Corey, Melanie Mayron, Lauren Jones, Garrett Morris, Antonio Fargas.

A brash, shamelessly vulgar comedy covering a single ten-hour period at a Los Angeles car wash. Under the harried leadership of Mr. B. (Boyar), the enterprise brings together a host of colorful characters, including ex-convict

Lonnie (Dixon), activist Duane (Duke), gay Lindy (Fargas), secretary Marsha (Mayron), and many others. Also on the crowded scene are a down-on-her luck hooker (Jones), a mad bomber (Corey), and best of all, "Daddy Rich" (Pryor), the founder and head of the Church of Divine Economic Spirituality. Plus nonstop rock music, for those who care.

## Car 54, Where Are You?

★ Orion, 1994, c, 89 min. Dir: Bill Fishman. SP: Erik Tarloff, Ebbe Roe Smith, Peter McCarthy, Peter Crabbe, b/o the television series created by Nat Hiken. Cast: David Johansen, John C. McGinley, Fran Drescher, Nipsey Russell, Rosie O'Donnell, Al Lewis, Daniel Baldwin, Jeremy Piven.

The unabashedly stupid television series, made into an unabashedly stupid movie, with some nineties vulgarity added for good measure. Here again are those irrepressible cops, the dim Gunther Toody (Johansen), crying "Ooh! Ooh!" but in a different context, and his prim partner Francis Muldoon (McGinley). There's a plot of sorts: something about a Godfather (Baldwin) who wants to kill the yuppie (Piven) whom the cops are assigned to protect. Fran Drescher (*The Nanny*) appears as a comic vamp named Velma Velour, and Rosie O'Donnell shows up as Toody's shrill wife.

## Clerks

★★★ Miramax, 1994, 89 min. Dir and SP: Kevin Smith. Cast: Brian O'Halloran, Jeff Anderson, Marilyn Ghigliotti, Lisa Spoonauer, Jason Mewes, Kevin Smith.

A cheaply made (about $27,000), foul-mouthed, outrageous, and yes, often funny little movie about a convenience store clerk (O'Halloran) in Asbury Park, New Jersey, and his grungy, antisocial friend (Anderson), who works in the video store next door. There's scarcely any plot—mostly about O'Halloran's relationship with girlfriends past and present—but there are some laughs with his bizarre customers and with Anderson's hostile attitude toward people and life. The idle chatter is best, especially the discussion of the finer points of *The Empire Strikes Back* and *Return of the Jedi*.

## Cool Runnings

★★★ Disney, 1993, c, 97 min. Dir: Jon Turteltaub. SP: Lynn Siefert, Tommy Swerdlow, Michael Goldberg. Cast: John Candy, Leon, Doug E. Doug, Rawle D. Lewis, Malik Yoba, Raymond J. Barry.

A bobsledding team from Jamaica? It sounds unlikely, yet there actually was such a team in the 1988 Winter Olympics in Calgary. But this movie turns the story into a familiar "underdog-achieves-victory" comedy. Still, it's entertaining as Jamaican Derice Bannock (Leon), disqualified from the track team because of a freak accident, organizes a bobsledding team. The recruits have their problems, and so does their reluctant coach, the once-honored, now-disgraced Irv Blitzer (Candy). Does the team triumph? Does Irv regain his self-esteem? Can you doubt it? The cast is willing, some scenes are quite funny, and you'll cheer on the team.

## Crazy People

★☆ Paramount, 1990, c, 90 min. Dir: Tony Bill. SP: Mitch Markowitz. Cast: Dudley Moore, Daryl Hannah, Paul Reiser, J. T. Walsh, Mercedes Ruehl, Bill Smitrovich, David Paymer, Alan North.

A perfect example of a Terrible Idea. Adman Dudley Moore cracks up under severe strain and opts for "truth" in advertising. (His ads are funny but wildly unlikely.) He is carted off to a mental hospital, where he meets the sort of "crazy people" Hollywood always finds lovable. It turns out that these benighted souls are born writers of advertising copy and under Moore's leadership, they thrive. That is, until the ad agency head and the hospital chief put their greedy heads together to control the operation. Hollywood has often advanced the notion that insane people are the world's true saints, and this movie is a wretched example.

## The Dream Team

★★☆ Universal, 1989, c, 113 min. Dir: Howard Zieff. SP: Jon Connolly, David Loucka. Cast: Michael Keaton, Christopher Lloyd, Peter Boyle, Stephen Furst, Dennis Boutsikaris, Lorraine Bracco, Milo O'Shea, James Remar.

In the movies, mental illness is usually treated as an explanation for aberrant or violent behavior *(Psycho)*, or as a source of wisdom in a crazy world *(King of Hearts)*. Here, the mentally ill are used for laughs, and therein lies the problem. Four hospitalized mental patients (Keaton, Lloyd, Boyle, and Furst) are separated from their doctor (Boutsikaris) on a trip to Manhattan. The doctor, it seems, is the target of two crooked cops because he has witnessed a murder. The patients harness their handicaps to rescue the doctor. Keaton leads the others as a man consumed with rage, and his pals also have serious hangups. (Boyle believes he is Jesus Christ.) The notion of mental illness as a source of hilarity seldom works in movies and *The Dream Team* is no exception.

## The End

★★ United Artists, 1978, c, 100 min. Dir: Melvin Frank. SP: Jerry Belson. Cast: Burt Reynolds, Joanne Woodward, Dom DeLuise, Sally Field, Pat O'Brien, Myrna Loy, Strother Martin, David Steinberg, Robby Benson, Norman Fell, Carl Reiner.

A jet-black comedy that's not half as funny as it thinks it is, *The End* stars Burt Reynolds as a real estate salesman who learns that he is dying of a toxic blood disease. After going to church (Robby Benson is the bewildered young priest) and telling his lawyer-friend (Steinberg), his ex-wife (Woodward), and his girlfriend (Field), he winds up in a mental hospital with paranoid-schizophrenic Dom DeLuise, whose idea of friendship is helping Reynolds kill himself. The Reynolds-DeLuise sequences take up a good part of the footage, and they draw scattered laughs. Carl Reiner is funny as a "death therapist." Veteran actors Pat O'Brien and Myrna Loy are saddled with the roles of Reynolds's dim parents.

## Fast Times at Ridgemont High

★★★ Universal, 1982, c, 92 min. Dir: Amy Heckerling. SP: Cameron Crowe, b/o his book. Cast: Sean Penn, Jennifer Jason Leigh, Judge Reinhold, Robert Romanus, Brian Baker, Phoebe Cates, Ray Walston, Scott Thomson, Vincent Schiavelli, Forest Whitaker.

Writer (later director) Cameron Crowe spent a year masquerading as a high school student and wrote a blunt, believable book on what he found. Adapted for the screen, *Fast Times at Ridgemont High* is a raucous, rowdy, and sometimes funny teenage comedy. Much of the action centers on the mall rather than the high school, where the students work and play, sometimes simultaneously, and where they try to sort out their disheveled lives. The cast of young actors is on the mark, but Sean Penn steals the movie as Jeff Spicoli, an off-the-wall surfer who has no use for authority and who moves to his very own peculiar drummer.

## A Fine Mess

★★ Columbia, 1986, c, 88 min. Dir and SP: Blake Edwards. Cast: Ted Danson, Howie Mandel, Richard Mulligan, Stuart Margolin, Maria Conchita Alonso, Jennifer Edwards, Paul Sorvino.

The phrase "a fine mess" is, of course, associated with comedians Stan Laurel and Oliver Hardy, and if this hectic farce was intended as some sort of homage, we can only say, courtesy of Donnie Brasco, "Forget about it." Smart-aleck Ted Danson and dim-bulb Howie Mandel tangle with two gangsters (Mulligan and Margolin), who pursue them through an endless series of chases, fights, pratfalls, and the like. The protracted climax is sheer bedlam and not funny. There is more style and perfect timing in any five minutes of a good Laurel and Hardy movie than in the entire hour and a half of *A Fine Mess*.

## A Fish Called Wanda

★★★ MGM, 1988, c, 108 min. Dir: Charles Crichton. SP: John Cleese, b/o story by John Cleese, Charles Crichton. Cast: Jamie Lee Curtis, John Cleese, Kevin Kline, Michael

Palin, Maria Aitken, Tom Georgeson, Patricia Hayes.

*A Fish Called Wanda* will never be accused of good taste—animal lovers and stutterers, among others, are sure to take offense—but you may be laughing too hard to care. A jewelry shop in London is robbed by a gang of thieves, including ringleader George (Georgeson), stammering Ken (Palin), sexy Wanda (Curtis), and Wanda's aggressively stupid lover Otto (Kline, in a hilarious, Oscar-winning performance). Before long, the thieves are turning on each other. Into the comic mix steps Archie Leach (Cleese), a very British barrister who becomes unwittingly involved with the thieves. (Incidentally, Archie Leach was Cary Grant's real name.) Some parts are forced, but there are funny lines and situations, and the movie was hugely popular.

## Flirting with Disaster

★★ Miramax, 1996, c, 92 min. Dir and SP: David O. Russell. Cast: Ben Stiller, Patricia Arquette, Tea Leoni, Mary Tyler Moore, George Segal, Alan Alda, Lily Tomlin, Richard Jenkins, Celia Weston, Josh Brolin.

Many reviewers were enthusiastic about this determinedly offbeat comedy, calling it sidesplitting and deliciously funny. You may agree, but then again you may not. Mel Coplin (Stiller), married to Nancy (Arquette) and a recent father, sets out to find his birth parents, joined by a sexy but bewildered adoption agency official named Tina (Leoni). One comic disaster after another follows, bringing him in contact with, among others, a middle-aged ex-hippie couple (Alda and Tomlin) and two government agents (Jenkins and Brolin) who are more than friends. Some unexpected touches win laughs, but most of the time the movie seems to believe that eccentric behavior by itself is hilarious. Mary Tyler Moore is woefully miscast as Mel's mother, and others barely skirt embarrassment.

## Gone Fishin'

★ Hollywood, 1998, c, 94 min. Dir: Christopher Cain. SP: Jill Mazursky, Jeffrey Adams. Cast: Joe Pesci, Danny

Glover, Rosanna Arquette, Lynn Whitfield, Nick Brimble, Carol Kane, Gary Grubbs, Edythe Davis.

Silly slapstick that might have served Abbott and Costello in days of yore, but now this kind of thing comes across as merely dumb. Joe Pesci and Danny Glover are lifelong friends who go on a yearly fishing trip that always ends in disaster. This time is no exception as they go off to the Everglades and trigger catastrophe wherever they go. Mostly they tangle with a murderous thief (Brimble) who has hidden a fortune in money and jewels stolen from his victims. Fires, explosions, near-misses, chases, and so on and so on. But no laughs.

## Good Burger

★★☆ Paramount, 1997, 94 min. Dir: Brian Robbins. SP: Dan Schneider, Kevin Kopelow, and Heath Seifert. Cast: Kenan Thompson, Kel Mitchell, Abe Vigoda, Carmen Electra, Dan Schneider, Jan Schwieterman, Shaquille O'Neal, Sinbad, Robert Wuhl.

Preteeners might find *Good Burger* a tasty meal; others will probably find it indigestible. Kel Mitchell and Kenan Thompson (reprising their roles as Ed and Dexter from the popular Nickelodeon show *All That*) are both workers at a woebegone burger joint called Good Burger: Ed is childlike, literal-minded, and totally weird, while Dexter is a schemer, always looking for the main chance. Good Burger becomes rivals with Mondo Burger, the flashy fast-food spot across the street, run by a scrawny neo-Nazi (Schwieterman). When Ed concocts a tasty sauce that threatens Mondo Burger's business, the plot (such as it is) thickens. Not much is funny for the adult trade (and one sequence in a mental institution is truly bizarre), but there are a few laughs along the way.

## Gross Anatomy

★★☆ Touchstone, 1989, c, 109 min. Dir: Thom Eberhardt. SP: Ron Nyswaner, Mark Spragg. Cast: Matthew Modine, Daphne Zuniga, Christine Lahti, Todd Field, John Scott Clough, Alice Carter, Zakes Mokae, Robert Desiderio.

Joe Slovak (Modine) is not your usual first-year

medical student. Pretending to be diffident, making outrageous jokes, cutting up everywhere (including the laboratory), Joe is the essence of cool. He is a challenge for tough teacher Dr. Woodruff (Lahti), a tribulation to the more serious students (Field, Clough), and a nuisance to the girl (Zuniga) he fancies. But is Joe really anxious and needy? Do you doubt it? *Gross Anatomy* becomes somewhat serious in the second half, but there are enough jokes about the travails of aspiring young doctors to keep the franchise.

## Happy Gilmore

★☆ Universal, 1996, c, 96 min. Dir: Dennis Dugan. SP: Tim Herlihy, Adam Sandler. Cast: Adam Sandler, Christopher McDonald, Julie Bowen, Carl Weathers, Frances Bay, Kevin Nealon, Ben Stiller (unbilled).

Yet another atrocious Adam Sandler comedy, this one concerning a sociopath named Happy Gilmore, who longs to be a professional hockey player but turns out to have a special gift for golf. To save his beloved grandmother's house, he enters professional tournaments, vying against a nasty top-rated golfer (McDonald) who detests him. Presumably, Happy's violent behavior is meant as a takeoff on clean-cut sportsmen, but he comes across as hopelessly obnoxious. (He also causes more than one death.) The extra half-star is awarded because at least Sandler doesn't sing.

## Heaven Help Us!

★★★ TriStar, 1985, c, 104 min. Dir: Michael Dinner. SP: Charles Purpura. Cast: Donald Sutherland, John Heard, Andrew McCarthy, Mary Stuart Masterson, Kevin Dillon, Jay Patterson, Malcolm Danare, Jennie Dundas, Kate Reid, Wallace Shawn, Philip Bosco, Christopher Durang.

The year: 1965. The place: St. Basil's parochial school for boys in Brooklyn. Here, teenage boys study under the super-strict rule of the Brothers, while enjoying a rowdy life away from the classroom. Young Michael Dunn (McCarthy) is the movie's center, trying to keep his small family intact while coping with the sadistic teacher, Brother Constance (Patterson). He also finds romance with Danni (Masterson), the tough but vulnerable girl who runs the local soda fountain. *Heaven Help Us!* is a surprisingly effective mixture of raffish comedy and poignant drama, with good detail of time and place. Funniest scene: Brother Abruzzi (Shawn) delivers a lecture on lust.

## Home Fries

★★☆ Warners, 1998, c, 93 min. Dir: Dean Parisot. SP: Vince Gilligan. Cast: Drew Barrymore, Luke Wilson, Catherine O'Hara, Jake Busey, Shelley Duvall, Kim Robillard, Daryl Mitchell.

A pitch-black comedy in a Texas setting, *Home Fries* strives to be off-the-wall but turns out to be mostly out of steam. It begins with a man literally scared to death, killed by his stepsons (Wilson and Busey) at the instigation of their mother (O'Hara). The victim, it seems, was a two-timing louse. The crime may have been overheard over the radio by workers at the Burger-Matic eatery, one of whom is the pregnant waitress (Barrymore) who turns out to be carrying the victim's child. From here on, viewers are on their own as the plot thickens. The movie strains to be both raucous and macabre, but it succeeds only intermittently.

## The Impostors

★★★ Fox Searchlight, 1998, c, 102 min. Dir and SP: Stanley Tucci. Cast: Stanley Tucci, Oliver Platt, Alfred Molina, Tony Shalhoub, Steve Buscemi, Allison Janney, Isabella Rossellini, Campbell Scott, Dana Ivey, Hope Davis, Billy Connolly, Teagle Wrougere.

How do you reconstruct a wild, knockabout slapstick farce of the thirties? Take one part Marx Brothers, add some Laurel and Hardy, and throw caution to the winds. The result: Stanley Tucci's occasionally hilarious comedy. Tucci and Oliver Platt play unemployed, Depression-era actors who accidentally get into a brawl with an egomaniacal star (Molina) and flee from his wrath aboard an ocean liner, where they pose as stewards. The trouble gets worse when Molina comes aboard as a passenger. On the boat are a group of zanies, most of whom are not what they seem to be. There are too many characters, and some of the jokes fall flat, but a number of the setups are funny. Favorite character: Steve Buscemi's seriously depressed band singer. Woody Allen turns up, unbilled.

# The Jerk

★★★ Universal, 1979, c, 94 min. Dir: Carl Reiner. SP: Steve Martin, Carl Gottlieb, Michael Elias, b/o story by Steve Martin, Carl Gottlieb. Cast: Steve Martin, Bernadette Peters, Catlin Adams, Mabel King, Richard Ward, Dick Anthony Williams, Bill Macy, Jackie Mason, Maurice Evans.

Steve Martin's first starring feature is a slapdash, monumentally silly—but sometimes outrageously funny—affair. He plays Navin Johnson, possibly the world's most stupid individual. (He begins by telling us, "I was born a poor black child.") The movie traces his idyllic life with his black adopted family, his various jobs with a carnival, his sudden rise to fame and fortune when he invents the "Opti-Grab" handle for eye glasses, and his descent back into poverty. Gags about Navin's dumbness are fired off regularly and some of them hit the mark. Favorites: Navin discovers his "special purpose." Navin's "sophisticated" mansion. And the horrors of cat juggling.

# Kingpin

★★ MGM, 1996, c, 113 min. Dirs: Peter and Bobby Farrelly. SP: Barry Fanaro, Mort Nathan. Cast: Woody Harrelson, Randy Quaid, Vanessa Angel, Bill Murray, Chris Elliott, Richard Tyson, Rob Moran.

Made after *Dumb and Dumber* but before *There's Something About Mary, Kingpin* is another comedy from the brothers Farrelly, but one with an added dose of indigestible sentiment. Woody Harrelson plays a once-legendary champion bowler who is destroyed by a treacherous rival (Murray). Years later, he finds a prospective new champion in a sweet-natured, naïve Amish man (Quaid), whom he exploits and corrupts thoughtlessly. The climax is a major bowling tournament at which Murray, Harrelson's old nemesis, reappears. Of course, Harrelson's benign feelings for Quaid finally surface in time for the ending.

# King Ralph

★★☆ Universal, 1991, c, 97 min. Dir and SP: David S. Ward, b/o novel by Emlyn Williams. Cast: John Goodman, Peter O'Toole, Camille Coduri, Julian Glover, Richard Griffiths, Joely Richardson, Leslie Phillips, James Villiers, Niall O'Brien.

Virtually every joke is telegraphed from miles away, but if you can go along with the absurd premise, this comedy may offer passable diversion. John Goodman plays beefy, vulgar lounge singer–pianist Ralph Jones who suddenly finds himself heir to the throne of England. Of course he bungles the position at first, causing dismay and embarrassment with his crass behavior—he even falls for a commoner (Coduri)—but eventually his decent character shows through. Goodman is likable as King Ralph but Peter O'Toole steals the movie as the king's aide and tutor, bringing a crisp delivery to his every line.

# License to Drive

★★☆ Fox, 1988, c, 88 min. Dir: Greg Beeman. SP: Neil Tolkin. Cast: Corey Haim, Corey Feldman, Richard Masur, Carol Kane, Heather Graham, Michael Manasseri, Harvey Miller, Nina Siemaszko, Grant Goodeve, Parley Baer.

The teenage audience at which this movie is squarely aimed should probably enjoy its rowdy humor. When sixteen-year-old Les (Haim) fails his driving test and gets a date with a beautiful girl, does he sit and sulk? No, he steals his grandfather's 1972 Cadillac and begins a comically catastrophic nighttime adventure. Goaded on by his best friend, Dean (Feldman), Les gets into trouble, but it's never very serious—this is one teenage movie where nobody gets drunk or uses drugs. In the morning, Les even drives his pregnant mother (Kane) to the hospital. (He drives backward, since the car will only go in reverse.)

# The Mighty Ducks

★★☆ Touchstone, 1992, c, 100 min. Dir: Stephen Herek. SP: Steven Brill and Brian Hohlfield. Cast: Emilio Estevez, Joss Ackland, Lane Smith, Heidi Kling, Josef Sommer, Joshua Jackson, Elden Ratliff, Shaun Weiss.

Yuppie lawyer Gordon Bombay (Estevez) is arrested for drunk driving, and as part of his community service sentence, he is assigned to coach an inner-city hockey team made up of tough-talking misfits and underachievers. This being a Disney film, can you doubt that Gordon will eventually bond with these kids and lead them to victory? As with *The Bad News Bears* and other movies *(Wildcats, Ladybugs, Sunset Park)*, the idea of an unlikely coach saddled with a ragtag sports team is apparently irresistible to filmmakers, and sometimes they are right. The success of this movie prompted two sequels, an animated series, and a television movie based on that series, as well as an actual Disney-owned hockey franchise.

# Mixed Nuts

★ TriStar, 1994, c, 97 min. Dir: Nora Ephron. SP: Nora Ephron, Delia Ephron. Cast: Steve Martin, Madeline Kahn, Anthony LaPaglia, Juliette Lewis, Rita Wilson, Rob Reiner, Adam Sandler, Robert Klein, Liev Schreiber, Parker Posey.

Probably this is the only movie you will ever see in which an unbilled—and dead—Garry Shandling is disguised as a Christmas tree. An excruciating black comedy, *Mixed Nuts* centers on the people who run Lifesavers, a suicide prevention center, and who are as desperately in need of help as the people who call them. Heading up this wretched group are Steve Martin, who knows they will soon be evicted; a prissy and humorless Madeline Kahn; and Rita Wilson, an empathetic girl who secretly loves Martin. Other characters who are supposed to be cheerfully ditsy are merely depressing. Worst offender: Adam Sandler and his ghastly "songs."

# Mouse Hunt

★★★ Dreamworks SKG, 1997, c, 97 min. Dir: Gore Verbinski. SP: Adam Rifkin. Cast: Nathan Lane, Lee Evans, Vicki Lewis, Maury Chaykin, Michael Jeter, Ernie Sabella, Christopher Walken.

*Home Alone* meets Laurel and Hardy, but this time the defender of the home is a cute, eminently resourceful little mouse. Nathan Lane and Lee Evans play the none-too-smart Smuntz brothers, who inherit a decrepit old mansion after the death of their eccentric father (Hickey, in his last role). They learn that the house is an architectural masterwork, and decide to auction it off for a fortune. First, however, they have to deal with the current tenant, that clever mouse. Mousetraps, a killer cat, and an exterminator (Walken) all fail to destroy the little critter who, like *Home Alone*'s Kevin, knows all the tricks. Children and even some adults might enjoy the nonstop slapstick, and Lane and Evans are funny performers.

# Naked Gun 2¹/₂: The Smell of Fear

★★☆ Paramount, 1991, c, 85 min. Dir: David Zucker. SP: Jim Abrahams, Pat Proft. Cast: Leslie Nielsen, Priscilla Presley, George Kennedy, O. J. Simpson, Robert Goulet, Jacqueline Brookes, Richard Griffiths, Lloyd Bochner.

If the first *Naked Gun* didn't satisfy your burning need for sight gags, double-entendres, pratfalls, and throwaway lines, here's another stiff dose. Idiot cop Lt. Frank Dreben (Nielsen) is back in this second entry, trying to thwart the sinister power brokers who are bent on destroying America's energy policy. Headed by Robert Goulet, they have kidnapped a major energy expert (Griffiths) and substituted a lookalike. Forget the plot and concentrate on Dreben's hideous and sometimes hilarious faux pas and destructive impulses. If you care, there's more of the same in *Naked Gun 33¹/₃: The Final Insult* (1994).

# Naked Gun 33¹/₃: The Final Insult

★★☆ Paramount, 1994, c, 88 min. Dir: Peter Segal. SP: Pat Proft, David Zucker, Robert LoCash. Cast: Leslie Nielsen, Priscilla Presley, George Kennedy, O. J. Simpson, Fred Ward, Kathleen Freeman, Anna Nicole Smith.

As usual, no gag is too outrageous or too silly for

this third and presumably last in the "Police Squad" series. This time brain-dead Lt. Frank Dreben (Nielsen) comes out of retirement to help stop terrorist Rocco Dillon (Ward) from detonating a bomb. Once again, Frank triggers disaster wherever he goes—he virtually demolishes a maximum security prison in one of the funnier sequences. (Prisoners at a riot: "What are we?" One querulous reply: "Homo sapiens?") The climax comes at the Academy Awards ceremony, with Frank saving the day despite himself. Some good jokes here (a musical about Mother Teresa and a movie called *Geriatric Park*).

## National Lampoon's Animal House

★★★ Universal, 1978, c, 109 min. Dir: John Landis. SP: Harold Ramis, Douglas Kenney, Chris Miller. Cast: Tim Matheson, John Belushi, Thomas Hulce, John Vernon, Verna Bloom, Peter Riegert, Karen Allen, Stephen Furst, Cesare Danova, Donald Sutherland.

Noisy, frenetic, and unsubtle, but you will probably find yourself laughing helplessly at the antics in this movie. The year is 1962, and at Faber College, the fraternity members of Delta House are despised by the nasty Dean (Vernon), who wants to expel them, and by snobbish Omega House, which would like to destroy them. At the forefront of Delta's parties, stunts, and practical jokes are lunatic slob Bluto (Belushi in his signature movie role) and makeout artist Otter (Matheson). The gags come thick and fast, and some of them actually hit their target. In the final sequence, the Delta men demolish the school's big homecoming parade, and there are laughs that rise above the din of crashing floats and shrieking bystanders. A television spinoff from the movie had a brief run in 1979.

## National Lampoon's Vacation

★★★ Warners, 1983, c, 98 min. Dir: Harold Ramis. SP: John Hughes. Cast: Chevy Chase, Beverly D'Angelo, Anthony Michael Hall, Imogene Coca, Randy Quaid, Dana Barron, Christie Brinkley, John Candy, Eddie Bracken.

The first in the series of "Vacation" farces and probably the best. Clark Griswold (Chase), terminally clumsy and virtually brain-dead, sets off with his family on a cross-country tour heading for California's amusement park, Wally World. Along the way, they have numerous misadventures, most of them precipitated by Clark's unwavering stupidity. Some of the gags are funny, and there's the welcome presence of the inimitable Imogene Coca as Aunt Edna, at least until she suffers a peculiar fate. Followed by *National Lampoon's European Vacation* (1985), *National Lampoon's Christmas Vacation* (1989), and *Vegas Vacation* (1997).

## Night Shift

★★★ Warners/The Ladd Company, 1982, c, 105 min. Dir: Ron Howard. SP: Lowell Ganz, Babaloo Mandel. Cast: Henry Winkler, Michael Keaton, Shelley Long, Gina Hecht, Pat Corley, Bobby DiCicco, Nita Talbot, Charles Fleischer, Richard Belzer.

"Is this a great country or what?" shouts Bill Blazejowski (Keaton) after he and cohort Chuck Lumley (Winkler) have successfully launched a prostitution ring out of a morgue. (No, this is not a misprint.) Bill is the irrepressible, cheerfully amoral idea man. *Night Shift* is all about what happens when Bill's nerdlike coworker Chuck goes along with his business idea, and eventually, of course, all hell breaks loose. Shelley Long is the improbably clean-cut prostitute with whom Chuck falls in love. The first part of the movie has some genuine laughs despite the dubious premise, and mostly because of Keaton's star-making performance. The rest is just okay. Look quickly for Kevin Costner in a bit role.

## 1941

★★☆ Warners, 1979, c, 118 min. Dir: Steven Spielberg. SP: Robert Zemeckis, Bob Gale. Cast: Dan Aykroyd, John Belushi, Ned Beatty, Robert Stack, Treat Williams, Nancy Allen, Tim Matheson, Toshiro Mifune, Christopher Lee, Warren Oates, Lorraine Gary, Murray Hamilton, Slim Pickens, John Candy.

There are a few scenes of well-wrought slapstick but not much else in this elaborate, noisy, and exhausting movie from Steven Spielberg. Following the attack on Pearl Harbor in December 1941, war panic breaks out in Los Angeles a few days later when a Japanese submarine surfaces out of nowhere. Among the many lunatics causing pandemonium are John Belushi as an out-of-control fighter pilot in pursuit of what he believes to be a Japanese Zero, Ned Beatty as a super-patriot in love with guns, Robert Stack as a dim general who sobs at a showing of *Dumbo*, and Slim Pickens as a Christmas tree vendor who is captured by the Japanese crew. Coauthor Zemeckis later turned to directing.

## Out to Sea

★★☆ Columbia, 1997, c, 106 min. Dir: Martha Coolidge. SP: Robert Nelson Jacobs. Cast: Jack Lemmon, Walter Matthau, Dyan Cannon, Gloria DeHaven, Brent Spiner, Elaine Stritch, Donald O'Connor, Hal Linden, Rue McClanahan, Edward Mulhare, Estelle Harris.

The Jack Lemmon-Walter Matthau routine may be frayed around the edges by this time, but *Out to Sea* gives it another spin, with mildly amusing results. Here they play brothers-in-law—Lemmon is a still-grieving widower, and Matthau is the ever-disreputable bachelor—who sign onto a cruise as dance hosts in lieu of paying the fare. Predictably, they get into all sorts of trouble with cruise director Brent Spiner (the movie's funniest character). Matthau catches the eye of Texas divorcée Dyan Cannon, while Lemmon finds romance with widow Gloria DeHaven. Most scenes are telegraphed well in advance, but there are some funny moments. The best feature is the welcome presence of such veteran performers as Gloria DeHaven and Donald O'Connor.

## Planes, Trains, and Automobiles

★★★ Paramount, 1987, c, 93 min. Dir and SP: John Hughes. Cast: Steve Martin, John Candy, Laila Robins, Michael McKean, Kevin Bacon, Dylan Baker, William Windom.

Steve Martin is an uptight, fastidious business executive. John Candy is a big, boorish shower-ring salesman. Both have one overriding goal: to get from New York's LaGuardia Airport to Chicago's O'Hare Airport. The two men meet when Candy usurps Martin's cab, and from then on they are tossed together in two days of comic misadventures in which trains, buses, trucks, and automobiles somehow play a role. Martin and Candy are funny in their contrasting styles, and they also manage to give their characters an unexpected measure of sweetness and decency. *Planes, Trains, and Automobiles* may not be world-class comedy, but it's fun.

## Police Academy

★★☆ Ladd, 1984, c, 95 min. Dir: Hugh Wilson. SP: Neal Israel, Pat Proft, Hugh Wilson, b/o story by Neal Israel, Pat Proft. Cast: Steve Guttenberg, George Gaynes, G. W. Bailey, Bubba Smith, Michael Winslow, David Graf, Andrew Rubin, Bruce Mahler.

The movie that started it all, precipitating no less than seven awful sequels. This first *Police Academy* is a raucous farce in which all sorts of weird and hapless candidates show up for training in the academy once all restrictions are lifted. Leading troublemaker is Mahoney (Guttenberg), who is reluctant to go through the training and is the bane of existence for nasty but stupid Lt. Harris (Bailey). Among the more noticeable candidates are Jones (Winslow), master of sound imitations, and Tackleberry (Graf), who will shoot at anything that moves. Funniest character: Commandant Lassard (Gaynes), the academy's dull-witted, totally clueless head.

## Private Parts

★★☆ Paramount, 1997, c, 108 min. Dir: Betty Thomas. SP: Len Blum, Michael Kalesniko, b/o book by Howard Stern. Cast: Howard Stern, Robin Quivers, Mary McCormack, Fred Norris, Jackie Martling.

Don't expect to find "shock jock" Howard Stern—the man who casts aspersions on

A tense moment for those daffy police recruits and their chief in their first caper, *Police Academy* (1984). Left to right: Steve Guttenberg, George Gaynes, Andrew Rubin, and Michael Winslow.

blacks, gays, lesbians, Asians, the disabled, and many others on his popular radio program—turning up very often in this movie. Instead you get a kinder, gentler Stern, a devoted family man who is greatly misunderstood. In broad, cartoonlike style, the movie takes the viewer through Stern's childhood, his courtship and marriage to his wife Alison (McCormack), and his rise from a disc jockey in Connecticut to his current status as the self-proclaimed "King of All Media." There is still enough of his raunchy, outrageous humor to please his fans, but for many others a little Stern is already too much.

## Revenge of the Nerds

★★☆ Fox, 1984, c, 90 min. Dir: Jeff Kanew. SP: Steve Zacharias, Jeff Buhai, b/o story by Tim Metcalfe, Miguel Tejada-Flores, Steve Zacharias, Jeff Buhai. Cast: Robert Carradine, Anthony Edwards, Timothy Busfield, Bernie Casey, Ted McGinley, Curtis Armstrong, Julie Montgomery, John Goodman, Jamie (James) Cromwell.

*Revenge of the Nerds* offers a wildly fanciful, low-comedy view of college life in which everything is controlled by odious jocks. Evidently nobody seemed to mind or care, since the movie was so popular that it inspired three sequels, including one for TV. Lewis (Carradine) and Gilbert (Edwards) are computer nerds who come to Adams College, where they and the other nerds are humiliated at every turn by the brain-dead jocks and their all-blonde girlfriends. They exact some revenge and finally get the chance to triumph at the annual homecoming carnival. However, there's more trouble until everyone on campus allies with the nerds. Some raucous amusement.

## Romy and Michele's High School Reunion

★★★ Touchstone, 1997, c, 91 min. Dir: David Mirkin. SP: Robin Schiff, b/o her play. Cast: Lisa Kudrow, Mira Sorvino, Alan Cumming, Julia Campbell, Janeane Garofalo, Mia Cottet, Kristin Bauer.

Longtime friends and world-class airheads Romy (Sorvino) and Michele (Kudrow) decide to attend their ten-year high school reunion in Tucson. Their class always perceived them as tasteless, overdressed losers and "weirdos," and so they decide to pose as successful Los Angeles businesswomen. At first the reunion seems like a triumph for the girls, until it turns out be their fantasy. In reality, they are mocked and humiliated at every turn, until they decide to relax and just enjoy themselves. In the end, of course, they triumph after all. Lightweight but surprisingly enjoyable, with some genuinely funny moments.

## Sister Act

★★★ Touchstone, 1992, c, 100 min. Dir: Emile Ardolino. SP: Joseph Howard. Cast: Whoopi Goldberg, Maggie Smith, Harvey Keitel, Kathy Najimy, Wendy Makkena, Mary Wickes, Bill Nunn, Robert Miranda, Joseph Maher.

*Sister Act* is something of a mess—much of it is contrived and the second half is incoherent. But this popular comedy has Whoopi Goldberg pretending to be a nun, and she's funny and engaging. She plays an improbable lounge singer named Delores who witnesses a murder committed by her gangster boyfriend (Keitel). The police arrange for her to be hidden in a convent, of all places, where she is introduced as Sister Mary Clarence. Hostile at first, she

warms to the nuns and teaches them to form a show-stopping choir. Then the gangster plot takes over and the movie collapses. Still, there's Whoopi and wonderful Mary Wickes as a tart-tongued nun. A sequel, *Sister Act 2: Back in the Habit,* was released in 1993.

## Slap Shot

★★★ Universal, 1977, c, 122 min. Dir: George Roy Hill. SP: Nancy Dowd. Cast: Paul Newman, Michael Ontkean, Lindsay Crouse, Jennifer Warren, Melinda Dillon, Strother Martin, Jerry Houser, Yvon Barrette, Steve Carlson, Swoosie Kurtz, Kathryn Walker.

*Slapshot,* George Roy Hill's rowdy movie about hockey, probably has more profanity per minute than any film in recent memory, but it's also great fun and a pungent commentary on the sorry aspects of professional American sports. Paul Newman gives a fine, measured performance as Reggie Dunlop, the aging coach of Charleston's professional hockey team. Although the team plays clean and only talks dirty, Reggie learns that the only way to rise to the top is to play a dirty, violent game accompanied by a lot of publicity hoopla. His Charleston Chiefs make it to the big time. Characters include Michael Ontkean as a rare good guy, a Princeton graduate turned pro, and Jennifer Warren as Reggie's estranged wife.

## Sour Grapes

★ Castle Rock, 1998, c, 92 min. Dir and SP: Larry David. Cast: Steven Weber, Craig Bierko, Matt Keeslar, Karen Sillas, Viola Harris, Robyn Peterman, Orlando Jones, Jennifer Leigh Warren.

It's inconceivable that Larry David, the co-creator of the long-running *Seinfeld* television series, could have written and directed a comedy as abysmal as *Sour Grapes.* A black comedy without a single redeeming feature, it revolves about two cousins, one (Weber) a heart surgeon, the other (Bierko) a designer of sportswear. When Bierko wins an Atlantic City jackpot using two of Weber's quarters, the consequences spin off in all directions, eventually

# FUNNY LADIES

Recent years have brought a number of talented actresses to the attention of moviegoers, not necessarily in leading roles but in roles that show their special talent for comedy. Here are only a few.

## Julie Kavner

Julie Kavner made her mark playing Rhoda Morgenstern's lovable, plain-speaking younger sister in the television series *Rhoda* (1974–78). She brightened many a *Tracey Ullman Show* as a variety of supporting characters and is also instantly recognizable as the voice of Marge Simpson on *The Simpsons*. Many of her movies have been with Woody Allen—she was featured prominently in *Hannah and Her Sisters* (1986) as Allen's assistant; in *Radio Days* (1987) as a Brooklyn mother in the 1940s; in *Alice* (1990) as a decorator; and other of his films. Look for Kavner performances, real and often touching, in *Awakenings* (1990), *I'll Do Anything* (1994), and, in her one starring role to date, as stand-up comedian Dottie Ingels in *This Is My Life* (1992).

## Joan Cusack

Joan Cusack won a well-deserved Supporting Actress nomination for her performance as Emily Montgomery, the bewildered bride-to-be, in the popular *In and Out* (1997). She made an impression as manic TV assistant Blair Litton in *Broadcast News* (1987) and also appeared notably in *Working Girl* (1988), *My Blue Heaven* (1990), *Toys* (1992), *Nine Months* (1995), and *Grosse Point Blank* (1997), with her brother John. The actress often projects an appealing, offbeat quality that makes her stand out in many scenes.

## Janeane Garofalo

Janeane Garofalo already has a legion of fans, and with very good reason. Her portraits of usually funny, blunt-speaking, yet intensely likable women have made viewers sit up and take notice. Starting as a stand-up comedian, she moved into television, playing a continuing role on the superb *Larry Sanders Show* and appearing as a regular performer on *The*

---

involving Bierko's overbearing mother (Harris), a television comic (Keeslar) who loses both testicles in a botched operation, and other crudely drawn characters. The dialogue is witless, the acting is inept (Bierko is a special offender), and the situations are stupid beyond belief. One star is too generous for this fiasco.

## Spies Like Us

★★ Warners, 1985, c, 109 min. Dir: John Landis. SP: Dan Aykroyd, Lowell Ganz, Babaloo Mandell, b/o story by Dan Aykroyd, Dave Thomas. Cast: Chevy Chase, Dan Aykroyd, Donna Dixon, Steve Forrest, Bruce Davison, William Prince, Bernie Casey, Tom Hatten, Frank Oz.

A poor-man's version of a Crosby-Hope "Road" movie (Hope even makes a guest appearance), *Spies Like Us* has a few laughs at the beginning, but quickly becomes just plain dull. Chase and Aykroyd, in their first starring vehicle, play low-level government desk jockeys in Washington who are used as disposable decoys in an elaborate spy operation. The operation involves one

*Ben Stiller Show* on Comedy Central. After her film debut in *Reality Bites* (1994), Garofalo attracted attention as the date from hell in *Bye Bye Love* (1995), as an acerbic Los Angeles talk-show host in *The Truth About Cats and Dogs* (1996), and as a brutally frank, terminally depressed attendee at *Romy and Michele's High School Reunion* (1997). She starred in *The Matchmaker* (1997) and had roles in *Clay Pigeons* (1998) and *Permanent Midnight* (1998). She is funny without being winsome or self-consciously "cute," and that's refreshing.

## Bonnie Hunt

Bonnie Hunt offers a delightful mixture of wit, irony, and wryness in her best roles. In the first few years of her film career, she played conventional roles in *Rain Man* (1988), the two *Beethoven* movies (1992 and 1993), and *Dave* (1993). Then her talent shone through in a large supporting role in the wispy romantic comedy *Only You* (1994)—as Kate, Marisa Tomei's sister-in-law and best friend, the actress used her sardonic way with a line to deflate the hurt and the anger she felt at her husband's cheating. She was also good as Renee Zellweger's sensible, cautionary sister in *Jerry Maguire* (1996). Other movies in which she appeared include *Jumanji* (1995), *Now and Then* (1995), and *Kissing a Fool* (1998), Her television program, *The Bonnie Hunt Show*, had a run of one season in 1997.

## Lisa Kudrow

Starting in 1994, Lisa Kudrow made her mark in television playing the adorably dim Phoebe in the television series *Friends*. In films she attracted attention briefly as Albert Brooks's vacuous date in *Mother* (1996), then costarred with Mira Sorvino as air-headed Michele in *Romy and Michele's High School Reunion* (1997). However, it was as Lucia in *The Opposite of Sex* (1998) that the actress won admiring notices that made her a contender for stardom. Playing a spinsterish schoolteacher whose acerbic manner concealed a lonely, romantic-minded woman jealous of other people's happiness, she evoked both laughter and compassion. She also played Billy Crystal's bride-to-be in *Analyze This* (1999).

of those ever-popular mad military schemes that gets out of hand and threatens the end of civilization. Can you guess who sets things right? One gimmick: minor roles are played by some well-known directors, including Costa-Gavras, Martin Brest, and Terry Gilliam.

## To Wong Foo, Thanks for Everything, Julie Newmar

★★ Universal, 1995, c, 108 min. Dir: Beeban Kidron. SP: Douglas Carter Beane. Cast: Patrick Swayze, Wesley Snipes, John Leguizamo, Stockard Channing, Arliss Howard, Chris Penn, Melinda Dillon, Blythe Danner, RuPaul, Quentin Crisp, Julie Newmar.

The first sight of three notably heterosexual actors as drag queens—Patrick Swayze as Vida Boheme, Wesley Snipes as Noxeema Jackson, John Leguizamo as Chi Chi Rodriguez—is startling and funny. Then the movie goes rapidly downhill. The three set off on a cross-country trip to Hollywood to participate in the national

Drag Queen of the Year pageant. Along the way their car breaks down in a midwestern town called Snydersville, and predictability sets in. The drag queens teach the townspeople to bring a little style and gumption into their lives and the townspeople learn something about tolerance. Inevitably, too, there's a gay-baiting policeman (Penn) for the trio to show up. Once a movie like this might have seemed "daring," but no more.

## Tommy Boy

★★ Paramount, 1995, c, 96 min. Dir: Peter Segal. SP: Bonnie Turner, Terry Turner. Cast: Chris Farley, David Spade, Bo Derek, Rob Lowe, Dan Aykroyd, Brian Dennehy. Julie Warner, Sean McCann, Zack Grenier.

When the father (Dennehy) of Tommy Callahan (Farley) dies suddenly, Tommy must take over his auto parts factory. Tommy, a recent college graduate who is overweight, overzealous, childlike, and monumentally clumsy, hasn't the vaguest notion of how to run a business. In addition, his father's brand-new wife (Derek) and her "son" (Lowe), are scheming to take over the business for rival Aykroyd. To save the factory, Tommy and caustic coworker Richard (Spade) take off on a cross-country tour to sell brake pads. *Tommy Boy* is not as bad as the follow-up Farley-Spade comedy, *Black Sheep* (see page 254), but neither is it any more than passable for undiscriminating viewers. Farley works hard to win laughs but after a while he is more exhausting than funny.

## Trading Places

★★☆ Paramount, 1983, c, 116 min. Dir: John Landis. SP: Timothy Harris, Herschel Weingrod. Cast: Dan Aykroyd, Eddie Murphy, Jamie Lee Curtis, Ralph Bellamy, Don Ameche, Denholm Elliott, Jim Belushi, Alfred Drake.

Eddie Murphy is virtually the only reason to see this contrived comedy. He plays Billy Ray Valentine, a street-wise hustler who finds himself part of a wager between the wealthy Duke brothers (Bellamy and Ameche). To resolve the

question about heredity and environment, the brothers manipulate stuffy financial wizard Louis Winthrope III (Aykroyd) into changing places with Billy Ray. Soon Louis has lost his job, his house, and his fiancée, while Billy Ray is enjoying life as a rich, successful businessman. When the two realize that they are merely ploys in a nasty scheme, they exact their own brand of revenge. The execution of this rather worn idea is heavy-handed, but Murphy moves it along, even when the comedy turns merely dumb, as in the climax on a train.

## Trapped in Paradise

★ Fox, 1994, c, 112 min. Dir and SP: George Gallo. Cast: Nicolas Cage, Jon Lovitz, Dana Carvey, John Ashton, Madchen Amick, Donald Moffat, Florence Stanley, Richard Jenkins, Angela Paton.

A brain-dead comedy with mostly brain-dead characters. Two larcenous brothers (Lovitz and Carvey) persuade a reluctant third (Cage) to travel to Paradise, Pennsylvania, where a bank is just waiting to be robbed. They rob the bank, but have great trouble making their getaway, mostly because the townspeople are so extremely naïve and just plain nice—that is, nice to the point of idiocy. There is hardly a believable moment in the whole witless enterprise, and no cast member is seen to advantage. Dana Carvey is especially irritating as the dumbest of the brothers.

## Trial and Error

★★★ New Line, 1997, c, 98 min. Dir: Jonathan Lynn. SP: Sara Bernstein, Gregory Bernstein, b/o story by Sara Bernstein, Gregory Bernstein, Cliff Gardner. Cast: Michael Richards, Jeff Daniels, Charlize Theron, Alexander Wentworth, Jessica Steen, Austin Pendleton, Rip Torn, Dale Dye.

The talent for knockabout physical humor that Michael Richards displayed on *Seinfeld* gets a new workout here in this amiable and occasionally very funny comedy. Richards is an almost unemployable actor (his audition for a mobster's role is hilarious) who finds himself impersonating a lawyer when his true-lawyer friend (Daniels) is incapacitated after a rowdy bachelor party. Richards's attempts to be lawyerly end in comic embarrassment or disaster when he defends an old con man (Torn) who sells pennies as copper engravings of Lincoln. In one brief scene, Dale Dye wins laughs as an expert witness who explains why Twinkies resemble cocaine. Lynn directed *My Cousin Vinny,* which also involved an imposter lawyer. Light and breezy fun.

## Twins

★★☆ Paramount, 1988, c, 112 min. Dir: Ivan Reitman. SP: William Davies, William Osborne, Timothy Harris, Herschel Weingrod. Cast: Arnold Schwarzenegger, Danny DeVito, Kelly Preston, Chloe Webb, Bonnie Bartlett, Hugh O'Brian, Nehemiah Persoff, Maury Chaikin.

As the result of a bizarre genetic experiment, Julius and Vincent Benedict (Schwarzenegger and DeVito) are the world's most unlikely twins. Julius is a gentle, innocent giant with a brilliant mind, and Vincent is a short, disreputable con artist. Their troubles begin when they finally meet. Julius's search for his mother leads them to odd places and people, while Vincent's involvement with a cache of stolen money and some murderous thieves puts their lives in danger. The plot takes some unlikely twists and turns, but *Twins* has its amusing moments, mostly created by the glaring differences in appearance and temperament between the two men.

## Uptown Saturday Night

★★☆ First Artists, 1974, c, 104 min. Dir: Sidney Poitier. SP: Richard Wesley. Cast: Sidney Poitier, Bill Cosby, Harry Belafonte, Richard Pryor, Flip Wilson, Calvin Lockhart, Rosalind Cash, Roscoe Lee Browne, Paula Kelly.

This raucous farce stars Sidney Poitier and Bill Cosby as friends who set out to recover a winning lottery ticket stolen from them during the pair's one visit to a fancy after-hours black club. Poitier's a factory worker and Cosby is a taxi driver, and they are both clueless innocents in

trouble as they encounter—among others—a powerful gang boss (Belafonte), a seedy, treacherous private detective (Pryor), a phony politician (Browne), and a rousing reverend (Wilson), whose oration is a highlight of the movie. Two more Poitier-Cosby teamings: *Let's Do It Again* (1975) and *A Piece of the Action* (1977), both also directed by Poitier.

## Used Cars

★★★ Universal, 1980, c, 111 min. Dir: Robert Zemeckis. SP: Robert Zemeckis, Bob Gale. Cast: Kurt Russell, Jack Warden, Gerrit Graham, Deborah Harmon, Frank McRae, Joseph P. Flaherty, David L. Lander, Michael McKean.

Imagine a wild climax involving 250 used cars, and you have some idea of the knockabout humor in this silly but often hilarious farce. It seems that twin brothers Luke and Roy Fuchs (Warden) are forever fighting each other over their facing used car lots. When nice Luke dies of a heart attack induced by his nasty brother Roy, his star salesman Rudy (Russell) takes over to wreak his revenge on Roy. Rudy is proudly crooked, and his wild schemes make up much of the movie's far-out comedy. No subtlety here, but raucous laughter induced by brain-dead car buyers, unscrupulous salesmen, and the like. And then there's that 250-car climax. . . .

## Vegas Vacation

★★ Warners, 1997, c, 95 min. Dir: Stephen Kessler. SP: Elisa Bell. Cast: Chevy Chase, Beverly D'Angelo, Randy Quaid, Ethan Embry, Marisol Nichols, Wayne Newton, Wallace Shawn, Sid Caesar, Christie Brinkley.

Hopefully, the last of the idiotic Griswold family shenanigans. This time, the Griswolds—brain-dead dad Clark (Chase), wife Ellen (D'Angelo), and their teenage kids (Embry and Nichols)—head for Las Vegas, where everything goes predictably haywire. Clark loses a fortune; Ellen is romanced by a self-parodying Wayne Newton; son Rusty is mistaken for a high roller; daughter Audrey gets to mix with the showgirls. The only laughs come from Quaid, repeating as Clark's cheerfully obnoxious cousin. The climax, with a chastened Clark rounding up his family, is especially stupid. Good-bye, Griswolds?

## Volunteers

★★ TriStar, 1985, c, 106 min. Dir: Nicholas Meyer. SP: Ken Levine, David Isaacs, b/o story by Keith Critchlow. Cast: Tom Hanks, John Candy, Rita Wilson, Tim Thomerson, Gedde Watanabe, George Plimpton.

It's 1962, and Lawrence Bourne III (Hanks) is a wealthy, irresponsible playboy who suddenly finds himself joining the Peace Corps to escape his heavy gambling debts. He lands in Thailand, where his principal cohorts are pretty Beth Wexler (Wilson) and the irrepressible "Tom Tuttle from Tacoma" (Candy). Their goal is to build a bridge with the natives but soon they are dangerously involved with a powerful war lord, Communist soldiers, and a treacherous CIA man (Thomerson). Hanks and Candy are always fun to watch, even this early in their careers, but the screenplay is low on laughter. Hanks and Wilson are paired romantically, and they later married in real life.

## The Waterboy

★★ Touchstone, 1998, c, 86 min. Dir: Frank Coraci. SP: Tim Herlihy, Adam Sandler. Cast: Adam Sandler, Kathy Bates, Henry Winkler, Fairuza Balk, Jerry Reed.

Adam Sandler fans may enjoy this extremely popular comedy; others beware. This time he plays Bobby Boucher, a thirty-one-year-old man who joins the Louisiana Mud Dogs, a losing football team, as waterboy. If you are surprised by a climax in which Bobby, angry at slights to his mother or his water supply, comes off the bench and leads the team to victory, you have never been to the movies. Kathy Bates wins a few laughs as his possessive mother who serves Bobby a snake roast in their bayou cabin. With his grating voice and moronic manner, Sandler is a taste that many moviegoers seem to have acquired. The question is, why?

## Wayne's World

★★ Paramount, 1992, 95 min. Dir: Penelope Spheeris. SP: Mike Myers, Bonnie Turner, Terry Turner, b/o characters created by Mike Myers. Cast: Mike Myers, Dana Carvey, Rob Lowe, Tia Carrere, Brian Doyle-Murray, Lara Flynn Boyle, Alice Cooper, Colleen Camp.

A feature-length extension of the popular "Wayne's World" skits on *Saturday Night Live*, this knockabout comedy can be recommended only to those who found the original amusing. Wayne (Myers) and Garth (Carvey), who cohost a weird, rambling program on public-access television, behave like unruly, not overly bright preteenagers as they move through a wisp of a plot. Gags abound, and some of them are so unexpected they are almost funny (like Wayne and his would-be girlfriend Carrere suddenly start speaking Cantonese). There was a sequel in 1993, but enter *Wayne's World* at your own risk.

## Weekend at Bernie's

★★ Fox, 1989, c, 97 min. Dir: Ted Kotcheff. SP: Robert Klane. Cast: Andrew McCarthy, Jonathan Silverman, Catherine Mary Stewart. Terry Kiser, Catherine Parks, Don Calfa.

This movie was popular enough to warrant a sequel, but it's silly stuff, with just one gimmick and that one isn't very funny. Two young men (McCarthy and Silverman) who work for an insurance company are invited to their boss's house, unaware that their boss, Bernie (Kiser), intends to kill them for uncovering some incriminating information. Instead their boss is murdered, and when a weekend party arrives, the two must frantically pretend that Bernie is still alive. Somehow everyone is too stupid to notice the obvious truth. Can you follow this? Do you care? Raucous and unamusing.

## Where's Poppa?

★★★ United Artists, 1970, c, 82 min. Dir: Carl Reiner. SP: Robert Klane, b/o his novel. Cast: George Segal, Ruth Gordon, Ron Leibman, Trish Van Devere, Barnard Hughes, Vincent Gardenia, Paul Sorvino, Garrett Morris.

Wayne Campbell (Mike Myers, left), host of his own late-night cable access TV show, joined by his sidekick Garth (Dana Carvey, right), welcomes Rob Lowe to *Wayne's World*

Considering the current film scene, Carl Reiner's off-the-wall black comedy may not shock viewers as it once did, but it has its outrageous moments. Gordon Hocheiser (Segal) is a thirty-five-year-old lawyer who despises his senile mother (Gordon), since she is not only ruining his career but also spoiling his current romance with a nurse (Van Devere). He turns for help to his younger brother, Sidney (Leibman), who has his own peculiar problems. Sidney's experiences in Central Park, and their consequences, are unexpected, harrow-

ing, and (yes) sometimes very funny. Segal skillfully plays yet another genial nerd, but Gordon is almost beyond endurance as Momma. Viewers in 1970 were either convulsed or revulsed. Take your pick.

## Which Way Is Up?

★★☆ Universal, 1977, c, 94 min. Dir: Michael Schultz. SP: Carl Gottlieb, Cecil Brown. Cast: Richard Pryor, Lonette McKee, Margaret Avery, Morgan Woodward, Marilyn Coleman, Bebe Drake-Hooks, Gloria Edwards.

Loosely adapted from Lina Wertmuller's Sicilian

comedy *The Seduction of Mimi, Which Way Is Up?* stars Richard Pryor as LeRoy Jones, an orange picker who becomes a union hero and leaves his wife and family at home to seek work in Los Angeles. In the city he finds himself a new woman, starts a second family, and eventually sells out to the capitalists. The Wertmuller movie doesn't translate well to an American setting, but Pryor is sometimes funny as LeRoy and even funnier playing two other roles, a hypocritical preacher and LeRoy's foul-mouthed old father.

## White Men Can't Jump

★★★ Fox, 1992, c, 114 min. Dir and SP: Ron Shelton. Cast: Woody Harrelson, Wesley Snipes, Gloria Perez, Tyra Ferrell, Cylk Cozart, Kadeem Hardison, Ernest Harden, Jr., John Marshall Jones.

At first glance, this pungent, entertaining movie would seem to be about basketball, but it's not. It is really about friendship, loyalty, and racial harmony. Wesley Snipes is Sidney, a basketball hustler with job and marital problems. Woody Harrelson is Billy, another basketball hustler with a nagging girlfriend (Perez). After Billy outhustles Sidney, the two join forces to hustle everyone else. They aim for the "big score," but trouble comes when they owe money to some dangerous hoods. Shelton's dialogue is swift, funny, and profane, and he extracts juicy performances from the cast, especially Rosie Perez, who is hilarious as a girl whose sole obsession is getting to be a contestant on *Jeopardy.*

# One of a Kind: Unclassifiable Comedies

Here are a number of movie comedies that defy easy classification. Some of them might fit with effort into a particular genre or subgenre. (Is *All About Eve* a satire of theatrical life?) Others, such as *Melvin and Howard* or *Who Framed Roger Rabbit,* stand alone as unique creations.

## After Hours

★★★ Warners, 1985, c, 97 min. Dir: Martin Scorsese. SP: Joseph Minion. Cast: Griffin Dunne, Rosanna Arquette, Teri Garr, John Heard, Verna Bloom, Thomas Chong, Cheech Marin, Catherine O'Hara, Bronson Pinchot, Dick Miller.

Is this a pitch-black comedy, or an urban horror story, or both? Critics and viewers have discussed *After Hours* without coming to any conclusion. At night, a young uptown word-processor (Dunne) travels to New York City's SoHo district, where he meets a woman in an all-night coffee shop. From that point his life becomes a series of bizarre, terrifying occurences. He comes upon a number of very strange people and ends up fleeing in terror from a crowd that believes he is a neighborhood thief. Cheech and Chong appear as burglars. Watch this oddball film but remember, you're on your own.

## All About Eve

★★★★ Fox, 1950, 138 min. Dir: Joseph L. Mankiewicz. SP: Joseph L. Mankiewicz, b/o story by Mary Orr. Cast: Bette Davis, Anne Baxter, George Sanders, Gary Merrill, Celeste Holm, Hugh Marlowe, Thelma Ritter, Gregory Ratoff, Marilyn Monroe.

Movies about the New York theater generally get it all wrong (overtures at dramatic plays and similar gaffes), but *All About Eve* gets it gloriously right. Joseph Mankiewicz's witty screenplay revolves about Margo Channing (Davis), a luminous stage star whose brittle manner conceals a deep insecurity. Along comes Eve Harrington (Baxter), a scheming minx pretending to be all sweetness and light. Eve covets not only Margo's next role but her director-boyfriend (Merrill) as well. Bette Davis was seldom more passionately involved in the heart of her role, and everyone else is just fine, especially Oscar winner George Sanders (Best Supporting Actor) as acid-tongued theater critic Addison De Witt. Other Oscars went to the movie, and to Mankiewicz for his screenplay and direction.

## Bean

★☆ PolyGram, 1997, c, 94 min. Dir: Mel Smith. SP: Richard Curtis, Robin Driscoll. Cast: Rowan Atkinson, Peter MacNichol, Pamela Reed, Harris Yulin, Burt Reynolds, Larry Drake, Chris Ellis, Johnny Galecki, Sir John Mills.

The character of Bean, embodied by Rowan Atkinson, was featured on a British sitcom that became hugely popular around the world. Eccentric (to put it mildly), mischievous, and infantile, Bean barely spoke as he spread disaster and havoc wherever he went. This feature-length comedy sends him to America as the representative of a British museum on the occasion of the return of the painting of "Whistler's Mother" to its native home. Everything goes horribly wrong as Bean ruins the painting and nearly ruins the life of museum curator MacNichol. The character of Bean is tolerable only in small doses, and fifteen minutes into this movie, you may want to strangle him. Be our guest.

A meeting of theater people from *All About Eve* (1950): playwright Hugh Marlowe, "friend" Anne Baxter, director Gary Merrill, and star actress Bette Davis (left to right).

## Better Off Dead

★★★ CBS Entertainment, 1985, c, 98 min. Dir and SP: Savage Steve Holland. Cast: John Cusack, David Ogden Stiers, Kim Darby, Diane Franklin, Curtis Armstrong, Dan Schneider, Amanda Wyss, Aaron Dozier.

An offbeat comedy with some original ideas. Lane (Cusack) is a teenager madly in love with Beth (Wyss). When she rejects him for the local jock (Dozier), he decides to end it all but fails after several tries. The movie's originality, however, does not come from this plot device but from some bizarre characters (an Asian exchange student who imitates Howard Cosell,

a newspaper delivery boy from hell) and a few touches of fantasy (working at a grubby fast-food restaurant, Lane imagines a kind of "Frankenburger," embodied by claymation). Eventually, Lane triumphs over the jock in a ski race and falls for Monique (Franklin), a pretty exchange student who lives next door. No sense or logic in this comedy, but some laughs.

## City Slickers

★★★ Castle Rock, 1991, c, 112 min. Dir: Ron Underwood. SP: Lowell Ganz, Babaloo Mandel. Cast: Billy Crystal, Bruno Kirby, Daniel Stern, Jack Palance, Patricia Wettig, Helen

Slater, Noble Willingham, Tracey Walter, Josh Mostel.

Three friends (Crystal, Stern, Kirby) are having a midlife crisis; each has his own disappointments or regrets. They decide to exchange New York City for the Wild West—to get away from it all by signing on as real, working cowboys charged with transporting a herd of cattle to a new home. Under a leathery trail boss (Palance in an Oscar-winning performance), the city slickers take on unexpected challenges and learn some life lessons. A very likable movie that avoids some expected clichés and offers a few clever variations on the old fish-out-of-water theme. Sequel: *City Slickers: The Legend of Curly's Gold* (1994).

## Desperately Seeking Susan

★★★ Orion, 1985, c, 104 min. Dir: Susan Seidelman. SP: Leora Barish. Cast: Rosanna Arquette, Madonna, Aidan Quinn, Mark Blum, Laurie Metcalf, Robert Joy, Will Patton, John Turturro.

An oddball switched-identity comedy, *Desperately Seeking* Susan features Madonna in one of her very few good roles in the eighties. She plays Susan, a shady, wildly offbeat, and possibly dangerous woman whose life becomes entangled with Roberta (Arquette), a bored surburban housewife. Roberta is the central character—she becomes obsessed with a personal ad headed "Desperately seeking Susan," and through a series of unlikely circumstances, she takes over Susan's identity. The ups and downs of the plot are not believable, but the movie is a watchable if eccentric mixture of slapstick, melodrama, and romance, and Madonna is genuinely amusing as the kooky Susan.

## Diner

★★★☆ MGM/UA, 1982, c, 110 min. Dir and SP: Barry Levinson. Cast: Steve Guttenberg, Daniel Stern, Mickey Rourke, Ellen Barkin, Kevin Bacon, Timothy Daly, Paul Reiser, Michael Tucker.

Featuring a group of young actors, some of whom would go on to starring roles, *Diner* is Barry Levinson's affectionate, winning tribute to his early years. (This was his first effort at directing). Set in Baltimore in 1959, the movie revolves around a group of friends who have just graduated from high school and are uneasy about what lies ahead for them. Gathering at the Fells Point diner, Eddie (Guttenberg), Boogie (Rourke), Fenwick (Bacon), and Shrevie (Stern) discuss topics that reveal their naïveté, their hopes, and their half-formed opinions. As their relationships shift and change, the movie becomes a funny, touching view of the shaky bridge between adolescence and maturity.

## Ed Wood

★★★☆ Touchstone, 1994, 124 min. Dir: Tim Burton. SP: Scott Alexander and Larry Karaszewski, b/o book by Rudolph Grey. Cast: Johnny Depp, Martin Landau, Sarah Jessica Parker, Patricia Arquette, Jeffrey Jones, Bill Murray, Vincent D'Onofrio, G. D. Spradlin, Lisa Marie.

Martin Landau's astonishing, Oscar-winning performance as horror film legend Bela Lugosi is easily the highlight of Tim Burton's delightfully offbeat film. Edward D. Wood, Jr. (Depp), was a phenomenon of the fifties: an outrageous, no-talent dreamer who persisted in making some of the worst movies of all times. *Ed Wood* shows him gathering his stock company of misfits and eccentrics who join him in creating such extraordinarily awful gems as *Glen or Glenda* (1953), *Bride of the Monster* (1955), and *Plan 9 from Outer Space* (1959). Johnny Depp is marvelous as Wood, but Martin Landau offers a memorable portrait, simultaneously comic and tragic, of a frail, drug-ridden but still flamboyant actor at the end of his life.

## The Freshman

★★★ TriStar, 1990, c, 102 min. Dir and SP: Andrew Bergman. Cast: Marlon Brando, Matthew Broderick, Penelope Ann Miller, Bruno Kirby, Frank Whaley, Joe Polito, Paul Benedict, Richard Gant.

Critics seemed to have a divided opinion about Marlon Brando's performance in this quirky, sometimes amusing comedy. Either they felt he was playing a brilliant variation on his *Godfather* character of Don Corleone, or they believed he was showing his usual contempt for acting, including his own career. His Carmine Sabatini is clearly modeled on his famous godfather, but placed here in a comic context. As the Mafia chieftain, he takes naïve film student Clark Kellogg (Broderick) under his wing, involving him in some shady business that centers on a rare Komodo dragon rather than on drugs. Andrew Bergman's screenplay has many clever touches and some offbeat casting (Maximilian Schell as the maitre d' at a climactic banquet), but it strains too hard to be different.

## The Fortune

★★☆ Columbia, 1975, c, 88 min. Dir: Mike·Nichols. SP: Adrien Joyce (Carol Eastman). Cast: Jack Nicholson, Warren Beatty, Stockard Channing, Florence Stanley, Scatman Crothers, Richard B. Shull.

There's no faulting the performances, particularly Jack Nicholson's, or the period ambiance and music (by David Shire), in this black comedy from Mike Nichols. The overall result, however, is mostly flat. Set in the 1920s, the movie centers on two fortune-hunters named Oscar (Nicholson) and Nick (Beatty). Their target is a dizzy heiress named Freddie (Channing, in her film debut). When Freddie, fed up with the antics of both men, decides to give her money to charity, they plot to kill her, but it all goes comically awry. Or at least the intention is comical. The stars work hard—Nicholson is quite funny as the manic Oscar—but the spark is missing.

## The Graduate

★★★★ Joseph E. Levine/Embassy, 1967, c, 105 min. Dir: Mike Nichols. SP: Buck Henry, Calder Willingham, b/o novel by Charles Webb. Cast: Anne Bancroft, Dustin Hoffman, Katharine Ross, Murray Hamilton, William Daniels, Elizabeth Wilson, Brian Avery, Norman Fell, Marion Lorne, Alice Ghostley.

A landmark comedy of the late sixties, and a movie that, after more than three decades, still defines a period and a generation. *The Graduate* centers on twenty-one-year-old Benjamin Braddock (Hoffman, in his star-making role), a recent college graduate who is unsure of where his life is heading. Trouble looms in the person of his parents's neurotic, alcoholic friend Mrs. Robinson (Bancroft), who lures Benjamin into her bed. When Benjamin falls for Mrs. Robinson's daughter Elaine (Ross), there's hell to pay. There are many reasons for the movie's classic status: the exceptionally clever screenplay; the songs on the soundtrack (written by Paul Simon; performed by Simon and Garfunkel); Oscar-nominated performances by Hoffman, Bancroft, and Ross; and Mike Nichols's assured direction, which won the Oscar. The word is plastics.

## The Great Race

★★★ Warners, 1965, c, 150 min. Dir: Blake Edwards. SP: Arthur Ross, b/o story by Arthur Ross, Blake Edwards. Cast: Tony Curtis, Jack Lemmon, Natalie Wood, Peter Falk, Keenan Wynn, Arthur O'Connell, Vivian Vance, Dorothy Provine, Larry Storch, George Macready, Marvin Kaplan.

A long, extravagant cartoon of a movie, *The Great Race* is Blake Edwards's tribute to old-time slapstick. Tony Curtis, dressed all in white and teeth sparkling in the sun, is the Great Leslie, the lionized front-runner in a turn-of-the-century automobile race from New York to Paris. His archenemy is dastardly Professor Fate (Lemmon), determined to destroy Leslie in any one of a number of ways and doomed to failure in all of them. Natalie Wood is Maggie DuBois, a militant reporter who mixes in the race and falls for Leslie. The elaborate sequences (a Western brawl, a pie-throwing melee, and others) grow monotonous after a while, but Lemmon is funny as Professor Fate and even funnier as an addled Prussian prince.

## Guarding Tess

★★★ TriStar, 1994, c, 98 min. Dir: Hugh Wilson. SP: Hugh Wilson, Peter Torokvei. Cast: Shirley MacLaine, Nicolas Cage, Austin Pendleton, Edward Albert, James Rebhorn, Richard Griffiths, John Roselius, David Graf, Susan Blommaert.

Young Benjamin Braddock (Dustin Hoffman) begins a clandestine affair with Mrs. Robinson (Anne Bancroft), his parents' neurotic, alcoholic friend, in *The Graduate* (1964).

Tess Carlisle (MacLaine) is a former First Lady, tough, demanding, and sarcastic, who is living in a farmhouse in Ohio, attended by her household staff and watched over by a Secret Service detail. Heading this detail is Doug Chesnic (Cage), who does his job well but who is often exasperated by Tess's behavior. When his tour of duty is over he wants to leave, but Tess insists that he stay. Their sparks of hostility, and their grudging affection, form the basis for this enjoyable comedy-drama, and the two stars are fine. Later in the film, melodrama takes over in conventional fashion, but the movie's chief pleasure lies in the Tess-Doug relationship.

## Handle with Care (Citizens Band)

★★★☆ Paramount, 1977, c, 98 min. Dir: Jonathan Demme. SP: Paul Brickman. Cast: Paul LeMat, Candy Clark, Ann Wedgeworth, Marcia Rodd, Roberts Blossom, Charles Napier, Bruce McGillis, Alix Elias.

A very funny, engaging—and highly original—comedy, *Handle with Care* centers around a group of happily obsessed ham radio operators and their CBs. One of their number, Paul LeMat, is a truck driver who must deal with a cantankerous father (Blossom), a resentful brother (McGillis), and an ex-girlfriend (Clark) with a surprising CB secret. There's a secondary plot involving a bigamous trucker (Napier) and his two wives (Rodd and Wedgeworth), which is by far the most hilarious portion of the movie. The film was a failure under the original title *Citizens Band,* but was rereleased as *Handle with Care* after some favorable reviews and industry buzz.

## I'll Do Anything

★★★ Columbia, 1994, c, 115 min. Dir and SP: James L. Brooks. Cast: Nick Nolte, Albert Brooks, Julie Kavner, Joely Richardson, Tracey Ullman, Whittni Wright, Jeb Brown, Ian McKellen, Rosie O'Donnell, Ken Page, Joely Fisher, Woody Harrelson.

*I'll Do Anything* will be remembered as the movie that was produced as a musical but then later had the songs excised by its writer-director. Actually, it's much better than that single fact suggests: a quirkily entertaining, often perceptive comedy-drama with an expert cast. The film is rather schizoid: one part deals with aspiring actor Matt Hobbs (Nolte) and his relationship with his difficult little daughter (Wright); the other part is a satirical view of Hollywood life. Much the best part of the film concerns insecure producer Burke Adler (Brooks) and his Girl Friday, Nan (Kavner), who loves him but who is compelled to tell him the unvarnished truth about his selfishness and insensitivity.

## In and Out

★★ Paramount, 1997, c, 92 min. Dir: Frank Oz. SP: Paul Rudnick. Cast: Kevin Kline, Joan Cusack, Tom Selleck, Debbie Reynolds, Wilford Brimley, Matt Dillon, Bob Newhart.

One of the first movies to deal with the "outing" of a repressed gay man, *In and Out* was hugely popular, which is not to say that it is any good. An English teacher in a small Indiana town, Howard (Kline) is about to be married to Emily (Cusack). At the Academy Awards ceremony, he is "outed" by a former student (Dillon), who has won the Oscar as Best Actor. A frantic Howard denies that he is gay, while everyone convulses about his true sexuality. Kline has fun with the role, but the idea that all gay men love to dance, dress neatly, and adore

Barbra Streisand is ridiculous, and the climax, in which almost everyone rallies to Howard's support, is so shameless that even Frank Capra would have shunned it. Oscar-nominated Joan Cusack is best as the unhinged bride-to-be.

## Ishtar

★★ Columbia, 1987, c, 107 min. Dir and SP: Elaine May. Cast: Dustin Hoffman, Warren Beatty, Isabelle Adjani, Charles Grodin, Jack Weston, Carol Kane, Tess Harper.

Well, anyway, the songs are funny. This legendary fiasco, released after much controversy and many costly delays, is not as awful as its reputation, but it's quite bad. Warren Beatty and Dustin Hoffman play Lewis and Clarke, aspiring songwriters whose songs give a new dimension to the word *terrible.* Out of desperation they accept a gig in Morocco, where they become embroiled in the civil war engulfing the area. Isabelle Adjani is the obligatory girl in distress (this is, in a sense, an updated "Road" movie), and Charles Grodin plays a duplicitous CIA agent. Much of the screenplay falls dismally flat, but there are tolerable portions, including Lewis and Clarke's adventures in the desert with a blind camel.

## L.A. Story

★★★☆ TriStar, 1991, c, 95 min. Dir: Mick Jackson. SP: Steve Martin. Cast: Steve Martin, Victoria Tennant, Richard E. Grant, Marilu Henner, Sarah Jessica Parker, Susan Forristal, Kevin Pollak, Sam McMurray.

A scrambled but highly diverting mixture of romantic comedy, fantasy, and satire. Writer-star Steve Martin casts an affectionate but still sharp-edged view of Los Angeles as he assembles his off-beat characters. Martin plays the "Kookie Weatherman" of an L.A. television station, who falls head over heels in love with a British reporter (Tennant) and finally wins her with the help and advice of a freeway traffic signal (yes, a traffic signal). The screenplay deftly spoofs some of the Los Angeles rituals, such as the high-toned lunch, and many of the jokes have to be caught on the run, such as the names of a

Sausalito motel and an expensive Hollywood restaurant. Sarah Jessica Parker is funny as an oddball girl who seems to spend all of her time on roller skates. In all, a most engaging original.

## Larger Than Life

★★ United Artists, 1996, c, 83 min. Dir: Howard Franklin. SP: Roy Blount, Jr. Cast: Bill Murray, Janeane Garofalo, Matthew McConaughey, Linda Fiorentino, Anita Gillette, Pat Hingle, Lois Smith, Tai.

*Larger than Life* takes the idea of Bill Murray transporting an elephant across America and somehow manages to come up mostly laugh-free. Murray plays a cynical motivational speaker (the first scenes in which he works at his job are at least marginally funny) who inherits Vera the elephant from his circus clown father and decides to transport her cross-country. Vera will end up either shipped to Sri Lanka by an environmental activist (Garofalo) or victimized by a nasty animal trainer (Fiorentino). Matthew McConaughey plays a manic cowboy trucker to absolutely no avail.

## Melvin and Howard

★★★☆ Universal, 1980, c, 95 min. Dir: Jonathan Demme. SP: Bo Goldman. Cast: Paul LeMat, Jason Robards, Mary Steenburgen, Pamela Reed, Jack Kehoe, Michael J. Pollard, Dabney Coleman, Gloria Grahame.

A genuine original, *Melvin and Howard* takes off from an actual incident. Melvin Dummar (LeMat), none-too-bright and generally broke, is driving across the Arizona desert when he finds and helps an apparent derelict (Robards) who claims to be billionaire Howard Hughes. After Hughes's death, Melvin comes upon a mysterious will that names him as one of Hughes's beneficiaries. Is is authentic or a fake? Nobody knows for sure. Actually, the movie is more about Melvin's haphazard life, particularly his relationship with wife Lynda (Steenburgen) and friends. Steenburgen won an Oscar for her funny, uncondescending performance as Lynda. Bo Goldman's screenplay also received an award, and Jason Robards was nominated as Best Supporting Actor.

## Million Dollar Legs

★★★☆ Paramount, 1932, 64 min. Dir: Edward Cline. SP: Henry Myers, Nick Barrows, b/o story by Joseph L. Mankiewicz. Cast: W. C. Fields, Jack Oakie, Andy Clyde, Lyda Roberti, Susan Fleming, Ben Turpin, Hugh Herbert, George Barbier, Billy Gilbert.

Truly a one-of-a-kind movie, a lunatic farce that makes little sense but will probably have you laughing with its barrage of sight gags and non sequiturs. Imagine W. C. Fields as the crackpot president of Klopstokia, a mythical country overrun with nuts and goats, mostly the former. To raise money, President Fields enters the country in the Olympics, with himself as a champion weight lifter and his majordomo (Clyde) as the world's fastest runner (the "legs" of the title). Also involved are Jack Oakie as a visiting brush salesman and Lyda Roberti as a spy named Mata Machree ("The Woman No Man Can Resist"). Favorite scene: the country's cabinet meets to arm-wrestle the president for control of the government.

## Moscow on the Hudson

★★★☆ Columbia, 1984, c, 115 min. Dir: Paul Mazursky. SP: Paul Mazursky and Leon Capetanos. Cast: Robin Williams, Maria Conchita Alonso, Cleavant Derricks, Alejandro Rey, Saveli Kramarov, Elya Baskin, Oleg Rudnik.

Mixing offbeat humor and flag-waving patriotism, *Moscow on the Hudson* manages to come up a winner, thanks in large part to Robin Williams's ingratiating performance. He plays Vladimir Ivanoff, a Russian musician who defects during his trip to America with the Moscow Circus. While preparing for American citizenship, he meets a number of helpful people, conveniently representing virtually every ethnic group. He also falls in love with a pretty Italian immigrant (Alonso). Director-coauthor Mazursky goes for sentiment rather than satire, but the movie is diverting entertainment. The best sequence by far is Vladimir's defection in Bloomingdale's, no less, with floorwalkers, members of the Soviet secret police, New York policemen, and others converging on the scene in comic confusion.

# Mr. Wrong

★ Touchstone, 1996, c, 92 min. Dir: Nick Castle. SP: Chris Matheson, Kerry Ehrin, Craig Munson. Cast: Ellen DeGeneres, Bill Pullman, Joan Cusack, Dean Stockwell, Joan Plowright, John Livingston, Polly Holliday, Robert Goulet, Maddie Corman, Ellen Cleghorne.

Didn't anyone notice how atrocious, how grotesquely unfunny this material is? In her feature film debut, Ellen DeGeneres plays Martha, a thirtyish woman, bright, attractive, and conspicuously single, who meets Whitman (Pullman), a man who seems to be the lover she's been waiting for. Instead, he turns out to be seriously unhinged, a persistent, even dangerous person who almost destroys her life. Ordinarily this plot would be played for chilling horror, but it's intended as black comedy, and the result is catastrophic. In all, an anti-romantic comedy that is noted here as One of a Kind—a kind we hope never to see again.

# The Opposite of Sex

★★★☆ TriStar, 1998, c, 100 min. Dir and SP: Don Roos. Cast: Christina Ricci, Martin Donovan, Lisa Kudrow, Lyle Lovett, Johnny Galecki, Ivan Sergei, William Scott Lee.

Dedee (Ricci) is sixteen and very bad news. Tough, amoral, totally self-absorbed—and pregnant—she narrates this decidedly offbeat movie and tells the viewer from the start, "If you think I'm just plucky and scrappy and all I need is love, you're in over your head." Dedee comes to visit Bill (Donovan), her gay half-brother, and sets in motion a series of events that affects the lives of a group of people in ways that cannot be summarized. Among the fascinating characters are Lucia (Kudrow in a wonderful performance), the acerbic sister of Bill's dead lover, and Matt (Sergei), Bill's current lover who is seduced into heterosexuality by Dedee. Emphatically quirky dialogue, good acting, and many small jolts of surprise make this movie a genuine original.

# Paper Moon

★★★☆ Paramount, 1973, 102 min. Dir: Peter Bogdanovich. SP: Alvin Sargent, b/o novel by Joe David Brown. Cast: Ryan O'Neal, Tatum O'Neal, Madeline Kahn, P. J. Johnson, John Hillerman, Burton Gilliam, Randy Quaid.

Young Tatum O'Neal's wonderful, Oscar-winning performance as little Addie is the mainstay of this delightful period comedy. In Depression America, beautifully evoked in black-and-white photography, Addie (Tatum O'Neal) attaches herself to Moze (Ryan O'Neal, Tatum's real-life dad), a fly-by-night con man and Bible salesman. Together, Moze and Addie roam the bleak countryside, selling Bibles mostly to unsuspecting widows. Along the way they encounter some colorful people, especially a flamboyant "entertainer" (Kahn) who calls herself Trixie Delight. The movie is flavorsome, funny, and even a bit poignant, but it's Tatum O'Neal's Addie that you're likely to remember. A short-lived television series based on the movie appeared in 1974.

# Pee-Wee's Big Adventure

★★ Warners, 1985, c, 1985. Dir: Tim Burton. SP: Paul Reubens, Phil Hartman, and Michael Varhol. Cast: Paul Reubens, Elizabeth Daily, Mark Holton, Diane Salinger, Tony Bill, Cassandra Peterson, James Brolin.

Viewers tend to find this movie either delightfully imaginative or terminally stupid; take your pick. Pee-Wee Herman (Reubens) is a nine-year-old in an adult's body, with a too-small gray suit, a large bow tie, and makeup. Pee-Wee lives in a house that might be called a combination of amusement park fun house and toy store. When his beloved bike is stolen, Pee-Wee roams across the country (especially to the Alamo in Texas) in a desperate search, meeting various weird characters along the way. Undoubtedly there are imaginative touches in the countless sight gags, but Pee-Wee wears out his welcome in a very short time.

# Pride and Prejudice

★★★★ MGM, 1940, 118 min. Dir: Robert Z. Leonard. SP: Aldous Huxley, Jane Murfin, b/o novel by Jane Austen. Cast: Greer Garson, Laurence Olivier, Mary Boland, Edmund Gwenn, Edna May Oliver, Maureen O'Sullivan,

Ann Rutherford, Melville Cooper, Frieda Inescort, Heather Angel, Karen Morley, Marsha Hunt.

This version of Jane Austen's comedy of manners was one of MGM's best literary adaptations, an enchanting film that only cries out for color to be entirely satisfactory. As in the novel, the story revolves around the Bennetts and their five marriageable daughters. Mostly it concerns the verbal sparring and eventual romance of the eldest Bennett girl, Elizabeth (Garson, a bit long in the tooth but radiant), and the insufferably snobbish Mr. Darcy (Olivier). There are many moments of delicious absurdity and some glancing comments on manners and morals. As Mrs. Bennett, Mary Boland is all dithering heedlessness, and Edmund Gwenn makes a sly, clear-eyed paterfamilias.

## Ruggles of Red Gap

★★★☆ Paramount, 1935, 92 min. Dir: Leo McCarey. SP: Walter De Leon, Harlan Thompson; adaptation by Humphrey Pearson, b/o novel and play by Harry Leon Wilson. Cast: Charles Laughton, Charlie Ruggles, Mary Boland, ZaSu Pitts, Roland Young, Leila Hyams, Maude Eburne.

Most famous for the sequence in which Charles Laughton delivers the Gettysburg Address to a group of awestruck cowboys and barflies, *Ruggles of Red Gap* is a lighthearted tale that has seen several incarnations over the years. Charles Laughton gives (for him) a restrained performance as Marmaduke Ruggles, the proper British butler who is won in a poker game by the Flouds (Ruggles and Boland), a vulgar, newly rich American couple. Brought to the American West, Ruggles learns about free enterprise and equality and even gets to court a tremulous widow (Pitts). The movie gets sluggish at times, but it's never less than genial. *Ruggles* was filmed twice in the silent years and remade (loosely) in 1950 as *Fancy Pants*, a vehicle for Bob Hope.

## Smoke Signals

★★★ ShadowCatcher Entertainment, 1998, c, 88 min. Dir: Chris Eyre. SP: Sherman Alexie, b/o his stories. Cast: Adam Beach, Evan Adams, Irene Bedard, Gary Farmer, Tantoo Cardinal, Michelle St. John, Robert Miano, Molly Cheek, Elaine Miles.

A small but diverting comedy, truly unlike any other, *Smoke Signals* offers insights into modern Indian-American life. On an Idaho reservation, sweet-natured, orphaned Thomas (Adams) is looked after by stoic Victor (Beach), whose father once saved Thomas in the fire that killed his parents. When the father dies, Victor and Thomas begin a journey together in which they come to understand each other. Victor also resolves his troubled feelings about his father and the past. Small details, many of them humorous and revealing about Indian culture, make *Smoke Signals* a movie worth watching.

## So I Married an Axe Murderer

★ TriStar, 1993, c, 93 min. Dir: Thomas Schlamme. SP: Robbie Fox. Cast: Mike Myers, Nancy Travis, Anthony LaPaglia, Brenda Fricker, Amanda Plummer; guest appearances by Alan Arkin, Phil Hartman, Michael Richards, Steven Wright, Charles Grodin.

Here is a comedy that gives new meaning to the word *dreadful*. The premise alone is warning enough: Charlie McKenzie (Myers) is a San Francisco self-styled "poet" who is unable to commit to any relationship. He meets, courts, and eventually marries an attractive girl (Travis), whom he comes to believe is a widely sought axe murderer. Eventually he even convinces his best friend, policeman Tony (LaPaglia), that the lady has homicide on her mind. The truth comes out in an utterly stupid climax. Myers's character is an objectionable fool, and his predicament has not one trace of authentic humor. Too bad so many good actors got caught up in this fiasco, some in small guest appearances.

## That Darn Cat

★★☆ Disney, 1997, c, 89 min. Dir: Bob Spiers. SP: S. M. Alexander, L. A. Karaszewski, b/o screenplay by Gordon Gordon, Mildred Gordon, Bill Walsh. Cast: Christina Ricci, Doug E. Doug, Michael McKean, Bess Armstrong, George

Dzunda, Peter Boyle, Dyan Cannon, Dean Jones, John Ratzenberger, Estelle Parsons, Mark Christopher Lawrence. A loose remake of the 1965 Disney movie, *That Darn Cat* might provide passable entertainment for young viewers, but hardly anyone else. Christina Ricci stars as Patti Randall, a dour teenager living in Edgefield, a suburb of Boston, with her cat D.C. When a housekeeper is kidnapped from the home of wealthy Dean Jones and Dyan Cannon, D.C. lets Patti know that the victim is being held in a nearby rundown house. Soon she is teaming up with bungling FBI agent Zeke Kelso (Doug), led by the ever-resourceful D.C., to foil the kidnappers. No third version required.

## Throw Momma from the Train

★★☆ Orion, 1987, c, 88 min. Dir: Danny DeVito. SP: Stu Silver. Cast: Danny DeVito, Billy Crystal, Anne Ramsey, Kim Greist, Kate Mulgrew, Branford Marsalis, Rob Reiner.

This movie takes Alfred Hitchcock's *Strangers on a Train* and turns it in the direction of farce. The result is not nearly as funny as it might have been. DeVito plays a childish man burdened with a monstrous, emasculating mother (Ramsey). Crystal is his creative writing teacher, a man who would love to destroy his hated ex-wife (Mulgrew). When Crystal seems to suggest that the two should commit each other's murder (in the way of Hitchcock's thriller), DeVito takes him seriously. Naturally, comic chaos erupts all over the place. Although there are some amusing moments, the screenplay veers out of control and begins to rely on such bewhiskered gimmicks as a runaway automobile. Anne Ramsey won an Oscar nomination as Best Supporting Actress.

## Tootsie

★★★★ Columbia, 1982, c, 116 min. Dir: Sydney Pollack. SP: Larry Gelbart, Murray Schisgal, b/o story by Larry Gelbart, Don McGuire. Cast: Dustin Hoffman, Jessica Lange, Teri Garr, Dabney Coleman, Charles Durning, Bill Murray (uncredited), Geena Davis, George Gaynes, Sydney Pollack, Doris Belack.

Obnoxious and argumentative, actor Michael Dorsey (Hoffman) is told by his agent (Pollack), "Nobody in New York or Hollywood will work with you." In desperation, Michael disguises himself as a woman and becomes a sensation on a soap opera as Dorothy Michaels. He falls for a beautiful soap-opera actress (Lange) and also becomes a better man by viewing the world through a woman's eyes. One of the sharpest, funniest comedies of the eighties, *Tootsie* aims a few satirical arrows at the frantic worlds of television and theater. Hoffman gives one of his best performances (he even makes Michael's pushiness winning), and Lange is enchanting in her Oscar-winning role.

## Who Framed Roger Rabbit

★★★☆ Touchstone, 1988, c, 103 min. Dir: Robert Zemeckis. SP: Jeffrey Price, Peter S. Seaman, b/o novel by Gary K. Wolf. Cast: Bob Hoskins, Christopher Lloyd, Joanna Cassidy, Stubby Kaye, Alan Tilvern, Joel Silver. Voice of Roger Rabbit: Charles Fleischer. Voice of Jessica Rabbit: Kathleen Turner (speaking), Amy Irving (singing).

This cinematic treat will have you believing in the interaction of living actors and cartoon characters (or Toons, as the movie calls them). Set in 1947 Los Angeles, the movie revolves about seedy detective Eddie Valiant (Hoskins), who is charged with proving that overwrought Toon-star Roger Rabbit did not kill the lover of his sexy wife, Jessica. Eddie's adventures involve him with the bizarre Judge Doom (Lloyd), a master criminal with a dastardly agenda. *Who Framed Roger Rabbit* brings in many famous cartoon characters in hilarious solo appearances and also includes a plethora of inside jokes, visual puns, and other touches guaranteed to keep you laughing. The movie won four Oscars, including a special Oscar for animation director Richard Williams.

## The World of Henry Orient

★★★☆ United Artists, 1964, c, 105 min. Dir: George Roy Hill. SP: Nora Johnson, Nunnally Johnson, b/o novel by Nora Johnson. Cast: Peter Sellers, Paula Prentiss, Tippy

Walker, Merrie Spaeth, Angela Lansbury, Tom Bosley, Phyllis Thaxter, Bibi Osterwald, Peter Duchin.

Both funny and touching, *The World of Henry Orient* is a unique movie that mixes comedy and sentiment, with accent on the comedy. Two teenage girls (Walker and Spaeth) get a wild crush on an egotistical, womanizing concert pianist named Henry Orient (Sellers). They drive poor Henry to distraction, even interfering with his daytime assignation with another man's wife (Prentiss). At the same time, the girls have their own problems at home— Walker is virtually ignored by her parents (Lansbury and Bosley) and Spaeth has to cope with a broken home. Sellers is hilarious as the beleagured musician, and the rest of the cast is just fine. A 1967 stage musical version called *Henry, Sweet Henry* failed to make the grade.

# Index

Abbott and Costello Meet Frankenstein, 42–43
Abbott and Costello Meet the Invisible Man, 43
About Last Night . . . , 82
Ace Ventura, Pet Detective, 46, 47
Ace Ventura: When Nature Calls, 46
Adam's Rib, 124
The Addams Family, 142
Addicted to Love, 82
The Adventure of Sherlock Holmes' Smarter Brother, 170
After Hours, 273
After the Thin Man, 235
Ah, Wilderness!, 194
Airheads, 253
Airplane!, 170
An Alan Smithee Film Burn Hollywood Burn, 170–171
Alice, 50
All About Eve, 273, 274
All in a Night's Work, 82
All Night Long, 83
All of Me, 213
The Americanization of Emily, 171
Amos & Andrew, 235
Analyze This, 235–236
Angels in the Outfield, 213
Animal Crackers, 10, 11
Annie Hall, 50, 51
Another You, 253
Any Wednesday, 194
The Apartment, 75–76
Armed and Dangerous, 236
Arsenic and Old Lace, 64
Arthur, 83–84
Article 99, 171
Artists and Models, 34
As Good As It Gets, 84
The Associate, 171
At the Circus, 10
At War with the Army, 34–35
Auntie Mame, 194–195
Austin Powers: International Man of Mystery, 171–172
Avanti!, 76
The Awful Truth, 124–125

Babes in Toyland, 25
Baby Boom, 142
Baby's Day Out, 142–143
The Bachelor and the Bobby-Soxer, 84
Bachelor Mother, 84
Bachelor Party, 253

Back to School, 143
Back to the Future, 213–214
The Bad News Bears, 143
Ball of Fire, 84–85
Bananas, 50–51
The Bank Dick, 18, 19
Barefoot in the Park, 195
BASEketball, 253–254
Bean, 273
Beat the Devil, 172
The Beautician and the Beast, 85
The Beautiful Blonde from Bashful Bend, 70
Beautiful Girls, 85
Bedtime for Bonzo, 143
Beethoven, 143
Before Sunrise, 85
Being There, 172
Bell, Book and Candle, 195
The Bellboy, 35
Belle of the Nineties, 22
Best Friends, 86
The Best Man, 248
Betsy's Wedding, 144
Better Off Dead, 274
The Beverly Hillbillies, 254
Beverly Hills Cop, 236
Big, 214
Big Bully, 144
Big Business, 254
The Big Lebowski, 236, 237
Big Night, 144
The Big Picture, 173
The Big Store, 10–11
Billy Madison, 254
Biloxi Blues, 195
The Birdcage, 144
The Black Bird, 173
Black Sheep, 254–255
Blank Check, 144–145
Blaze, 248
Blazing Saddles, 59
Blind Date, 86
Blondie, 45
Bluebeard's Eighth Wife, 126
Bob & Carol & Ted & Alice, 126
Bob Roberts, 248
Bombshell, 173
Bonnie Scotland, 25
Boomerang, 86
Born Yesterday, 195–197
Boy Meets Girl, 196
The Brady Bunch Movie, 173
Brain Donors, 255

Breaking Away, 145
Breaking In, 236
The Bride Came C.O.D., 86
Bringing up Baby, 86–87
Broadcast News, 88
Broadway Danny Rose, 51–52
Brother Orchid, 236–237
The Brothers McMullen, 145
Buck Privates, 43
Buck Privates Come Home, 44
Buddy Buddy, 76
Buffy the Vampire Slayer, 214
Bull Durham, 88
Bullets over Broadway, 52
Bulworth, 249
The 'Burbs, 173
Bus Stop, 196, 198
Bustin' Loose, 145
Butterflies Are Free, 198
Bye Bye, Love, 126

Cabin Boy, 173–174
The Cable Guy, 46
Cactus Flower, 198
Caddyshack, 255
Cadillac Man, 237–238
California Suite, 198
The Candidate, 249
The Cannonball Run, 255
Captain Newman, M.D., 228
Captain Ron, 145–146
Carbon Copy, 174
Car 54, Where Are You?, 256
Carnal Knowledge, 126
Car Wash, 255–256
Casanova's Big Night, 28
Casper, 214
The Cat and the Canary, 28
Cat Ballou, 174
Catch-22, 175
Caught in the Draft, 28
Celebrity, 52
The Cemetery Club, 198–199
Chances Are, 214
A Change of Seasons, 127
The Cheap Detective, 175
Christmas in Connecticut, 88
Christmas in July, 70
Cinderfella, 35–36
Citizen Ruth, 175
City Slickers, 274–275
Clean Slate, 215
Clerks, 256
Clifford, 146

Clueless, 175
The Cocoanuts, 11–12
Cocoon, 215
Cold Turkey, 175–176
Come Blow Your Horn, 199
Come September, 88
Coming to America, 88–89
Compromising Positions, 238
Coneheads, 215
Continental Divide, 89
Cookie, 146
Cool Runnings, 256
Cops and Robbers, 238
Cops and Robbersons, 146
Coupe de Ville, 146–147
The Court Jester, 38
Cousins, 147
Crazy People, 256
Critical Care, 176
Critic's Choice, 28–29
Crossing Delancey, 89

Dave, 249, 250
A Day at the Races, 12–13
Dead Men Don't Wear Plaid, 176
Death Becomes Her, 215
Deconstructing Harry, 52
Defending Your Life, 216
The Delicate Delinquent, 36
Dennis the Menace, 147
Designing Woman, 127
Desire, 89
Desk Set, 89–90
Desperately Seeking Susan, 275
Diary of a Mad Housewife, 127
Diner, 275
Dinner at Eight, 199
The Disorderly Orderly, 36
Disorganized Crime, 238
The Distinguished Gentleman, 249–250
The Divorce American Style, 127–129
Doc Hollywood, 90
Doctor Dolittle, 216
Dr. Strangelove or How I Learned to
    Stop Worrying and Love the Bomb,
    176–177
The Doctor Takes a Wife, 90
Don't Drink the Water, 199
Down and Out in Beverly Hills, 147
Down Periscope, 228
Dracula: Dead and Loving It, 59
Dragnet, 178
The Dream Team, 257
Duck Soup, 12, 14–15
Dumb & Dumber, 48
Dutch, 147–148

Easy Living, 70
Ed Wood, 275
The Egg and I, 148

18 Again!, 216
The End, 257
Enter Laughing, 199–200
Every Day's a Holiday, 22
Every Girl Should Be Married, 90
Everyone Says I Love You, 52–53
Everything You Always Wanted to
    Know About Sex (But Were Afraid
    to Ask), 53

The Fabulous Baker Boys, 90–91
The Facts of Life, 29
Family Business, 148
The Family Jewels, 36
Fancy Pants, 29
The Farmer's Daughter, 250
Fast Times at Ridgemont High, 257
Fatal Instinct, 178
Father of the Bride, 148, 149
Father's Day, 148–149
Father's Little Dividend, 149–150
Father Was a Fullback, 150
Fatso, 150
Ferris Bueller's Day Off, 150
A Fine Mess, 257
First Monday in October, 200
The First Wives Club, 128
A Fish Called Wanda, 257–258
The Flamingo Kid, 150–151
Fletch, 238
Flirting with Disaster, 258
Flubber, 216
The Flying Deuces, 25
Folks!, 151
A Foreign Affair, 76
Forget Paris, 130
For Love or Money, 91
For Pete's Sake, 130
For Richer or Poorer, 130
The Fortune, 276
The Fortune Cookie, 76–77
40 Carats, 200
Foul Play, 239
The Four Seasons, 130
Four Weddings and a Funeral, 91
Francis the Talking Mule, 45
Freaky Friday, 217
French Kiss, 91
The Freshman, 275–276
The Front, 53
The Fuller Brush Man, 40
Full of Life, 131
Funny About Love, 131
Funny Farm, 151
Fun with Dick and Jane, 131
Fuzz, 239

Garbo Talks, 151
George of the Jungle, 178
George Washington Slept Here, 200

Get Shorty, 239
Getting Even with Dad, 151–152
Ghost, 217
The Ghost Breakers, 29
Ghostbusters, 217
Goin' to Town, 22
The Golden Child, 217
Gone Fishin', 258
Good Burger, 258
Goodbye, Columbus, 178
The Goodbye Girl, 91–93
Good Morning, Vietnam, 228–229
Good Neighbor Sam, 131
Go West, 15
Go West, Young Man, 22–23
The Graduate, 276, 277
The Grass Is Greener, 131–132
The Great Dictator, 68
The Great McGinty, 70–71
The Great Outdoors, 152
The Great Race, 276
The Great White Hype, 178–179
Greedy, 152
Green Card, 93
Gross Anatomy, 258–259
Grosse Point Blank, 239–240
Groundhog Day, 218
Grumpier Old Men, 152
Grumpy Old Men, 152
Guarding Tess, 276–277
Guess Who's Coming to Dinner, 153
A Guide for the Married Man, 132

Hail the Conquering Hero, 71
Hairspray, 179
Handle with Care (Citizens Band),
    277–278
Hands Across the Table, 93
Hanky Panky, 240
Hannah and Her Sisters, 53
Happiness, 153
Happy Gilmore, 258
Harold and Maude, 93
Harry and the Hendersons, 218–219
Harvey, 200–201
Having Wonderful Time, 201
H.E.A.L.T.H., 179
The Heartbreak Kid, 94
Heaven Can Wait, 179
Heaven Help Us!, 258
Hello Again, 219
Here Comes Mr. Jordan, 219
He Said, She Said, 93
High Anxiety, 59–60
His Girl Friday, 201
History of the World—Part 1, 60
Hold That Ghost, 44
A Hole in the Head, 64
Holiday, 201
Hollywood or Bust, 36

Hollywood Shuffle, 180
Home Alone, 153
Home for the Holidays, 153–154
Home Fried, 258
Honey, I Shrunk the Kids, 219
Honky Tonk Freeway, 180
Hopscotch, 240
Horse Feathers, 15
The Hospital, 180
The Hot Rock, 240
Hot Shots!, 180
House Calls, 94
Housequest, 154
HouseSitter, 94
How to Marry a Millionaire, 94–95
The Hudsucker Proxy, 181
Husbands and Wives, 53–54

If Lucy Fell . . . , 95
I'll Do Anything, 278
I Love You Again, 132
I Love You, Alice B. Toklas!, 181
I Love You to Death, 154
I Married a Witch, 219–220
I'm No Angel, 23–24
I'm Not Rappaport, 202
The Impostors, 258–259
In and Out, 278
The Incredible Mr. Limpet, 220
The Incredible Shrinking Woman, 220
Indiscreet, 95
The In-Laws, 154
Innerspace, 220
The Inspector General, 38
In the Mood, 181
In the Navy, 44
I Ought to Be in Pictures, 201–202
I.Q., 95
Irreconcilable Differences, 132
Ishtar, 278
It Could Happen to You, 95
It Happened One Night, 64–65
It's a Gift, 18
It Should Happen to You, 96
It's My Turn, 96
It Started with Eve, 96
It Takes Two, 154
I Was a Male War Bride, 229

Jeffrey, 202
The Jerk, 260
Jerry Maguire, 96
Jingle All the Way, 154–155
Joe Versus the Volcano, 96–97
Jumping Jacks, 36–37
June Bride, 97
Junior, 220–221

Keep 'Em Flying, 44
Kicking and Screaming, 181

The Kid from Brooklyn, 38
The King of Comedy, 181–182
Kingpin, 260
King Ralph, 260
Kissing a Fool, 97
Kiss Me, Stupid, 77
Kiss Me Goodbye, 221
Klondike Annie, 24
Kotch, 155
Krippendorf's Tribe, 155

Ladybugs, 155
The Lady Eve, 71
Lady for a Day, 65–66
A Lady Takes a Chance, 97
Larger Than Life, 279
The Last Detail, 229
The Last Married Couple in America, 132–133
Last of the Red Hot Lovers, 202
L.A. Story, 278–279
Leave It to Beaver, 155–156
Legal Eagles, 97–98
The Lemon Drop Kid, 29–30
A Letter to Three Wives, 133
Liar Liar, 48
Libeled Lady, 98–99
License to Drive, 260
Life with Father, 202–203
Life with Mikey, 182
Life Stinks, 60
Like Father, Like Son, 221
Living in Oblivion, 182
The Lonely Guy, 100
The Long, Long Trailer, 133
Look Who's Talking, 156
Lost and Found, 133
Lost in America, 182
Love and Death, 54
Love at First Bite, 221
The Love Bug, 221
Love Crazy, 133–134
The Loved One, 182–183
Love Finds Andy Hardy, 156
Love Happy, 15
Love in the Afternoon, 77
Lover Come Back, 100
Lovesick, 100
Love! Valor! Compassion!, 203
Lucky Partners, 100
Luv, 203

Ma and Pa Kettle, 45
Mad Dog and Glory, 240
Made for Each Other, 100–101
Made in America, 101
Madhouse, 156
Mafia!, 183
Maid to Order, 221–222
The Main Event, 101

The Major and the Minor, 77
Major Payne, 156–157
Making Mr. Right, 222
The Male Animal, 203
Manhattan, 54–55
Manhattan Murder Mystery, 55–56
Mannequin, 222
Man of the House, 157
Man on the Flying Trapeze, 18
Man's Favorite Sport?, 101
The Man with Two Brains, 183
The Man Who Came to Dinner, 203–204
The Man Who Knew Too Little, 183
Married to It, 134
Married to the Mob, 240–241
The Marrying Kind, 134–136
The Marrying Man, 136
Mary, Mary, 204
M*A*S*H, 229
The Mask, 48
The Matchmaker, 204
Matilda, 222
Matinee, 183–184
Maverick, 184
Max Dugan Returns, 157
Maxie, 222–223
McHale's Navy, 229–230
Melvin and Howard, 279
Memories of Me, 157
Miami Rhapsody, 157–158
Michael, 223
Micki & Maude, 136
Midnight, 77–78
A Midsummer Night's Sex Comedy, 56
Mighty Aphrodite, 56
The Mighty Ducks, 261
Milk Money, 101–102
Million Dollar Legs, 279
The Miracle of Morgan's Creek, 71
The Mirror Has Two Faces, 102
Miss Firecracker, 204
Mixed Nuts, 261
Modern Times, 68, 69
The Money Pit, 158
Monkey Business (Cary Grant), 223
Monkey Business (Marx Brothers), 15–16
Monsieur Beaucaire, 30
Monsieur Verdoux, 68
The Moon Is Blue, 205
Moon over Parador, 250–251
Moonstruck, 102
The More the Merrier, 102
Moscow on the Hudson, 279
Mother, 158
Mouse Hunt, 261
Movers and Shakers, 184
Movie Movie, 184
Moving, 158

Mr. and Mrs. Smith, 136
Mr. Blandings Builds His Dream House, 158–159
Mr. Deeds Goes to Town, 66
Mr. Hobbs Takes a Vacation, 159
Mr. Mom, 159
Mister Roberts, 204–205
Mr. Smith Goes to Washington, 66
Mr. Wonderful, 102–103
Mr. Wrong, 280
Mrs. Doubtfire, 159
Multiplicity, 223
Murder by Death, 184–185
Murphy's Romance, 103
My Best Friend's Wedding, 103
My Blue Heaven, 241
My Cousin Vinny, 241
My Favorite Blonde, 30
My Favorite Brunette, 30–31
My Favorite Spy, 32
My Favorite Wife, 136–137
My Favorite Year, 185
My Fellow Americans, 251
My Little Chickadee, 19, 20–21
My Man Godfrey, 103
My Sister Eileen, 205
My Stepmother Is an Alien, 223–224

Naked Gun 2½: The Smell of Fear, 261
Naked Gun 33⅓: The Final Insult, 261–262
National Lampoon's Animal House, 262
National Lampoon's Loaded Weapon I, 185
National Lampoon's Vacation, 262
Neighbors, 160
Never Give a Sucker an Even Break, 20–21
Never Wave at a WAC, 230
A New Leaf, 137
A New Life, 137
New York Stories ("Oedipus Wrecks"), 56
A Night at the Opera, 16–17
A Night in Casablanca, 17
Night Shift, 262
Nine Months, 103–104
1941, 262–263
Ninotchka, 104
Nobody's Fool, 104
Noises Off, 205
Nothing in Common, 160
Nothing Sacred, 185
Nothing to Lose, 241
No Time for Sergeants, 230
The Nutty Professor, 37

The Object of My Affection, 104
The Odd Couple, 205–206
The Odd Couple II, 160
Office Space, 185–186

Oh, God!, 224
Once Around, 160
One Fine Day, 104, 106
One, Two, Three, 78
Only When I Laugh, 206
Only You, 106
Operation Mad Ball, 230–232
Operation Petticoat, 232
Opportunity Knocks, 241–242
The Opposite of Sex, 280
Other People's Money, 206
Our Relations, 25
Out Cold, 242
Out of Sight, 242
The Out of Towners, 137
Outrageous Fortune, 242
Out to Sea, 263
Overboard, 106
The Owl and the Pussycat, 106

The Paleface, 32
The Pallbearer, 106–107
The Palm Beach Story, 71, 73
Paper Moon, 280
Parenthood, 161
The Parent Trap, 161
Paris—When It Sizzles, 186
Passed Away, 161
Pat and Mike, 107
Paternity, 107
Paulie, 161
Pee-Wee's Big Adventure, 280
Pete 'n' Tillie, 137–138
Phffft!, 138
The Philadelphia Story, 206
Picture Perfect, 107
Pillow Talk, 107–109
The Pink Panther, 242–243
The Pink Panther Strikes Again, 243
Planes, Trains, and Automobiles, 263
Playing by Heart, 109
Play It Again, Sam, 56
Plaza Suite, 206–207
Pleasantville, 224–225
Please Don't Eat the Daisies, 163
Police Academy, 263, 264
Postcards from the Edge, 163
Prelude to a Kiss, 207
Pretty Woman, 110
Pride and Prejudice, 280–281
Primary Colors, 251
The Princess and the Pirate, 32
The Princess Bride, 186
The Prisoner of Second Avenue, 207–208
Private Benjamin, 232–233
Private Parts, 263–264
Prizzi's Honor, 243
The Producers, 60–61
Protocol, 251
The Purple Rose of Cairo, 57

Quick Change, 243–244

Rabbit Test, 225
Radio Days, 57
Raising Arizona, 244
Ready to Wear (Prêt-à-Porter), 186
Reality Bites, 110
The Ref, 163
Renaissance Man, 233–234
Revenge of the Nerds, 264–265
Richie Rich, 163
Risky Business, 186–187
Road to Singapore, 32–33
Robin Hood: Men in Tights, 61–62
Roman Holiday, 110
Romantic Comedy, 208
Romy and Michele's High School Reunion, 265
Room Service, 17
Roxanne, 110
Roxie Hart, 187
Ruggles of Red Gap, 281
Rush Hour, 243
Rushmore, 111
The Russians Are Coming! The Russians Are Coming!, 187
Ruthless People, 138

Sabrina, 79
Same Time, Next Year, 208
The Santa Clause, 225
Saps at Sea, 26, 27
Say Anything . . . , 164
Scenes from a Mall, 57
The Secret Life of an American Wife, 138
The Secret Life of Walter Mitty, 38–39
The Secret of My Success, 187–188
Seems Like Old Times, 138–139
The Senator Was Indiscreet, 251–252
Send Me No Flowers, 208
Serial Mom, 188
The Seven Year Itch, 79
Sex and the Single Girl, 111
Sgt. Bilko, 234
Shadows and Fog, 57
The Shaggy Dog, 225
Shakespeare in Love, 111
Shampoo, 188
She-Devil, 139
She Done Him Wrong, 24
She's Having a Baby, 139
She's the One, 164
A Shock to the System, 244
The Shop Around the Corner, 111–112
A Shot in the Dark, 208
The Show-Off, 40
Sibling Rivalry, 164
Silent Movie, 62
Silver Streak, 244, 245
A Simple Wish, 225–226

Singles, 112
The Sin of Harold Diddlebock, 73
Sister Act, 265
Sitting Pretty, 164
Six Days, Seven Nights, 112
Six of a Kind, 21
Sixteen Candles, 165
Skin Deep, 112
Slap Shot, 265
Sleeper, 58
Sleepless in Seattle, 112–113
Sliding Doors, 113
Slums of Beverly Hills, 165
Smile, 188
Smoke Signals, 281
Sneakers, 244
Soapdish, 188–189
S.O.B., 187
So Fine, 165
So I Married an Axe Murderer, 281
Some Kind of Wonderful, 165
Some Like It Hot, 79–80
Something to Talk About, 139
Son of Paleface, 33
Sons of the Desert, 26
Sorrowful Jones, 33
Sour Grapes, 265–266
A Southern Yankee, 40, 41
Spaceballs, 62
Speechless, 113
Spies Like Us, 266–267
Splash, 226
Stakeout, 244–245
Stalag 17, 80
Stardust Memories, 58
Starting Over, 113
State of the Union, 252
The Sting, 245–246
Stir Crazy, 246
Strange Bedfellows, 139
Stripes, 234
Stuart Saves His Family, 165–166
The Stupids, 166
Sullivan's Travels, 72–74
Summer Rental, 166
Sunday in New York, 113–114
The Sunshine Boys, 209
Support Your Local Sheriff, 189
The Sure Thing, 114
Surrender, 114
Sweet Liberty, 189
Swimming with Sharks, 189
Swingers, 189–190
Swiss Miss, 26
Switch, 226
Switching Channels, 209

Take the Money and Run, 58
Taking Care of Business, 246

Taking Off, 190
The Talk of the Town, 114, 116–117
Teachers, 190
Teacher's Pet, 114–115
The Teahouse of the August Moon, 209
That Darn Cat, 281–282
That Old Feeling, 140
That's Life!, 166
That Touch of Mink, 115
Theodora Goes Wild, 115
There's Something About Mary, 115, 118
They All Laughed, 118
They Got Me Covered, 33
The Thin Man, 246
This Is My Life, 167
This Is Spinal Tap, 190
A Thousand Clowns, 209
¡Three Amigos!, 190–191
Three Men and a Baby, 167
The Thrill of It All, 140
Throw Momma from the Train, 282
'Til There Was You, 118
The Time of Their Lives, 44
Tin Cup, 118
To Be or Not To Be, 191
To Die For, 191
Tom, Dick and Harry, 118–119
Tommy Boy, 268
Tootsie, 282
Topper, 226
Topper Returns, 226–227
A Touch of Class, 119
Tough Guys, 246
To Wong Foo, Thanks for Everything,
    Julie Newmar, 267–268
Trading Places, 268
Trapped in Paradise, 268
Trial and Error, 268–269
True Love, 167
The Truman Show, 48
The Truth About Cats and Dogs, 119
Tunnel of Love, 210
Turner & Hooch, 247
The Twelve Chairs, 62
Twentieth Century, 210–211
Twins, 269
Two-Faced Woman, 140
Two for the Road, 140
Two for the Seesaw, 210, 212

Uncle Buck, 167
Undercover Blues, 247
Under the Yum Yum Tree, 212
Unfaithfully Yours, 74
Up in Arms, 39
Uptown Saturday Night, 269
Used Cars, 269

Vampire in Brooklyn, 227
Vampire's Kiss, 191
Vegas Vacation, 269–270
Victor/Victoria, 119
Vivacious Lady, 119–120
Volunteers, 270

The Wackiest Ship in the Army, 234
Wagons East!, 191–192
Wag the Dog, 252
Walk, Don't Run, 120
The War of the Roses, 141
The Waterboy, 270
Wayne's World, 270, 271
Way Out West, 26
A Wedding, 167–168
The Wedding Singer, 120
Weekend at Bernie's, 270
Welcome to the Dollhouse, 168
We're Not Married, 141
What About Bob?, 168
What's Up, Doc?, 120
When Harry Met Sally..., 120–121
Where's Poppa?, 270–271
Which Way Is Up?, 271–272
While You Were Sleeping, 121
Whistling in the Dark, 40
White Men Can't Jump, 272
Who Done It?, 44
Who Framed Roger Rabbit, 282
Who Is Killing the Great Chefs of
    Europe?, 247
Wholly Moses, 192
Wide Awake, 168
Will Success Spoil Rock Hunter?, 192
Without a Clue, 192
Without Love, 212
Without Reservations, 121
With Six You Get Eggroll, 169
The Woman in Red, 141
A Woman of Distinction, 121
Woman of the Year, 121–122
The Women, 212
Wonder Man, 39
Working Girl, 122
The World of Henry Orient, 282–283
The World's Greatest Lover, 192–193
Wrongfully Accused, 193

The Yellow Cab Man, 41
You Can't Cheat an Honest Man, 21
You Can't Take It with You, 66–67
Young Frankenstein, 62–63
You're Never Too Young, 37
Yours, Mine, and Ours, 169
You've Got Mail, 122–123

Zelig, 58
Zorro the Gay Blade, 193